McGill's Legal Aspects of Life Insurance

Huebner School Series   *Walter J. Woerheide, Editor*

Individual Medical Expense Insurance
Thomas P. O'Hare

Meeting the Financial Need of Long-Term Care
Burton T. Beam, Jr., and Thomas P. O'Hare

Fundamentals of Insurance for Financial Planning
Burton T. Beam, Jr., Barbara S. Poole, David L. Bickelhaupt, and Robert M. Crowe

Readings in Financial Planning
David M. Cordell and Barbara S. Poole (eds.)

Fundamentals of Financial Planning
David M. Cordell (ed.)

Fundamentals of Income Taxation
James F. Ivers III (ed.)

McGill's Life Insurance
Edward E. Graves (ed.)

McGill's Legal Aspects of Life Insurance
Edward E. Graves and Burke A. Christensen (eds.)

Group Benefits: Basic Concepts and Alternatives
Burton T. Beam, Jr.

Planning for Retirement Needs
David A. Littell and Kenn Beam Tacchino

Fundamentals of Investments for Financial Planning
Walt J. Woerheide and David M. Cordell

Fundamentals of Estate Planning
Constance J. Fontaine

Estate Planning Applications
Ted Kurlowicz

Planning for Business Owners and Professionals
Ted Kurlowicz, James F. Ivers III, and John J. McFadden

Financial Planning Applications
Thomas P. Langdon and William J. Ruckstuhl

Financial Decision Making at Retirement
David A. Littell, Kenn Beam Tacchino, and David M. Cordell

The Practitioner's Guide to Advanced Pension Topics
John J. McFadden, David A. Littell, and Kenn Beam Tacchino

Executive Compensation
John J. McFadden (ed.)

Huebner School Series

McGill's Legal Aspects of Life Insurance

Sixth Edition

Edward E. Graves and Burke A. Christensen, Editors

The American College Press/*Bryn Mawr, Pennsylvania*

This publication is designed to provide accurate and authoritative information about the subject covered. While every precaution has been taken in the preparation of this material, the editors and The American College assume no liability for damages resulting from the use of the information contained in this publication. The American College is not engaged in rendering legal, accounting, or other professional advice. If legal or other expert advice is required, the services of an appropriate professional should be sought.

Library of Congress Control Number 2008925901
ISBN 1932819630

Printed in the United States of America

Dr. Dan M. McGill, PhD, CLU, whom we honor by including his name in the title of this book, is professor emeritus at The Wharton School of the University of Pennsylvania. He has been one of the most influential educators and scholars in the field of insurance for more than 40 years. Considered by many to be the nation's leading life insurance scholar, Dr. McGill taught at The Wharton School for more than three decades and served as chairman of The Wharton School's prestigious insurance department for 25 years. He also served as executive director of the Solomon S. Huebner Foundation for Insurance Education.

Contents

Preface

This is a basic text on the legal aspects of life insurance. Eleven of the chapters are a reprint of the legal material from the 2002 edition of *McGill's Life Insurance*. These 11 chapters have been supplemented with six chapters on legal topics not covered in *McGill's Life Insurance*. Chapter 18 addresses procedural and emotional issues concerning death and dying, while chapter 19, the final chapter, is a collection of short essays on ethics from the *Journal of Financial Service Professionals*. The result is a concise and readable book of which we are proud.

We wish to thank Robert Murphy for his excellent editorial help and Evelyn Rice for her production assistance. In addition, Bruce Worsham deserves credit for making this a separate volume rather than part of a massive 1,200-page edition of *McGill's Life Insurance*.

Finally, this book would not have been possible without the pioneering work of Dr. Solomon Stephen Huebner and Dr. Dan M. McGill.

Every attempt has been made to ensure that this volume is accurate and up-to-date. Since we have full confidence in Murphy's Law and expect that you will find some errors or shortcomings, we would appreciate your critical reactions and suggestions for improvement. With your help we can make future editions of this book even better.

Edward E. Graves
Burke A. Christensen

About the Editors

Edward E. Graves, CLU, ChFC, associate professor of insurance at The American College and holder of the Charles J. Zimmerman Chair in Life Insurance Education, has served on The College's faculty since 1976. He is responsible for the courses in the Chartered Life Underwriter (CLU) and Chartered Financial Consultant (ChFC) designation programs that deal with individual life insurance products and life insurance law. Mr. Graves has published articles on these subjects in industry journals and is the coauthor of a number of textbooks for both The American College and the American Institute for Chartered Property and Casualty Underwriters. He is consulting editor on life insurance products for the *Journal of Financial Service Professionals*, and he served on the Insurance Task Force of the Financial Products Standards Board from 1987 to 1989. More recently Mr. Graves was a member of the task force that created the Life Insurance Illustration Questionnaire (IQ) for the American Society of CLU & ChFC. He earned his BS degree from California State University at Los Angeles. He holds a master's degree from the University of Pennsylvania.

Burke A. Christensen, JD, CLU, has 25 years of experience as an insurance, tax, and estate planning lawyer. He was awarded the Chartered Life Underwriter designation in 1987. In April 1995, he became a life insurance agent and was appointed vice president of A.W. Ormiston & Co., a 64-year-old insurance brokerage agency, which specializes in providing life and health insurance to large law firms throughout the United States. From 1984 to 1995, Mr. Christensen was vice president and general counsel for the Society of Financial Service Professionals in Bryn Mawr, Pennsylvania. He has served on the drafting committees for the Society's Life Insurance Illustration Questionnaire and the policy Replacement Questionnaire (RQ). He is a frequent author and lecturer on insurance and estate planning. Since 1979, his column, "Law & Life Insurance," has appeared monthly in *Trusts & Estates* magazine. He was a contributing author for the 1994 edition of *McGill's Life Insurance,* and he has written other articles for the *Journal of Insurance Regulation, Trusts & Estates, Probate & Property,* and the *National Law Journal.* Since 1985, he has been the author of the Society's column on business and professional ethics, "Strictly Speaking," which is published in the *Journal of Financial Service Professionals*. Mr. Christensen is a graduate of Utah State University and the University of Utah College of Law. He is a member of the Pennsylvania and American Bar Associations, and he is admitted to practice before the United States Supreme Court.

McGill's Legal Aspects of Life Insurance

1

Fundamental Legal Concepts

Dan M. McGill
Revised by Burke A. Christensen

Learning Objectives

An understanding of the material in this chapter should enable the student to

---

1-1. Distinguish between the two basic forms of American law.

1-2. Describe the nature and functions of each of the forms of legislative law.

1-3. With respect to case law, explain what it is composed of, how new law is made by the courts, how common law differs from civil law, the distinction between law and equity, and the role of the courts in interpreting legislative law.

1-4. Describe the nature and jurisdiction of the various federal and state courts.

1-5. Explain how the courts attempt to deal with problems involving conflicts of law.

Chapter Outline

The following chapters are designed for the student of the principles of law that govern the creation and marketing of life and health insurance contracts. They are not intended to turn the student into an insurance lawyer. The goal is to enable the student to become sufficiently expert in the topics covered so that he or she may legitimately lay claim to the title of insurance professional.

It is not sufficient that a student or practitioner of life insurance understand only the economic and mathematical bases of the subject; he or she must also have a firm grasp of the basic legal relationships that have largely shaped its formal structure and influenced its content. The law of life insurance is derived predominantly from the general law of contracts; yet, contract law as applied to insurance contracts has been profoundly modified by the needs of the insurance business. On the one hand, insurance companies have sought to condition and limit the risks they assume; on the other hand, the insuring public has required and obtained protection against insurance companies' excessively legalistic interpretations of policy provisions. The resulting law is a compromise between these conflicting demands. The core of our study will be contract law, but one who knows only contract law will not fully grasp the law of insurance contracts.

This chapter is not concerned with legal abstractions and esoteric concepts. It deals with concrete legal principles and situations that field and home office representatives are certain to meet in the ordinary course of business. Most of the principles are encountered on a recurring—if not daily—basis. Recognition of situations and actions that have legal significance will enable life insurance company representatives to provide better service to the insuring public and more protection to their company against involuntary assumption of risk and unfavorable litigation.

Through a brief summary of the forms of law, the American judicial system, the general principles of contract interpretation, and the unique legal characteristics of a life insurance contract, this chapter will enhance the student's comprehension of the basic legal principles underlying life insurance.

FORMS OF LAW

law

> *law:* The collection of rules of conduct recognized as binding on the members of a community for the violation of which a sanction is provided

legislative law

case law

American law, despite its varied and complex nature, can be classified into two broad, all-inclusive forms: (1) *legislative law*, which takes the form of legislation as enacted by parliamentary bodies and as promulgated by governmental agencies, and (2) *case law*, which is developed by courts and administrative agencies.

Legislative law, which we have defined to include regulations, consists of the general rules of conduct promulgated by a legally constituted body vested with the authority and power to issue such rules for all or a given portion of the population. For example, representatives of the people create constitutions; legislatures enact statutes; agencies issue regulations. All of these are forms of legislative law. Legislation is found chiefly in statute books and is generally identified as a "law" or an "act."

Case law consists of the narrow rules of conduct promulgated by the courts and administrative tribunals in the adjudication of particular controversies. Case law is located in the published and unpublished reports of judicial and administrative decisions.

The rule of law represented by legislation and regulation is stated in an official, explicated, textual form. Its future application to the acts of the public is generally quite clear.

This is not true of case law. Although case law settles controversy between the parties to that case, its application to other future cases may be uncertain. In fact, a proposition of case law that may have an impact on the general public is not always directly stated but often must be inferred from the published opinions of a judicial or an administrative decision. Thus case law is flexible in form, while legislation is rigid.

Legislation[1]

The forms of legislative law presented here are in descending order of political authoritativeness as follows:

- the federal Constitution
- treaties
- federal statutes
- federal executive orders and administrative regulations
- state constitutions
- state statutes
- state administrative regulations
- local ordinances

The Federal Constitution

The primary functions of a constitution are to establish the framework of the government and to set forth the fundamental legal and political principles of a society. Thus the Constitution of the United States provides for a national government of three coordinate branches—the legislative, executive, and judicial—and sets down in some detail the powers and functions of each. At the same time it provides safeguards against infringement by the government of the basic human rights, such as freedom of speech, freedom of religious worship, and freedom of peaceful assemblage. In short the federal Constitution prescribes the powers of the various branches of the federal government and imposes limitations on those powers as they affect private individuals and the states.

The federal government of the United States came into being when the Constitution was ratified by the original 13 sovereign and individually independent states. Thus the federal government is a creation of the people of those states through a delegation of power by them to the federal government. As a result, no powers can be exercised by the federal government unless they exist in the federal Constitution. This is not true of the states. The states retain all powers not granted to the federal government. This principle is recognized by the Tenth Amendment to the federal Constitution: "The powers not delegated to the United States by the Constitution, nor prohibited by it to the States, are reserved to the States respectively, or to the people."

Nevertheless, pursuant to Article VI, Section 2 of the federal Constitution, the supreme law of the land in the United States is the Constitution and the federal laws and treaties created under the authority of the federal Constitution. This is known as the *supremacy clause*. Only in those areas where the federal Constitution is silent are the states supreme.

supremacy clause

Treaties

The treaties entered into between the government of the United States and foreign governments sometimes contain provisions as to aliens' rights that conflict with local law. In that event, such treaties take precedence over state constitutions or statutes. For example, a treaty in 1850 between the United States and Switzerland provided that the heirs of a Swiss citizen who died owning land in the United States should be entitled to inherit the land. This treaty was upheld by the Supreme Court of the United States in the face of a contrary legal doctrine of the state of Virginia, in which the land was located. In so holding, the court said, "It must always be borne in mind that the Constitution, laws and treaties of the United States are as much a part of the law of every state as its own local laws and Constitution. This is a fundamental principle in our system of complex national policy."[2]

Federal Statutes

The federal Constitution was, of necessity, couched in general terms. It was intended that Congress would address itself to matters requiring specialized rules and regulations. The statutes enacted by Congress within the scope of the powers given to the federal government by the supremacy clause therefore are of higher authority than any state constitution or statute.

Not all acts of Congress, however, create "law" in the sense in which the term is generally used. Some acts are directed at one individual by name or at a specifically identified group of individuals and are known as *private laws*. They do not purport to lay down general rules of human conduct. Statutes of general application are labeled *public laws*.

private laws

public laws

Federal Executive Orders and Administrative Regulations

Under Article II of the Constitution, the President of the United States has a power of rather indefinite scope to issue executive orders that, if they prescribe general rules of conduct, are laws, legislative in form. Within their proper scope, executive orders are paramount to state law. In addition, many federal administrative bodies, such as the Internal Revenue Service, have the power to make general rules, ordinarily identified as regulations. These are legislative in character, and when issued pursuant to a constitutional federal statute, are superior to all forms of state laws.

State Constitutions

A state constitution is, within the proper sphere of its operation, the "supreme law" of the state—subject, of course, to the priority of federal legislative law in its proper sphere. There is a significant theoretical difference between the state governments and the federal government. A federal governmental power exists only if it has been granted by the federal Constitution. The states, however, are the sovereign representatives of their people and possess all governmental powers that have not been delegated by the people to the federal government or limited by the state constitution. As a result a federal law is constitutional only if it is based on a delegation of power found within the federal Constitution. In contrast, a state law is always presumed to be valid unless the state or federal constitutions specifically prohibit the state from exercising such a power.

In addition to outlining the framework of government and limiting the authority of state officials, state constitutions often prescribe general rules of conduct of the kind normally associated with acts of the state legislature. The purpose of such a provision is to place the rules contained therein beyond the power of alteration by the legislature.

State Statutes

This is a voluminous body of legislative law, because state legislatures have residuary powers to prescribe general rules of conduct. As explained above, state governments have all powers not specifically denied them by the federal Constitution, federal treaties, federal statutes, and the appropriate state constitution. The operations of life insurance companies and the contents of their policies are greatly affected by state statutes. In fact, all states have enacted so-called standard provisions that must be included, in substance, in all life insurance policies issued in the states.

State Statutes Limited By

- federal Constitution prohibitions
- federal treaties
- federal statutes
- applicable state constitution

To assist the states in preparing well-designed legislation that responds to the complexities of the life insurance business, the National Association of Insurance Commissioners (NAIC) has developed numerous model acts and regulations. These models may be considered by the state legislatures and insurance departments as they develop the laws that will be enacted in each state.

State Administrative Regulations

administrative
case law

Administrative bodies or officials as a group are endowed with some of the characteristics of all three branches of government—judicial, executive, and legislative. They sometimes have authority, granted by statute, to adjudicate particular controversies and claims, and in so doing perform judicial or quasijudicial functions. Their decisions, with their accompanying explanations, become precedents of *administrative case law*. In their capacity as prosecuting and law enforcement officials, they exercise executive powers. Finally, they are frequently empowered by statute to make general rules of conduct in their particular areas of responsibility; these general rules, as "regulations," have the force and effect of law.

State Administrative Bodies

- create regulations
- enforce regulations and statutes
- resolve some controversies
- coordinate regulations with other states

Regulations, orders, opinions, and rulings issued by the various state insurance departments constitute one of the most important sources of law for insurance companies. Similar regulations issued by state and federal securities regulatory authorities are also important to the business of insurance because many types of insurance products are subject to state and federal securities laws.

Local Ordinances

The right to govern certain subordinate units of the state—for example, cities, towns, and counties—is delegated by the state to local governmental entities that have legislative powers limited to matters of purely local concern. The general rules enacted by these municipalities are usually called "municipal ordinances."

stare decisis

stare decisis: a Latin term that means that a court can be expected to follow a previous decision of that court or a higher appellate court in the same jurisdiction

JUDICIAL DECISIONS

When a court is called upon to decide a case involving a point on which there is no legislation or for which there is no clear legislative answer, it will look to the appropriate state or federal Constitution and to prior cases for precedents. If there is no clear statutory answer, the prior case law will control. If the court finds an applicable case law precedent, it will ordinarily decide the current dispute on the basis of the principles enunciated in the earlier case. If it finds no precedent squarely in point or applicable by analogy, it must originate a rule to resolve the dispute. Presumably the rule will reflect proper consideration of history, customs, morals, and sound social policy.

Example: **Some Types of Laws**

- *treaty*—The United States is a signatory to the Nuclear Nonproliferation Treaty of 1968 to limit the spread of nuclear weapons capability to other nations.
- *federal statute*—The Securities Exchange Act of 1934 regulates the purchase and sale of certain securities.
- *federal executive order*—A working group was created by a federal executive order to coordinate, promote, and facilitate the effective use of dispute-resolution processes within federal agencies.

- *state statute*—Many states have enacted laws requiring automobile drivers to carry auto bodily injury and property damage liability insurance.
- *state administrative regulation*—A state administrative body may have responsibility for the licensing and oversight of child day-care facilities.
- *local ordinances*—A city council passes a law controlling the number and size of signs that may appear on commercial buildings in the town.

Considerations Guiding Judicial Decisions

- history
- customs
- morals
- laws
- sound social policy

In creating new rules, courts are making case law. The more situations coming before the courts for which there are no existing rules, the more new case law there will be. Moreover, each new rule becomes an integral part of the whole body of rules that the courts may use in the future.

American case law is rooted in the law of England as it existed at the time of the colonization of America. This is natural, since the early settlers brought with them the only law they knew. This law was composed of the rules followed by the English courts in the settlement of disputes and the existing statutory enactments of Parliament. Because the decisions of the English courts were assumed to reflect those principles, maxims, usages, and rules of action that had regulated people's affairs from time immemorial, they were designated as the "common law" of England. The influence of the common law of England on the development of American law continued well into the 19th century. Since the English common law was the fountainhead of American case law, the latter likewise came to be known as the "common law." In this sense the term common law distinguishes case law from statutory or constitutional law.

common law

common law: originally the unwritten law as derived from the customs or ideas of justice in England and now the collection of judicial decisions, customs, and concepts of justice that define what is considered to be right and wrong. In contrasting them with legislative (or statutory) law, court decisions are often referred to as the common law. England, Canada, and the United States are common law countries.

civil law

civil law: the law derived from the law of Rome (in contrast with common law). Civil law is not based on court decisions (as is common law) but on the enactment of a comprehensive code. Italy and France are civil law countries. In contrast with criminal law, civil law refers to the obligations and rights created between private parties.

Common Law Compared to Civil Law

A broader use of the term common law distinguishes the entire system of English law from the legal systems developed in other parts of the world. It has acquired special significance in distinguishing between the English legal system—and systems based on it—and the code developed in the Roman Empire that today serves as the foundation of the legal systems in continental Europe and in the state of Louisiana.

The Roman civil law originated as the law of the city of Rome but was gradually extended to the entire Roman Empire. After the fall of the Roman Empire in the 5th century, this law was compiled into a code called "Corpus Juris Civilis." Since the compilation was carried out during the reign of Justinian, it is often referred to as the "Justinian Code."

The Justinian Code attempted to develop a rule to cover every possible type of legal conflict. One example is the rule to settle the question of survivorship when two people perished under circumstances that made it impossible to determine who died first. While there are many substantive differences between the Roman civil law and the Anglo-American common law, the most significant difference lies in the impact on the entire legal system of the adjudication of a particular case. Under the civil law code, a case is brought within one of the general provisions and is settled by application of the rule contained therein to the facts of the case. The decision in a particular case is little influenced by previous litigation on the point involved and, in turn, will exert little—if any—influence on similar disputes arising in the future. Under the system of common law, however, a controversy not covered by legislation is decided only after a guiding rule has been sought in previously litigated cases, and—more important—once a decision has been made, it forms the basis for the settlement of future disputes. The more frequently a decision is used as a guide to action, the stronger it becomes as a precedent.

equity

> *equity:* a body of law developed to provide relief where legal remedies have failed

Law versus Equity

The term common law is also used to designate the rules applied by the courts of common law as contrasted with the rules applied by courts of equity.

The term "equity" is peculiar to Anglo-American law. It arose because of the failure of the common law to give adequate and proper remedy in some cases. In the early courts of England, the procedure for pursuing a legal remedy was very rigid. There were a fixed number of "forms of action," and every remedial right had to be enforced through one of these forms. The first step in any action was to apply to the king for a writ, which was a document addressed to the person responsible for the alleged wrong. This writ gave a brief summary of the facts upon which the right of action was based, and it contained certain technical formulas indicating the form of action being brought and the amount of money damages sought. The nature of these writs was fixed and could not be substantially altered. A writ had been developed not only for each form of action but also for the facts, circumstances, and events that would constitute the subject matter of the particular action. If no writ could be found that corresponded substantially to the facts constituting the basis for complaint, the injured party could obtain no relief in the courts. The only course of action available was a direct appeal to the conscience of the king.

Over a period of time the number of direct petitions became so great that the king had to delegate responsibility for dealing with them. Since the appeal was to the king's conscience, he began to refer such matters to his spiritual adviser, the chancellor, who, being an official of the Church, usually favored the ecclesiastical law or the civil law over common law. Once begun, the practice of delegating cases to the chancellor for his sole decision rapidly became the established method of dealing with such controversies. Eventually a separate court functioning under the chancellor, called the Chancery Court, was created.

courts of law
court of equity

Following the English precedent, the American colonies (and later the states) established two sets of courts, one applying the rules of common law, called *courts of law*, and the other applying rules of equity and good conscience, called *courts of equity*. England still maintains separate courts of law and equity, but in this country, the two systems have been merged to the extent that the same court can hear both types of cases. Whether the case is heard in law or equity depends on the remedy sought. If there is a legal remedy, the action must be brought in law; if there is no legal remedy or the legal remedy is inadequate, the suit can be brought in equity.

legal remedy

legal remedy: attempt to seek money damages for a failure to perform a contract as written

equitable remedy

equitable remedy: attempt to enforce performance in a contract, to modify its terms, or to excuse performance for some reason

The distinction between law and equity is extremely important to life insurance companies. Equity gives them access to remedies that are otherwise unavailable and that are essential to their operation. Among the equitable remedies frequently invoked by life insurance companies are suits for rescission and restitution, suits for reformation of contracts, and bills of interpleader. (All of these terms will be explained later in this book.) Suits in equity are usually tried without a jury, which—in view of the traditionally hostile attitude that juries usually have toward insurance companies—is considered to be a major procedural advantage.

Example: ***Legal versus Equitable Remedies***

Jack and his business partner, Jill, have entered into a binding buy-sell agreement whereby, on the death of either, the decedent's estate is obligated to sell the business interest to the survivor, and the survivor is obligated to buy it. Jill dies and Jack, unable to come up with the purchase price, reneges on his promise to buy. Jill's heirs could bring an action in law, seeking money damages. More likely, they would bring an action in equity, seeking enforcement of the contract against Jack.

Equitable Remedies Sought by Insurers

- rescission
- restitution
- reformation of contract
- bills of interpleader

Administrative Decisions

Administrative agencies are normally created by legislative enactment and are charged with the administration of laws that are general in character and that affect the rights and privileges of private citizens. When administrative agencies apply a law to a particular set of facts, they are making case law. Their decisions, when officially or unofficially reported and published, have the status of precedents. Precedents in this area, however, are regarded with less sanctity than are judicial decisions and are less likely to be applied to a different set of facts. An administrative tribunal, unlike the usual court of law, has jurisdiction over a limited class of cases.

RELATIONSHIP OF THE JUDICIARY TO LEGISLATIVE LAW

In our governmental system of checks and balances, the courts have the right to interpret or construe the law created by the legislative branch and enforced by the executive branch. The courts determine the meaning of the words used in the statute and decide whether a particular set of facts comes within the scope of the law created by the statute. The same function is exercised with respect to the federal and state constitutions. As a part of this function the courts determine whether or not a particular statute conflicts with a particular constitutional provision.

rules of statutory construction

In the process of determining the scope and meaning of statutory and constitutional provisions, the courts have developed a number of rules. These are known as *rules of statutory construction*. The fundamental purpose of all these rules is to ascertain and give effect to the intention of the legislature.

One of the most basic rules is that if the language of the statute is plain and unambiguous and its meaning clear and definite, there is no room for judicial construction. The statute is said to have a "plain meaning," which the courts must enforce irrespective of their opinion of the wisdom or efficacy of the statute. Normally the meaning of a statute is sought from the words used by the legislature to express its intent. But if the language of the statute is ambiguous and may have more than one meaning, matters that are extraneous to the statute—such as its title, legislative history, conditions leading to its enactment, and so forth—can be taken into account in an attempt to arrive at the statute's true meaning.

It stands to reason that all parts of a statute must be considered in any attempt to ascertain its meaning. Furthermore, the interpretation adopted by a court must be one that will give effect to the whole statute. Reflecting the traditional conflict between common and statutory law, the courts have decreed that statutes in derogation of the common law shall be strictly construed. This means that in order to change the common law, a statute must do so clearly and explicitly or it will not be enforced. Finally, if there are two statutes dealing with the same subject matter, the more recent one is to be given effect as the last expression of legislative intent.

jurisdiction	*jurisdiction:* the power to interpret and apply the law. There are several types of jurisdiction.
geographical jurisdiction	*geographical jurisdiction:* the area governed by the legislative unit that created the court's jurisdiction. The courts of Pennsylvania, for example, have no jurisdiction in Utah.
original jurisdiction	*original jurisdiction:* the power to decide a case when it is first heard by a judge or jury
appellate jurisdiction	*appellate jurisdiction:* the power to review the decision of a lower court
jurisdiction over the subject matter	*jurisdiction over the subject matter:* the power of a court to decide cases including certain subjects. For example, a state court has no subject matter jurisdiction to decide a case involving a treaty between the United States and France.
jurisdiction over the person	*jurisdiction over the person:* the power of a court to enforce its decision over a party to a lawsuit

CLASSIFICATION OF COURTS

Federal Courts

According to Article III of the federal Constitution, "The judicial power of the United States shall be vested in one Supreme Court and in such inferior courts as the Congress may, from time to time, ordain and establish." Pursuant to this constitutional power, the Congress has created numerous federal courts. At the head of the hierarchy stands the Supreme Court of the United States. The Supreme Court has original jurisdiction over all cases involving ambassadors, ministers, and consuls, and those in which a state is a party. In all other cases that can properly be brought before the Supreme Court, the court has appellate jurisdiction. Hence the principal jurisdiction of the court is appellate. It is the court of last resort for all cases involving federal law and for all cases coming to it from the inferior or lower federal courts involving questions of state law.

In 1891 Congress made provisions for intermediary courts of appeal in order to lessen the burden on the Supreme Court. These tribunals are known as the Courts of Appeals, of which there are now 13. Each Court of Appeals is assigned to a specified circuit that serves a certain number of states. Each of these courts has a minimum of three judges, who preside as a group. The jurisdiction of the Courts of Appeals is exclusively appellate. The decision of a Court of Appeals is subject to review only by the Supreme Court. For most cases, the decision of the Supreme Court to hear an appeal from a Court of Appeals, or any other court, is purely discretionary.

The federal courts of original jurisdiction for most matters are the District Courts. The country is presently divided into more than 90 judicial districts, each state having at least one district, and no district embracing territory in more than one state. There is one District Court for each judicial district, but most courts have more than one judge. The District Courts have jurisdiction over all cases arising under the federal Constitution or laws of Congress and over cases involving litigants with diversity of citizenship where the amount in dispute exceeds $75,000 per plaintiff (Title 28, Part IV, Chapter 85, Sec. 1332). For purposes of federal jurisdiction, *diversity of citizenship* is considered to exist whenever the litigating parties are citizens of different states in the United States or one is a citizen of the United States and the other is a citizen of a foreign country. For this purpose a corporation is considered to be a citizen of the state in which it is chartered. If the jurisdiction of the federal courts is based on diversity of citizenship, the subject matter of the dispute may be state law.

diversity of citizenship

In addition to these courts of general jurisdiction, there are a number of federal courts that have jurisdiction—not always exclusive—over certain types of disputes. Among such courts are the Court of Claims, the Tax Court, the federal military courts, and the Court of Customs and Patent Appeals.

State Courts

In each state, there exists—by state constitutional provision and legislative enactment—a system of judicial tribunals, which embraces various courts of original jurisdiction and one or more of appellate jurisdiction. Usually there is one court of unlimited original jurisdiction that has the power to entertain any action, regardless of the amount involved or the nature of the relief requested, although it does not ordinarily have authority over the probate of wills or administration of deceased persons' estates. This state court of general original jurisdiction usually hears cases at the county seat of the various counties in the state, and is known variously as the District, Circuit, Superior, or Common Pleas Court.

Federal Court Levels

- U.S. Supreme Court
- Courts of Appeal (13 courts)
- District Courts (90 districts)

Example: ***State Court Systems***

The Wisconsin court system is made up of three levels of courts, each with a different function:

- *Supreme Court* is a law-developing appellate court that decides cases that have statewide significance and involve issues that require interpretation of the law.
- *Court of Appeals* hears appeals of cases that have already been decided by a Circuit Court.

To view a summary of the court systems of other states, click on www.yahoo.com and search under "State Court Systems."

The name of the state court does not necessarily indicate its place in the judicial hierarchy. In New York, for example, the general court of original jurisdiction (the trial court) is known as the Supreme Court, while the court of last resort is known as the Court of Appeals. In most states, however, the court of last resort is called the Supreme Court.

JURISDICTION OF COURTS

A court's jurisdiction refers not only to its power to hear a case but also its power to render an enforceable judgment. The constitutional or statutory provision creating a particular court defines its jurisdiction as to subject matter, parties, geographical area, and amounts involved. Jurisdiction over the person of the defendant is especially important. This jurisdiction is given effect by a summons from the court in which the case is to be tried. The summons, usually delivered to the sheriff to be served upon the individual or organization made defendant to the suit, must be served within the geographical area subject to the jurisdiction of the court issuing the summons. If a person comes into the state or county and is served with a summons while he or she is there, that person is then under the authority and jurisdiction of the court.

If the defendant is a nonresident of the place where the suit is brought, service of process may be accomplished by publication. This, however, does not normally give the court authority to render a personal judgment for damages. Accompanied by proper attachment proceedings, however, service by publication brings under the court's jurisdiction all attached property of a nonresident that lies within the territorial limits of the court; such attached property therefore is liable for the judgment debt and may be used to satisfy the judgment. Moreover, under the Unauthorized Insurers Service-of-Process Act, which is discussed in the following chapter, a policyowner residing in one state may obtain and enforce a judgment against an out-of-state insurance company by serving the summons on the insurance commissioner or other designated official of the state of the insured's domicile.

If a particular controversy falls within the jurisdiction of the federal courts, the plaintiff may bring his or her action in a federal court. If the plaintiff brings the action in a state court and the defendant acquiesces in the choice of jurisdiction, the case will be tried in the state court. If, however, the defendant does not wish the case to be heard in the state court, he or she can have it removed to the appropriate federal court. If a case involving a federal question is adjudicated in a state court, the decision of the state court on that question is subject to review by the Supreme Court of the United States, according to the conditions and limitations imposed by Congress.

CONFLICT OF LAWS

conflict of laws

A court's jurisdiction refers to its power to hear a controversy and enforce its decision. Jurisdiction, however, is not determinative of the law that will be applied. A court of one state may have to apply the law, either statutory or common, of another state. The manner in which this could come about involves the *conflict of laws*—one of the most complex branches of the law.

The conflict of laws concept can be better understood if it is renamed "choice of laws." The latter is a more appropriate term because the issue is which law is to be applied when the laws of two or more jurisdictions seem relevant but are not in agreement.

The question of which law will govern the validity and interpretation of a life insurance contract is extremely important, because states have different attitudes toward various company practices and policy provisions and thus different laws on these issues. Broadly speaking, the matter is resolved on the basis of the *contacts* that a life insurance contract has with various territorial sovereigns that might be deemed to have an interest in determining the rights and duties of the parties to—and beneficiaries of—the contract. These contacts might arise out of the state's relationship to the home office, a branch office, the insured, or the beneficiary, to mention only the major possibilities. Theoretically, if a state has *any* relationship to—or contact with—an insurance contract, it has some (though perhaps only slight) claim to a voice in the determination of the rights and duties thereunder. In a typical case, there will be at least two states concerned with the policy—the state in which the home office is located and the state in which the insured is domiciled. But there can easily be more, so regardless of where the case may be heard, rules must be developed to determine which state has the paramount interest in interpreting and enforcing the contract.

The traditional rule followed by the majority of jurisdictions is that unless the parties agree otherwise, questions concerning the *validity* and *interpretation* of a life insurance contract will be resolved by the law of the state in which the contract was made and in which the last act necessary to bring the contract into existence took place. This is sometimes called the *place-of-making rule.* Since, under the usual circumstances, the contract becomes effective at the moment it is delivered by the agent to the insured and the first premium is collected, the place of making is typically the state in which the insured resides because that is where delivery was made. On the other hand, if the first premium is paid with the application and a conditional receipt is issued contingent on approval at the company's home office, the act that brings the policy contract into existence occurs at the home office of the company, producing a different result.

place-of-making rule

The traditional rule is that matters relating to *performance* of the contract are controlled by the law of the state where the contract is to be performed. However, this rule seems inappropriate for insurance contracts and has not been adopted.

Disturbed by the arbitrary nature of the place-of-making rule and convinced that all policyowners should be protected by the laws of their states, some states have enacted statutes and some courts have adopted rules to the effect that all policies shall be governed by the laws of the state in which the insured is domiciled, regardless of where the contract came into existence. Other courts—feeling that the control of a state over a company incorporated under its laws assures equality of treatment of all policyowners, wherever they live—follow the rule that the laws of the insurer's state of incorporation will be applied in determining the validity and interpretation of a life insurance contract. In all these cases, the choice of the governing law is determined by the conflict-of-law rule of the state in which the case is being adjudicated.

A life insurance policy may contain a provision that its validity and interpretation will be governed by the law of a designated state, which may be neither the insured's state of domicile nor the state in which the home office is located. It appears that, while the insured or beneficiary can enforce this provision if the laws of the designated state are more favorable to him or her than the laws that would apply under the conflict-of-law rule, the insurance company is not permitted to invoke the provision.[3]

center-of-gravity

grouping-of-contracts theory

In more recent years there has been a tendency for the courts to follow a different doctrine, known as the *center-of-gravity theory*, or *grouping-of-contracts theory*, to resolve conflicts-of-law problems, whether the matter in dispute involves the validity, interpretation, or performance of a contract. Under this theory, the courts, instead of regarding the parties' intention, place of making, or performance as conclusive, give emphasis to the law of the state that has the most significant contacts with the matter in dispute. The merit of this approach is that it gives the state with the most interest in the dispute paramount control over the legal issues. The principal disadvantage is the possibility that it will afford less certainty and predictability than the more rigid rules traditionally applied.

Choice of Laws When They Differ in Applicable Jurisdictions

- place of contract completion
- place of performance
- place of domicile
- designated state statute
- conflict-of-laws rule in state of jurisdiction
- center of gravity

Note that when the courts of one state apply the laws of another state, they apply *their* interpretation of what the law is in the other state. This may differ from the interpretation adopted by the courts of the other state.

In creating the federal judiciary,[4] the Judiciary Act of 1789 provided that when trying cases based on diversity of citizenship, federal courts would be bound by the applicable laws of the state in which they were sitting (assuming no conflict of laws). In the famous case of *Swift v. Tyson*, decided by the United States Supreme Court in 1842, it was held that the word "laws" used in the act referred to statutory law and not to case law. Thus the federal courts were free to apply their own version of the common law in settling disputes not involving a federal or state statute. This ruling turned out to be highly significant for insurance companies, inasmuch as federal precedents were more favorable to the companies in many respects than the common law of the various states. This happy state of affairs was ended in 1938, when the United States Supreme Court in *Erie Railroad Company v. Tompkins* overruled its earlier doctrine and held that the federal courts were obliged to apply the common law, as well as the statutory law, of the state in which the case is being heard. Three years later, the Supreme Court held that the federal courts would also have to follow the conflict-of-law rules of the state in which they sit. Thus, for purposes of diversity jurisdiction, a federal court is in effect only another court of the state.

CHAPTER REVIEW

Answers to the review questions and the self-test questions can be found in the Supplement.

Key Terms

law	courts of law
legislative law	courts of equity
case law	geographical jurisdiction
supremacy clause	original jurisdiction
privacy laws	appelate juridiction
public laws	jurisdiction over subject matter
administrative case law	jurisdiction over the person
precedent	diversity of citizenship
stare decisis	conflict of laws
common law	place-of-making rule
civil law	center-of-gravity (grouping of
equity	contracts) theory

Review Questions

1. Compare the two basic forms of American law—legislative law and case law—in terms of
   a. the types of rules of conduct they consist of
   b. by whom they are promulgated
   c. where they are located
   d. the certainty of their application to future situations

2. Describe the nature and function(s) of each of the following forms of legislative law (listed in descending order of political authoritativeness):
   a. the federal Constitution
   b. treaties
   c. federal statutes
   d. federal executive orders and administrative regulations
   e. state constitutions
   f. state statutes
   g. state administrative regulations
   h. local ordinances

3. Describe the difference between the federal government and the state governments in terms of the powers they have and what this difference in powers implies concerning the validity (constitutionality) of their laws.

4. Describe the ways in which administrative bodies or officials (such as state insurance commissioners) are endowed with some characteristics of each of the following three branches of government:
   a. judicial
   b. executive
   c. legislative

5. What are the two important sources of case law?

6. Describe the process by which judicial decisions and thus new case law are made.

7. Compare common law to civil law in terms of
   a. what each system is based on
   b. how a case is decided
   c. how a decision in one case applies to future disputes

8. Explain the distinction between law and equity and why this distinction is extremely important to life insurance companies.

9. Explain the role the courts play relative to legislative law.

10. With respect to the rules of statutory construction developed by the courts,
   a. explain the fundamental purpose they serve
   b. describe briefly several of the basic rules

11. Describe the types of cases over which each of the following federal courts has jurisdiction and indicate whether the jurisdiction is original and/or appellate:
   a. Supreme Court of the United States
   b. Courts of Appeal
   c. District Courts
   d. other federal courts

12. What are the typical state courts, and what type of jurisdiction (original or appellate) do they normally have?

13. Explain how courts may gain jurisdiction over the person of the defendant in each of the following situations:
   a. if the defendant is a resident of the place where the suit is brought
   b. if the defendant is a nonresident of the place where the suit is brought

14. If a particular controversy falls within the jurisdiction of the federal courts, under what circumstances may the case be tried by a state court?

15. Describe the rules followed traditionally and in more recent years by the courts to resolve conflicts-of-law problems.

Self-Test Questions

T   F   1. The law of life insurance is derived predominantly from the general law of contracts.

T   F   2. Case law consists of narrow rules of conduct promulgated by the courts and administrative tribunals in the adjudication of particular controversies.

T   F   3. With rare exceptions, both legislative law and case law are quite rigid and thus are applied to future situations with predictable certainty.

T   F   4. No powers can be exercised by the federal government unless they exist in the federal Constitution.

T   F   5. Many federal administrative bodies have power to make general rules (regulations) that are legislative in character and, when issued pursuant to a constitutional federal statute, are superior to all forms of state laws.

T   F   6. State administrative bodies or officials are often able to perform judicial and quasijudicial functions, to exercise executive powers, and to make general rules of conduct that have the force and effect of law.

T   F   7. Both the courts and administrative agencies are sources of case law.

T   F   8. Under the system of common law, a decision in a particular case is little influenced by previous litigation on the point involved, and in turn will exert little influence on similar disputes in the future.

T   F   9. Equitable remedies are attempts to seek money damages for a failure to perform a contract as written.

T   F   10. Equity gives life insurance companies access to remedies (such as suits for rescission and suits for reformation of contracts) that are otherwise unavailable and that are essential to their operations.

T   F   11. When administrative agencies apply a law to a particular set of facts, they are making legislative law.

T   F   12. The fundamental purpose of the rules of statutory construction is to permit the courts to apply their own interpretation (that is, judicial construction) to the language of a statute regardless of how clear and unambiguous the language may be.

T   F   13. All federal courts have both original and appellate jurisdiction over cases.

T   F   14. District courts at the federal level have jurisdiction over all cases in which the litigating parties are citizens of different states in the United States and the amount in dispute exceeds $75,000 per plaintiff.

T   F   15. If the jurisdiction of the federal courts is based on diversity of citizenship, the subject matter of the dispute may be which state's law to apply.

T   F   16. If a particular controversy falls within the jurisdiction of the federal courts, the case may be tried in a state court under certain circumstances.

T   F   17. In more recent years, the courts have tended to follow the place-of-making rule to resolve conflicts-of-law problems, whether the matter in dispute involves the validity, interpretation, or performance of a contract.

NOTES

1. The materials in this section were drawn largely from Noel T. Dowling, Edwin W. Patterson, and Richard R. Powell, *Materials for Legal Method* (University Casebook Series) (Chicago: Foundation Press, Inc., 1946), pp. 14–29. The classification of laws set forth in this section of the chapter was taken from that source.
2. *Havenstein v. Lynham,* 100 U.S. 483, 490 (1879).
3. See Edwin W. Patterson, *Essentials of Insurance Law,* 2d ed. (New York: McGraw-Hill Book Co., Inc., 1957), pp. 54 and 55, pp. 114 and 116, for citations.
4. Judiciary Act of 1789 SS 34, 1 Stat. 92 (1879) 28 U.S.C., SS 725 (1952).

Basic Principles of Contract Law

Dan M. McGill
Revised by Burke A. Christensen

Learning Objectives

An understanding of the material in this chapter should enable the student to

---

2-1.   Explain the general rules of contract law relating to the nature of a contract, the parties to a contract, the requirements for a contract to exist, and the alternative remedies available to the promisee if the promisor fails to perform as agreed in the contract.

2-2.   Describe the various characteristics that may apply to contracts in general.

2-3.   Explain what contract characteristics apply to life insurance policies and how these characteristics have resulted in modifications of the general rules of contract law when the courts have applied them to life insurance.

Chapter Outline

contract   *contract:* an agreement enforceable at law

A life insurance policy is a special kind of contract. To be extremely specific, it is an informal, aleatory, unilateral contract of adhesion to pay a stated sum subject to a condition precedent. This means, of course, that an insurance policy is not a formal, commutative, bilateral, negotiated, indemnitory, unconditional contract with right of subrogation. To understand what all these terms mean, a short course in contract law is necessary.

A Life Insurance Contract Is

- an informal contract
- aleatory
- unilateral
- a contract of adhesion
- subject to a condition precedent

Many promises can be broken without penalty. But a contract creates a binding promise for which the law creates a duty of performance. This duty is imposed on the one who makes the promise, who is known as the *promisor*. The person to whom the promise is made is known as the *promisee*. Pursuant to a life insurance contract, the insurance company promises to pay a death benefit if the policyowner pays the premium. Since only the insurer makes a promise, it is the promisor. The policyowner is the promisee. To enforce that duty, the law provides a remedy to the promisee. If the promisor fails to perform as agreed in the contract, the promisee has two alternatives. He or she may sue for money damages on the contract. This is an action at law. Or if money damages are insufficient, the promisee may sue to require the promisor to fulfill its obligation under the contract. This is known as an equitable action.

In order for a contract to exist, the parties must fulfill certain requirements, which may change depending on the type of contract being created. For all contracts, however, three elements must exist: (1) a valid offer, (2) an acceptance of that specific offer, and (3) an exchange of consideration. There must also be a legal purpose for the contract, and the parties to the agreement must be legally competent.

promisor
promisee

offer

offer: the manifestation of willingness to enter into a bargain, so made as to justify another person's understanding that his or her assent to that bargain is invited and will conclude it

acceptance

acceptance: a manifestation of assent to the terms of an offer made in a manner invited or required by the offer

consideration

consideration: something of value bargained for and requested by the promisor and given by the promisee in exchange for the promise

For purposes of determining whether there has been an offer and an acceptance of that offer, it used to be said that for a contract to exist there must be evidence of a "meeting of the minds" between the parties involved. Since it is difficult for anyone (even judges) to read minds, this concept is no longer used. It is more precise to say that an agreement exists when there has been a "manifestation of mutual assent." This new standard merely requires an examination of the available evidence to determine whether each party had indicated an acceptance of the agreement.

GENERAL NATURE OF A LIFE INSURANCE CONTRACT

policy

A valid agreement between a life insurance company and the applicant for insurance, represented by an instrument called the *policy* (from the Italian word polizza, meaning "a rolled document"), is a contract and, as such, is subject to the general rules of contract law. However, in adapting these rules, which are familiar to all students of business law, to the life insurance contract, the courts have introduced substantial modifications because of certain peculiar characteristics of the life insurance contract. These characteristics—which, with one exception, are common to all types of insurance contracts—are briefly described in this chapter.

Aleatory Contract

aleatory contract

aleatory contract: an agreement that conditions the performance by one party on the happening of an uncertain event

commutative contract

commutative contract: an agreement where each party expects to receive benefits of approximately equal value

Example:

Aleatory versus Commutative Contract

Chuck pays $500 for a block of lottery tickets. If Chuck's number comes up, he will win $1 million. Otherwise, he will get nothing. This is an aleatory contract.

Chuck also pays $500 for a sofa. In return, he gets a sofa that presumably is worth approximately $500. This is a commutative contract.

The agreement contained in a life insurance policy is *aleatory* in nature, rather than *commutative*. In a commutative agreement, each party expects to receive from the other party, in one way or the other, the approximate equivalent of what he or she undertakes to give. Thus in an agreement to purchase real estate, the buyer agrees to pay a sum of money that represents the approximate value of the property to him or her, while the seller agrees to sell the property for a price that represents its approximate value to him or her. In other words, both parties contemplate a fairly even exchange of values. The courts generally will not consider whether the value exchanged would be equal to an objective observer unless there is such a huge discrepancy that it amounts to evidence of undue influence by one party or incompetence by the other. For most purposes, the worth of a thing is the price it will bring.

In an aleatory agreement, on the other hand, both parties realize that, depending on chance, one may receive a value out of all proportion to the value that he or she gives. The essence of an aleatory agreement is the element of chance or uncertainty. The prime example of such a contract is the wagering agreement. The term may also be applied to an endeavor where the potential gain or loss is governed largely by chance. Thus, the oil industry's exploration and drilling functions may be described as aleatory in nature. So is prospecting for gold, silver, or uranium.

In a life insurance transaction, the present value of the potential premium payments at the inception of the agreement is precisely equal, on the basis of the company's actuarial assumptions, to the present value of the anticipated benefits payable under the contract. In this sense the life insurance transaction is not aleatory. Moreover, the sum total of insurance transactions for a company, or for the entire life insurance industry, is not aleatory because of the predictability and stability provided by the theories of probability and the law of large numbers.

It remains true, however, that a particular policyowner may pay in to the insurance company a sum of money considerably smaller than the sum promised under the contract. Indeed, the face amount of the policy may become payable after the insured has paid only one installment of the first premium. This *chance* of obtaining a disproportionate return from an "investment" in a life insurance policy has motivated—and continues to motivate—many unscrupulous persons to seek life insurance through fraudulent means and for illegal purposes. The remedies for breach of warranty, misrepresentation, and concealment are invoked by the companies to protect themselves and society against fraudulent attempts to procure insurance. The requirement of an insurable interest is also designed to deal with the problems created by the fact that the life insurance policy is an aleatory contract. The aleatory nature of the insurance contract accounts in large measure for the modifications of general contract law as it is applied to the field of insurance contract law.

Unilateral Contract

unilateral contract

> *unilateral contract:* an agreement in which only one party makes a promise

bilateral contract

> *bilateral contract:* an agreement in which promises are made by both parties

---

Example: ***Unilateral versus Bilateral Contract***

Jane's father promised to give her $100,000 on her 25th birthday if Jane does not marry prior to that date. Only Jane's father can be sued if the agreement is breached, so this is a unilateral contract.

Jane's father also agreed to sell to her his antique Chevrolet Corvette for $50,000 on her 21st birthday. Jane agreed to the arrangement. Either Jane's father or Jane can be sued if the agreement is breached, so this is a bilateral contract.

Most contracts in the business world are *bilateral* in nature. This means that each party to the contract makes an enforceable promise to the other party. The consideration for such a contract is the exchange of mutual promises. Thus an order from a wholesaler to a manufacturer for a specified quantity of a particular item at a specified price, if accepted, is a bilateral contract. The manufacturer agrees (promises) to deliver the desired merchandise at an agreed-upon price, while the wholesaler agrees (promises) to accept and pay for the merchandise when delivered. Either party can sue if the other fails to perform as promised.

Under a *unilateral* contract, on the other hand, only one party makes an enforceable promise. A contract is created because the nonpromising party to the contract performs his or her part of the bargain *before* the contract comes into existence. For instance, if the wholesaler in the example above had remitted cash with his or her order, the transactions would have become unilateral in nature, inasmuch as only the manufacturer (who made a promise to deliver) had anything to perform. In general, unilateral contracts are confined to situations in which one party is unwilling to extend credit to the other or to take the other's word for future performance.

As a general rule, a life insurance policy is a unilateral contract, in that only the insurance company makes an enforceable promise thereunder. The insurer's promise is given in exchange for performance by the policyowner of a certain act—payment of future premiums. As the consideration demanded by the company—namely, the application and the *first* premium or the *first* installment thereof—is given by the applicant, the contract goes into effect. Under the life insurance contract, the policyowner has made no promise to pay premiums subsequent to the first and is under no legal obligation to do so. If he or she does not pay additional premiums, the company will be released from its original promise to pay the face amount of the policy. Nevertheless, the policyowner incurs no legal penalties through failure to continue premium payments. On the other hand, the insurance company is obligated to accept the periodic premiums from the payer and to keep the contract in force in accordance with its original terms.

A life insurance contract may become a bilateral contract in some circumstances. For example, assume an agent of an insurer has authority to waive cash payment of the first premium. If an insurance policy is delivered by such agent in exchange for the applicant's promissory note or for the applicant's oral promise to pay premiums, a *bilateral* contract is created. In this situation the insurer's promise is exchanged for the applicant's promise.

Conditional Contract

condition precedent

condition precedent: an act or event that must occur before a duty is imposed or a right exists

condition subsequent

condition subsequent: an act or event that will terminate an existing right

---

Example: ***Condition Precedent versus Subsequent***

Ted, an insured, failed to pay a life insurance premium on time, and the policy lapsed. Ted dies. The insurer never became obligated to pay the face amount because of breach of a condition precedent.

Pat, an insured, paid life insurance premiums when due, so the policy remained in force. Pat died while on a training mission as a crew member of an Air National Guard helicopter that crashed. The policy contains an exclusion for death resulting from flight on a military aircraft. The insurer's liability is discharged because of breach of a condition subsequent (the military flight exclusion).

Closely related to the foregoing is the fact that the life insurance policy is a *conditional* contract. This means that the company's obligation under the contract is contingent on the performance of certain acts by the insured or the beneficiary. This does *not,* however, make the contract bilateral.

A condition is always inserted in a contract for the benefit of the promisor (the insurer) and hence is disadvantageous to the promisee (the policyowner). The following is a simple example of a conditional unilateral contract: Able promises to pay Baker $10 if she washes Able's car. The promised payment of the money is conditioned upon the performance of the act.

Conditions are not confined to unilateral contracts; a party to a bilateral contract can condition his or her promise in any manner acceptable to the other party. The following is an example of a conditional bilateral contract: Able promises to deliver 10 red rocking chairs, and Baker promises to accept them and pay Able $100 each if they are delivered prior to May 1st.

Conditions are classified as either precedent or subsequent. A condition precedent must be satisfied before legal rights and duties are created or continued, whereas a condition subsequent must be fulfilled in order to prevent the extinguishment of rights and duties already created in the contract. Whether a condition is precedent or subsequent depends on the intention of the parties to the contract. When the intention is not clear, the courts' tendency is to classify a condition as precedent in order to avoid a forfeiture.

The legal significance of a condition is quite different from and less burdensome than that of a promise. Failure to perform a contractual promise subjects the promisor to liability for damages to the promisee. Failure to perform or fulfill a condition does not subject the person involved (the promisee) to liability for damages but merely deprives him or her of a right or privilege that he or she otherwise would have had or might have acquired. It releases the promisor from his or her obligation to perform.

The promise of a life insurance company is conditioned on the timely payment of premiums. Payment of these premiums is considered to be a condition precedent to the continuance of the contract under its original terms. If this condition is not fulfilled, the company is relieved of its basic promise but remains obligated to honor various subsidiary promises contained in the surrender provisions and the reinstatement clause.

The company's promise to pay the face amount of the policy is always conditioned on the insured's forbearance from committing suicide during a specified period (usually one or two years) after the policy's issue and may be conditioned on the insured's death from causes not associated with war or aviation. Finally, the insurance company has no liability until satisfactory proof of death has been submitted by the beneficiary or the insured's personal representative.

Life Insurance Conditions Precedent

- timely payment of premiums
- forbearance from committing suicide during initial specified period
- proof of death submitted to insurance company

Contract of Adhesion

contract of adhesion

contract of adhesion: a contract drafted by one party that must be accepted or rejected by the other party as it is written. There is no negotiation over the terms of the agreement.

A life insurance policy is also a contract of adhesion. This means that the terms of the contract are not arrived at by mutual negotiation between the parties, as would be the case with a *bargaining* contract. The policy, a complex and technical instrument, is prepared by the company and, with minor exceptions, must be accepted by the applicant in the form offered to him or her. The prospective insured may or may not contract with the company, but in no sense is the applicant in a position to bargain about the terms of the contract. The applicant must reject the contract entirely or "adhere" to it. Any bargaining that precedes the issuance of a life insurance contract has to do only with whether or not the contract is to be issued, the plan and amount of insurance, and to some degree the terms of the settlement agreement, although the settlement agreement itself is actually drafted by the insurance company.

The adhesive nature of the life insurance contract is highly significant from a legal standpoint. This importance derives from the basic rule of contract construction that a contract is to be construed or interpreted most strongly against the party who drafted the agreement. The avowed purpose of this rule is to neutralize any advantage that might have been gained by the party that prepared the contract. This means that if there is an ambiguity in a life insurance policy, the provision in question will be given the interpretation most favorable to the insured or his or her beneficiary. A rather prevalent view in insurance circles is that the courts, in their zeal to protect the insured, often find ambiguities in contracts where none exist.

Some who readily admit the soundness of this rule of construction in general and of its application to life insurance policies prior to the turn of the century question its continued application to policies currently being issued, considering the large number of provisions that are required by state statutes to be incorporated in such policies. Although these statutes do not prescribe the exact language to be used, many states require that the language of all policy provisions, including those voluntarily included, be approved by the state insurance department before sale of the policy form to the public. Such a requirement has the purpose, among others, of preventing the use of any deceptive or misleading language or of any provisions that would be unfair to policyowners. These factors have produced a relaxation of the strict rule of construction in some courts, but generally, all ambiguous provisions of the policy continue to be construed against the insurer.

Contract to Pay Stated Sum

contract of indemnity

contract of indemnity: an insurance contract that reimburses the insured only for actual losses incurred

right of subrogation

right of subrogation: the right of an insurer to take the place of the injured insured and sue the party responsible for the damages incurred

---

Example: ***Subrogation***

Andy carried life insurance on his own life as well as uninsured motorists coverage in his personal auto insurance policy. Andy dies in an auto accident caused by an uninsured driver, and Andy's heirs are paid both by his life insurer and his auto insurer. The life insurer will not have a right of action against the uninsured driver, but the auto insurer will.

Contracts issued by property and casualty insurance companies are usually contracts of indemnity. This means that the insured can collect only the amount of his or her loss, irrespective of the face of the policy—except, of course, that the recovery cannot exceed the face of the policy. Moreover, upon payment by an insurer of a loss caused by the negligence of a third party, as in the case of an automobile accident, the insurer acquires the insured's right of action against the negligent third party up to the amount of its loss payment and any expenses incurred in enforcing its rights. This is known as the doctrine of subrogation. While a provision giving effect to this doctrine is included in virtually every property and casualty insurance policy, the doctrine applies even in the absence of a policy provision.

A life insurance policy therefore is not a contract of indemnity, but one to pay a *stated sum* (even if the sum may fluctuate under the provisions of a variable life insurance policy). This is presumably based on the assumption that because the value of a person's life to that person is without limit, no sum payable upon his or her death will be in excess of the loss suffered. Thus even though the insured has reached an age or a circumstance where he or she no longer has an economic value, upon his or her death the insurance company will still have to pay the sum agreed upon. The practical significance of this principle is that the insurance company, after paying the face amount of the policy, is not subrogated to the right of action of the decedent's estate when his or her death was caused by the negligence of a third party.

CHAPTER REVIEW

Answers to the review questions and the self-test questions can be found in the Supplement.

Key Terms

contract	commutative contract
promisor	unilateral contract
promisee	bilateral contract
offer	condition precedent
acceptance	condition subsequent
consideration	contract of adhesion
policy	contract of indemnity
aleatory contract	right of subrogation

Review Questions

1. Suppose Joe Smith, aged 25, has just purchased a $100,000 whole life policy from ABC Life Insurance Company covering his life. In addition to being the applicant and the insured, Joe is the policyowner. He named his wife, Bonnie, as primary beneficiary and his children as contingent beneficiaries. Use this information to indicate your understanding of the general nature of a contract by answering each of the following questions.
    a. Who is the promisor?
    b. Who is the promisee?
    c. What requirements must have been fulfilled in order for a contract to be created?
    d. If the promisor fails to perform as agreed in the contract, what legal remedies does the promisee have?

2. What standard tends to be applied by the courts today in determining whether there have been an offer and an acceptance of that offer in order for a contract to exist?

3. Explain the reason why a life insurance policy is an aleatory rather than a commutative contract.

4. What steps do life insurance companies take in attempting to deal with the problems created because a life insurance policy is an aleatory contract?

5. Explain why a life insurance contract is generally a unilateral rather than a bilateral contract and what obligations this does and does not create for the policyowner and the insurance company with respect to premiums and coverage.

6. Under what circumstances might a life insurance contract become a bilateral contract?

7. Explain how the legal consequence of failing to perform a contractual promise differs from that of failing to perform or fulfill a condition.

8. List several conditions generally found in life insurance policies.

9. Explain why a life insurance contract is considered to be a contract of adhesion and what impact this generally has if a policy provision is found to be ambiguous by the courts.

10. Explain how and why an insurer's right of subrogation differs under a life insurance contract from what it would be under a typical property or liability insurance contract.

Self-Test Questions

T   F   1. In a typical life insurance contract, the insurer is the promisee and the policyowner is the promisor.

T   F   2. All that is required for a contract to exist is a valid offer and an acceptance of that offer.

T   F   3. A life insurance policy is an aleatory contract because there is a chance that the amount of the premiums paid may be considerably smaller than the amount of the benefit promised in the policy.

T   F   4. Because both the insurer and the applicant typically make enforceable promises, life insurance contracts are usually bilateral contracts.

T   F   5. A condition is always inserted in a contract for the benefit of the promisor.

T   F   6. Failure to perform a condition in a contract subjects the promisee to liability for damages.

T   F   7. Timely payment of premiums after the first premium is considered a condition precedent to the continuance of a life insurance contract under its original terms.

T   F   8. Because a life insurance policy is a contract of adhesion, the courts generally construe ambiguous policy provisions against the insurer.

T   F   9. Unlike policies typically issued by property and casualty insurance companies, life insurance policies are contracts of indemnity.

Formation of a Life Insurance Contract: Part 1

Dan M. McGill
Revised by Burke A. Christensen

Learning Objectives

An understanding of the material in this chapter should enable the student to

3-1. Distinguish between persons (legal entities) who are parties to a life insurance contract and those who are not.

3-2. Explain why a life insurer may lack the capacity to contract and what the possible legal consequences are of violating various state laws for the enforceability of its contracts.

3-3. Explain whether various special groups of life insurance applicants—minors, the mentally infirm, and foreigners—either have or do not have the capacity to contract, and in each case, what this implies for the enforceability of life insurance policies they may purchase.

3-4. Explain the role of the application in the formation of a life insurance contract.

3-5. Explain when and how a life insurance contract comes into existence and, accordingly, when coverage under a life insurance policy becomes effective in each of the following situations:

    a. when the applicant does not tender the first premium with the application
    b. when the applicant tenders the first premium with the application and is given an insurability type of conditional receipt by the agent
    c. when the applicant tenders the first premium with the application and is given an approval type of conditional receipt by the agent
    d. when the applicant tenders the first premium with the application but is not given a conditional receipt by the agent

3-6. Explain how the courts have tended to interpret the typical conditions precedent to the existence of a life insurance contract.

3-7.   Explain how the courts have dealt with the key issues related to an unreasonable delay by the insurance company in determining the insurability of a prospective insured.

3-8.   State the rules generally applied by the courts in dealing with questions related to premium due dates and the dates from which certain benefits and clauses begin to run when a life insurance policy has been backdated.

Chapter Outline

To be enforceable, the agreement between a life insurance company and the person seeking insurance, represented by a written instrument called the policy, must meet all the requirements prescribed by law for the formation of a valid contract. In this and the following chapter, the manner in which each of the requirements is satisfied in forming a life insurance contract will be explained in specific terms.

LEGAL CAPACITY OF THE PARTIES

Parties to the Contract

There are two parties to the life insurance contract: the insurance company and the owner. The applicant is normally, but not necessarily, the owner and the person whose life is the subject matter of the contract. The person on whose life a policy is issued is the *insured*. A person or entity who takes out insurance on a person's life is referred to as the *applicant* or *owner*. The person whose life is insured is not a party to the contract unless he or she is also the owner. Two or more persons or entities may jointly apply for insurance on the life of another person, as is the case with some business

insured
applicant
owner

Parties to Life Insurance Contract

- policyowner
- insurance company

---

continuation agreements. In the case of joint life policies (either last-to-die or first-to-die), a person or entity may own a policy insuring more than one life.

Example: ***Parties to the Contract***

Ramon applied for and owns a life insurance policy on the life of his wife, Tess, with their only child, Miguel, as primary beneficiary. Recently, Ramon made a collateral assignment of the policy to Local State Bank as security for a loan. The insurer, Whatta Life Insurance Company, was properly notified of the assignment. Who are the legal parties to the insurance contract? Only the policyowner, Ramon, and the insurer, Whatta Life.

---

third-party beneficiary

    The designation of a *third-party beneficiary* to receive the proceeds upon the policy's maturity does not make such a person a party to the contract. The third-party beneficiary need not know of the contract at its inception, may disclaim any benefits thereunder, and incurs no duties by virtue of his or her designation. The beneficiary may acquire certain rights that are enforceable against the company, but he or she acquires them only through the agreement between the company and the applicant or owner. Furthermore, the beneficiary's rights can be negated by any defenses available to the insurer against the owner. Even the rights of an irrevocable beneficiary may be defeated. This may be accomplished by policy loans (absent a policy provision requiring the beneficiary's consent) or by allowing the policy to lapse.

assignee

assignee: an entity to whom any right or interest is transferred (assigned)

    An assignee, while possessing rights quite distinct from those of a beneficiary, occupies a position similar to that of the beneficiary in that he or she is an *interested* party, but is not a party to the contract unless there has been an absolute assignment that has been consented to by the other party. It is worth noting that the voluntary payment of premiums by a person having no other relationship with the policy bestows no contractual rights or privileges on the premium payor.

The contractual relationship between the insurance company and the owner of the policy is that of conditional debtor and creditor. The insurance company incurs obligations only if certain conditions are fulfilled, and then its duty is only to carry out the terms of the contract. The insurance company is not a trustee in any sense of the word and is under no legal obligation to render an accounting of the premiums received or, absent a showing of bad faith, of the apportionment of dividends.

Competency of the Insurer

person
natural person
artificial person

> *person:* a legal entity. In the law, a *natural person* is a human being. An entity that exists only because the law creates it is an *artificial person.* Examples are trusts, corporations, and partnerships.

Without specific legislation to the contrary, there is no reason why any person who has the legal capacity to enter into a contract cannot become the insurer under a life insurance contract. Freedom of contract is a constitutional and common-law privilege that must not be abridged unless the nature of the contract's subject matter makes it a proper subject for the exercise of the state's police power. Insurance—because of its magnitude, nature, and intimate bearing on the welfare of society—has been adjudged a proper subject for the exercise of such power.

The U.S. Supreme Court has ruled that a state may prohibit the making of insurance contracts by persons, either natural or artificial, who have not complied with the requirements of the state's law. In many states, statutes specifically prohibit natural persons (that is, human beings) from acting as life insurers. Even in states that have not so legislated, the nature of the business—with its need for continuity and permanence of the insurer—has brought about the same result. Hence, while individual insurers were common in the early days of life insurance, today the legitimate insurance business is conducted exclusively by corporate insurers. If a corporation seeking to write life insurance in a particular state is legally organized, the only question that can arise regarding its capacity to contract is whether the corporation has complied with all the requirements for doing business in that state.

A contract issued by an unlicensed insurer is usually enforceable by the policyowner. This rule of law recognizes that a person who is solicited to buy insurance cannot be expected to inquire into the affairs of the insurance company to determine whether or not it has complied with all the statutory and regulatory requirements governing its operations, and is fully qualified to enter into the proposed contract. On the contrary, the prospective insured is permitted to assume that the insurer is legally competent to enter into the proposed contract. In the event of a dispute, the insurer will not be permitted to use its own violation of statutory requirements as a defense against claims.

In order to assist the insured in enforcing claims against an unauthorized out-of-state insurer, all of the states (but not the District of Columbia) have enacted the *Unauthorized Insurers Service-of-Process Act.* This legislation designates the insurance commissioner or some other state official as the agent of the unauthorized insurer for the purpose of accepting service of process. Designed to deal with companies that do business by mail, these statutes permit the insured to secure a judgment against the insurer in the courts of his or her own state. This judgment must be given "full faith and credit" by the courts of all other states in which the insurer has assets. Agents of unauthorized insurers are subject to both criminal and civil penalties and, in some states, are personally liable for claims under contracts they sold. It hardly seems necessary to add that an unlicensed insurer cannot maintain an action to enforce any claim arising out of an insurance contract that violates the laws of the state in which the suit is brought.

Unauthorized Insurers Service-of-Process Act

Unlicensed or Unauthorized Insurers

- Contracts may be enforceable by policyowner.
- Litigation against insurer may be initiated and tried in state of policyowner.
- Litigation against out-of-state insurer may be coordinated through insurance regulator in policyowner's own state.

If the insurer is duly authorized to do business in a particular state but has failed to comply with some other requirement of the state law, the validity of its contracts will usually not be affected by the noncompliance. The contracts will be binding on both parties, but the insurer will be subject to whatever penalties are imposed for the violation of the law. If the statute requires certain provisions in such a contract, the contract will be deemed to contain such provisions.

Competency of the Applicant

All individuals are presumed to have legal capacity except those belonging to clearly defined groups that are held by law to have no capacity or only limited capacity to contract. For example, an alien enemy and a person judicially determined insane are wholly incompetent to enter into a contract. Others, such as minors and those who are mentally infirm but not adjudicated incompetent, have varying levels of contractual capacity.

Minors—or infants, as they are known to the law—do not lack capacity in the absolute sense and may enter into contracts that are binding on the other party. However, subject to certain restrictions, a minor can disaffirm a contract at any time during minority and demand a return of the monetary consideration that passed to the other party. Limitations on the right of a minor to void contracts are found in the general rules stipulating that an infant is bound to pay the reasonable value of necessities actually furnished to him or her. If the minor can make restitution for that which he or she received, it must be done.

American courts have held that a life insurance policy is not a necessity for a minor in the legal sense of the word. Hence, absent a statute to the contrary, a minor can disaffirm a life insurance contract at any time during minority and recover all premiums paid. Most courts permit full recovery of premiums with no deduction for the cost of protection, while a few courts authorize the company to retain that portion of the aggregate premiums applied toward the cost of protection. In the latter case, recovery is limited to the policy's cash value or reserve. It is clear that only by permitting the insurer to deduct the cost of protection does the court compel the minor to make restitution to the insurer.

Recognizing the importance of life insurance and of the unfavorable position of a life insurance company in dealing with minors, most states have enacted statutes conferring the legal capacity to enter into valid and enforceable life insurance contracts covering their own lives on minors of a specified age and older. The age limit varies from 14 to 18, with age 15 predominating. A minor who satisfies the age requirement is permitted not only to purchase a life insurance policy but also to exercise all ownership rights in the contract. The statutes usually require that the beneficiary be a close relative; the eligible relationships are set forth in each state's law. Some of the statutes bestow legal capacity on a minor only for the purpose of negotiating insurance on his or her own life; the minor (in those states) still lacks legal capacity to become the owner of a policy on the life of another person.

Limited Contracting Capacity of Minors

- Minor may disaffirm a contract at any time during minority.
- Minor may demand return of monetary consideration paid before disaffirming contract.
- Most states grant legal capacity to contract for life insurance at age 15 (age 18 in a few states).

A life insurance contract entered into between an American company and a resident of a foreign country is just as valid as one made with an American citizen unless the two countries are at war, in which case the contract is null. In the first instance, the resident of the foreign country would be described as an alien friend; in the second, as an alien enemy. A contract made with an alien friend is valid in all respects, while one with an alien enemy is void. No difficulties are likely to arise unless an alien friend with whom a contract has been made becomes an alien enemy through the outbreak of hostilities. In that event, it will generally be impossible, as well as contrary to public policy, for the parties to carry out the terms of the contract. In the case of life insurance, premium payments could not be made (unless the company had a branch office in the foreign country), and a question would arise as to the status of the policy.

Court rulings involving this problem have been diverse. In Connecticut and a few other states, it is held that all rights in such contracts are terminated and all equities forfeited. This is a harsh rule, and permits the enrichment of the insurance company at the expense of one whose nonperformance was beyond his or her individual control.

Many more states, including New York, hold that the contract is merely suspended during hostilities and can be revived by payment of all past-due premiums. Under this rule, the policy of a deceased policyowner can be revived and the company forced to pay the face amount. This rule obviously exposes the company to a high degree of adverse selection.

A third rule, established in 1876 by the U.S. Supreme Court, holds that a contract is terminated for nonpayment of premiums caused by the outbreak of hostilities, but the policyowner is entitled to the reserve value computed as of the date of the first premium in default. The reserve is paid to the governmental agency responsible for assembling and holding property belonging to alien enemies. Under this rule, no action can be brought to recover the face amount of the policy; nor is the company under any obligation to revive the policy.

Although none of these solutions to the problem is completely satisfactory, the basis of settlement prescribed by the Supreme Court in 1876 seems to be the most equitable. However, that case was decided before nonforfeiture values were a common provision. It was also based on federal common law, which no longer exists. Today, the practice would likely be to apply the automatic nonforfeiture provisions and perform the contract as written.

MUTUAL ASSENT

As in the case of other simple contracts, there must be a manifestation of mutual assent before a life insurance contract can be created. One party must make an offer to enter into an insurance transaction, and the other must accept the offer. One would naturally assume that the company, through one of its soliciting agents, makes the offer, which the prospective insured is free to accept or decline. That is not necessarily the case.

In many situations, the prospect is considered to have made the offer. As a general rule, and subject to the exceptions noted later, the prospect is considered to have made the offer whenever the application is accompanied by the first premium; the company is regarded as the offeror whenever the first premium is not paid (or at least not definitely promised) with the application. In the first situation, the prospect has indicated his or her unqualified willingness to enter into a contractual relationship with the company, even to the point of putting up the consideration. In the second situation, the prospect may refuse, without any legal penalties, to accept and pay for the contract issued by the company. The question of who is the offeror and who the offeree is important in determining the exact time at which the contract takes effect, which may be of crucial significance. (This matter is dealt with later in this book.)

Example: ***Offer and Acceptance***

Stan applied for insurance on his own life but did not pay the first premium with the application. Two weeks later, the insurer issued the policy exactly as applied for and forwarded it to the soliciting agent. On his way to deliver the policy, the agent learned that Stan had died in a plane crash that morning. Is the policy in force? No, because Stan had invited an offer. The insurer made the offer, but acceptance of it never took place.

Many states now require that the policyowner be given a "10-day free look" after delivery of the policy. During that time the contract is in effect, but its continuation is subject to the policyowner's right to cancel the policy within the 10 days and receive a full refund of his or her premiums.

The Application

The chain of events that culminates in a life insurance contract begins with a conversation between the company's soliciting agent and a prospect for insurance, during the course of which the prospect is invited or—more accurately—urged to extend an offer to the company. Such invitations to deal have no legal consequences in the formation of the contract, although they may contain representations that will have consequences after the contract is made. If the invitation to deal comes from a broker, the representations will have no legal effect before or after formation of the contract because a broker is considered the applicant's agent for the purpose of procuring insurance.

The applicant's offer to the company, or an applicant's invitation to the company to make him or her an offer, as the case might be, is communicated in the form of an application. Unless there is a specific state statute requiring that the application be in writing, it is clear that the application and the contract can be either oral or written. Written applications for life insurance policies, however, are required as a matter of company practice.

The application for a life insurance contract serves the following purposes:

- It requests the insurer to issue a specific type of policy, providing a designated amount of insurance in exchange for a specified premium.
- It gives the name and address of the applicant (and person to be insured if different from the applicant), the name and relationship of the person or persons to whom the proceeds are to be paid, and the manner in which the company's obligation is to be discharged.
- It provides a detailed description of the risk that the insurer is asked to underwrite, including statements or representations as to the applicant's (or person to be insured's) occupation, travel plans, family history, personal medical history, present physical condition, and habits.
- It puts the applicant on notice and requires an acknowledgment from him or her that the soliciting agent has no authority to modify any terms of the application or of the policy to be issued pursuant to that (the *nonwaiver clause*).
- It authorizes the insurer to obtain information from other sources (including the Medical Information Bureau) about the health, lifestyle, and finances of the person to be insured.

The contents of the application relating to the first two functions constitute the offer in the technical sense since they fix the terms of the policy to be issued by the company as an acceptance of the offer. While the identification of the person whose life is to be insured is a necessary part of the offer, the detailed description of the risk is not actually a part of the offer. From a legal standpoint, the applicant's representations as to his or her medical history, present physical condition, and so on are merely inducements to the insurer; they are not promises or conditions of the contract. Neither does the nonwaiver clause relate to the offer. It is intended merely to prevent the applicant from successfully contending afterward that he or she was misled as to the agent's apparent authority.

In the typical commercial transaction, the offer becomes a part of the contract ultimately consummated. This is not true of the offer leading to a life insurance contract unless the application is specifically made a part of the contract (a common insurance practice). It has long been established—first by court decisions and later by statutes—that once a life insurance policy is issued, the entire contract is contained in the policy. This rule, known historically as the *parol evidence rule,* has been stated as follows:

> All preliminary negotiations, conversations, and oral agreements are merged in and superseded by the subsequent written contract and unless fraud, accident, or mistake be averred, the writing constitutes the agreement between the parties, and its terms cannot be added to or subtracted from by parol evidence.[1]

A typical state statute provides that "every policy of life, accident or health insurance, or contract of annuity delivered or issued for delivery in this state shall contain the entire contract between the parties." In addition, most insurance policies contain a provision to this effect, as in this example:

> This policy, the attached copy of the initial application, any application for reinstatement, all subsequent applications to change the policy and any endorsements or riders are the entire contract. No statement will be used in defense of a claim unless such statement is contained in the application(s).

A Life Insurance Policy Includes

- policy itself
- initial application
- any endorsements or riders to the policy
- any subsequent applications to change the policy
- any application for reinstatement

Because the company relies on the information contained in the application, and in the event of a contested claim would undoubtedly want to introduce evidence from it, it customarily incorporates the application into the contract, by reference as well as by physical attachment of a copy (usually a photostat) of the application to the policy. In most states there are statutes requiring that a copy of the application be physically attached to the policy if the statements in the application are to be treated as representations and are to be introduced into evidence in the event of litigation. Typical statutory language provides that "no application for issuance of any life, accident or health insurance policy, or contract of annuity shall be admissible in evidence unless a true copy of such application was attached to such policy when issued."

Effective Date of Coverage

The coverage under a life insurance policy becomes effective the instant the contract comes into existence. This, however, takes place only after certain conditions have been fulfilled, and those conditions can be fulfilled in more than one manner. The procedure by which a contract is brought into existence after the application's submission depends on whether the application is regarded as an offer or only as an invitation to the company to make an offer. That, in turn, depends on the time at which and the circumstances under which the first premium is paid. In that regard it is necessary to distinguish among three different sets of circumstances. The first set of circumstances is one under which the application is submitted without payment of the first premium.

Application without First Premium

Recall that when the applicant does not tender the first premium with the application, no offer has been made. The application is regarded as only an invitation to deal. The approval of the application and the issuance of the policy constitute an offer from the company to the prospective insured, which is normally communicated by delivery of the policy. The applicant conveys his or her acceptance of the company's offer by accepting delivery of the policy and paying the first premium. This assumes that the soliciting agent does not have authority to extend credit. If the agent has authority to take a promissory note or even an oral promise of the insured in lieu of cash, an application accompanied by such a promise is an offer from the applicant to make a *bilateral* contract—an exchange of the applicant's promise for the insurer's promise.

Most companies specify in the application that the prospective insured must be in good health at the time of delivery of the policy, and some insurers condition the contract on the absence of any medical treatment during the interim between the application's submission and the policy's delivery. All these requirements—delivery of the policy, payment of the first premium, good health of the applicant, and absence of any interim medical treatment—are treated as conditions precedent that must be fulfilled before the contract comes into existence and the coverage becomes effective. Each of these requirements will be discussed below.

Conditions Necessary to Create Life Insurance Coverage

- delivery of the policy
- payment of the first premium
- good health of applicant
- absence of any interim medical treatment

Delivery of the Policy. Delivery of the policy is a legal prerequisite to the validity of the life insurance contract only because many companies specifically make it so. Neither by statute nor by common law is the delivery of a formal policy requisite to the completion, validity, or enforceability of a contract of insurance. This is contrary to real estate law, for example, which holds that legal title to real estate is not transferred until the deed is delivered. The company could conceivably communicate its offer to the applicant in some other manner, and the applicant could manifest acceptance by notifying the company or the soliciting agent.

The controlling reason why many insurance companies make delivery of the policy a condition precedent to the formation of the contract is that it provides a way to establish the precise moment at which coverage under the contract becomes effective. Some carriers make no special provision in the application to set the date when coverage begins. Some provide that coverage begins when the policy is issued and the entire first year's premium has been paid. Several other actions of the company—such as approval of the application by the underwriting department, issuance of the policy, or mailing the policy to the soliciting agent for delivery—might be used to mark the inception of coverage. This could lead to much confusion and litigation unless the parties agree in advance that a definite determinable event, such as delivery of the policy, marks the beginning of coverage.

Despite this attempt to achieve certainty, litigation has developed over the meaning of the word "delivery." The issue is whether the condition can be satisfied only by a manual delivery or whether constructive delivery is sufficient. If it is clearly evident from the terms of the application and the policy that actual manual delivery is expected, the requirement will be strictly enforced. If, however, the requirement is couched in terms of a simple "delivery," the general rule is that the condition can be fulfilled by constructive delivery.

constructive delivery

Constructive delivery has been held to take place whenever a policy, properly stamped and addressed to the company's agent, is deposited in the mail, intended to be delivered unconditionally. There are a number of decisions, however, that hold that the requirement of delivery—and especially "actual delivery"—is itself a condition precedent that cannot be met by constructive delivery. (It should be noted that the issue of constructive delivery is not material if the other conditions—notably, payment of the first premium and the applicant's good health—are not met.)

To a large extent delivery is a matter of the parties' intention. It is a question of who has the *right* to possession of the policy, rather than who has actual possession. That being true, possession of the policy by the insured is at most only *prima facie* evidence of its delivery. The presumption of proper delivery can be rebutted by evidence that the insured obtained possession of the policy by fraud or for the purpose of inspecting it, or in any other manner manifesting a lack of intention on the company's part to effect a legal delivery of the policy. On the other hand, it has been held that if the first premium has been paid, the applicant is in good health, and the company has implicitly expressed its intention of being legally bound under the contract by delivering the policy to the agent to be unconditionally passed on to the applicant, the contract is in force. Even though the insured may die without actual possession of the policy, the company is liable for payment of the insured amount.

In view of the foregoing presumption, an agent must observe proper safeguards in relinquishing physical possession of a policy to an applicant before all conditions precedent have been fulfilled. The need for caution is greatly magnified if the policy, on its face, acknowledges receipt of the first premium, which is sometimes the case. The most common circumstance under which the agent may find it necessary to relinquish control over a policy without making a legal delivery is when the applicant expresses a desire to study the policy. In that event, the applicant is asked to sign a receipt acknowledging that the policy has been delivered only for examination and approval and that the first premium has not been paid. This acknowledgment is called an *inspection receipt.*

inspection receipt

Payment of First Premium. It is customary for the application—and sometimes the policy itself—to stipulate that the first premium must be paid before coverage becomes effective. Payment of the full amount in cash is usually specified, and unless the company agrees to extend credit, any payment smaller than the full premium will fail to satisfy the requirement. The agent is usually not authorized to extend credit on behalf of the company, but he or she may pay the premium for the insured and seek reimbursement on a personal basis. If an agent is authorized to accept an applicant's promissory note in payment of the first premium, the applicant's tendering such a note will satisfy the condition precedent. Failure of the applicant to pay the note at maturity may cause the policy to lapse.

Payment by check may be taken as absolute or conditional payment, depending on the parties' intention. If the check is accepted as absolute payment of the first premium, the bank's failure to honor the check would not affect the validity of the policy but merely give the insurance company the right to sue the applicant for the amount of the check. On the other hand, if the check is accepted only as conditional payment, nonpayment of the check would cause the contract to fail. Most companies stipulate that checks are accepted subject to being honored by the bank, which is the common law rule in the absence of evidence that the check was accepted as absolute payment.

delivery-in-good-health clause

Good Health of Applicant. The delivery-in-good-health clause is a by-product of the process by which risks are underwritten in life insurance. In most lines of property and casualty insurance, the local agent is given the authority to underwrite the risk and bind the coverage. There need be no lag between the inspection of the risk and the binding of the coverage. In life insurance, however, all underwriting information is forwarded to the home office, and the right to bind the risk rests solely with the executive officers of the company. Under such a system, which seems to be the only feasible one, there is an inevitable time lag between the submission of the application and the assumption of the risk by the insurer. In some cases, where the investigation of the applicant or the insured is very comprehensive and the collection of medical data involves correspondence with attending physicians and requests for supplemental diagnostic procedures, the lag might be as long as several weeks. Obviously the company would like to be protected against a deterioration of the applicant's health during the time it is considering the application. The way that insurance companies have chosen to accomplish this objective is the delivery-in-good-health clause.

While the exact wording of the good-health clause varies from company to company, the gist of the clause is that the policy will not take effect unless, upon the date of delivery, the applicant is alive and in good health. Some clauses provide that unless the first premium is paid with the application, the applicant must be alive and in good health upon payment of the first premium. This clause has the effect of making the applicant's good health a condition precedent to the effectiveness of the contract. Under the laws of some states, including Pennsylvania, if the applicant underwent a medical examination at the request of the insurer, the good-health requirement can be invoked only with respect to changes in the applicant's health occurring after the medical examination.

The fact that the good-health requirement is a condition precedent and has been enforced by the majority of courts has great significance in protecting life insurance companies against fraud. Even so, the protection of the good-health clause must be sought by the insurer during the policy's period of contestability. Once that period has expired, the good-health clause is void.

In attempting to rescind a contract on the grounds of misrepresentation or concealment, insurance companies are frequently required to prove that the applicant deliberately misrepresented the facts of the case. In fact, most states have enacted legislation that stipulates that no misrepresentation will void a policy unless the misrepresentation was made with an actual intent to deceive or unless it would increase the risk. To prove intent to defraud is always difficult and frequently impossible. With the good-health clause, however, insurance companies can avoid that difficulty since intent is not involved. The clause is concerned with the existence of a condition and not what may or may not have been known to the applicant. If the company can prove to the court's satisfaction that the applicant was not, in fact, in good health at the date of delivery of the policy, it can avoid liability under the contract. In practice, however, companies generally raise the issue only when they suspect that the applicant did not act in good faith or when there has been a material deterioration in the applicant's or proposed insured's health in the interval between the date of the medical examination and the date the policy is delivered.

As might be expected, the courts have frequently been called upon to define the meaning of the terms "good health" and "sound health." The courts have ruled that "good health," as used in the context of the clause under discussion, is a relative term, meaning not absolute freedom from physical infirmity but only such a condition of body and mind that one may discharge the ordinary duties of life without serious strain upon the vital powers. The term does not mean perfect health, but a state of health free from any disease or ailment that seriously affects a person's general physical soundness. Good health is not impaired by a mere temporary indisposition, which does not tend to weaken or undermine the constitution. One of the most comprehensive definitions was supplied by a Kansas court:

> [Good health] is not apparent good health, nor yet a belief of the applicant that he is in good health, but it is that he is in actual good health. Of course, slight troubles or temporary indisposition which will not usually result in serious consequences, and which do not seriously impair or weaken his constitution, do not establish the absence of good health, but, if the illness is of a serious nature, such as to weaken and impair the constitution and shorten life, the applicant cannot be held to be in good health.[2]

There has been a tendency on the part of some courts to narrow the application of the clause to cases where a change in the applicant's health occurs between the time of the medical examination and delivery of the policy to the applicant. This line of decisions is exemplified by a Pennsylvania case, in which the court stated that the good-health clause has no application to a disease the applicant may have had at the time of the medical examination unless fraud or misrepresentation can be proved, since presumably the applicant's physical condition was satisfactory to the company; otherwise, the policy would not have been issued. According to the court, "The legal scope of that provision is restricted to mean only that the applicant did not contract any new disease impairing his health, nor suffer any material change in his physical condition between the time of such examination and the date of the policy. . . ."[3]

This interpretation of the good-health clause is certainly at variance with the common understanding of the term good health and with the legal definition cited earlier, but it is consistent with the apparent purpose of the clause. As a matter of fact, companies have usually invoked the clause as a defense against a claim only where there has been a change in the applicant's health, or where there has been fraud or misrepresentation in the application. Moreover, the burden of proving that the applicant was not in good health at the time the policy was delivered is usually on the insurance company, although a minority of courts have held that the insured or the beneficiary must prove compliance with the clause.

Medical Treatment after Submission of Application. Some policies issued today contain a clause that provides that the life insurance policy will not take effect if the applicant has received medical or hospital treatment between the time that the application was signed and the date the policy was delivered.[4] Like the good-health clause, this clause is designed to deal with a change in the applicant's physical condition during the time the application is being processed. It is intended to be a condition precedent, and the courts generally treat it as such. In other words, if during the contestable period, the company can prove that the applicant received medical or hospital treatment between the date of the application and delivery of the policy, and failed to disclose that fact to the company, the company can avoid liability under the contract. If the medical treatment is disclosed at the time the policy is delivered, the company, after consideration of the ailment, may conclude that the applicant's insurability is not impaired and waive the clause. The courts are very zealous in seeking a waiver of the clause if the conduct of life insurance companies or their agents implied such a waiver.[5]

Justification of Conditions Precedent. When the premium is not paid with the application, all conditions precedent must be fulfilled before the contract becomes effective. In general this means that the policy must be delivered by the agent while the applicant is alive and in good health, and the full amount of the first premium must be paid in cash or by a valid check at the moment of delivery. Delivery of the policy and payment of the first premium are supposed to be simultaneous transactions.

Recognizing the advantages to both the applicant and the company of having the coverage attach at the date of application, insurance companies have devised a procedure to accomplish this objective. This procedure, involving the use of a conditional receipt, is described in the following section.

Prepayment of First Premium

The applicant can avoid the legal consequences of some conditions precedent by remitting the first premium with the application for insurance. Companies generally acknowledge receipt of the premium with a document called a *conditional receipt,* which binds the coverage without reference to delivery of the policy. There are several forms of conditional receipt in general use today,[6] but the two basic types are the insurability type and the approval type. The insurability type is the most common by a large margin.

conditional receipt

The approval type is no longer widely used because it offers far less protection to the applicant than the insurability type.

insurability type of conditional receipt

Insurability Type. The *insurability type of conditional receipt* (see figure 3-1) makes the coverage effective at the time of the application, provided the applicant is found to be insurable in accordance with the company's general underwriting rules. Some receipts make coverage effective on the date of the application or the medical examination, whichever is later.

Example: ***Insurability Type of Conditional Receipt***

On January 4, Ben applied for a life insurance policy. He paid the first premium at that time and was given a conditional receipt of the insurability type. On January 11, he underwent the medical examination as required by the insurer. On January 13, Ben died suddenly of a massive heart attack. On January 16, the insurer's underwriting department evaluated Ben's application and medical examination results, neither of which gave any indication of health problems for Ben. Unless fraud can be shown, the insurer must pay the face amount of the policy to the beneficiary.

FIGURE 3-1
Insurability Premium Receipt

Face of the Receipt

RECEIVED FROM _____, Applicant,

Name of Proposed Insured if other than Applicant _____
   Amount of cash settlement received $............................ in connection with the initial premium for the proposed insurance for which an application is this day made to the Ajax Life Insurance Company.
   Life Insurance and any additional benefits in the amount applied for (but not exceeding a maximum liability of $50,000, including all additional benefits on all pending applications to the company combined) shall be deemed to take effect as of the date of this receipt, subject to the terms and conditions printed on the reverse side hereof.
   The amount of settlement received shall be refunded if the application is declined or if a policy is issued other than as applied for and is not accepted. Any check, draft, or money order is received subject to collection.

_____   _____

   Date of Receipt   Signature of Agent

Back of the Receipt

Subject to the limitations of this receipt and the terms and conditions of the policy that may be issued by the company on the basis of the application, the life insurance and any additional benefits applied for shall not be deemed to take effect unless the company, after investigation and such medical examination, if any, as it may require, shall be satisfied that on the date of this receipt each person proposed for insurance was insurable for the *amount* of life insurance and any additional benefits applied for according to the company's rules and practice of selection; provided, however, that approval by the company of the insurability of the Proposed Insured for a plan of insurance other than that applied for, or the denial of any particular additional benefit applied for, shall not invalidate the terms and conditions for this receipt relating to life insurance and any other additional benefit applied for.

(Not to be detached unless issued under the requirements for using Conditional Receipt)

Source: *Law and the Life Insurance Contract,* 6th ed., Irwin Professional Publishing, 1989, p. 148.

Coverage under such a clause, however, is not automatic. The applicant is considered to have made an offer to the insurer. The insurer, by issuing the conditional receipt, accepts the offer, subject to a condition—the condition that the applicant is found to be insurable. If the home office finds the applicant to have been insurable in accordance with its general underwriting rules on the date of the application or medical examination, the coverage attaches retroactively to the date cited. If the company finds that the applicant was not insurable at the time he or she submitted the application, the coverage never attaches under the policy applied for and the premium is refunded. For the coverage to be binding as of the date of application, the risk must be acceptable to the company under its underwriting rules on the plan and for the amount applied for and the premium rate on the application. If the risk is acceptable, but only on a plan or at a premium rate different from that on the application, the company is construed to have made a counteroffer that must be accepted by the applicant before the coverage can become effective.

If the applicant is found to have been insurable at the date of application, coverage attaches retroactively even though, in the meantime, the applicant may have died or suffered a deterioration in health. Companies are frequently called upon to consider the application of a person known to have died since applying for insurance, and they are careful not to permit knowledge of that fact to influence their underwriting decision. The same code of ethics is followed in reviewing the prepaid applications of persons who have subsequently suffered heart attacks or other physical impairments. If the applicant is to receive the fullest benefit of the conditional receipt, it is absolutely essential that the company apply general underwriting standards, rather than standards tailored to fit the individual case.

approval type of conditional receipt

Approval Type. The *approval type of conditional receipt* (see figure 3-2) states that the coverage is effective from the completion of the application, provided the company approves the application. The receipt usually makes no reference to the criteria that will be applied in the company's consideration of the application. Under the present state of the law, however, it is clear that the company must act reasonably and apply its customary underwriting standards.

Under the approval type of receipt, the company is not at risk if the applicant dies before the application is acted upon. Nevertheless judicial opinion is divided as to whether the insurer should be held liable for payment of the policy's face amount if the applicant dies before the company acts on the application.

FIGURE 3-2
Approval Premium Receipt

Face of the Receipt

RECEIVED FROM _____ , Applicant,

Name of Proposed Insured if other than Applicant _____

    Amount of cash settlement received $...................... in connection with the initial premium for the proposed insurance for which an application is this day made to the Ajax Life Insurance Company.

    Life Insurance and any additional benefits in the amount applied for shall be deemed to take effect as of the date of approval of this application at the home office of Ajax Life Insurance Company.

    The amount of consideration received shall be refunded if the application is declined or if a policy is issued other than as applied for and is not accepted. Any check, draft, or money order is received subject to collection.

_____	_____
Date of Receipt	Signature of Agent

Back of the Receipt

    Subject to the limitations of this receipt and the terms and conditions of the policy that may be issued by the company on the basis of the application, the life insurance and any additional benefits applied for shall not be deemed to take effect unless the company, after investigation and such medical examination, if any, as it may require, shall be satisfied that on the date of this receipt each person proposed for insurance was insurable for the *amount* of life insurance and any additional benefits applied for according to the company's rules and practice of selection; provided, however, that approval by the company of the insurability of the Proposed Insured for a plan of insurance other than that applied for, or the denial of any particular additional benefit applied for, shall not invalidate the terms and conditions for this receipt relating to life insurance and any other additional benefit applied for.

(Not to be detached unless issued under the requirements for using Conditional Receipt)

Source: *Law and the Life Insurance Contract,* 6th ed., Irwin Professional Publishing, 1989, p. 148.

There is a judicial trend, noticeable with respect to both the insurability and approval types of receipts, to find an ambiguity and to hold that there is coverage from the date of the receipt until approval or declination of the application. In recognition of this trend, a minority (but a growing minority) of insurers use a form of conditional receipt that places the company unconditionally at risk from the date of application, usually for a limited face amount and period of time, such as 60 days. The insurance remains in full effect unless and until the application is declined. Under this form of receipt, the applicant enjoys coverage for a brief period even when he or she is definitely an uninsurable risk.

Properly construed, the conditional receipt arrangement offers real benefits to both the insured and the insurer and is widely used. It protects the applicant against loss of insurability while the application is being processed, and it protects the company against a declination of the policy by the applicant after it has been issued—at considerable expense. The arrangement is feasible, since all applicants using the plan pay their premiums in advance, and the company is not exposed to adverse selection. Moreover, the arrangement does not involve any relaxation of underwriting standards.

The majority of courts interpret conditional receipts strictly in accordance with the language used by the insurer. Nevertheless, even these courts have a clear preference to find that coverage does exist, and to do so they are sometimes creative in discovering an ambiguity that can be construed in favor of the applicant. The minority of courts take a much more liberal view in favor of the applicant. They tend to ignore the language of the conditional receipt and find that coverage exists because the applicant, having paid the premium, would have reasonably expected it to exist. A decreasing number of courts seem to be willing to go so far as to rewrite the terms of the conditional receipt.

However, some insurers expect that some courts will find temporary coverage effective regardless of the conditions stipulated in the receipt. In some jurisdictions, to eliminate the possibility of unintended temporary coverage, a few insurers have stopped accepting a premium payment with the application.

Advance Payment of First Premium without Conditional Receipt

The first premium is rarely remitted with the application without a conditional receipt being issued to the applicant. Under such circumstances, coverage does not attach until the application has been approved and the policy has been delivered.[7] The applicant is considered to have made an offer that can be withdrawn at any time before acceptance by the company. Acceptance is manifested by delivery of the policy.

As with policies whose premiums are not paid in advance, delivery can take the form of an actual physical transfer of the policy from the agent to the applicant or transmission through the mail in such manner as to constitute constructive delivery. However, if the application requires that the policy be delivered to the applicant while he or she is in good health, mailing the policy to the agent for delivery to the applicant is not likely to be regarded as constructive delivery since a condition has been imposed on its release. Mailing the policy directly to the applicant, regarded as a waiver of the delivery requirement, would be treated as a waiver of the good-health requirement only if the insurer had knowledge of a breach of the condition. The contract would become effective the instant the policy is placed in the mail, even if the insured never receives it.

Delay in Consideration of the Application

A life insurance company owes a moral duty (and in a minority of the states, a legal duty) to the insuring public to consider all applications within a reasonable period and to render prompt decisions on the insurability of those seeking insurance. These two questions may arise in case of an unreasonable delay by the company in determining the insurability of an applicant:

- Does the unreasonable delay constitute an acceptance of the applicant's offer?
- Is the insurer liable for the damages caused by its delay if the applicant dies before the application is either accepted or rejected?

It seems clear that no presumption of acceptance should be allowed when the application is not accompanied by the first premium. In that event, no offer has been made to the company, and the company's silence could hardly be construed as acceptance of a nonexistent offer. A different situation exists, however, when the applicant remits the first premium with the application and thus makes a valid offer to the company.

As a general rule, silence is not construed as acceptance of an offer. To the contrary, after a reasonable time, the offeror can assume that the offer has been rejected and that he or she is free to deal with another party. If this were not the rule, people with goods to sell could flood the country with offers that the recipients would be obliged to reject so that they would not become obligated to buy the goods. The writing of rejections could become an intolerable burden. A majority of courts have applied this general rule to the insurer's silence and have held that no matter how long the company delays, its silence will not bind it to a contract of insurance.

A few courts have made a distinction between *unsolicited* offers, the usual kind, and those made in response to the activities of agents who are paid to solicit offers, as is the case in life insurance. These courts have held that the insurer's unreasonable delay in rejecting an application constitutes an acceptance that completes the contract.

tort

While in most states, delay in consideration of an application does not make an insurer liable under *contract,* some courts have recognized a liability of the company in *tort*—that is, a civil liability arising from other than a contract. Although they are distinctly in the minority (and it is believed that this is no longer an important trend in the law), these courts have held that since the company is operating under a franchise from the state, it is under duty to act promptly and with due care on all applications received by it. They argue that the state issues a charter or license in order that the public may have access to an important form of protection that, in the public interest, should be made available to all who can qualify for it. These courts believe that after the company solicits the application and obtains it along with the applicant's consideration, the company is bound to furnish the insurance that the state has authorized or to decline to do so within a reasonable time. An Iowa court ruled, "Otherwise the applicant is unduly delayed in obtaining insurance he desires and for which the law has afforded the opportunity, and which the insurer impliedly has promised if conditions are satisfactory."[8] Failure to live up to this obligation makes the insurer liable to the applicant for damages.

If an applicant who was insurable at the time of application dies before the insurance company—in disregard of its duty to act promptly—has approved the risk, many courts would hold that the applicant's estate could recover the amount of insurance applied for. It would seem that if the insurer is adjudged guilty of a tort, the beneficiary would be the logical person to receive damages. With a few exceptions, however, the courts hold that the beneficiary is not a party at interest until coverage becomes effective and thus cannot recover. (The question of tort liability is not likely to arise under a conditional receipt because the conditional receipt forms in general use provide for retroactive coverage.)

Operative Date of Policy

The foregoing discussion was concerned with determining the date on which coverage under a life insurance contract becomes effective. This date is usually referred to as the *effective date* of the policy. It may or may not be the same date as that on the face of the policy, which is significant for other reasons. The date on the policy governs the status of various policy provisions after the contract has gone into effect, and it is sometimes referred to as the *operative date* of the policy.

effective date

operative date

The policy may bear the date on which it was issued, the date on which the coverage becomes effective, or the date on which it was applied for. The most common practice is to date the policy as of the date of issue unless there is a conditional receipt. In this event the policy will bear the date of the application or the medical examination, whichever is later.

Backdating

backdating
(antedating)

Occasionally a policy carries a date earlier than the date of application. This is known as *backdating (antedating)* the policy and is done only at the request of or with the consent of the applicant, usually to produce a lower insurance age and hence a lower premium.[9] The practice is not generally regarded to be in conflict with antirebating laws, but several states prohibit it when an age change is involved. Other states have attempted to control the practice by forbidding the issue of a policy that bears a date more than 6 months earlier than the date of the application, a limitation that many companies have voluntarily adopted.

The practice of backdating policies—which, from a legal standpoint, refers to the use of any date earlier than the effective date of the policy—raises these three important questions:

- When does the next premium fall due?
- From what date does extended term insurance run?
- From what date do the incontestable and suicide clauses begin to run?

Example: **Effect of Backdating**

On September 7, 2003, Jack applied for and paid an annual premium for a life insurance policy. To gain a lower rate associated with a lower age, Jack requested that the policy carry a date of June 12, 2003. The policy was issued as applied for on September 29, 2003. Jack's renewal premium for the policy will be due on June 12, 2004.

Premium Due Dates. When the antedating was done at the applicant's request and resulted in his or her lower contract age, the overwhelming majority of both state and federal courts hold that the due date of the next premium is established by the date of the policy. Even when the antedating does not benefit the applicant—that is, no age change is involved—the majority of the courts support the view that the policy date establishes the due date, on the grounds that certainty is preferable to uncertainty. In some jurisdictions, especially Missouri, it is held that the payment of an annual premium entitles the insured to a full year of protection and that the due date of the next premium is determined by reference to the effective date of coverage. For this reason, many companies do not refer to the first premium as an annual or quarterly premium but indicate the exact period that premium covers and the due date of the second premium.

Date of Extended Term Insurance. Fixing the period of extended term insurance in the event that there is a default in premium payments is closely related to the problem of determining the due date of the second and subsequent premiums. It would clearly be to the advantage of the insured and his or her beneficiaries to calculate the date of default from which the period of extended term insurance runs in reference to the effective date of the contract rather than from an earlier date of issue. If the insured dies, the choice of beginning date for the term insurance could make the difference between payment of the face amount of the policy and total avoidance of liability by the company. It is generally held, however, that the anniversary date fixed for premium payments also controls the inception date for extended term insurance.

Incontestable and Suicide Clauses. The general view regarding the incontestable and suicide clauses is that the date of issue establishes the point of departure. A few courts, however, arguing that the suicide clause is completely independent of the provisions dealing with premium payment, hold that the effective date of the policy controls. Some policies specify a certain date as being the "date of issue" for the purpose of these two clauses; courts usually recognize this date.

In summary, backdating, if done without fraud or mistake and not in violation of a state statute, is given effect whether it benefits the insured or the insurer.

CHAPTER REVIEW

Answers to the review questions and the self-test questions can be found in the Supplement.

Key Terms

insured	constructive delivery
applicant	inspection receipt
owner	delivery-in-good-health clause
third-party beneficiary	conditional receipt
assignee	insurability type of conditional
person	receipt
natural person	approval type of conditional receipt
artificial person	tort
Unauthorized Insurers Service-of-Process Act	operative date
	backdating (antedating)
parol evidence rule	

Review Questions

1. Bill Johnson purchased a $250,000 life insurance policy on his own life from ABC Life Insurance Company. As policyowner, Bill named his wife, Janet, as the beneficiary. Subsequently, Bill made a collateral (not an absolute) assignment of the policy to East Bank as security for a $10,000 loan. Who are the parties to the contract?

2. XYZ Corporation owns a $1 million life insurance policy purchased from ABC Life Insurance Company on the life of Pete Harrington, one of XYZ's young executives. Pete's wife, Sally, is named as beneficiary. Who are the parties to the contract?

3. What is the nature of the contractual relationship between the parties to a life insurance contract?

4. In each of the following cases, indicate whether the life insurance contract is enforceable, and if so, by whom:
    a. a policy issued by an unlicensed insurer
    b. a policy issued by an insurer that is duly authorized to do business in the state but has failed to comply with some other requirement of state law

5. Explain how the Unauthorized Insurers Service-of-Process Act assists the insured in enforcing claims against an unauthorized out-of-state insurer.

6. Indicate the extent to which each of the following has the capacity to contract:
    a. a person who is mentally infirm but is not adjudicated incompetent
    b. a person judicially determined insane

7. With respect to minors as applicants for life insurance contracts, explain
    a. the general rules of law concerning a minor's capacity to contract and right to disaffirm a contract
    b. how the American courts have generally applied these rules in cases involving life insurance policies
    c. how statutes enacted in most states affect the legal capacity of minors applying for life insurance

8. With respect to a life insurance contract entered into between an American life insurance company and a resident of a foreign country, explain how the validity of the contract would be influenced by whether or not a state of war exists between the two countries.

9. State the general rule that distinguishes between when the prospect and when the insurance company are considered to have made the offer to enter into a life insurance contract.

10. Explain the legal consequences of each of the following in connection with the formation of a life insurance contract:
    a. a conversation between the company's soliciting agent and a prospect for insurance during which the prospect is encouraged to purchase insurance
    b. the application for a life insurance contract

11. List the purposes served by the application for a life insurance contract and then, for each purpose listed, explain whether or not the contents of the application related to that purpose constitute part of the offer in the technical sense.

12. Why is it important for a copy of the application for a life insurance contract to be attached to the policy at the time it is issued?

13. In general, when does the coverage under a life insurance policy become effective, and on what factors does this depend?

14. Jason Manders applied to purchase $100,000 of life insurance on his own life from ABC Life Insurance Company but did not give the agent the first premium with the application. Assuming the agent does not have the authority to extend credit, answer the following questions:
    a. What is the application regarded as in this case?
    b. What will constitute the offer, and how will it normally be communicated in this case?
    c. Who will accept the offer in this case, and how will that acceptance be manifested?
    d. In this case, what conditions precedent must commonly be fulfilled before the contract becomes effective?
    e. Assuming ABC Life Insurance Company had already found Jason to be insurable according to its general underwriting rules, how much would the company be obligated to pay if Jason was killed in a car accident before the policy was delivered?
    f. How would offer and acceptance differ if the agent had authority to extend credit and accepted Jason's promissory note for the first premium at the time the application was completed?

15. For each of the following key issues litigated in an attempt to ascertain the meaning of "delivery" of a life insurance policy, state the general rules established by the courts:
    a. whether the condition can be satisfied only by manual delivery or whether constructive delivery is sufficient
    b. whether actual possession of the policy indicates that the condition precedent of delivery has been fulfilled

16. With respect to the delivery-in-good-health clause, explain the following:
    a. the purpose of including the clause in the life insurance application

    b. how the courts have interpreted the meaning of the terms "good health" and "sound health"

    c. the types of situations in which companies usually invoke the clause as a defense to a claim

17. Explain how the courts have generally interpreted the clause included in some life insurance policies that provides that the policy will not take effect if the applicant-insured has received medical or hospital treatment between the time the application was signed and the date of the policy's delivery.

18. Alan Frank applied to purchase $50,000 of life insurance on his own life from ABC Life Insurance Company. At the time he completed the application, Alan paid the agent the first premium and was given a conditional receipt (insurability type) by the agent. Given this information, answer the following:

    a. Who is considered to have made the offer in this case?

    b. Who accepted the offer in this case, and how was that acceptance manifested?

    c. Assuming ABC Life Insurance Company had already found Alan to be insurable according to its general underwriting rules, how much would the company be obligated to pay if Alan was killed in a car accident before the policy was delivered?

    d. Assuming Alan would have been found to be insurable according to the insurer's general underwriting rules on the date of the application, how much would the ABC Life Insurance Company be obligated to pay if Alan was killed in a car accident before the underwriting review of his case was completed and, accordingly, before a policy was issued?

    e. How would the answer to question d. differ if the agent had given an approval type of conditional receipt rather than an insurability type receipt to Alan when the first premium was paid?

19. What benefits do the conditional receipts offer to each of the following?
    a. the applicant
    b. the insurance company

20. Jean Jones applied to purchase $250,000 of life insurance on her own life from ABC Life Insurance Company. At the time she completed the application, Jean gave the agent a personal check for the first premium but was given no receipt by the agent. Given this information, answer the following questions:
    a. Who is considered to have made the offer in this case?
    b. Who will accept the offer in this case, and how will that acceptance be manifested?

21. State the rules applied by the majority of the courts and by the minority of the courts in dealing with each of the following issues related to an

unreasonable delay by the insurance company in determining the insurability of a prospective insured:

    a.   whether the unreasonable delay constitutes acceptance of the applicant's offer

    b.   whether the insurer is liable for damages caused by its delay if the prospective insured dies before the application is either accepted or rejected

22.   State the rules generally applied by the courts in resolving the following issues in cases where policies have been backdated:

    a.   When does the next premium fall due?

    b.   From what date does extended term insurance run?

    c.   From what date do the incontestable and suicide clauses begin to run?

Self-Test Questions

T   F   1.   The parties to a life insurance contract are the insurance company, the insured, and the third-party beneficiary.

T   F   2.   The applicant is normally, but not necessarily, the owner of a life insurance policy.

T   F   3.   The contractual relationship between the insurance company and the owner of a life insurance policy is that of conditional debtor and creditor.

T   F   4.   A contract issued by an unlicensed insurer is usually enforceable by the policyowner.

T   F   5.   The Unauthorized Insurers Service-of-Process Act permits the insured to seek a judgment against an unauthorized out-of-state insurer in the courts of his or her own state.

T   F   6.   If the state statute requires certain provisions to be included in a life insurance policy, a contract issued without those provisions will generally be deemed invalid and thus unenforceable by either party.

T   F   7.   Mentally infirm persons always lack the capacity to contract.

T   F   8.   If there is no statute to the contrary, a minor can disaffirm a life insurance contract at any time during minority and recover all premiums paid.

T   F   9.   Most states have enacted statutes that permit minors of at least a specified age to enter into valid and enforceable life insurance contracts covering their own lives.

T   F   10.   As a general rule, the prospect is considered to have made the offer whenever the application is accompanied by the first premium.

T   F   11.   As a matter of common practice in life insurance, the offer does not become part of the contract.

T   F   12.   Coverage under a life insurance policy becomes effective once the policy is delivered.

T   F   13.   When the applicant does not tender the first premium with the application, the application is regarded as the offer and the issuance of the policy by the insurer is considered the acceptance of the offer.

T   F   14.   Even when the terms of the application and policy clearly indicate that actual delivery of the policy is expected, the courts generally hold that constructive delivery is sufficient to fulfill the condition precedent.

T   F   15.   Usually the courts base their decisions concerning the delivery of a life insurance policy on whom has actual possession of the policy.

T   F   16.   Most insurance companies today take a check as absolute payment of the first premium.

T   F   17.   In interpreting the delivery-in-good-health clause, the courts have generally ruled that "good health" is a relative term that does not require absolute freedom from every physical infirmity.

T   F   18.   When the first premium is not paid with the application, all conditions precedent must be fulfilled before the contract becomes effective.

T   F   19.   When the insurability type of conditional receipt is used to acknowledge receipt of the first premium, the company has accepted the applicant's offer subject to a condition.

T   F   20.   When the approval type of conditional receipt is used to acknowledge receipt of the first premium, the insurance company is generally obligated to pay the death benefit if the insured dies before the application is acted upon, as long as the insured would have been insurable according to the company's general underwriting rules on the date of the application.

T   F   21.   If the first premium is remitted with the application without a conditional receipt being issued to the applicant, coverage generally does not attach until the application has been approved and the policy has been delivered.

T   F   22.   Most courts have construed an unreasonable delay by the insurer in acting on the application as an acceptance of an offer that binds the insurer to the contract.

T   F   23.   The date on the face of a life insurance policy is always the same as the date on which coverage under the contract becomes effective.

T   F   24. When backdating has been done at the applicant's request, the majority of courts hold that the policy date establishes the premium due date even when the backdating does not benefit the applicant

T   F   25. The general view of the courts is that the date of issue establishes the point of departure for the incontestable and suicide clauses.

NOTES

1. H. M. Horne and D. B. Mansfield, *The Life Insurance Contract,* 2d ed. (New York: Life Office Management Association, 1948), p. 46.
2. *Klein v. Farmers and Bankers Life Insurance Co.,* 132 Kan. 748, 753, 297 Pac. 730, 732 (1931).
3. *Davidson et al. v. John Hancock Mutual Life Insurance Co.,* 159 Pa. Super. 535, 49 A. 2d 186 (1946).
4. Industrial life insurance policies usually contain a provision that permits the company to void the contract (within the contestable period) if within 2 years prior to application for the policy the insured received hospital or medical treatment that he or she failed to disclose or to prove immaterial to the risk.
5. Some companies invoke the doctrine of continuing representations to deal with changes in insurability during the interim between submission of the application and delivery of the policy. The landmark case in this area of law is *Stipcich v. Metropolitan Life Ins. Co.,* 277 U.S. 311, 45 Sup. Ct. 512, 72 L.Ed. 895.
6. Muriel L. Crawford and William T. Beadles, *Law and the Life Insurance Contract,* 6th ed. (Homewood, IL: Irwin Professional Publishing, 1989), pp. 154–165.
7. A few courts have held to the contrary. Moreover, California has a statute that binds the insurer as of the moment of premium payment if the risk meets the underwriting requirements of the company.
8. *Duffie v. Bankers Life Assn.,* 160 Iowa 19, 27, 139 N.W. 1087, 1090 (1913).
9. A person's insurance age for ordinary insurance is his or her age at the nearest birthday. For insurance purposes, he or she becomes 1 year older 6 months and 1 day after his or her last birthday. It is possible to obtain a lower insurance age by dating a policy back only 1 day, but most cases involve a much longer period.

Formation of a Life Insurance Contract: Part 2

Dan M. McGill
Revised by Burke A. Christensen

Learning Objectives

An understanding of the material in this chapter should enable the student to

---

4-1. Distinguish between the consideration for a unilateral life insurance contract and a bilateral contract.

4-2. Distinguish between the roles of the first premium and premiums after the first in connection with the formation and continuance of a life insuranccontract.

4-3. Explain the grounds on which insurers accept checks and promissory notes for payment of the first premium on life insurance contracts and what rights the insurer has under various circumstances when it does so.

4-4. State the general rule regarding what contracts must do and must not do to satisfy the requirement of legal purpose, and describe the exception to this general rule for life insurance contracts.

4-5. List three behaviors contrary to public policy that might be encouraged by the purchase of life insurance, and describe the various safeguards to deter such behavior.

4-6. With respect to the requirement of insurable interest in life insurance, explain

   a. what is meant by insurable interest
   b. when insurable interest must exist
   c. who is required to have an insurable interest in the life of the insured (1) when the policy is procured by the insured and (2) when the policy is procured by someone other than the insured
   d. what types of relationships may give rise to an insurable interest when the policy is procured by someone other than the insured and what the interest may be based on for each of these relationships
   e. how the courts treat life insurance contracts that are not supported by an incipient insurable interest and thus are illegal

4-7.   Explain when the consent of the person to be insured is usually required by the law and by insurers when a life insurance contract is taken out by someone other than the prospective insured.

4-8.   Describe the factors that influence the form a life insurance contract may take.

Chapter Outline

CONSIDERATION

consideration

consideration: any benefit to the promisor or detriment to the promisee

Nature of the Consideration

The life insurance contract, like other contracts, must be supported by a valid consideration. In a unilateral contract, consideration is always given in exchange for a promise, and in the case of a bilateral contract is itself a promise. Since only the company makes an enforceable promise, the life insurance contract is a unilateral contract. The consideration for the insurer's promise is the first premium, or if premiums are to be paid more frequently than annually, the first installment of the first premium. Most life insurance policies state that the company's promise is given in consideration of the *application* and the first premium. This is apparently intended to give greater legal effect to the application, on which the company places great reliance.

Your policy and the application make up the entire contract. We relied on the application in issuing this policy. A copy was attached to the policy when it was issued. Please examine it and let us know if there are any errors or omissions. The only statements that may be used to contest the policy are those in the application. In the absence of fraud, they will be representations, not warranties.

The consideration for this policy is the application and payment of the total initial premium on or before policy delivery.

condition

condition: a provision in a legal agreement that makes one event contingent upon the occurrence of another

condition precedent

condition precedent: an event that must occur *before* another duty or right exists

condition subsequent

condition subsequent: an event that terminates an existing duty or right

Premiums after the first are not part of the legal consideration since otherwise the contract could not come into existence until they are all paid. Rather, payment of such premiums is a condition precedent to the continuance of the contract. This means that the insurer's promise is conditioned on the continued payment of periodic premiums. In other words, the contract contains a provision that makes the continued payment of premiums a condition that must occur before the insurer will have to perform on its promises. If the insured defaults in the payment of a fixed premium after the life insurance contract is in force, the company is released (subject to the nonforfeiture laws) from its original promise to pay the face amount of the policy. But it remains obligated to honor various subsidiary promises that are contained in the surrender provisions and the reinstatement clause. For flexible premium policies, the required condition is that premium payments must be adequate to satisfy the specified minimum cash value (commonly 2 month's mortality charges) or else the insurer is released from its promise to pay a death benefit.

Form of the Consideration

The insurance company is entitled to receive the first premium, or the first installment thereof, in cash; it may, however, agree to accept any valuable property. The premium may be paid in cash, by check, by promissory note, or—in the absence of a prohibitive statute—by services, such as printing work or advertising. Some states forbid an insurance company to accept payment of any premium in services, presumably because the practice lends itself too readily to rebating. By placing an excessive value on the services rendered, a company or its agent could, in effect, refund a portion of the contractual premium charge. Today, payment of premiums by any method other than cash, policy loans, or financing programs (in the case of some college senior or graduate student plans) is generally prohibited.

Checks are readily accepted by insurance companies, but they are generally treated as conditional payments. That is, crediting the premium is usually conditioned on the bank upon which the check is drawn honoring the instrument. If the check is not honored when presented and the company holds that the premium has not been paid, its promise is no longer operative for a fixed premium policy. This is true even if the check was tendered to the insurer in good faith by the insured. However, when the insured had sufficient funds in the bank to cover the check and the bank's failure to honor the check was based on a technical defect in the instrument, such as an improper signature or an incorrect date, or on a clerical error on the part of the bank, insurance companies are inclined to recognize a contractual obligation, provided that the premium is subsequently paid in cash or by valid check.[1]

A company or its properly authorized agent may agree that the check constitutes an absolute payment of the premium. That is, the company accepts the liability of the parties to the instrument in satisfaction of the premium. Although this is not normal procedure, it may occur when the agent gives the applicant an unconditional premium receipt in exchange for his or her check. In this case, if the check is not paid when presented, the company may enforce its rights on the instrument, but it cannot validly claim that the premium has not been paid.

promissory note   *promissory note*: a written promise to pay a sum of money

While it is no longer a common practice, a company may also authorize some or all of its agents to accept the insured's promissory note in payment of the first premium (and subsequent premiums, for that matter). If the note is honored at maturity, there are no complications, but there is a real question about the status of the policy in the event that the note is not paid when due. Anticipating this complication, a company may stipulate on the note, on any premium receipt, on the policy, or on all three that if the note is not paid at maturity, the policy will be forfeited. If such a provision is included, it will be enforced according to its terms. As soon as the maturity date of the note arrives, if the note remains unpaid, the company is entitled to repudiate the contract.

If the stipulation is included in the note or in the premium receipt *but not in the policy,* there is a conflict of opinion as to the rights of the company.[2] Some courts hold that the provision is invalid because it violates the statute in most states that says that the policy and the application constitute the entire contract between the parties. Other courts uphold the provision by recognizing that the statute means simply that the policy contains the entire contract as of the time it was issued. The courts that entertain this view feel that the statute does not prevent the execution of subsequent agreements. They point out that if the policy is construed to contain all possible agreements relating to the contract, it would be contrary to the statute for the company to agree to an extension of time to pay a premium, whereas such agreements are generally recognized. Upholding the provision seems to be in accord with the evident intention of the parties.

If the forfeiture provision is contained in the policy but not in the note or the premium receipt, there is also a conflict of opinion. In states in which the entire-contract statute is strictly followed, the provision contained in the policy will be enforced according to its terms. In other states the decision turns on the interpretation of the note and the receipt. If the note and the receipt evidence an intention on the part of the insurer to accept the note as an unconditional payment, this subsequent agreement will override the provision contained in the policy. On the other hand, if there is no indication of an intention to accept the note as an unconditional payment, the provision in the policy will prevail.

If there is no forfeiture provision in the policy, the note, or the premium receipt, the note is considered to be an absolute payment of the premium, and the insurance company is limited to its rights on the note in the event that it is not paid at maturity. This is the usual case.

It should be observed that if the insurer or its authorized agent extends credit to the insured, the contract will be bilateral rather than unilateral. In this case, the consideration for the insurer's promise is the insured's promise to pay the amount of the first premium.

An agent who is not authorized to extend credit on behalf of the company may pay the premium for the applicant. In doing so, he or she is acting as the applicant's agent, and failure of the applicant to reimburse the agent will not invalidate the policy.

LEGALITY OF PURPOSE

General Considerations

To be enforceable a contract must be entered into for a legal purpose. All contracts are assumed to have a legal purpose, except those that contemplate a course of action that would contravene a statute or some other rule of law. It is not sufficient, however, that the agreement refrain from an act specifically prohibited by law; it must not tend to encourage illegality, immorality, or other conduct contrary to public policy. There is an exception to this rule. An insurance contract issued by an insurer unlicensed to do business in that state is an illegal contract. However, the law that makes such a contract illegal was enacted to protect the citizens of the state. Consequently, the law permits the insured, but not the life insurance company, the option to either avoid or enforce the contract.

Life insurance clearly does not require either party to perform an illegal act and, in that respect, qualifies as a perfectly valid contract. As a matter of fact, it is universally recognized as having a purpose highly beneficial to society and worthy of favorable legislative treatment. On the other hand, it has been acknowledged that without adequate safeguards, life insurance could lend itself to behavior that would be socially harmful and contrary to public policy. Specifically, it could provide the motivation for wagering, murder, and suicide.

Inducement to Wagering

Regarding the first of these dangers, remember that life insurance is an aleatory contract. This means that it offers the potential of a return out of all proportion to the investment in the contract. This characteristic quickly attracted elements of the population who hoped to enrich themselves through the operation of the laws of chance. In 18th century England, life insurance became the means of satisfying a mania for gambling, which was discouraged but not prohibited. Speculative life insurance was likely to be taken out on anyone who was in the public eye. Persons accused of crimes punishable by death and those in disfavor with the royal court were favorite subjects for life insurance contracts. Prominent people became the object of speculative insurance as soon as press notices revealed them to be seriously ill, and the premium for new policies on such persons fluctuated from day to day in accordance with the reports or rumors of their condition. Newspapers of the day even carried premium quotations on the lives of persons known to be the object of speculative insurance, with the consequences described by a contemporary writer. "This inhuman sport affected the minds of men depressed by long sickness; for when such persons casting an eye over a newspaper for amusement, saw their lives had been insured in the Alley at 90 p.c., they despaired of all hopes, and thus their desolution [sic] was hastened."[3]

The situation became so intolerable that in 1774 Parliament enacted a law stating that a person contracting for insurance had to have an insurable interest in the life of the person to be insured. The statute added an indemnity element; upon the death of the insured, it was illegal to recover a sum in excess of the monetary interest that the policyowner had in the life of the insured.

In this country an insurable interest has always been required in all jurisdictions, but with the exceptions noted later, no attempt has been made to apply the indemnity concept that existed for a time in England. As late as 1960, the requirement of insurable interest was not based upon statute but resulted from a judicial application of the public policy against enforcing wagering contracts. All states require that an insurable interest between the applicant-owner and the prospective insured exist at the contract's inception.

Example: ***Life Insurance as a Wagering Contract***

Alex, a U.S. Marine, may soon be sent to the Philippines to assist in the U.S. war against a group of terrorists there. Gordon, a friend of Alex, convinces Janine, Alex's wife, to take out a life insurance policy on Alex. Gordon secretly agrees with Janine that Gordon will pay all the premiums, in return for which Janine will name Gordon as beneficiary of 50 percent of the proceeds. Because Gordon has no insurable interest in Alex's life, the policy is, for Gordon, purely a wagering contract.

Murder of Insured by Beneficiary

The insurable interest requirement originated as a means of controlling wagering on human lives, and still finds its greatest significance in that function. But it was also intended to reduce the threat of murder created by insuring one person's life for the benefit of another. The thought was that, if the class of persons who can legally insure the life of another is restricted to those who are closely related to the proposed insured by blood, or possess such a financial relationship that they stand to gain more by his or her continued life than by the insured's death, the temptation to murder the insured would be greatly curtailed. A further safeguard is that a person whose life is to be insured by another must give his or her consent to the transaction. Presumably, a prospective insured will not permit his or her life to be insured in favor of a person whose integrity or motives are questionable.

Relationships Supporting an Insurable Interest

- close family member
- spouse
- financial dependency
- business partnership
- debtor-creditor

The same reasoning underlies the rule, discussed later, that the beneficiary of a policy applied for or owned by the insured need not have an insurable interest in the insured. The law presumes that the insured, whose life is at stake, is capable of choosing beneficiaries who will not be motivated to commit murder to enjoy the insurance proceeds sooner.

The foregoing deterrents are supplemented not only by criminal penalties for murder but also by statutes and judicial rulings that prohibit the payment of insurance proceeds to a beneficiary who murders the insured. This restriction is based on a general rule of law that a wrongdoer is not permitted to profit by his or her wrongdoing. The insurance company is not relieved of its obligation to pay, because the proceeds will be owed to contingent beneficiaries or to the insured's estate, depending on the policy language and the law in the particular jurisdiction involved.

suicide

> *suicide*: the intentional killing of oneself. For insurance purposes, it makes a difference whether the person was sane or insane at the time of the suicide.

Suicide

A final area in which there is the possibility of a conflict between life insurance and the public interest is the treatment of suicide. Suicide is contrary to many religious laws, and attempted suicide is ordinarily a penal offense. Thus suicide is contrary to public policy. Any contract that would encourage suicide or act as an inducement to commit suicide would, by the same token, be contrary to public policy.

To protect against people who might apply for insurance with the deliberate intention of committing suicide, insurers adopted the precaution of inserting a clause in their policies that limited their liability to a return of premiums if the insured committed suicide within a specified period—usually one or 2 years—after the date of issue. It was felt that such a clause would properly protect the insurers' interests and after a preliminary period during which any abnormal impulse toward self-destruction should have passed, would provide coverage against a peril to which all people are subject.

Such a clause was adjudged by the U.S. Supreme Court to conserve the public interest, and most of the states have enacted statutory restrictions on the insurer's right to avoid liability because of suicide during a limited period after the life insurance policy is issued. Although most states permit suicide exclusions for 2 years or less, a few states limit the maximum length of the suicide exclusion clause to one year.

Exception to Suicide Exclusion. An exception to this philosophy is the Missouri statute that precludes the defense of suicide at any time unless it can be proved that the insured was contemplating suicide at the time he or she applied for the insurance. The Missouri statute provides as follows: "In all suits upon policies of insurance on life hereafter issued by any company doing business in this state, to a citizen of this state, it shall be no defense that the insured committed suicide, unless it shall be shown to the satisfaction of the court or jury trying the case, that the insured contemplated suicide at the time he made his application for the policy, and any stipulation in the policy to the contrary shall be void." This statute has been upheld by the U.S. Supreme Court as not being in conflict with the state constitution or the federal Constitution, but the court intimated that the statute was inconsistent with public policy and sound morality.

The insured's state of mind at the time of the suicide can determine whether the death benefit is payable. New York, for example, prohibits exclusion of suicide while the insured is insane. Suppose the policy has a suicide clause, but the clause does not contain the phrase, "while sane or insane." If the insured commits suicide while sane, the company will not be required to pay the death benefit. However, if the insured was insane at the time of the suicide, the insurer will be required to pay the death benefit. This rule is based on the theory that insanity is a disease that may infect all insureds, and the insurer has assumed that risk. Consequently, to avoid that risk, suicide clauses usually specifically exclude liability for a suicide whether the insured was sane or insane. A sample suicide clause reads as follows:

> If the insured, while sane or insane, dies by suicide within two years after the date of issue, the death proceeds under this policy will be an amount equal to the premiums paid less any loan against this policy.

Note that if there is no suicide exclusion clause in the policy, the death benefit is payable even if the insured commits suicide and intended to do so when the policy was purchased. Note also that the insured's accidental death is not excluded even if it occurs as the result of the insured's sane or insane act.

Insurable Interest

insurable interest

> *insurable interest:* a relationship between the person applying for insurance and the person whose life is to be insured in which there is a reasonable expectation of benefit or advantage to the applicant from continuation of the life of the insured or an expectation of loss or detriment from the cessation of that life

A typical insurable interest statute is the following Pennsylvania law: "The term 'insurable interest' is defined as meaning, in the case of persons related by blood or law, an interest engendered by love and affection, and in the case of other persons, a lawful economic interest in having the life of the insured continue, as distinguished from an interest which would arise only by the death of the insured." In its broadest sense, insurable interest is a "relation between the insured and the event insured against such that the occurrence of the event will cause substantial loss or harm of some kind to the insured."[4] Note that the life insurance definition does not require a *pecuniary* interest; it is broad enough to recognize a sentimental interest based on love and affection. Some cases support the opinion that a relationship by blood or marriage alone constitutes an insurable interest. Among blood relationships, only parent and child, grandparent and grandchild, and siblings have been recognized as sufficiently close to establish an insurable interest. Among relationships based upon marital ties, only the relationship between husband and wife is sufficient to establish an insurable interest. Beyond these four narrow categories, it is the majority role that sentimental attachment based upon relationship alone is insufficient to establish an insurable interest. Note further that a pecuniary interest need not be capable of exact measurement. Nor need it be based on a legal right. It is sufficient that there be a *reasonable expectation* of some financial gain or advantage.

Family Insurable Interests

- parent–child
- grandparent–grandchild
- spouse–spouse (same marriage)
- siblings

Before a discussion of the various relationships that can give rise to an insurable interest, it is necessary to explain when the interest must be present.

Incidence of Insurable Interest

In property and casualty insurance, an insurable interest need not be present at the inception of the contract, but it must exist at the time of loss if there is to be any recovery under the contract. The requirements are reversed in the case of life insurance. In life insurance an insurable interest must exist at the inception of the contract but need not be present at the time of the insured's death. This striking difference in the application of the requirement results from the fact that property insurance is based on the principle of indemnity, while a life insurance contract is not. To use property insurance terminology, a life insurance policy is a *valued policy*. It is a contract to pay

valued policy

a stated sum upon the occurrence of the event insured against. The stated sum may be unrelated to the dollar value of the loss. Since the beneficiary has a legal claim to a fixed sum of money upon the insured's death, he or she need not prove that a loss was sustained by reason of the death.

Example: ***Incidence of Insurable Interest***

For several years, Ed, the sole owner of a small business, has carried key employee life insurance on Dan, Ed's leading salesperson, with Ed as the designated beneficiary. Three years ago, Dan retired from the company due to failing health. Ed continued to make the premium payments until Dan died. Although he no longer has an insurable interest in Dan's life, Ed is nevertheless entitled to the full death proceeds.

One may concede that the insurable interest of one person in another person's life should not be the *measure* of recovery and still argue that if the former's interest has become *wholly* extinguished, his or her right to the face amount of the policy should likewise be extinguished. To permit a person whose interest in the life of the insured has been completely terminated to collect the proceeds at the insured's death gives the appearance of speculation and offends many people's sense of justice. However, the rule was adopted by the English courts at a time when surrender values were not available, and termination of a policy before maturity meant forfeiture of all accumulated values. For the courts to force a policyowner to lapse a policy and forfeit the entire investment element because an interest that was perfectly valid at the time the policy was issued had been extinguished would have been harsh. The courts were faced with the alternative of permitting the owner of the policy to collect the full face amount of the policy or nothing at all.

If the matter were being adjudicated today without regard to precedent, the courts would probably hold that extinguishment of insurable interest terminates a policy, and the policyowner would be permitted to recover the cash value as of the date of extinguishment, together with premiums paid thereafter in mistaken reliance on the contract. As the matter now stands, an incipient insurable interest is all that is necessary to sustain the validity of a life insurance contract. Thus if a creditor procures insurance on the life of his or her debtor and the debt is subsequently extinguished, the creditor may keep the policy in force and collect the full amount of the policy when the insured dies. A policy procured by a partnership on the life of a partner is unaffected by the dissolution of the partnership and the transfer of the policy to a former member of the firm who no longer has an insurable interest. A corporation that procures a policy on the life of a valuable manager may collect the full amount of insurance, despite the fact that the manager had previously been discharged. A divorce does not deprive a spouse-beneficiary of the right to the proceeds of his or her former spouse's life insurance, even though he or she no longer has an insurable interest in the former spouse's life.

When Insurable Interest Is Required

- for property insurance—at time of loss
- for life insurance—at formation of policy (note Texas exception)

The foregoing rules are not followed in Texas. The Texas courts have traditionally required a continuing interest. That is, a person who takes out insurance on the life of another person must have an insurable interest in the insured at the maturity of the contract in order to receive the proceeds. Prior to 1953, Texas case law also required that any beneficiary or assignee in a policy procured by the insured must have an insurable interest at all times. A later statute modified the requirement by stating that any beneficiary or assignee named by the insured will be *deemed* to have an insurable interest, but it left undisturbed the mandate of a continuing interest for the person who procures insurance on another's life.

This discussion has made no reference to life insurance policies procured by the person whose life is to be insured since in such cases there is no question of a continuing interest. If the view is accepted that a person has an insurable interest in his or her own life, then certainly that insurable interest continues throughout his or her life.

Relationships Evidencing Insurable Interest

In considering the relationships that give rise to an insurable interest, it is helpful to distinguish between the cases in which the applicant is applying for insurance on his or her own life and those where the applicant is seeking insurance on the life of another.

Policy Procured by the Insured

The question of insurable interest is not involved when a person, on his or her own initiative, applies for a policy on his or her own life. It is commonly said that a person has an unlimited insurable interest in his or her own life, but the expression is technically inaccurate since a person does not suffer a financial loss by his or her own death—or at least that person does not survive to claim indemnity for a loss. Hence it seems preferable to state that the issue of insurable interest is immaterial when a person applies for insurance on his or her own life. Regardless of how the status of the insured is characterized, the law considers the insurable interest requirement to have been met—for any amount of life insurance.

For underwriting purposes, however, insurers do not accept the view that the applicant has an unlimited insurable interest or that the question is immaterial. An applicant's financial circumstances are carefully investigated, and the company limits the amount of insurance to that which can be justified by the applicant's financial status and earning capacity.

The law is well settled that when a person procures a policy on his or her own life, it is not necessary that the beneficiary have an insurable interest in the insured's life, either at the inception of the contract or at the time of the insured's death. U.S. law is unanimous on that point, the rationale being that insureds should be permitted to dispose of their human life value with the same freedom that they can exercise in disposing of their other property at death. The temptation to murder is considered minimized by the insured's judgment in choosing the objects of his or her bounty. As a matter of fact, the insured enjoys much greater latitude in disposing of his human life value, since insurance proceeds are not subject to restrictions on bequests to charitable organizations or claims of creditors (if properly set up). Some restrictions do exist in the community-property and quasi-community-property states, however.

Applications at Beneficiary's Instigation. The courts take a different view of the situation when the policy is applied for at the beneficiary's instigation. Such a transaction may arise out of a legitimate business relationship and have a useful purpose, or it may serve as a cloak for a wagering contract. When the application does not stem from a business or personal situation that would seem to justify the designation of the particular beneficiary as payee, and the beneficiary agrees in advance to pay all premiums under the policy, the courts are inclined to regard the transaction as speculative in nature. For example, when a woman was induced to apply for insurance on her life in favor of the mortgagee of her husband's land, her employer, her sister-in-law, and the beneficiary in each case was paying all premiums, the contract was declared to be a wager.

The payment of premiums by the beneficiary is not conclusive proof of wagering, but it gives rise to a strong inference. Since the question of insurable interest is important only at the policy's inception, it is immaterial whether later, because of a change of circumstances, the beneficiary assumes responsibility for premium payments in order to keep the policy in force.

In 1893, a North Carolina court ruled that a policy procured at a college's instigation covering the life of a wealthy man (a prospective donor) was invalid because the college had no insurable interest in his life. This changed during the 1900s, however, and it became an acceptable practice for donors to encourage charities and other nonprofit institutions to apply for life insurance on their lives, with the donors providing a means of paying the premiums, often using trusts. It was widely believed that the various state statutes regarding insurable interest included the relationship between a charity or nonprofit organization and its donors.

However, the IRS issued a private letter ruling in 1991 to a New York taxpayer disallowing income tax, gift tax, and estate tax deductions related to an intended gift of life insurance to a charity. The basis of the denial was an IRS interpretation that the charity lacked an insurable interest in the life of the donor under New York law. In swift reaction to the IRS's private letter ruling, New York and many other states amended their insurable interest statutes to acknowledge an insurable interest between charities and their prospective donors. Although there is disparity from one state to another, most of these revised statutes specifically recognize the relationship between donors and many classifications of nonprofit organizations as an insurable interest. As some tax authorities point out, a few of these statutes do not, however, explicitly express the donee organization's right to apply for the life insurance policy directly. Some tax advantages may be lost if an existing policy is donated to the organization, rather than purchased by the donee organization.

In practice, an insurer makes no distinction between applications submitted at the prospective insured's initiative and those submitted at the prospective beneficiary's instigation. In all cases, the insurer requires that the original beneficiary have an insurable interest of some sort as a precaution against wagering, homicide, or other mortal peril. If the prospective beneficiary does not appear to have a legitimate insurable interest, the company will request an explanation of the relationship; if the explanation is unsatisfactory, it will almost certainly reject the application.

Once the policy is issued, however, the company has no right to withhold approval of a change of beneficiary because the proposed beneficiary lacks an insurable interest—or on any other grounds, for that matter, except failure to comply with the prescribed procedure for effecting such a change. Of course, if the circumstances surrounding the request for a change of beneficiary indicate an attempt to evade the underwriting requirements of the company or the legal requirement of insurable interest, the insurer may be permitted to rescind the policy on the basis of fraud or because the entire transaction was a subterfuge for procurement of insurance by a person lacking an insurable interest in the insured.

Policy Assignments. The insured may make the policy payable to a third party by means of an assignment, and as a general rule, it is not necessary for the assignee to have an insurable interest. The position of the courts is that it is immaterial whether the insured designates the payee of the policy within the contract itself, as with a conventional beneficiary designation, or with a separate instrument—an assignment.

Very few states, however, require the assignee to have an insurable interest, at least under certain circumstances. All states require an insurable interest if the insured was induced by the assignee to take out the policy since that would be tantamount to the assignee's applying for the insurance directly. If there is any indication at the time of application that an assignment is contemplated, the insurance company, as a matter of underwriting practice, will usually require evidence of the prospective assignee's insurable interest.

Under the doctrine adopted by the majority of American courts, there is nothing to invalidate successive assignments of a life insurance policy once it is validly issued. None of the assignees need have an insurable interest, and the insured need not give his or her consent to the assignments. This rule is based on the doctrine that a life insurance policy is a form of personal property and should be freely transferable. If a life insurance contract could be sold only to persons having an insurable interest in the insured's life, the market would be severely limited, and the owner of the policy would be handicapped in disposing of it.

Accelerated-Benefit Provisions. In recent years there were instances where persons suffering from full-blown AIDS sold their life insurance policies to a *viatical settlement company* (a company that keeps the policy to collect the death benefit) in order to help them finance needed health care during the terminal stage of their illness. Such policy sales prompted some life insurers to introduce accelerated-benefit provisions for life insurance policies. The IRS has even set forth requirements for tax-free treatment of life insurance proceeds that are paid during the last 12 months of life for terminally ill insured persons under these accelerated-benefit provisions.

Some states have imposed insurance regulations on viatical settlement companies to discourage unregulated commercial trading of life insurance policies covering terminally ill individuals. There is a concern that desperate people with few options may be taken advantage of by unregulated persons wagering on life insurance policies.

It seems repugnant and contrary to public policy for existing life insurance policies to be sold on the auction block to the highest bidder. (Such a market actually developed in England before the development of cash values in life insurance policies.) If the buyers of these policies had an insurable interest in the insured's life, there would be less of a public policy concern. However, purchasers of existing policies do not need an insurable interest.

A recent development in the United States is the emergence of a secondary market to purchase life insurance policies that the owner no longer

viatical settlement company

life settlements

wishes to continue. The purchaser pays more than the cash surrender value that the life insurer is willing to pay. The purchaser assumes payment of premiums and becomes the beneficiary. These secondary policy sales are often called *life settlements*. They are most likely to involve policies for large face amounts covering insureds over the age of 70. Once a policy has been sold, it can be resold multiple times, and subsequent purchasers are likely to request a preliminary assessment of the insured person's health each time the policy changes ownership.

A special set of rules is applicable when a policy is made payable to a creditor of the insured, whether the designation is as beneficiary or as assignee. Creditor situations will be discussed in the next section of this chapter.

Most policies are issued upon the application and at the initiative of the person to be insured. Hence the foregoing principles govern the typical situation. The rules applicable to the exceptional cases, in which the applicant and the insured are not one and the same, are set forth below.

Policy Procured by Person Other than Insured

In most jurisdictions, consent of the person to be insured is usually essential to the validity of a life insurance contract taken out by a person other than the prospective insured. However, these jurisdictions usually make an exception for applications submitted by a spouse on the life of the other spouse or by a parent on the life of a child too young to apply for insurance in his or her own right. As a practical matter, the prospective insured's signature is needed on the application to affirm the accuracy of the information in it. Hence insurers always require the signature of the person whose life is to be insured, except when that person is a minor.

In all jurisdictions, a third-party applicant must have an insurable interest in the life of the person to be insured. This statement presupposes that the applicant will be the owner of the policy and the person to receive the proceeds upon maturity of the contract. A more accurate statement of the requirement—as it is prescribed in some states, at least—is that the *person who procures the policy and is to receive the proceeds* must have an insurable interest in the insured. The New York Insurance Law, for example, states the requirement in such terms and provides that, if the proceeds are paid to a person not having an insurable interest in the insured *at the time the contract was made,* the insured's personal representative may maintain an action to recover such proceeds from the person receiving them.

The insurable interest required may arise out of either a family or a business relationship. As explained earlier, if it arises out of a family relationship, it may be based on *love and affection* or on a legal or factual expectation of *financial* advantage from continuance of the life of the insured. Interests originating in business relationships are regarded as economic in nature.

Family Relationships. The doctrine that an emotional attachment constitutes a sufficient insurable interest, apart from financial considerations, has been expounded in various judicial opinions and incorporated into the statutes of some states. It seems that the doctrine serves both of the insurable interest requirement's major objectives: to minimize wagering and to prevent murder.

In applying the doctrine, the closeness of relationship needed to satisfy the requirement is critical. The relationship of husband and wife is universally conceded to be close enough, although it is virtually always accompanied by an economic interest. The relationship of parent and child, based on both economic and familial ties, is generally regarded as sufficient to satisfy the law. A growing minority of courts have also recognized the relationships of sibling to sibling and grandparent and grandchild as sufficient.[5] Blood relationships more remote than the above, such as uncle and niece, uncle and nephew, and cousin of any degree, have generally been rejected as insufficient. Aside from that of husband and wife, no tie growing out of affinity alone—such as an interest of an individual in his or her father-in-law, mother-in-law, brother-in-law, stepfather, or stepchild—has been recognized as a sufficient insurable interest.

Family Relationships Generally Not Supportive of Insurable Interest

- cousins
- uncle–nephew
- uncle–niece
- aunt–nephew
- aunt–niece
- father-in-law
- mother-in-law
- stepchild

The courts that do not subscribe to the belief that a sentimental value alone will satisfy the insurable interest requirement still find a valid insurable interest in close family relationships, apparently on the assumption that a legal or factual expectation of pecuniary value exists in such cases. Thus the legal obligation of spouses to support each other gives them an insurable interest in each other's life. A parent is entitled to the services of a minor child and hence has an insurable interest in the child's life. A woman has an insurable interest in the life of her fiancé, at least in states where the agreement to marry is a legal obligation.

factual expectation
An expectation of financial advantage from the continued life of a person that is not based on a legal obligation is referred to as a *factual expectation*. A

factual expectation is generally not sufficient to support a contract of indemnity, such as those found in the property and casualty insurance branches, but it has long been regarded as sufficient in life insurance. In the earliest reported American decision involving life insurance, the Supreme Judicial Court of Massachusetts upheld a policy in favor of the insured's sister on the reasoning that the insured had been voluntarily supporting her and probably would have continued to do so had he lived. A foster child, though not legally adopted and hence without legal claim to support, has been held to have an insurable interest in the life of his foster father. A woman living with a man under the honest but mistaken belief that she was lawfully married to him was held to have had an insurable interest in his life because of her expectation (possibly misplaced) that he would have continued to support her. An illegitimate child is considered to have an insurable interest in the life of his or her putative father, who has contributed to the child's support.

Example:	***Factual Expectation of Financial Advantage***
	Patricia, aged 55, is unmarried with no children. She has, however, developed a great affection for Lee Ann, Patricia's niece and a single parent, and Lee Ann's son, Todd, aged 6. In fact, Patricia has promised Lee Ann on several occasions that Patricia will pay all of the costs of Todd's college education when Todd is ready for it. In this situation, Lee Ann probably would be deemed to have an insurable interest in Patricia's life based on a factual expectation of financial advantage from Patricia's continued life.

When an insurable interest is based on a family relationship, there is no legal limit to the amount of insurance that may be validated by it. This is based on the concept that a life insurance policy is not a contract of indemnity and hence does not purport to reimburse a beneficiary for a specific pecuniary loss. Insurance companies, however, have their own strict guides limiting the amount of insurance they will underwrite. It would be extremely difficult, if not impossible, to place a precise valuation on an interest based on love and affection. Interests arising out of a legal entitlement to support could perhaps be valued, but those based on a factual expectation could be measured only in the roughest terms. Interests based on business relationships can usually be valued and, in general, can support only an amount of insurance that bears a reasonable relationship to the value of the interest.

Business Relationships. A variety of business relationships create an insurable interest. One of the most common is a contractual arrangement calling for unique or distinctive personal services. There are numerous examples of such arrangements in the entertainment world. A theatrical producer has an insurable interest in the life of an actor who has contracted to perform over a definite period and who would be extremely difficult to replace in the role. Likewise, a film producer has an insurable interest in the lives of the principal performers, which escalates as the film gets into production and the death of a star would disrupt operations and require refilming all scenes in which the deceased appeared. Professional sports teams have an insurable interest in the lives of their players.

The examples above are based on contractual or legal obligations, but factual expectations may also support an insurable interest. The importance of the business manager has led to the recognition that a corporation or other form of business enterprise has an insurable interest in the life of a manager or some other official whose services and skills are vital to the prosperity of the enterprise. This is so even though the person has not assumed a legal obligation to work for the firm for any specified period of time. A firm's interest in its key officers and employees has been recognized by statute in many states and judicially sanctioned in the other states. Insurance taken out to protect such an interest is called *key person insurance* and is widely sold.

Another business relationship that gives rise to an insurable interest exists among partners in a partnership and stockholders in a closely held corporation. The consequences of the death of a general partner or active stockholder can be so detrimental that the parties involved frequently enter into an agreement for the disposition of the business interest of any individuals who might die while still active in the management of the firm. Specifically, the agreement binds the firm's surviving members to purchase the deceased member's interest at a specified price. It also obligates the deceased member's estate to sell his or her interest to the surviving members. The agreements are usually financed by insurance on the lives of the individuals involved, and either the other members of the firm or the firm itself applies for the insurance on any particular individual. In such cases, the courts have recognized an insurable interest, based on the factual expectation of a loss if the business has to be liquidated upon a general partner's or stockholder's death.

Perhaps the most common business or commercial transaction that produces an insurable interest is by lending money.[6] Despite the fact that the obligation to repay a loan is not discharged by the death of a debtor—the obligation is enforceable against the deceased's estate—a creditor is universally conceded to have an insurable interest in the life of the debtor. This rule is based on the recognition that the creditor may not be able to collect the sum of money due from the debtor's estate because of insufficiency of assets. The creditor may protect his or her interest by taking out insurance on the debtor's life or by requiring the debtor to designate the creditor as payee under a policy taken out by the debtor.

If the creditor takes out insurance on the debtor's life *and pays the premiums,* he or she is permitted to retain the full amount of the proceeds, even though they exceed the amount of the debt, plus accumulated interest. In fact, the creditor can retain the full amount of the proceeds even if the debt has been completely extinguished. The only limitation imposed in most jurisdictions is that the amount of insurance must not be disproportionate to the amount of the debt as it existed at the time the policy was issued or as it was reasonably expected to be thereafter. The purpose of this requirement is to prevent using a debt as a cloak for a wagering transaction. In a leading case, for example, a policy for $3,000 taken out on the basis of a $70 debt was held to be a wager and hence invalid. Yet policies have been upheld when the amount of insurance was several times the debt. A Maryland court upheld a policy for $6,500 on a debt of $1,000, while a New York court validated a policy for $5,000 taken out to protect a debt of $2,823. These decisions are largely due to the notion that a creditor should be allowed to insure the debtor's life for a sum estimated to be sufficient to reimburse the creditor at the debtor's death for premiums paid on the policy, with interest thereon, plus the debt and accumulated interest. There is no clear rule on how much in excess of the debt can be taken out in life insurance on the debtor. The only guideline is that the amount of insurance must bear a reasonable relationship to the size of the debt.

If a debtor assigns an existing policy to the creditor as security for a loan, the creditor is permitted to retain only the amount of the creditor's interest and must pay the excess, if any, to the insured's estate or third-party beneficiary, as the case may be.[7] The creditor's interest is construed to comprise the unpaid portion of the loan, accumulated interest on the loan, and expenses connected with the loan, including any premiums paid on the policy. The same rule applies when the creditor is designated beneficiary if it is clear that the arrangement was intended to serve as security for the debt. In general, the creditor's rights are the same when the debtor procures new insurance and assigns it as collateral, provided the debtor pays the premium.

Occasionally a policy is assigned to the creditor in satisfaction of the debt and not as security for it. In those instances, the creditor is allowed to keep all the proceeds, even though they greatly exceed the amount of the debt canceled. The validity of such an arrangement has been upheld even when the creditor has induced the debtor to procure the policy.

Legal Effect of Lack of Insurable Interest

A life insurance contract not supported by an incipient insurable interest is a wagering contract and hence illegal. This does not mean, however, that the contract cannot be carried out according to its terms. The courts will not enforce an illegal contract, but they do not necessarily forbid the parties to observe the promises made under the illegal agreement.

If an insurance company feels that the applicant honestly believed that he or she had an insurable interest in the life of the person to be insured, it may honor its promise despite later evidence that there was no insurable interest. On the other hand, if the company feels that the applicant knew that no insurable interest existed and sought the insurance for speculative purposes, it may deny liability on the grounds of illegality. If the court sustains the company's contention, there will be no obligation under the contract. Not only will the company be relieved of paying the face amount of the policy (if the insured has died), but in some states it will also not be obligated to return the premiums paid under the contract.

Several states have relaxed the rule against nonenforcement of illegal contracts to allow the applicant or personal representative to recover all premiums paid if he or she applied for insurance in the honest belief that he or she had an insurable interest. In all jurisdictions, recovery of premiums is permitted if the insurer's agent induced the applicant to apply for insurance by falsely leading the applicant to believe that he or she had a legitimate insurable interest.[8]

Moreover, in cases involving wagering policies, the courts have not strictly applied the doctrine that a partial illegality taints the entire transaction and makes it void for all purposes. The rule is frequently modified when a person applies for insurance on his or her own life at the instigation of a third party who lacks an insurable interest in the applicant but who pays the premiums and is designated beneficiary. From a strict legal standpoint, such a contract is illegal. Nevertheless, the courts may direct the insurance company to pay the proceeds to the insured's estate and nullify the interest of the offending beneficiary. Under such circumstances, however, the courts are practically unanimous in permitting the beneficiary to recover the premiums he or she paid on the policy out of the proceeds. The courts take the same attitude toward cases in which a policy is assigned to a third party who induced the insured to apply for the policy but has no insurable interest.

LEGALITY OF FORM

Some types of contracts have to be in a particular form in order to be legal. From a practical standpoint, this aspect of the formation of a contract refers to whether or not the contract has to be in writing or can be oral.

The Statute of Frauds—which was originally enacted in England in the 17th century and has become a part of the statutory law of nearly all the states of the United States—requires certain types of contracts to be in writing to be enforceable. The only section of the statute that might be construed to apply to a life insurance contract is that which requires written and signed proof of an agreement that by its terms cannot be performed within one year from its effective date. Since the insurer's promise may have to be fulfilled within one year or even one day from issuance of the policy, a life insurance contract falls outside the statute. Hence, in the absence of specific legislation requiring a life insurance contract to be in writing, such a contract can be oral in form.

Some states specifically require life insurance contracts to be in writing, while others construe statutes prescribing standard provisions in the contract to mean that the contract itself must be in writing. All states have prescribed a set of standard provisions that must be included—in substance—in all contracts of life insurance. This requirement does not necessarily invalidate oral contracts; standard provisions are simply assumed to be a part of the oral agreement.

Statutes invalidating any terms in a policy that appear in a type face smaller than a designated size, and statutes requiring a policy to be signed, have been interpreted as not requiring a written contract. Charter provisions requiring all contracts to be in writing are usually disregarded by the courts if proof is furnished that an agent of the company led the "insured" to believe that he or she was covered under an oral agreement.

As a practical matter, oral contracts are rare; they usually occur only when an agent oversteps his or her authority and the company is estopped from denying responsibility for the agent's conduct. Because oral contracts are a potential source of misunderstanding and litigation, they are completely unsuitable for a transaction involving life insurance.

CHAPTER REVIEW

Answers to the review questions and the self-test questions can be found in the Supplement.

Key Terms

consideration

condition

condition precedent

condition subsequent

promissory note

suicide

insurable interest

valued policy

viatical settlement company

life settlements

factual expectation

Review Questions

1. What is the consideration given in exchange for the life insurer's promise in each of the following cases?

    a. when, as is commonly the case today, a life insurance contract is a unilateral contract

    b. when, as is less common, a life insurance contract is a bilateral contract

2. What legal role do renewal premiums play with regard to the continued operation of a life insurance contract?

3. Explain what rights an insurer has if a check taken for payment of the first premium on a life insurance policy is not paid when presented and the check was accepted by the company as

    a. a conditional payment of the premium

    b. an absolute payment of the premium

4. Explain what rights the insurer has under each of the following sets of circumstances when the first premium for a life insurance policy was paid with a promissory note but the note was not paid when due:

    a. if the company had authorized the agent to extend credit on its behalf and the note, the premium receipt, and/or the policy contained a forfeiture provision (a provision stating that the policy will be forfeited if the note is not paid at maturity)

    b. if the company had authorized the agent to extend credit on its behalf, but there is no forfeiture provision in the note, the premium receipt, or the policy

    c. if the agent was not authorized to extend credit on behalf of the company, but the agent pays the premium for the applicant and takes the applicant's promissory note

5. With respect to the general legal principle that, to be enforceable, a contract must be entered into for a legal purpose,

    a. explain the general rule concerning what an agreement must do and what it must not do in order to satisfy this requirement of legal purpose and thus be enforceable

    b. describe an exception to this general rule for insurance contracts and explain why the exception is made

6. List three behaviors contrary to public policy that might be encouraged by the purchase of life insurance, and for each, describe the various safeguards imposed by the law and by insurance companies in an effort to deter such behavior.

7. With respect to the application of the concept of insurable interest to life insurance, explain each of the following:

    a. whether or not a *pecuniary* interest is required to have insurable interest

    b. whether or not insurable interest must be based on a *legal* right

    c. when insurable interest generally must exist, how this differs from the requirement applicable to property and casualty insurance, and why the difference exists

8. While Joe Jones was working for LL Corporation as a senior manager, the company took out a $1 million life insurance policy on Joe's life and named itself the beneficiary. As part of a "downsizing" program, Joe left the company. Just prior to Joe's departure, the company had paid the annual premium for the policy. Explain how and why the existence of insurable interest would affect LL Corporation's right to collect the policy death benefit when Joe died a month after leaving the company.

9. Indicate whether or not each of the following persons is required by law and/or by life insurance companies to have an insurable interest when a life insurance policy is procured by the insured:
   a. the insured
      (1) by the law
      (2) by insurers for underwriting purposes
   b. the beneficiary
      (1) by the law
      (2) by insurers for underwriting purposes
   c. an assignee
      (1) by the law
      (2) by insurers for underwriting purposes

10. Explain what rights a life insurance company generally has in each of the following situations where a life insurance policy was procured by the insured:
   a. once the policy has been issued, to withhold approval of a change in beneficiary on the ground that the proposed beneficiary lacks an insurable interest
   b. once the policy has been validly issued, to invalidate successive assignments of the policy on the grounds of either a lack of insurable interest by the assignees or a lack of consent given to the assignments by the insured

11. Explain when the consent of the person to be insured is usually required and when it is usually not required by each of the following when a life insurance contract is taken out by a person other than the prospective insured:
   a. by most jurisdictions
   b. by insurers

12. Explain who must have an insurable interest in the life of the person to be insured when a life insurance policy is procured by a person other than the prospective insured.

13. List the two general types of relationships that may give rise to insurable interest when a life insurance policy is procured by a person other than the prospective insured, and describe what the insurable interest may be based on for each of these relationships.

14. List the family relationships that have been recognized by the courts as being sufficiently close to satisfy the requirement for insurable interest when a life insurance policy is procured by a person other than the prospective insured.

15. When a family relationship is not sufficiently close in itself to satisfy the requirement for insurable interest, on what other basis may an insurable interest be established?

16. When an insurable interest is based on a family relationship, what limits, if any, does each of the following place on the amount of insurance that may be validated by it?
    a. the law
    b. insurance companies

17. Describe the various business relationships that commonly give rise to an insurable interest.

18. Explain how much of the life insurance proceeds a creditor is permitted to retain upon the debtor's death in each of the following cases:

    a. where the creditor took out the insurance on the debtor's life and paid the premiums
    b. where the debtor assigned an existing policy to the creditor as security for a loan (or where the creditor was designated as the beneficiary and it was clear that the arrangement was intended to serve as security for the debt)

19. Explain how the courts treat a life insurance contract not supported by incipient insurable interest with respect to each of the following:
    a. attempts to enforce the contract
    b. the rights of the parties to observe the promises made under the illegal agreement
    c. the right of the insurer to deny liability on the ground of illegality
    d. the rights of the insurer to keep, and of the applicant or personal representative to recover, premiums paid
    e. a situation in which a person applies for insurance on his or her own life at the instigation of a third party who lacks insurable interest in the applicant but who pays the premiums and is the designated beneficiary

20. Describe the factors that influence the form (written or oral) a life insurance contract may take.

Self-Test Questions

T   F   1. With a life insurance contract, the consideration is usually the applicant's promise to pay the first premium.

T   F   2.   Payment of premiums after the first one is a condition precedent to the continuance of a life insurance contract.

T   F   3.   Generally, if a life insurance company accepts a check for the premium, and the check is not honored when presented to the bank for payment because of insufficient funds, the company may enforce its rights on collecting the check, but cannot validly claim the premium was not paid and therefore its promise is no longer operative.

T   F   4.   If an agent who is authorized to do so accepts a promissory note for the first premium and the note is not paid when due, the insurer is not entitled to repudiate the contract but rather is limited to its right to attempt to collect the note.

T   F   5.   When a life insurance contract is bilateral, the consideration for the insurer's promise is the applicant's promise to pay the amount of the first premium.

T   F   6.   Because a life insurance policy issued by an insurer unlicensed to do business in that state lacks legal purpose, it is not enforceable by either party.

T   F   7.   All of the states require that there be an insurable interest between the applicant-owner and the prospective insured at the inception of a life insurance contract.

T   F   8.   In an effort to reduce the threat of murder of the insured by the beneficiary, the courts generally have held that the insurance company is relieved of its obligation to pay if the beneficiary murders the insured.

T   F   9.   Because suicide is contrary to public policy, it is not covered by life insurance policies.

T   F   10. In life insurance, insurable interest must be based on a pecuniary interest.

T   F   11. In life insurance, generally insurable interest need not exist at the time of the insured's death but rather only at the inception of the contract.

T   F   12. A divorce does not deprive a spouse-beneficiary of the right to the proceeds of his or her former spouse's life insurance, even though he or she no longer has an insurable interest in the former spouse's life.

T   F   13. When a life insurance policy is purchased by the insured, the law considers the issue of insurable interest to be immaterial.

T   F   14. When a life insurance policy is purchased by the insured, the law generally requires that the beneficiary have an insurable interest in the insured's life at the inception of the contract.

T   F   15. Once a life insurance policy has been issued to the insured, the insurance company has no right to withhold approval of a change of beneficiary on the ground that the proposed beneficiary lacks an insurable interest.

T   F   16. In most jurisdictions, consent of the person to be insured is usually essential to the validity of a life insurance contract taken out by a person other than the prospective insured.

T   F   17. When a life insurance policy is purchased by a person other than the insured, the required insurable interest may arise out of either a family or a business relationship.

T   F   18. When an insurable interest is based on a family relationship, there is no legal limit to the amount of insurance that may be validated by it.

T   F   19. If a creditor takes out insurance on the debtor's life and pays the premiums, the creditor is permitted to retain only the amount of the creditor's interest when the debtor dies and must pay the excess proceeds, if any, to the debtor-insured's estate or third-party beneficiary, as the case may be.

T   F   20. While the courts will not enforce a life insurance contract that is not supported by incipient insurable interest, they also will not necessarily forbid the parties from carrying out the illegal contract according to its terms.

T   F   21. When no insurable interest existed at the inception of a life insurance contract, the insurer may deny liability on the ground of illegality, but it must always return all premiums paid under the contract.

T   F   22. In the absence of specific legislation requiring a life insurance contract to be in writing, such a contract can be oral in form.

T   F   23. State statutes that prescribe a set of standard provisions that must be included in all contracts of life insurance invalidate oral life insurance contracts.

NOTES

1. See 50 ALR 2d, 630 (1956).
2. Muriel L. Crawford and William T. Beadles, *Law and the Life Insurance Contract,* 6th ed. (Homewood, IL: Irwin Professional Publishing, 1989), p. 315.
3. David Scott, *Every Man His Own Broker* (1761), quoted in C. Walford, *Insurance Cyclopaedia* (London: Charles and Edwin Layton, 1876), vol. IV, p. 187.
4. Edwin W. Patterson, *Essentials of Insurance Law*, 2d ed. (New York: McGraw-Hill Book Co., 1957), p. 154.
5. Buist M. Anderson, *Anderson on Life Insurance* (Boston: Little, Brown & Co., 1991), Sec. 12.5, p. 364.
6. *Ibid.,* Sec. 12.12.
7. *Ibid.,* Sec. 12.11.
8. Crawford and Beadles, *Law and the Life Insurance Contract*, p. 48.

5

Avoidance of the Contract by the Insurer

Dan M. McGill
Revised by Burke A. Christensen

Learning Objectives

An understanding of the material in this chapter should enable the student to

5-1. Define a warranty and a representation and explain the difference between them.

5-2. Explain why warranties are no longer of major importance in the law of life and health insurance.

5-3. List the general characteristics of representations and describe the exceptions applicable to life insurance.

5-4. Explain what remedies are available to an insurer in the case of a misrepresentation.

5-5. Explain the steps an insurer must take and what it must prove to rescind a life insurance contract on grounds of misrepresentation.

5-6. Explain the concept of materiality as applied to misrepresentation in life insurance, and describe the standards used by the courts in testing the materiality of misrepresented facts.

5-7. Explain how state statutes have modified the common law effect of misstatements by an applicant for life insurance.

5-8. For the various subject areas in a life insurance application, indicate whether each is generally construed to be a statement of fact or opinion and the extent to which it tends to be invoked by insurers as a defense in litigation.

5-9. Explain the nature and legal effect of a concealment in general law and in the various branches of insurance law.

5-10. Describe how the scope of the doctrine of concealment has been narrowed in life insurance and how the doctrine is principally applied to nondisclosures in the formation of life insurance contracts.

Chapter Outline

A warranty is a clause in an insurance contract that prescribes, as a condition of the insurer's liability, the existence of a fact affecting the risk assumed under the contract.

warranty

warranty: a statement that becomes part of the contract and is guaranteed by the maker to be true in all respects[1]

representation

representation: a statement [(made) at the time of the making of a contract] that induces a party to enter into a contract. It is not part of the contract.[2]

When a contract is created between two parties, it makes a great deal of difference whether the statements made by each side are warranties or representations. If a statement is a warranty and it later turns out to be untrue in any respect, the other party may rescind the contract. If the same statement is a representation that later turns out to be untrue, the other party may rescind the contract only if the representation was material to the formation of the contract.

The doctrine of warranties originated in marine insurance more than 200 years ago, and it still plays an important role in that branch of insurance. It was developed for the purpose of controlling the risk associated with a particular insurance venture. If a certain state of affairs was deemed to be a risk-reducing factor and insurance was arranged on the assumption that such a state of affairs would continue throughout the term of the policy, the policy would condition the coverage on the existence of the favorable state of affairs. The policy would *warrant* that the desired conditions would prevail. For example, the frequent wars during the 18th century made it highly desirable that British merchant vessels sail under the convoy of British warships, and it was customary for marine insurers to require an insured vessel to sail under convoy or pay a higher premium. If a shipowner warranted that his vessel would sail only under convoy and then permitted it to sail alone, his coverage would be nullified. It was not necessary for the insurer to prove that the breach—the failure to sail with a convoy—materially increased the risk; materiality was assumed. Neither was it necessary to establish bad faith or fraud on the part of the insured. The insurer had only to prove that the warranty was breached.

The use of warranties gradually spread to other branches of insurance where they were less suitable. They were no longer confined to contracts sold to businesses familiar with trade and insurance practices but were liberally interspersed in contracts sold to the general public, who had no concept of the significance of warranties. Abuses inevitably developed. The situation was particularly bad in fire insurance where there was no incontestable clause to ameliorate the effect of a breach of warranty.

Warranties are no longer of major importance in the law of life and health insurance. It used to be that statements made by the applicant for life insurance were warranties. But this is no longer the case. In the 1800s insurance companies developed a bad reputation because they strictly enforced their contractual right to rescind contracts if they discovered that any statement made by the applicant was inaccurate in the slightest respect. The courts strained the law in an effort to protect the insuring public, but most states found it necessary to provide statutory relief for those persons procuring life and health insurance and, less commonly, those seeking other types of insurance. The general effect of the statutory modifications is that no breach of warranty will void a contract unless it increases the risk, contributes to the loss, or occurs with fraudulent intent.

The special legislation directed at life insurance—and, in many states, at health insurance—was brought about by the fact that, for one reason or another, most companies had begun to incorporate the application into the policy, which, according to common law doctrine, made all statements in the application warranties. To make doubly sure of this result, some companies, by express provision, made the applicant warrant the truth of all statements in the application. This meant that the company was in a position to void the contract if any one statement in the application was not literally true.

REPRESENTATIONS

Generally speaking, a representation is an oral or written statement made by a party to a contract prior to or contemporaneously with the formation of the contract.[3] It is not a part of the contract but is an inducement to the contract. It refers to facts or conditions existing at the time the statement is made.[4] It may be a fact within the knowledge of the person making the statement or merely an expression of opinion or belief. It does not bind the party making it to anything that may happen after the contract is made. If it did, it would be a promise or condition of the other party's promise and would have to be embodied in the contract. It would be the equivalent of a warranty. Finally, a representation need be only substantially true when made.

In life insurance, representations are made by both the applicant and the soliciting agent, but for all practical purposes, only the applicant's statements have legal significance. Hence, the discussion in this chapter will be concerned only with the applicant's representations.

Since representations do not purport to change the terms of a contract, they are not subject to the parol evidence rule, discussed earlier, and in the absence of a prohibitory statute or policy provision, can be oral in form. However, most states have enacted statutes, directed at life insurance and

referred to as *entire-contract statutes,* which state, in substance, that the policy and the attached application constitute the entire contract between the parties.[5] These statutes have been interpreted by the courts to exclude all of the insured's representations other than those contained in the application attached to the policy. In other words, the application or a copy thereof must be attached to the policy if the company is to treat the statements in the application as representations. In addition, most states require that every policy include a provision that excludes all of the applicant's statements other than those contained in the application from consideration. A typical provision reads as follows:

> No statement of the insured shall avoid this policy or be used in
> defense of a claim hereunder unless it is contained in the application
> and a copy of such application is attached to the policy when issued.

Technically, when the application is made a part of the contract, either by physical attachment to the policy or by reference to it in the policy, all the statements in the application pertaining to the risk become warranties. To avoid this untoward result, more than half of the states have enacted laws that convert statements in the application from warranties to representations. Other states have removed the sting from warranties by requiring that the matter misrepresented be material or, stricter still, have contributed to the loss, before a company can use the breach of warranty as a basis for voiding the contract.

Apart from statute or judicial ruling, most companies' policies provide that all statements in the application are deemed representations and not warranties. As a matter of fact, it is customary for insurance companies to incorporate into one omnibus clause provisions that state that the policy and the application attached thereto constitute the entire contract, that statements in the application are deemed representations, and that no statement of the insured will be used to void the policy or to contest a claim unless it is contained in the application attached to the policy. A typical provision is as follows:

> This policy is a contract between the owner and (name of insurer). This policy, the attached copy of the initial application, any applications for reinstatement, all subsequent applications to change the policy, and any endorsements or riders are the entire contract. No statement will be used in defense of a claim unless such statement is contained in the application. All statements contained in the application shall, in the absence of fraud, be deemed representations and not warranties.

Statements in Application Deemed

- property insurance—warranties
- liability insurance—warranties
- life insurance—representations
- health insurance—representations

Legal Consequences of a Misrepresentation

A representation has legal consequences only if a person, acting in reliance thereon, is induced to enter into a contract to which he or she would not otherwise have become a party. If the representation turns out to be false, the aggrieved party can sue to recover damages from the person who made the misstatement or to rescind the contract that he or she was induced to make. The first remedy is available against anyone who *fraudulently* or *deceitfully* makes a misrepresentation. The second remedy is available only if the person who makes the misrepresentation is a party to the contract.

Remedies for Material Representation

- recovery of damages

  or
- rescission of the contract if misrepresentation was made by a party to the contract

Thus if a life insurance company is induced to issue a policy because of the fraudulent misrepresentation of the medical examiner, it can recover damages, if any, from the medical examiner, but it cannot rescind the policy unless it can prove that the applicant conspired with the doctor to have the misrepresentation made or at least knew of the fraud before the policy was issued. Cases of this sort are occasionally unearthed, but the typical remedy for a misrepresentation in a life insurance application is rescission of the contract.

rescission

> *rescission:* termination of a contract. The contract is declared void because of a material misrepresentation by one party. It is an equitable, not a legal, remedy.

voidable contract
void contract

> *voidable contract* and *void contract:* A contract is voidable if one party has the right to disaffirm it and thereby terminate the agreement. A "void contract" is unenforceable by either party. In fact, the term is an oxymoron. Since a contract is a legally enforceable agreement, it is either valid, voidable, or does not exist.

Notice of Rescission

A misrepresentation does not of itself make a contract void; it only makes it voidable. The difference is that with a voidable contract the aggrieved party may elect to affirm the contract, in which event he or she is bound by its terms (but not precluded from suing for damages for any fraud involved), or he or she may elect to rescind the contract. The party is under an obligation to exercise this option within a reasonable time after discovering the falsity of the representation. In this respect, a misrepresentation differs from a breach of warranty, in that a breach of warranty can be offered in defense of a claim even when the company has delayed making its election between affirmation and rescission beyond a reasonable period. However, this distinction has lost some of its significance because of a number of court decisions that treat the insurer's retention of premiums after discovery of either a misrepresentation or a breach of warranty as a *waiver* or *estoppel* (see chapter 6). In any event, the insurer's delay bars its power to rescind on the ground of misrepresentation only if the insured was prejudiced by the delay.

An insurance company's notice of rescission must be accompanied by a tender of all premiums paid under the contract. This is necessary because the purpose of rescission is to wipe out the contract and restore the parties to the positions they occupied before the contract was made. If the insured owns the contract and is still alive, the tender of premiums is made to the insured, but if the insured is deceased it is usually made to the beneficiary, and in legal effect, is an offer of settlement. In those circumstances, a prudent insurer seeks a release from both the beneficiary and the insured's estate.

To make its rescission conclusive, the insurance company must obtain an adjudication of its power to rescind. It may do this by defending a judicial proceeding brought by the beneficiary to recover on the policy or by instituting a suit in equity to obtain a decree of rescission. In the former, the question of misrepresentation is usually left to a jury if there is any conflicting evidence, since the beneficiary's suit to recover the sum payable by the policy's terms is an *action at law*.[6] Suits in equity are usually tried by a judge who determines both the law and the facts. Insurance companies prefer suits in equity because they avoid juries and their tendency to favor the adversary of an insurance company.

Statements of Fact

To obtain a rescission of a life insurance policy on the ground of a misrepresentation, the company must prove that one or more statements of *fact* in the application were both *false* and *material* to the company's decision to accept the risk or set the premium. It is not necessary, unless required by statute, to prove that the statement was made with intent to deceive the insurer. While considerable authority can be found for the argument that only a *fraudulent* misrepresentation of a material fact will provide ground for rescission, a majority of cases hold that an innocent misrepresentation of a material fact suffices to make a policy voidable. The doctrine is well established that the test of a misrepresentation is the *effect* on the insurer, not the *culpability* of the insured or the agent in making it. By the same token, it is held that a fraudulent misstatement of an immaterial fact will not make a policy voidable. The purpose of rescission is to protect the company—and, indirectly, its policyowners—against an increase in risk arising out of a misrepresentation, not to punish the insured whose dishonesty caused the company no harm.

Matters of Opinion

An important exception to the rule that a misrepresentation need not be fraudulent to obtain a rescission exists when the misstatement is a matter of opinion, belief, or expectation. It is not sufficient that the applicant's belief about the status of a matter material to the risk turns out to be erroneous. If the applicant's statement accurately reflects his or her state of mind at the time of the assertion, no misrepresentation occurs. A statement of opinion is false only if the person making it does not have that opinion at the time the statement is made. Therefore, to void a policy on the ground of a false statement of opinion, the insurer must prove that the insured spoke fraudulently. This leads to the conclusion that a statement of opinion must be *false*, *material*, and *fraudulent* before it makes a policy voidable.

If the statement in the application is qualified by such words as "in my opinion," or "to the best of my knowledge and belief," or "the above is as near correct as I can recall," it is clearly one of opinion or belief. However, even unqualified statements will be construed by the courts to be statements of opinion if the fact to which they relate is deemed to be one not susceptible to the insured's accurate and conclusive determination. In other words, an unqualified assertion about a situation or event for which there may obviously be differences of opinion may be construed as a statement of opinion.

A statement that the applicant "is in good health" has been held to be a statement of opinion[7] since it calls for an inference rather than a report on observed facts. Statements about the future are construed as expressions of intent or expectation and thus are also opinions, rather than representations of facts. The following are typical questions taken from the application form of a large life insurance company calling for a declaration of intentions:

- Do you intend to travel or reside outside the United States?
- Do you have any intention of becoming a pilot, student pilot, or crew member of any type of aircraft?
- Do you have any intention of becoming a member of a military organization?
- Do you contemplate any change in occupation?

Negative answers to such queries are of no avail in litigation unless the insurer can prove that at the time of application, the applicant had a definite intention of doing the thing that was the subject of the inquiry.

Rule of Continuing Representation

rule of continuing representation

Moreover, a representation need be true only at the time it is made; it is not necessary that it continue to be true until the contract is consummated. At one time, the federal courts and some state courts accepted the view that a representation had to be true at the moment the contract became effective, a doctrine referred to as the *rule of continuing representation.* With some exceptions, however, the view today is that the intervening falsity of a representation will provide the ground for rescission only if notice of the changed circumstances is fraudulently withheld from the insurer.[8] In other words, the applicant must be aware of the change, must realize that the change is material to the company's underwriting decision, and must deliberately withhold notice of the change to the company.

However, no such duty to disclose exists if the insurer has already accepted the risk. This would be the case if the applicant had paid some or all of the first premium and a conditional receipt had been issued. Legally, such subterfuge by the applicant is not construed to be a misrepresentation, but a concealment, which is discussed later in this chapter.

Example: ***Intervening Falsity of a Representation***

On July 14, Hank applied for nonmedical life insurance and truthfully answered all the questions in the application. Hank's answers all suggested that he was in excellent health and that his application would be approved by the insurer as submitted. On July 17, during a routine visit to his family doctor to get a tetanus shot, Hank was found to have a large spot on his left lung. Hank decided not to notify the insurer of this new development. On July 26, the policy was issued as applied for. One year later, Hank died of lung cancer, at which time the insurer learned about the discovery of the spot on the lung several months earlier. Can the insurer deny the claim?

The insurer probably is entitled to deny the claim—*unless* Hank paid the first premium with the application and received a conditional receipt for it.

Concept of Materiality

A representation of the insured is significant only if it is communicated to the insurer and in some way influences the insurer's decision with respect to a contract. If a statement of the insured induces the insurer to enter into a contract that it would not have made had it known the true statement of the fact, or would have made only on different terms, the statement is *material*. More accurately, the facts misrepresented in the statement are material.

material

Extent of Falsity

A distinction must be made between the materiality of the subject matter of a question in the application and the materiality of a misrepresentation made in the answer to the question. Not all statements the insured makes in response to the insurer's questions about matters of consequence to the risk are material. To void a policy on the ground of a material misrepresentation, the company must prove not only that the insured made a misstatement about a matter of concern to the company, but also that the *extent* of the falsity was substantial enough to be significant. In other words, the *difference* between the actual facts relating to a matter material to the risk and the facts as falsely represented must be sufficient to induce the company's decision to accept the risk. This is simply another way of saying that knowledge of the facts would have caused the company to reject the risk or to accept it only on different terms.

The distinction between a material matter and the materiality of a false response relative to the matter can be illustrated by any number of questions in the typical application form. For example, one large company's application form contains the following question: "Have you now or have you ever had or been treated for any disease or disorder of the nose, throat, lungs, or pleura?" Suppose that an applicant gives a negative answer to that question when, in fact, he or she had suffered an attack of tonsillitis 10 years earlier that was severe enough to require medical treatment. Obviously, the condition of the applicant's throat is material to the company's consideration of the risk, but is the undisclosed attack of tonsillitis 10 years ago of sufficient consequence to justify rescission of the policy?

Tests of Materiality

prudent-insurer standard
individual-insurer standard

In adjudicating cases involving a misrepresentation, the courts may attempt to test the materiality of the misrepresented facts by referring to the underwriting practices of insurers generally or by referring to the practices of the particular company involved in the litigation. The first test has been characterized as the *prudent-insurer standard*, while the second has been designated the *individual-insurer standard.*

Prudent-Insurer Standard. The prudent-insurer standard has been adopted in the majority of jurisdictions, presumably because it is thought to provide objective standards for issues in which judgments are likely to be subjective or emotional. It is argued that the judgment of the litigating company's officers is likely to be warped by their assumption that anyone who dies within one or 2 years after issuance of the policy must have concealed some physical impairment. Under the prudent-insurer standard the judgment of objective experts on underwriting practices—usually officials of other companies—is substituted for the subjective opinions of the officers of the company that accepted the risk. A fundamental weakness of this standard is that it presupposes a uniformity of opinion and practice that does not exist. For example, medical directors of various insurance companies disagree about the significance of many types of impairments. Furthermore, relying exclusively on the testimony of outside experts may impose liability on an insurer, particularly a conservative one, for a risk that the company would unquestionably have rejected if it had had knowledge of the facts misrepresented.

Individual-Insurer Standard. The individual-insurer test, which is applied in many jurisdictions, has been adopted by statute in several important states. The New York Insurance Law, for example, states, "No misrepresentation shall be deemed material unless knowledge by the insurer of the facts misrepresented would have led to a refusal by the insurer to make such contract."[9] This test conforms to the basic principle of rescission for misrepresentation and has considerable support in judicial precedents involving transactions other than insurance contracts.

One would naturally assume that in applying this test, the courts would place great reliance on testimony of officials associated with the company involved in the litigation. Most states, by statute or court ruling, permit testimony as to the practices of the insurer involved in the litigation. The New York Insurance Law, for example, expressly permits the admissibility of the litigating insurer's underwriting practices as follows: "In determining the question of materiality, evidence of the practice of the insurer which made such contract with respect to the acceptance or rejection of similar risks shall be admissible."[10] Under this provision, the insurer's medical director (or some other qualified official) is permitted to testify in court that it is the company's practice to reject applications that reveal facts similar to those proved in the case under consideration. In fact, if qualified, the witness will be permitted to testify that had the insurer had knowledge of the facts misrepresented, the company would have rejected the application in dispute. If the testimony is uncontroverted, the evidence (if not patently absurd) is ordinarily deemed conclusive, and the question of materiality will not be addressed by the court. In several other states, while the insurer is permitted to prove what it would have done had it known the facts later disclosed, such evidence is not deemed conclusive.

The individual-insurer test enables an insurer to apply its standards of insurability in all cases, including those in which the applicant did not disclose all the facts that the insurer requested. This, of course, assumes that the insurer is permitted to prove its standards of insurability, rather than leaving the matter to the conjecture of the judge. Maintaining underwriting standards benefits not only the insurer but also the host of honest policyowners who have made no misrepresentations. Moreover, the test of what a particular insurance company would have done in a specific factual situation can be more accurately formulated and more reliably proved than the test of what insurance companies in general would have done.[11]

The principal disadvantage of the individual-insurer test is that the proof of materiality comes from the files of the insurance company and the testimony of its officials, and the counsel for the beneficiary has little chance of controverting it. His or her only hope is to prove that the company has not consistently followed its alleged practices.

Some recent decisions have ruled that misrepresented facts are material if knowledge of the facts *might* have caused the insurer to reject the application. This is a much stricter standard from the insured's standpoint and a much more difficult one to apply in practice. Facts that would have caused the company to further investigate the applicant even though, in the end, the company would have approved the application, would be treated as material. A California statute even holds that misrepresented facts are material if knowledge of them would have led the company to make further inquiries or to delay acceptance of the application.[12]

Statutory Modification of the Common Law

The common law effect of misstatements by an applicant for life insurance has been modified by statute in many states. The most significant modification is by statutes enacted in most states (and discussed earlier) that convert statements in the application from warranties into representations. The effect of these statutes is to eliminate the conclusive presumption of materiality of statements in the application, forcing the company to prove the statements' materiality.

Other statutes, which are far less prevalent, permit companies to void a contract only if the matter misrepresented increased the risk of loss. Such statutes usually apply only to representations. They were apparently intended to provide a more objective test of materiality than that furnished by the common law definition. However, any fact that would be considered an inducement to contract under the common law concept of materiality would, if so unfavorable as to be misrepresented by the applicant, tend to increase the risk. Hence, these statutes by judicial construction have been given the same effect as the prudent-insurer test of materiality.

A few states[13] have statutes that require the misrepresented fact to have contributed to the loss. The Missouri statute illustrates this type of legislation:

> No misrepresentation made in obtaining or securing a policy of insurance on the life or lives of any person or persons, citizens of this state, shall be deemed material or render the policy void, unless the matter misrepresented shall have actually contributed to the contingency or event on which the policy is to become due and payable, and whether it so contributed in any case shall be a question for the jury.[14]

Under this type of statute, an applicant can conceal or misrepresent a condition that, had it been known to the insurer, would have unquestionably caused it to decline the risk. Yet, the company will be held liable if the insured's death resulted from a cause not related to the misrepresented condition. For example, if an applicant concealed a serious heart impairment and later died in an automobile accident not caused by his or her heart condition, the company would have to pay the face amount of the policy, despite the fact that it would not have been at risk if the heart condition had been revealed at the time of application.

Sources of Litigation

Any statement in the application that is designed to elicit information directly relevant to the risk is a potential source of litigation. Yet some of the application's subject areas seldom serve as the basis for denial of a claim, while others are a frequent source of dispute. Whether the applicant's answer to a particular question is construed to be a statement of fact or a statement of opinion makes a significant difference.

Fact versus Opinion

Answers to questions concerning the amount of insurance the applicant carries and the disposition of applications he or she submitted to other companies are generally regarded to be statements of fact rather than of opinion. In recent years, however, insurance companies have rarely been successful in invoking a false answer to this group of questions as a material misrepresentation. Since the companies that do the bulk of the life insurance business are members of the Medical Information Bureau (MIB), they will ordinarily have access to information about impairments discovered by other companies. If a company was notified about detrimental information in the MIB files, it would be permitted to void the contract only if there was other material information that the applicant should have disclosed.[15]

Unequivocal answers to questions about the applicant's past and present occupation are regarded as statements of fact. Yet there are few reported cases where the insurer attempted to void the contract on the basis of a misrepresentation as to occupation. The chief explanation for this is probably that the inspection report is likely to uncover any discrepancy in the applicant's statement as to occupation. Statements about a change of occupation are considered to be declarations of expectation and could serve as a basis for voiding the contract only if false and fraudulent.

Answers to questions about family history that call for information about events that occurred many years before or happened to relatives long separated from the applicant are deemed to be opinions. Rarely have answers to such questions been used as a basis for litigation. It would ordinarily be difficult for the insurer to prove the materiality of the facts misrepresented without also proving that the applicant suffered from a serious medical impairment traceable, in part, to family history. In that event, it would be simpler to void the contract on the ground of the physical impairment. Answers to questions about exposure to contagious diseases, while significant for underwriting purposes, are of little value in litigation because of the difficulty of proving the materiality of the exposure.

The applicant's statements about his or her habits are usually treated as opinions. Questions directed at the applicant's use of intoxicating beverages or narcotics call for distinctions of degree, such as infrequent, moderate, or excessive use. Moreover, the applicant is asked for a self-evaluation, which he or she cannot be expected to do objectively. For these reasons, and because the inspection report reveals the most serious cases of addiction to alcohol or drugs, the applicant's statements as to habits seldom constitute the basis for litigation.

Medical Treatment

Answers to questions about specific ailments or diseases are in most—but not all—jurisdictions deemed to be statements of fact and not merely statements of opinion. An applicant is expected to know whether or not he or she has ever had or been treated for disorders of critical organs of the body. Some courts infer the applicant's knowledge of the falsity and materiality of the answer from the serious consequences to him or her of the disease and the treatment.[16] On the other hand, if the evidence indicates that the applicant's physician did not inform the applicant about the nature of his or her ailment—for instance, that it is an incurable disease—the applicant's statement as to that particular disease may be treated as an opinion and not be sufficient to permit the insurer's voiding the contract.

Answers to general questions about medical treatment, consultation, or hospitalization have been the ones most frequently invoked as defenses in litigation. The questions are usually regarding treatment that has taken place only during the last 5 years, and the applicant is expected to have a sufficiently keen awareness of the events to provide the insurer with accurate information. With some exceptions, the answers are treated as statements of fact and not of opinion. Except in states that have adopted the physician-patient privilege, the facts can be proved by the testimony or records of the physician or of the hospital.

Of course, the applicant's failure to disclose, or convey positive misrepresentation of, an instance of medical treatment is of itself neither material nor immaterial. The thing that is material is what the company would have learned, with the full cooperation of the physician or the hospital, if it had been put on notice as to the medical treatment and had made inquiry as to its nature. In order to avoid any disputes or disagreements about the materiality of an applicant's misrepresentation of his or her recent medical history, the New York Insurance Law states as follows:

A misrepresentation that an applicant for life, accident, or health insurance has not had previous medical treatment, consultation or observation, or has not had previous treatment or care in a hospital or other like institution, shall be deemed, for the purpose of determining its materiality, a misrepresentation that the applicant has not had the disease, ailment or other medical impairment for which such treatment or care was given or which was discovered by any licensed medical practitioner as a result of such consultation or observation.[17]

It does not follow that in all cases the facts misrepresented by the applicant's failure to disclose a medical consultation will be sufficient to void the contract. If the consultation were for the purpose of obtaining treatment for a common cold or some other slight temporary ailment, the facts misrepresented would not, because of their immateriality, constitute grounds for avoidance of the contract.

There is a federal statute that regards information about a patient's physical condition obtained by a physician through medical treatment or professional consultation as a *privileged communication*, which can be divulged only with the consent of the patient, or if deceased, his or her personal representative. A physician is not permitted to give testimony about the medical treatment of an applicant for insurance unless the applicant or his or her personal representative agrees that the physician's findings be made public. If the physician is not permitted to testify, a suspicion arises that the ailment was one material to the defense of misrepresentation. The suspicion is so strong that since 1940, the New York Insurance Law has contained a provision that, if the insurer proves that an applicant misrepresented the facts relating to a medical consultation, and the applicant or any other person claiming a right under the insurance contract prevents full disclosure and proof of the nature of the medical impairment, such misrepresentation will be presumed to have been material.[18] The presumption can be rebutted by evidence from the claimant that the ailment was not material to the risk.

This provision, which followed a decision of the highest court of New York to the same effect, has been successfully invoked in New York courts and in federal cases governed by New York law.

CONCEALMENT

The doctrine of concealment is the final legal defense of the insurance company in its efforts to avoid liability under a contract that was obtained through the misrepresentation or concealment of material facts. Of the three basic grounds for avoidance (breach of warranty, misrepresentation, and concealment), concealment is the narrowest in scope and the most difficult to prove.

Nature and Legal Effect of a Concealment

concealment

In general law, concealment connotes an affirmative act to hide the existence of a material fact. In insurance law, however, a *concealment* is essentially a nondisclosure; it is the failure of the applicant for insurance to communicate to the insurer his or her knowledge of a material fact that the insurer does not possess.

It is general law of long standing that one party to a contract is under no legal obligation during the period of negotiation to disclose to the other party information that the first party knows is not known to the second party and, if known, would be deemed material to the contract. The rationale of this rule is that prices in the marketplace should be set by the best-informed buyers and sellers, and as a reward for performing this economic function, they should be permitted to profit by their special knowledge of affairs. For some years, however, there has been a marked trend in the other direction. Among the numerous exceptions to the general rule are the requirements that one party not actively try to prevent the second party from discovering facts known only to the first party or give deliberately misleading answers to questions designed to elicit information material to the contract.

In insurance, the law of concealment, like the other two doctrines discussed earlier in this chapter, developed during the 18th century out of cases involving marine insurance. The relative inaccessibility of the property to be insured and the poor communication facilities, combined with the aleatory nature of the contract, caused Lord Mansfield, the father of English commercial and insurance law, to hold that the applicant for insurance was required by good faith to disclose to the insurer all known facts that would materially affect the insurer's decision about acceptance of the risk, the amount of the premium, or other essential terms of the contract, whether or not the applicant was aware of the materiality of the facts. Even though conditions affecting marine insurance have changed, the law has not. The person seeking marine insurance today, whether the shipowner or shipper, must disclose all known material facts in his or her possession to the insurer. Failure to do so, even though innocent, will permit the insurer to void the contract.

In English law, the doctrine of innocent concealment is strictly applied to all branches of insurance. In the United States, it is applied only to marine insurance. American courts have felt that the circumstances surrounding fire and life insurance are so different from those in marine insurance—particularly true in 1766 when the marine rule originated—that a different rule is justified. Under American law, except for marine insurance, a concealment will permit the insurer to void the contract only if the applicant, in refraining from disclosure, had a fraudulent intent.[19] In other words, *except for marine insurance, a concealment must be both material and fraudulent.* In marine insurance, it need only be material.

Test of Materiality

The doctrine of concealment may be regarded as a special manifestation of the doctrine of misrepresentation. The relationship between a misrepresentation and a concealment has been compared with that existing between the heads and tails of a coin. If a misrepresentation is the heads of a coin, a concealment is the tails. One is affirmative; the other is negative.

A concealment is misrepresentation by silence. It has legal consequences for the same reason that a misrepresentation does—namely, that the insurer was misled into making a contract that it would not have made had it known the facts. Hence, the general concept of materiality applied to a concealment is the same as that applicable to a misrepresentation: the effect on the underwriting decision of the insurer. "Fraudulent intent" is a subjective concept that is difficult to prove; many courts take the attitude that if the fact not disclosed by the applicant was *palpably material*, this is sufficient proof of fraud.[20]

palpably material

The degree of relevance to a risk required of a fact to be palpably material has never been judicially defined. An illustration was provided in a famous 1896 decision by William Howard Taft,[21] then a judge of the 8th Circuit Court of Appeals, who indicated that an applicant for life insurance who failed to reveal to the insurer that he was on his way to fight a duel would be guilty of concealing a palpably material fact. This illustration was almost contradicted by a 1938 decision that an applicant's failure to disclose that he was carrying a revolver because of his fear of being killed by his former partner, whom he had accused of committing adultery with his wife, was not a palpably material concealment, even though the applicant was murdered a few months later by a person unknown.[22] Experts are occasionally called upon to testify as to the materiality of a concealed fact, but in cases settled in favor of the insurer, the judge has usually decided from his or her own knowledge that the fact concealed was palpably material.

The palpable materiality test is applied to the applicant's knowledge of materiality, while both the prudent-insurer and individual-insurer tests of materiality apply only to the *effect* on the insurer. In concealment cases, which are governed by statutes only in California and states that have adopted its laws, the prudent-insurer test seems to be the prevailing one.

Test of Fraud

The test of fraud is whether the applicant believed the fact that he or she did not disclose to be material to the risk. This test was approved long ago by the highest court of New York in a case involving the applicant's failure to disclose that he had once been insane.[23] The concealment was held not to be fraudulent. The insurer therefore must prove that an undisclosed fact is, *in the applicant's own mind,* material to the risk. As a general proposition, the insured's awareness of the materiality of the fact concealed can be proved by establishing that the fact was palpably material, a characteristic that would be apparent to any person of normal intelligence.

However, in concealment cases, as with warranties and representations, the law takes into account the powers of understanding and state of knowledge of the particular applicant involved. Thus the failure of an applicant who was the state agent for the company to notify the insurer of a cancerous condition of the spleen, discovered after submission of the application but before issue of the policy, was held to be fraudulent in view of the applicant's exceptional knowledge of the materiality of such a condition.[24] On the other hand, the failure of a less sophisticated applicant to disclose a toxic condition of the heart muscle, likewise discovered in the interim between submission of the application and issue of the policy, was held not to be fraudulent when evidence revealed that the applicant had refused to take additional insurance offered to him and had changed the basis of premium payments from monthly to semiannually.[25]

Scope of the Doctrine of Concealment in Life Insurance

The requirement that a concealment be proved by the insurer to have been fraudulent has narrowed the scope of the doctrine in all forms of nonmarine insurance. Its scope has been further narrowed in life insurance through the use of a detailed written application and, in larger cases, a medical examination. There is a presumption that the application elicits information about every matter that the insurer deems material to the risk, and if the applicant answers all questions asked in the application fully and truthfully, he or she is under no duty to volunteer additional information. This presumption can be overcome by evidence that the applicant willfully concealed other information that was material to the risk and that the applicant knew to be material. In practice, however, the doctrine is seldom invoked except for nondisclosure of a material fact discovered by the applicant between the time he or she signed the application and the time the contract was consummated.

The general (but not unanimous) view of the courts is that the applicant under the doctrine of continuing representations must communicate promptly to the insurer his or her discovery of such interim facts if they are so obviously material that the applicant could not fail to recognize their materiality. In one of the early cases on the subject, the insurance company was permitted to deny liability under a policy issued in ignorance of the fact that the applicant had undergone an operation for appendicitis during the period the application was being considered by the home office, even though the applicant was in the hospital at the time the disclosure should have been made.[26] In a later case involving the interim discovery of a duodenal ulcer, the Supreme Court of the United States had the following to say:

Concededly, the modern practice of requiring the applicant for life insurance to answer questions prepared by the insurer has relaxed this rule (of disclosure) to some extent since information not asked for is presumably deemed immaterial.

But the reason for the rule still obtains, and with added force, as to changes materially affecting the risk that comes to the insured's knowledge after the application and before delivery of the policy. Even the most unsophisticated person must know that, in answering the questionnaire and submitting it to the insurer, the applicant is furnishing the data on the basis of which the company will decide whether, by issuing a policy, it wishes to accept the risk. If, while the company deliberates, the applicant discovers facts that make portions of the application no longer true, *the most elementary spirit of fair dealing* would seem to require him or her to make a full disclosure.[27]

Since not all courts impose the duty of disclosure of interim changes and, in any event, violation of the duty must be proved fraudulent, many companies rely on the delivery-in-good-health and medical treatment clauses to protect themselves against interim changes in the applicant's physical condition. These clauses create conditions or warranties that must be fully satisfied before the company can be held liable under the contract. The applicant is under no obligation to disclose interim developments, however material on their face, when the first premium is paid with the application and a binding receipt, conditioned on insurability at the date of application, is issued. Under such circumstances, the coverage becomes effective as of the date of application—or medical examination, if later—and changes in the applicant's insurability after that date are supposed to be immaterial to the insurer's deliberations. Of course, interim changes in the insured's physical condition can be used as evidence to support the company's contention that the insured concealed or misrepresented facts known to him or her when the application was made.

CHAPTER REVIEW

Answers to the review questions and the self-test questions can be found in the Supplement.

Key Terms

warranty	rule of continuing representation
representation	material
entire-contract statutes	prudent-insurer standard
rescission	individual-insurer standard
voidable contract	concealment
void contract	palpably material

Review Questions

1. Why does it make a difference whether a statement made by a party to a contract is a warranty or a representation if the statement later turns out to be untrue?

2. Why are warranties no longer of major importance in the law of life and health insurance?

3. List the general characteristics of representations, and indicate where exceptions are applicable to life insurance law.

4. When the application is made part of the life insurance contract, statements in the application pertaining to the risk technically become warranties. Explain how this result has been modified by
   a. statutes and judicial rulings
   b. common life insurance policy provisions

5. List the remedies that may be available to an aggrieved party when a representation turns out to be false, and indicate under what circumstances each remedy is available.

6. In completing the application for a life insurance policy issued a few months ago, Paul Fellers (the insured) misrepresented an answer to a question regarding medical treatment that had taken place during the last 5 years. Does this misrepresentation make the life insurance contract void?

7. What obligations does a life insurance company generally face with respect to promptness of action and return of premiums when it seeks to rescind a policy on ground of misrepresentation?

8. Describe the options available to an insurance company for obtaining an adjudication of its power to rescind a life insurance contract, and indicate which alternative insurers generally prefer.

9. Indicate what a life insurer must prove about each of the following types of statements to obtain a rescission of a life insurance policy on the ground of misrepresentation:

   a. a statement of fact
   b. a statement of opinion, belief, or expectation

10. In completing the application for a life insurance policy issued a few months ago, Janet Jacobs (the insured) made a false statement in answering a question concerning the amount of life insurance she already carried at that time. What would the insurance company generally have to prove about her statement to obtain a rescission of her policy on the ground of misrepresentation, and why?

11. In completing the application for a life insurance policy issued a few months ago, Bill Williams (the insured) made a false statement in answering a question concerning any contemplated change in his occupation. What would the insurance company generally have to prove about his statement to obtain a rescission of his policy on the ground of misrepresentation, and why?

12. When facts represented in the application change prior to the time a life insurance contract becomes effective, what must an insurance company generally demonstrate to provide a ground for rescission of the contract?

13. What must a life insurance company prove to void a policy on the ground of material misrepresentation?

14. In completing the application for a life insurance policy issued a few months ago, Dean Smith (the insured) misrepresented an answer to a question regarding medical treatment that had taken place during the last 5 years. More specifically, he gave a negative answer to a question asking whether he had a checkup, consultation, illness, injury, or surgery within the past 5 years. He forgot that he had gone to the doctor once 3 years ago for the flu. Does this misrepresentation provide a sufficient ground for rescinding the life insurance contract?

15. Compare the two standards the courts apply to test the materiality of facts misrepresented in life insurance applications, and describe the potential shortcomings of each standard.

16. Describe the ways in which the common law effect of misstatement by an applicant for life insurance has been modified by state statutes.

17. For each of the following types of information typically gathered in life insurance applications, indicate (1) whether it is generally construed to be a statement of fact or a statement of opinion, and (2) the extent to which it is invoked by insurers as a defense in litigation:

    a. answers to questions concerning the amount of insurance the applicant carries and the disposition of applications he or she submitted to other companies
    b. answers to questions about the applicant's (prospective insured's) past and present occupation
    c. statements about a change of occupation
    d. answers to questions about family history that call for information about events that occurred many years before
    e. answers to questions about exposure to contagious diseases
    f. statements about the prospective insured's habits
    g. answers to questions about specific ailments or diseases
    h. answers to general questions about medical treatment, consultation, or hospitalization during the last 5 years

18. How does a concealment in insurance law differ from a concealment in general law?

19. Explain the tests of materiality and fraud generally applied by the courts in determining whether an insurer can void a life insurance contract on the ground of concealment.

20. Explain how the scope of the doctrine of concealment has been narrowed in life insurance and when the doctrine tends to be invoked by life insurers in practice.

21. Explain under what circumstances the applicant for life insurance is and is not obligated to disclose facts discovered between the time the application was signed and the time the contract was consummated in order to avoid having the contract voided on the ground of concealment.

Self-Test Questions

T F   1. Unlike a representation of a fact, which must be both false and material, a warranty need be only untrue in order for a contract to be rescinded.

T F   2. A warranty is a statement that induces a party to enter into a contract but is not part of the contract.

T F   3. Because of statutes enacted in most states, warranties have become increasingly important in the law of life insurance.

T F   4. Although a representation may be either oral or written under general contract law, representations in life insurance—to be used by the insurer to rescind the contract—must be written and contained in the application attached to the policy.

T F   5. When a representation turns out to be false, the aggrieved party always has a choice of remedies, either suing the person who made the misstatement for damages or rescinding the contract.

T F   6. A misrepresentation by a party to a contract makes the contract voidable (rather than void) because the aggrieved party may elect to either affirm or rescind the contract.

T F   7. An insurer's delay bars its power to rescind a life insurance contract on the ground of misrepresentation only if the owner-insured was prejudiced by the delay.

T F   8. To make its rescission of a life insurance contract conclusive, the insurer's notice of rescission must be accompanied by a tender of all premiums paid under the contract.

T   F   9.   A statement of fact in the application must be false, material, and fraudulent to make a life insurance policy voidable on the grounds of misrepresentation.

T   F   10.   A majority of cases have held that an innocent misrepresentation of a material fact suffices to make a policy voidable, because the test of a misrepresentation is the effect on the insurer and not the culpability of the insured in making it.

T   F   11.   To obtain rescission of a life insurance policy based on a statement in the application about the applicant-insured's intention of becoming a student pilot, an insurer generally must prove the statement to be false, material, and fraudulent.

T   F   12.   The facts misrepresented in a statement in a life insurance application are material if they have induced the insurer to enter into a contract that it would not have made had it known the true statement of the facts, or would have made only on different terms.

T   F   13.   Under the prudent-insurer standard, the courts attempt to test the materiality of misrepresented facts by referring to the underwriting practices of the particular insurance company involved in the litigation.

T   F   14.   Most states have enacted statutes that convert statements in the life insurance application from warranties to representations.

T   F   15.   Because the applicant-insured's statements about his or her habits are usually regarded as statements of fact (rather than opinions), they frequently constitute the basis for litigation alleging misrepresentation.

T   F   16.   Answers to questions in the application about specific ailments or diseases are in most jurisdictions deemed to be statements of fact and not merely statements of opinion.

T   F   17.   Answers to general questions about medical treatment, consultation, or hospitalization during the last 5 years are generally treated as statements of fact and have been the ones most frequently invoked as defenses in litigation.

T   F   18.   In insurance law, a concealment connotes an affirmative act to hide the existence of a material fact.

T   F   19.   Except for marine insurance, a concealment need generally only be material in order for an insurer to void the contract.

T   F   20.   A concealment is misrepresentation by silence.

T   F   21.   The general concept of materiality applied to concealment is the same as that applied to misrepresentation—the effect on the underwriting decision of the insurer.

T   F   22. To rescind a life insurance contract on the ground of concealment, the insurer must prove that the undisclosed fact is, in the applicant's own mind, material to the risk.

T   F   23. Although an insurer generally can prove the applicant-insured's awareness of the materiality of a fact that has been concealed by establishing that the fact was *palpably material* (a characteristic that would be apparent to any person of normal intelligence), the courts also take into account the powers of understanding and state of knowledge of the particular applicant involved.

T   F   24. Because the applications currently used in the life insurance business are very comprehensive, there can no longer be any concealment in connection with the purchase of life insurance as long as the applicant answers all the questions asked in the application fully and truthfully.

T   F   25. If the applicant for life insurance discovered a material fact between the time the application was signed and the time the contract came into existence, the applicant would be under no obligation to disclose the fact if the first premium was paid with the application and a receipt conditioned on insurability at the date of application was issued.

NOTES

1. Muriel L. Crawford and William T. Beadles, *Law and the Life Insurance Contract,* 6th ed. (Homewood, IL: Irwin Professional Publishing, 1989), p. 678.
2. *Ibid.*, p. 676.
3. *Ibid.*, p. 243.
4. Buist M. Anderson, *Anderson on Life Insurance* (Boston: Little, Brown & Company, 1991), pp. 243–244.
5. *Ibid.*, p. 245.
6. Sec. 4101 of the New York Civil Practice Law and Rules permits an insurer when sued by a beneficiary to have its equitable defense or counterclaim for rescission tried before a judge without a jury.
7. *Sommer v. Guardian Life Insurance Co.,* 281 N.Y. 508, 24 N.E. 2d 308 (1939). A *statement* that the applicant is in good health must be distinguished from the requirement that the applicant *be* in good health upon delivery of the policy, which requirement, as a condition precedent, is strictly enforced.
8. Anderson, *Anderson on Life Insurance,* pp. 243–244.
9. New York Insurance Law, Sec. 149 (2). For purposes of this statute, a contract issued on the basis of a higher premium is considered a different contract.
10. *Ibid.*, Sec. 149 (3).
11. *Crotty v. State Mutual Assur. Co. of Am.,* 80 A.D. 2d 801, 437 N.Y.S. 21 103 (1981).
12. California Insurance Code, Sec. 334.
13. Missouri, Kansas, Oklahoma, and Rhode Island require that the misrepresented fact must have contributed to the company's loss in order to be considered material. However, these statutes do not apply if the insurer can show that the answers in the application were made with intent to deceive.
14. Mo. Ann. Stat. Sec. 376.800 (reman 1968).

15.   *Columbian National Life Insurance Co. of Boston, Mass. v. Rodgers,* 116 F. 2d 705 (10th Cir. 1941), certiorari denied, 313 U.S. 561 (1941).

16.   See, for example, *Mutual Life Insurance Co. of New York v. Moriarity,* 178 F. 2d 470 (9th Cir., 1949).

17.   New York Insurance Law, Sec. 149 (4).

18.   *Ibid.*

19.   This is not true in California. The Insurance Code (Sec. 330) of that state provides that "concealment, whether intentional or unintentional," entitles the insurer to rescind the contract.

20.   If the undisclosed fact is palpably material—that is, if its importance would be obvious to a person of ordinary understanding—it can be inferred that the applicant was aware of its materiality, an essential element in fraud.

21.   *Penn Mutual Life Insurance Co. v. Mechanics Savings Bank & Trust Co.,* 72 Fed. 413 (6th Cir. 1896).

22.   *New York Life Insurance Co. v. Bacalis,* 94 F. 2d 200 (5th Cir. 1938).

23.   *Mallory v. Travelers Insurance Co.,* 47 N.Y. 52 (1871).

24.   *McDaniel v. United Benefit Life Insurance Co.,* 177 F. 2d 339 (5th Cir. 1941).

25.   *Wilkins v. Travelers Insurance Co.,* 117 F. (2d) 646 (5th Circ. 1941).

26.   *Equitable Life Assurance Society of United States v. McElroy,* 83 Fed. 631 (8th Cir. 1897).

27.   *Stipcicli v. Metropolitan Life Insurance Co.,* 277 U.S. 311, 316-17 (1928). (Italics supplied.)

6

Waiver, Estoppel, and Election by the Insurer

Dan M. McGill
Revised by Burke A. Christensen

Learning Objectives

An understanding of the material in this chapter should enable the student to

6-1. Explain the effect the doctrines of waiver, estoppel, and election may have on a life insurer's ability to avoid liability under a policy.

6-2 Describe the general state of affairs in the field of waiver law, and explain why this situation exists.

6-3. Describe the general rules of agency law concerning the creation of an agency relationship, the types of authority that may be involved, the responsibility of the principal for the acts and knowledge of its agent, and the ability of the principal to effectively limit the powers of an agent; and explain how each of these rules is applied or modified in the life insurance business.

6-4. Distinguish between an insurance broker and an insurance agent in terms of the nature of their agency relationships.

6-5. Explain how the courts tend to distinguish between waiver and estoppel.

6-6. Distinguish between equitable estoppel and legal or promissory estoppel.

6-7. Explain what is meant by election, and describe the extent to which it has been applied to life insurance.

6-8. Describe various typical waiver situations, and explain what steps life insurers should take in an effort to avoid losing their rights to assert otherwise valid legal defenses in these cases.

Chapter Outline

As discussed in the preceding chapter, a life insurance company may be able to avoid liability under a policy on the grounds of a breach of condition, a misrepresentation, or a concealment. Another possible insurer defense to a suit is lack of coverage under the terms of the policy. An insurer may not be permitted to assert any of these defenses, however, if additional facts show that it has waived the defense, has taken actions that amount to an estoppel, or has conclusively elected not to take advantage of it.

Various factual situations constitute the basis for a waiver, an estoppel, and an election (examples of each will be shown later in this chapter). Although they are legally distinct concepts, it is customary to refer to them all generically as a waiver and to describe any situation that could lead to the loss of an otherwise valid legal defense as a waiver situation. Simply and broadly stated, a *waiver situation* is one in which an insurance company's presumably valid defense to a policy claim has been—or may be found to have been—waived by the company.

waiver situation

If the foregoing definition of a waiver situation seems vague and general, it was intended to be. The boundaries of waiver law are indistinct, and the concepts employed tend to be amorphous.

This state of affairs is largely attributable to the underlying purpose of waiver law, which, in the case of life insurance, is to protect the policyowner and his or her beneficiaries against a harsh and overly legalistic interpretation of the life insurance policy and application. In perhaps no other branch of the law is there such a universal tendency to make the law fit the facts, and if that is impractical, to create new law. A waiver has been described as "a kind of legal mercy, a way of tempering the wind to the shorn lamb."[1] In the process of providing mercy, the courts "have devised doctrines and asserted principles which are sometimes more creditable to the ingenuity and subtlety of the judges than easily harmonized with decisions rendered, under less violent bias, in other departments of the law."[2]

Edwin W. Patterson, Cardozo Professor Emeritus of Jurisprudence, Columbia University, and an eminent authority on the law of waiver, ascribed the state of confusion existing in this field to the use of "flexible concepts to analyze the significance of foggy facts."[3] Seeing hope for improvement, however, Patterson concluded that "the doctrines of waiver, once used as judicial whitewash to cover a multitude of minor defaults, are now used more sparingly and with more discrimination."[4] Nevertheless, in the years since these statements were made, the lack of clarity about the distinctions between waiver and estoppel has not improved.

Inasmuch as the law of agency is at the foundation of most waiver situations in life insurance, it is helpful to review the pertinent elements of that branch of the law before considering the more specific aspects of waiver.

LAW OF AGENCY

principal

principal: one for whom an agent acts

agent

agent: a person who acts for another

agency

Agency can be defined as the relationship that results from the manifestation of consent by one person or entity (the principal) that another party (the agent) will act on the principal's behalf. The agent is subject to the principal's control. There must also be a manifestation of consent to the agency by the agent.

Almost any person can be an agent. A person is not required to have contractual capacity in order to act as an agent. For example, a minor who cannot sign a binding contract for himself or herself can still serve as an agent and may sign a binding contract for his or her principal. However, only a person or an entity with contractual capacity to perform a certain act may act as a principal and appoint an agent. Thus a corporation may be a principal but a partnership may not. One who appears to be an agent of a partnership is at best an agent of the partners themselves.

Life Insurance Agents Must

- be licensed by the state
- have contractual capacity
- have agreed to the agency representation
- satisfy a state-imposed minimum age
- be subject to the principal's control

These general rules of agency law are modified when applied to the life insurance business. For example, life insurance agents must be of a certain minimum age, have contractual capacity, and be licensed by the state.

Example: ***Who May Be an Agent or Principal***

A person who has not reached the age of legal majority can be appointed as an agent to sell his or her neighbor's car. That minor could not, however, appoint a neighbor who has reached the age of legal majority as an agent to sell the minor's car.

In the case of a life insurance company, the agents—in the legal sense—include the directors (acting as a body), the officers, home office supervisory personnel, agency supervisors, and soliciting agents. In the business sense, only agency field supervisors and soliciting agents are regarded as agents. In this chapter the term "agent" will be used in its broader, legal meaning, with the expression "soliciting agent" used to designate field sales personnel. Most waiver situations involve actions of soliciting agents.

General Rules

power

power: the ability to say or do something. This ability may be inherent, given, implied, or derived.

authority

authority: the power to act that is given to someone by another party

The following four general rules of the law of agency are particularly relevant to life insurance:

- presumption of agency
- apparent authority of agents
- responsibility for acts of agents
- limitations on powers of agents

Presumption of Agency

There is no presumption that one person acts for another. There must be some tangible evidence of an agency relationship. Thus if a person claims to represent a certain life insurance company and collects a premium with which he or she later absconds, the company is not responsible for that person's actions if it has done nothing to create the presumption that the person is its authorized agent. If, however, the company has by its conduct permitted the person to have the appearance of an agency relationship (such as leaving that person in possession of company property, application blanks, and receipt forms), a presumption can be raised that the person is in fact representing the company. (The presumption can be overcome by proof that the company materials were improperly acquired.)

Note that agency must be created by the principal. It cannot be created unilaterally by the purported agent.

The scope of authority for an agent's actions can be considerably broader than one might expect. There are three types of agency authority:

express authority

- *Express authority* is the power specifically given to the agent by the principal either orally or in writing.

implied (incidental) authority

- *Implied authority* refers to those powers not expressly given by the principal to the agent that are necessary to exercise the powers that are expressly given. This type of authority is sometimes also referred to as *incidental authority.*

apparent authority

- *Apparent authority* is the authority that the public reasonably believes the agent possesses based on the actions of the principal. Apparent authority may arise regardless of whether the agent has been given any express authority by the principal.

Apparent Authority of Agents

Most agency relationships are evidenced by a written instrument that expressly confers certain powers on the agent; it may also expressly withhold certain powers. A life insurance company's agency contract usually authorizes the field representative to solicit and take applications for new

---

Life Insurance Agency Contracts Usually Deny Agents the Power To

- create a contract
- alter a contract
- discharge a contract
- extend time limits on payment of premiums
- waive any obligations
- waive any conditions
- extend any obligations
- extend any conditions
- accept predated or postdated checks
- deliver the policy to applicants not in good health

business, arrange medical examinations, and collect first-year premiums. It also sets forth a number of powers specifically denied the agent, including the right to make, alter, or discharge a contract; to extend the time for payment of premiums; to accept payment of premiums in other than current funds; to waive or extend any obligation or condition; and to deliver any policy unless the applicant is in good health and insurable condition at that time.

The agent's contract for one insurer, for example, provides that the company authorizes the agent to solicit applications for its insurance products. The contract then prescribes a substantial list of limitations on that authority as shown in the following example.

Example: The Agent shall have no authority for or on behalf of the Company to accept risks of any kind; to make, modify, or discharge contracts; to extend time for paying any premium; to bind the Company by any statement, promise, or representation; to waive forfeitures or any of the Company's rights or requirements, or to place the company under any legal obligation by any act that is not within the authority granted by the Company in this contract or otherwise in writing.

Another insurer uses this coverage to limit the scope of authority granted by its agent's contract, as follows in the example below.

Example: The Agent shall have no power or authority other than as herein expressly granted, and no other or greater powers shall be implied from the grant or denial of powers specifically mentioned herein.

An agent's power to bind his or her principal, however, may well exceed the scope of the principal's express authorization. This is because express authority is construed to convey authority to perform all incidental acts necessary to carry out the agency's purposes. Such acts fall under the heading of implied powers. For example, if an agent is expressly authorized to deliver a life insurance policy that can be properly delivered only upon the payment of the consideration, the agent has the implied power to collect the amount due and issue a receipt.

An agent's authority can also be expanded by conduct of the principal or agent that creates a justifiable belief by third parties dealing with the agent that he or she possesses powers that have not been vested in the agent and may—unknown to the third parties—have been expressly withheld by the principal. If third parties can prove that they were justified in relying on the presumption that the agent was acting within his or her authority, the principal will be estopped (precluded) from denying that the agent had such powers. In proving justifiable reliance, third parties need to demonstrate only that they exercised due diligence in ascertaining the agent's real authority. Authority created in this manner is referred to as apparent authority.

The doctrine of apparent authority can be illustrated by this example.

Example:	An agent has habitually granted his or her policy-owners extensions of time to remit premiums. Because the company has not taken action to deal with this infraction of its rules in the past, it would be precluded from denying that the agent had such authority until it notified the policyowners involved of the limitations on the agent's powers. The company's action with regard to one policyowner, however, would not create any presumption as to the agent's power to deal in a similar manner with other policyowners.

Responsibility for Acts of Agents

The principal is responsible for all acts of its agent when the agent is acting within the scope of express, implied, or apparent authority. This responsibility embraces wrongful or fraudulent acts, omissions, and misrepresentations, provided the agent is acting within the authority granted or implied by the principal. The principal is likewise responsible for any libel committed by an agent in the pursuit of his or her official duties. While there is no unanimity in the decisions, the weight of authority is that—in the absence of restrictions—a company is liable not only for the acts of its agents, but also for the acts of the subagents and employees to whom the agent has delegated responsibility. The liability of the company in such situations may depend on whether it has given the agent actual authority, or its actions have created an apparent authority, to delegate responsibility.

Secret limitations on the agent's authority are, under the doctrine of equitable estoppel, inoperative as to third persons. They are, of course, effective between the agent and the principal, and if the agent exceeds the actual authority given, he or she will be liable to the principal for any loss or damage. The agent, as might be expected, will also be liable to the principal for any loss or damage caused through the agent's fraud, misconduct, or mere negligence.

In the course of their daily business, insurance agents are frequently asked to express their opinion about the meaning of a particular provision. The general rule is that no legal effect is to be given to such opinions. This holding is based on the theory that an agent's opinion as to the meaning of any section does not create new obligations or modify old ones. This rule is followed particularly when the agent's authority is limited and the provision involved is clear and unambiguous. In certain jurisdictions, however, a company is bound by its agents' opinions, especially when the opinion is not inconsistent with the language of an ambiguous clause in the policy and the agent's opinion is relied on by the insured.[5]

Knowledge the Principal Is Presumed to Have

- information obtained by agents
- information obtained by medical examiners (even if it has not been communicated to the principal)

The agent's knowledge about matters within the agency's scope is presumed to be knowledge of the principal. This rule is applied even though matters coming to the agent's attention are not, in fact, communicated to the principal. This rule is of critical importance, since in all their dealings with prospective and actual policyowners, soliciting agents and medical examiners are regarded to be the legal agents of the company. Hence loyalty to the company, as well as common decency, demand that field representatives communicate to the company all matters of underwriting or other significance that come to their attention.

Example:

Agent's Knowledge Presumed to Be Principal's Knowledge

In the process of applying for insurance on her own life, Mary Ann disclosed to the soliciting agent that her father died at an early age due to kidney disease. The agent told her this was not important information and need not be reported on the application. The agent then forwarded the application to the insurer, which issued the policy as applied for. Several months later, Mary Ann developed kidney disease, at which time her father's cause of death became known. Unless the insurer can prove fraud or collusion on Mary Ann's part, it is obligated to keep the policy in force. The insurer is presumed to have had knowledge of the father's cause of death when it issued the policy.

Limitation on Powers of Agents

nonwaiver clause

Limitations on an agent's powers are generally effective when the limitations have been properly communicated and do not conflict with existing law. All companies communicate to their policyowners through a clause in the application blank or in the policy (or both) the customary limitations on the powers of soliciting agents and other company representatives with whom the policyowner may come in contact. This provision, generally referred to as the *nonwaiver clause*, usually states that only certain specified representatives of the company (executive officers) have the power to extend the time for payment of a premium or to modify the terms of the contract in any other respect. The clause further requires that any modification of the contract must be evidenced by a written endorsement on the contract. For example, such a provision might read as follows: Only our president or one of our vice presidents can modify this contract or waive any of our rights or requirements under it. The person making these changes must put them in writing and sign them.

A nonwaiver clause will not be enforceable against acts or statements occurring prior to the policy's issue unless it is contained in the application and the application is attached to the policy. In other words, the applicant cannot be presumed to have knowledge of a limitation in an instrument that comes into his or her possession only after the transaction has been consummated. On the other hand, the assumption follows that limitations on the agent's authority contained in the application or the policy are effective with respect to acts occurring subsequent to delivery of the policy. Unfortunately for the insurance companies, experience has not always borne out this assumption.

Brokers as Agents

insurance broker

An *insurance broker* is a person (individual, partnership, or corporation) who acts as an agent of the insured in negotiating for insurance and in procuring the issuance of an insurance contract. In the eyes of the law, the broker is requested by the prospective insured to act for him or her, although in practice, the "request" is usually solicited by the broker. The broker usually receives all his or her compensation (in the form of commissions) from the insurance company, delivers the policy for the company, and collects the premium from the insured. As a consequence, the broker has come to be regarded as the agent of the company for the purpose of delivering the policy and collecting the premium. In fact, this status is recognized by statute in some states.

When the broker is regarded as the agent of the company only for these limited purposes, the broker's knowledge as to facts affecting the risk is not imputed to the company for the purpose of establishing a waiver or estoppel, or for the purpose of obtaining reformation of the contract because of mistake.[6] In most states, however, there is legislation that provides that any person who solicits insurance for anyone other than himself or herself and procures a policy from the insurer will be deemed the agent of the insurer with respect to that policy.

MEANING OF WAIVER, ESTOPPEL, AND ELECTION

The legal concepts and rules employed in the adjudication of waiver situations have often lacked strong logic and consistency. The result is that the distinctions among waiver, estoppel, and election have become decidedly blurred, perhaps irretrievably so. Basically, however, the legal conceptions of waiver, estoppel, and election are derived from these two elemental principles:

- An individual should be bound by that to which he or she assents.
- An individual whose conduct has led another to act or not to act in reliance upon a belief as to a fact or an expected future performance, ought not to be allowed to act in a way contrary to a belief or expectation he or she created.[7]

The first principle is at the foundation of waiver and election, while the second suggests the basis for several varieties of estoppel.

Waiver

waiver

waiver: the voluntary and intentional giving up of a known right

The term "waiver" has been used with so many meanings that it almost defies analysis. Some courts try to distinguish it from estoppel, while other courts treat it as synonymous or interchangeable with estoppel. For example, one court might hold that the failure to demand an answer to an unanswered question in an application for life insurance constitutes a *waiver* of the right to make the demand, whereas another might hold that the company was *estopped* from demanding the answer. When a court does attempt to distinguish between waiver and estoppel, it ordinarily treats waiver as an act that indicates a manifestation of assent to something. For example, if a company elects to issue a policy even though the medical questions were not answered, it will be presumed to have waived the right to get the answers. On the other hand, an estoppel is treated as nonconsensual. This is because the purpose of the concept of estoppel is to redress a wrong and to prevent inequitable treatment of one party to a contract by the other. Thus if waiver is to be given a specific meaning, it would probably be appropriate to define it as a "manifestation of intent to relinquish a known right or advantage."[8] This meaning is similar to the definition provided many years ago by the highest court of New York: "A waiver is the voluntary abandonment or relinquishment by a party of some right or advantage."[9]

While the foregoing definitions set waiver apart from estoppel, they do not distinguish it clearly from *election,* which, as noted in the discussion later in this chapter, likewise connotes a voluntary act.

Estoppel

estoppel

> *estoppel:* a loss of the ability to assert a defense because of prior actions that are now inconsistent with that defense

The doctrine of estoppel, developed centuries ago in the English courts, is a limitation on a person's right to change his or her mind. The law recognizes the right of individuals to change their minds, but it imposes certain restraints on that right when a contract has been created or when parties have acted reasonably in reliance on another person's representations or promises. The law of contracts attempts to distinguish the serious promise from the casual or jesting promise by means of a *consideration*. In the law of estoppel, a detrimental reliance or change of position by the other party is the test.

There are two broad types of estoppel: (1) equitable estoppel (also called estoppel by representation and estoppel in pais) and (2) legal or promissory estoppel.

Equitable Estoppel

equitable estoppel

Historically, *equitable estoppel*, so called because it originated in the equity courts, was the first to develop. It was confined to a representation of past or present fact; it did not apply to promises about future behavior. This original meaning has been preserved through the years and is reflected in the following comprehensive definition: "An [equitable] estoppel is a representation of fact made by one person to another which is reasonably relied upon by that other in changing his position to such an extent that it would be inequitable to allow the first person to deny the truth of his representation."[10]

The essence of the equitable estoppel is that if a party purports to make a true statement about a past or present fact to another party who relies on the truth of the statement to his or her substantial detriment, the first party will not be permitted to later deny the truth of the statement. The case is tried on an assumption contrary to fact. Thus equitable estoppel is a rule of evidence rather than one of substantive law.

Legal or Promissory Estoppel

legal (promissory) estoppel

The doctrine of *legal (promissory) estoppel* has developed within the last century and is concerned with a statement of *future* conduct. It has been defined as "a statement as to his future conduct made by one person to another which is reasonably and foreseeably relied upon by that other in changing his position to such an extent that it would be inequitable to allow the first person to conduct himself differently from that which he stated."[11] In other words, if you make a promise in some circumstances, you won't be allowed to change your mind.

The example that follows illustrates a promissory estoppel.

Example:	Suppose P promises to give C $25,000 if C enters a particular college and receives a bachelor's degree. Suppose further that C matriculates at the designated college and completes all the requirements for the degree except passing the examinations for the final term when P notifies C of an intention to revoke the promise. Since C has made a substantial sacrifice in effort and money to attend college in reliance on P's promise, the courts would not permit P to revoke the promise. P's promise would be enforced, despite the fact that it was not supported by a consideration.[12] In other words, the law would recognize a valid contract. Some would even argue that C's actions in reliance on P's promise provide the consideration (or at least an equitable substitute) to support the contract.

The foregoing example illustrates the creation of a new obligation through a promissory estoppel. Some courts will not go that far in applying the doctrine, limiting its application to modifications of existing contracts, which is the typical application in life insurance situations. This application of promissory estoppel is of growing importance.

Election

election

In its original sense, *election* means a voluntary act of choosing between two alternative rights or privileges. Thus if a married man dies testate (with a will), his widow usually has the right to take under the will or under the appropriate intestate law. These are alternative rights, and the widow's act of choosing one is a voluntary relinquishment of the other. The similarity of an election to a waiver is readily apparent.

The concept of election has had only limited application in life insurance. Despite the fact that an election is an overt, manifested intent to be bound, the courts have occasionally found an election to exist in the inconsistent conduct of an insurer.

> *Example:*   A company's acceptance of a premium after the discovery of a material misrepresentation has been viewed as an election by the company not to void the contract.

WAIVER SITUATIONS

In the remainder of this chapter, no attempt will be made to distinguish between waiver, estoppel, and election. The practical effect is the same, irrespective of the particular doctrine the court uses to justify its decision. The emphasis hereafter is on the types of factual situations in which the courts are likely to invoke one of the doctrines outlined above to deprive a life insurance company of a defense that would have enabled it to avoid paying a claim.

Breach of Condition Precedent

The validity of most life insurance policies is contingent on the fulfillment of three conditions precedent:

- the payment of the first premium
- the good health of the applicant at the time the policy is delivered
- the absence of new elements affecting insurability (for example, medical treatment) in the interim between the submission of the application and the delivery of the policy

Payment of First Premium

The existence of a life insurance policy is usually conditioned on payment of the first premium, or the first installment thereof, *in cash.* The cash-premium clause is typically coupled with the delivery-in-good-health clause.

The requirement that the first premium be paid in cash has been strictly enforced by the courts. Upon proof that the soliciting agent delivered the policy without payment of the premium, or any part thereof in any form, the courts in most jurisdictions hold that the policy is not in force, even though the agent orally assured the applicant that it would take effect at once. The view is that an agent having authority merely to solicit insurance and to collect premiums in cash has no actual or apparent authority to extend credit.

In reaching this conclusion, the courts seem to place great emphasis on the existence of a nonwaiver clause in the application, as opposed to the policy. In a leading New York case on the subject,[13] the court, holding that the cash payment requirement had not been satisfied through the payment of the premium by the soliciting agent on behalf of the applicant, stressed that the insured *agreed* in the application that the insurance would not take effect unless the premium was paid at the time the policy was delivered. In another case,[14] the taking of a promissory note payable to the soliciting agent was not deemed a waiver of the cash-premium clause because there was also a nonwaiver clause in the application.

The nonwaiver clause will not prevent a finding of waiver in all cases; it is merely notice to the applicant of the agent's limited authority. If it can be proved that the agent actually had authority to extend credit for all or a part of the premium, the agent's doing so will, in most courts, constitute an effective waiver of the cash-premium requirement. Thus an agent who had the power to employ subagents, and had received detailed instructions from the home office as to how to deal with premium notes, was held to have authority to issue a binding receipt in exchange for the applicant's note.[15]

In another case, it was proved that the insurer followed the practice of requiring its soliciting agents to remit only the difference between the gross premium and the agent's commission. It was held that the agent had authority to extend credit for the balance to an applicant who had paid the agent more than the amount remitted but less than the full amount due—despite the existence of cash-premium and nonwaiver clauses in the application.[16] In cases like this, the company's formal printed instructions to the agency force are not conclusive proof of an agent's actual authority. To avoid a waiver, the company's action must be consistent with its announced policy.

It is common practice, of course, for premiums to be paid by check. If the check is honored by the bank upon which it is drawn, the premium—for all intents and purposes—has been paid in cash. A check is considered to be a cash payment if an applicant has sufficient funds in his or her bank account to cover the check for a reasonable period of time.[17] If a check tendered in payment of the first premium is not honored upon presentation within a reasonable time, however, the status of the policy depends on the terms under which the check was accepted. If the premium receipt states that the check is accepted as payment only on the condition that it be honored (a common practice), the policy will not go into force if the check is not honored. If the premium receipt does not so state, however, some courts have construed the issuance of a premium receipt to be an *election* to treat the check as payment of the premium. In that event, the condition of the policy has been fulfilled, and nonpayment of the check merely entitles the insurer to sue the drawer of the check.

Delivery-in-Good-Health and Medical Treatment Clauses

Insurance contracts are normally issued subject to a good-health clause, which is usually found in the application. This clause is made a part of the contract at the time the application is attached to the policy when it is issued and delivered to the policyowner.

Example 1:   A typical good health clause reads as follows:

> The Company shall incur no liability under any policy issued on this application unless and until any policy is delivered to the Owner, and the first premium is paid prior to any change in the Proposed Insured's good health and insurability.

Example 2:   Some companies accomplish this goal with such language as:

> No insurance shall take effect on this application until a policy is delivered, the full initial premium is paid, and unless the statements in all parts of the application continue to be true, complete, and without material change.

The policy may be delivered to an insured who is not in good health when that fact is known by the agent, or when the agent does not inquire as to the state of the insured's health. Has the insurer waived its rights to contest the breach?

It is clear that either waiver or estoppel may prevent the insurer from asserting the good-health clause as a defense. This may be avoided if the insurer has warned the policyowner about the good-health clause and the limitations on the agent's power to alter the contract. Thus both of those clauses are usually prominently printed on the insurance application. Nevertheless, one court has held that the agent's failure to inquire about the insured's health resulted in a waiver of the carrier's right under the good-health clause.

Misrepresentation in Application

The applicant for a life insurance policy must submit a written application that supplies various types of information, including information about the applicant's past and present health. The applicant may also have to undergo a medical examination, including an interrogation by the medical examiner. It is standard practice for the soliciting agent to fill out the application for the applicant and for the medical examiner to write in the answers to the questions that he or she asks the applicant.

There is always the possibility that the agent or medical examiner may incorrectly record information supplied by the applicant in the application. This may occur inadvertently or by design. Unless there is collusion, the medical examiner has little or no reason to falsify the medical records. The agent, however, because he or she is paid on a commission basis, does have an incentive to falsify information—either with or without the applicant's knowledge—that might adversely affect the application's acceptance.

If there is collusion between the applicant and any agent of the insurer to falsify the application, the insurer loses none of its defenses. If, on the other hand, the agent is acting alone and tells the applicant that an item of information is not being recorded correctly, the agent is likely to imply that the information is immaterial and should not be permitted to complicate home office underwriting officials' consideration of the application. In cases where the applicant's truthful answers have been falsely recorded in the application by the agent (or the medical examiner), it becomes important to determine the legal effect of these misstatements.

It is a well-settled rule that one who signs and accepts a written instrument with the intention of contracting is bound by its terms. However, if the instrument contains false statements, the aggrieved party has the right to avoid the contract. Hence, in accordance with strict contract law, material misstatements in the application should give the insurance company power to avoid the contract, regardless of the circumstances surrounding the statements' falsification. However, the courts, recognizing that a life insurance policy is a contract of adhesion that the insured seldom reads, do not apply strict contract law in these cases. The rule supported by the weight of authority is that if the application is filled out by an agent of the company who—without fraud, collusion, or the applicant's knowledge—falsely records information that the applicant had provided truthfully, the company cannot rely on the falsity of such information in seeking to avoid liability under the contract.[18] According to one court, "To hold otherwise would be to place every simple or uneducated person seeking insurance at the mercy of the insurer who could, through its agent, insert in every application, unknown to the applicant, and over his signature, some false statement which would enable it to avoid all liability while retaining the price paid for supposed insurance."[19]

The key to the rule is that the agent, in filling out the application, is acting for the company, not for the insured. In other words, the soliciting agent is, in a legal sense, the agent of the company, the principal. This finding can support either of two legal theories, both of which have been used by the courts to justify their decisions. The first theory holds that there is no deception of the insurance company since it knew through its agent that the written statement or statements were not true.[20] The second theory, more widely used, recognizes that there is deception but holds that since the company, through the knowledge of its agent, knowingly issued a voidable policy, it is estopped from voiding it. In both theories, the insurer has a right of action against the agent for breach of his or her duty to the principal.

To find an estoppel against the insurer, the courts must permit testimony, usually from the beneficiary, as to the answers the applicant provided to the agent. This would seem to be in violation of the parol evidence rule, but the general holding is that the parol evidence rule does not exclude oral testimony to establish waiver or estoppel.

The courts are likewise inclined to find a waiver or an estoppel when the applicant knows an answer is false but the agent asserts that it is immaterial. The view is that the applicant is entitled to rely on the superior knowledge of the agent or medical examiner, as the case may be. Even a stipulation in the application that oral statements made to the agent will not be binding on the company has been held unenforceable. However, when the applicant knows that the agent or medical examiner is not truthfully reporting obviously material facts to the company, the applicant is guilty of fraud and cannot invoke the doctrine of estoppel, which requires honest reliance. The applicant's behavior in this situation is regarded as collusive.

Waiver Subsequent to Issuance of Policy

If a condition is breached after a policy has gone into effect, the breach can be waived by the insurer in either of two ways:

- by an express statement, usually in writing, from a representative of the insurer having the authority to waive the condition
- by the inconsistent conduct of the company and its representatives

With waiver by an express statement, attention must again be directed to the clause embodied in the application for a life insurance policy, stipulating that no provision of the contract can be waived except by a *written* endorsement on the contract signed by a designated officer of the company. This restriction is likely to be enforced with respect to *express* waivers, although the courts occasionally find that the company bestowed the waiver authority on representatives not designated in the nonwaiver clause, even local agents. Moreover, oral statements may be accepted as evidence of waiver. Note that this is not inconsistent with the parol evidence rule, which applies only to oral statements made prior to or contemporaneously with the formation of the contract. Most of the litigation concerning express waivers involves the authority of the person who allegedly approved the waiver. It is clear that if an important official of the company purports to waive a breach of condition, the waiver will be recognized and enforced by the courts. The validity of other alleged waivers will depend on the actual or apparent authority of the company representative making the statement.

A waiver after the policy is issued is more likely to be found in the inconsistent conduct of the company. When the company has knowledge of a breach or nonperformance of a condition and wishes to avoid the contract on that ground, it must pursue a course of conduct consistent with that intention. In their zeal to protect policyowners, the courts will seize upon inconsistent conduct on the part of the insurer as evidence of an intention not to exercise its power of avoidance. For example, if a company has followed a general practice of accepting and retaining premiums tendered after the expiration of the grace period, it will be estopped from denying the punctuality of any premiums so paid. Perhaps more important, it will be estopped from insisting on the timely payment of premiums in the future, unless it makes unmistakably clear to policyowners from whom overdue premiums have customarily been accepted that future payments must be made before expiration of the grace period. Any attempt by the company to collect a premium after the grace period has expired might be held to be a waiver unless accompanied by an invitation to the insured to submit an application for reinstatement.

The same rule applies when a company has established a practice of sending premium notices, although they are not required by statute or the policy. If, without adequate notice to policyholders, the company discontinued this practice, it would probably be held to have waived its right to insist on payment within the grace period, provided payment is tendered within a reasonable time. It used to be the practice of many companies to send out two premium notices—the second sometimes during the grace period. When those companies discontinued the second notice, they were careful to notify their policyowners of the change in practice in order to avoid the possibility of being charged with a waiver of the timely payment condition.

CHAPTER REVIEW

Answers to the review questions and the self-test questions can be found in the Supplement.

Key Terms

waiver situation
principal
agent
agency
power
authority
express authority
implied (incidental) authority

apparent authority
nonwaiver clause
insurance broker
waiver
estoppel
equitable estoppel
legal (promissory) estoppel
election

Review Questions

1. List three types of actions that might prevent a life insurer from avoiding liability under a policy on the grounds of a breach of condition, misrepresentation, concealment, or a lack of coverage under the terms of the policy.

2. Explain why the boundaries of waiver law are indistinct and the concepts employed tend to be amorphous.

3. State the general rules of agency law regarding who may serve as an agent, and explain how these general rules are modified when applied to the life insurance business.

4. Distinguish between those who are agents of a life insurance company in the legal sense and those who are agents in the business sense.

5. List the powers a life insurance agency contract usually confers on a company's field representative, and list those powers it generally withholds from the agent.

6. Explain why a life insurance soliciting agent's powers may well exceed the scope of the company's express authorization given in its agency contract.

7. Give an example of each of the following:
   a. a life insurance agent's implied powers
   b. a life insurance agent's apparent authority

8. Describe the extent to which a principal is responsible for the acts of its agents.

9. Explain whether a life insurance company is bound by an opinion given by its soliciting agent about the meaning of a particular policy provision.

10. Explain why it is critical for the legal agents of a life insurance company to communicate all significant information to the company.

11. What requirements must be satisfied in order for a nonwaiver clause to be enforceable against acts or statements occurring prior to the policy's issue?

12. For what purposes may an insurance broker be viewed in the eyes of the law as an agent of the insurance company?

13. List the two principles from which the legal concepts of waiver, estoppel, and election are derived, and indicate which principle is at the foundation of each legal concept.

14. Explain the situation that exists with respect to the efforts of various courts to distinguish between waiver and estoppel.

15. Distinguish between equitable estoppel and legal or promissory estoppel.

16. Indicate the extent to which each of the following is applied in life insurance:
    a. legal or promissory estoppel
    b. election

17. Describe what steps life insurance companies should take in an effort to keep the courts from invoking the doctrines of waiver, estoppel, or election to prevent their defenses based on breaches of the following conditions precedent:
    a. the payment of the first premium
    b. the good health of the applicant-insured at the time the policy is delivered

18. Describe the sets of circumstances under which the courts are inclined to find a waiver or an estoppel if the agent or medical examiner incorrectly records information provided by the applicant in the application.

19. List and explain the two ways a breach of a condition can be waived by the insurer after the policy has gone into effect.

20. Explain what an insurance company must do when it has knowledge of a breach or nonperformance of a condition and wishes to avoid the contract on that ground.

Self-Test Questions

T   F   1. Waiver, estoppel, or election may prevent an insurer from avoiding liability under a policy on the grounds of a breach of a condition, a misrepresentation, or a concealment.

T   F   2. When waiver law is applied to life insurance, the courts tend to make the law fit the facts; and if that is impractical, they often create new law to protect policyowners and beneficiaries against a harsh and overly legalistic interpretation of the policy and application.

T   F   3. Under the general rules of agency law, a person or entity must have contractual capacity in order to be either an agent or a principal.

T   F   4. Under the general rules of agency law, a corporation may be a principal.

T   F   5. Only soliciting agents and agency field supervisors are agents of a life insurance company in the legal sense.

T   F   6. The authority of a life insurance agent is limited to those powers expressly conferred on the agent by the company's agency contract.

T   F   7. Apparent authority refers to those powers not expressly given by the principal to the agent that are necessary to exercise the powers that are expressly given.

T   F   8. Both implied and apparent authority can exist only if the agent has been given some express authority by the principal.

T   F   9. The principal is responsible for all acts of its agent when the agent is acting within the scope of express, implied, or apparent authority.

T   F   10. The principal is responsible for the wrongful or fraudulent acts, omissions, and misrepresentations of its agent, provided the agent is acting within the authority granted or implied by the principal.

T   F   11. An agent is liable to the principal for any loss or damage caused by the agent exceeding the actual authority given by the principal or through the agent's fraud, misconduct, or mere negligence.

T   F   12. Life insurance companies generally are bound by the opinions expressed by their agents about the meanings of particular policy provisions.

T   F   13. A life insurance company is not presumed to know information of significance to the underwriting decision that has come to the attention of a soliciting agent or medical examiner but has not been communicated to the company.

T   F   14. The nonwaiver provision usually states that only certain specified representatives of the company (executive officers) have the power to extend the time for payment of a premium or to modify the terms of the contract in any other respect.

T   F   15. An insurance broker acts as an agent of the insured in negotiating for insurance and in procuring the issuance of an insurance contract.

T   F   16. The insurance broker has come to be regarded as the agent of the insurance company for the purpose of delivering the policy and collecting the premium.

T   F   17. While some courts try to distinguish waiver from estoppel, other courts treat waiver as synonymous or interchangeable with estoppel.

T   F   18. Estoppel is defined as the voluntary and intentional giving up of a known right.

T   F   19. When a court does attempt to distinguish between waiver and estoppel, it ordinarily treats waiver as an act that indicates a manifestation of assent to something and treats estoppel as nonconsensual.

T   F   20. Legal estoppel is confined to a representation of past or present fact, whereas equitable estoppel is concerned with a statement of future conduct.

T   F   21. The concept of election has been applied extensively in life insurance.

T   F   22. When the application contains both cash-premium and nonwaiver clauses, the courts tend to hold that the policy is not in force if the soliciting agent delivered the policy without payment of the premium, even though the agent orally assured the applicant that the policy would take effect at once.

T   F   23. As a general rule, if the application is filled out by an agent of the insurance company who—without fraud, collusion, or the applicant's knowledge—falsely records information that the applicant had provided truthfully, the company cannot rely on the falsity of such information in seeking to avoid liability under the contract.

T   F   24. When the applicant knows that the agent or medical examiner is not truthfully reporting obviously material facts to the insurance company, the applicant is guilty of fraud and cannot invoke the doctrine of estoppel, which requires honest reliance.

T   F   25. After a policy has been issued, the only way a breach of a condition can be waived is by an express statement in writing from a representative of the insurer having the authority to waive the condition.

NOTES

1. Edwin W. Patterson, *Essentials of Insurance Law,* 2d ed. (New York: McGraw-Hill Book Co., Inc., 1957), p. 476.
2. John Skirving Ewart, *Waiver Distributed* (Cambridge, MA: Harvard University Press, 1917), p. 192.
3. Patterson, *Essentials of Insurance Law,* p. 494.
4. *Ibid.,* p. 483.
5. *Couch Cyclopedia of Insurance Law,* 2d ed. rev. (Rochester, NY: The Lawyers Cooperative Publishing Co., 1993), sec. 531.
6. *Mishiloff v. American Central Insurance Co.,* 102 Conn. 370, 128 Atl. 33 (1925); *Ritson v. Atlas Assurance Co.,* 279 Mass. 385, 181 N.E. 393 (1932).
7. *Couch Cyclopedia of Insurance Law,* secs. 71.1–71.3.
8. Patterson, *Essentials of Insurance Law,* p. 495.

9. *Draper v. Oswego County Fire Relief Assn.,* 190 N.Y. 12, 14, 82 N.E. 755, 756 (1907).

10. Patterson, *Essentials of Insurance Law,* p. 496.

11. *Ibid.*

12. H. M. Horne and D. B. Mansfield, *The Life Insurance Contract,* 2d ed. (New York: Life Office Management Association, 1948), p. 81.

13. *Drilling v. New York Life Insurance Co.,* 234 N.Y. 234, 137 N.E. 314 (1922).

14. *Bradley v. New York Life Insurance Co.,* 275 Fed. 657 (8th Cir. 1921).

15. *Schwartz v. Northern Life Insurance Co.,* 25 F. (2d) 555 (9th Cir. 1928).

16. *New York Life Insurance Co. v. Olliclh,* 42 F. (2d) 399 (6th Cir. 1930).

17. *State Life Insurance Co. v. Nolan,* 13 S.W. 2d 406 (Tex. Civ. App. 1929).

18. In New York, the insured is bound by false answers entered by the agent or medical examiner if the insured certifies as to the answers. *Bollard v. New York Life Insurance Co.,* 228 N.Y. 521, 126 N.E. 900 (1920).

19. *State Insurance Co. of Des Moines v. Taylor,* 14 Colo. 499, 508, 24 Pac. 333, 336 (1890).

20. *Heilig v. Home Security Life Insurance Co.,* 222 N.C. 21, 22 S.E. 2d 429 (1942).

The Incontestable Clause

Dan M. McGill
Revised by Burke A. Christensen

Learning Objectives

An understanding of the material in this chapter should enable the student to

---

7-1.   Explain the nature and purpose of the incontestable clause.

7-2.   Explain what constitutes a contest within the meaning of the incontestable clause, and describe the types of proceedings that can be used to contest a life insurance policy.

7-3.   Indicate when the contestable period is considered to begin running under various common life insurance policy situations.

7-4.   Describe the various types of incontestable clauses that have been used by life insurance companies, and explain how the insured's death during the contestable period does or does not affect the insurer's rights regarding a contest of the policy under each type of clause.

7-5.   Explain whether the incontestable clause does or does not apply to nonpayment of premiums, disability and accidental death benefit provisions, hazards excluded from a policy, nonfulfillment of the delivery-in-good-health requirement and other such conditions precedent, misstatement of age and sex provisions, a suit for reformation to correct a clerical error in a policy, and reinstatement of a policy.

Chapter Outline

The preceding chapter discussed the impact of the doctrines of waiver, estoppel, and election on the right of a life insurance company to avoid liability under a policy because of fraud, misrepresentation, or breach of condition at the contract's inception. This chapter will consider an even more restrictive influence—the incontestable clause. This clause, without counterpart in any other type of contract, was once the source of considerable misunderstanding and litigation. A commonly held opinion is that no other provision of a typical life insurance contract has been the center of so much "controversy, misinterpretation, and legal abuse" as the incontestable clause.[1] While the incontestable clause is no longer the source of much litigation, the provision has a vital bearing on the protection afforded by a life insurance contract, and it is worthy of careful study.

NATURE AND PURPOSE OF THE CLAUSE

incontestable clause

incontestable clause: a provision in the insurance contract that waives most of the insurance company's rights to dispute the validity of the contract after a certain period of time

In its simplest form the incontestable clause states that a policy is incontestable from its date of issue, except for nonpayment of premium. The purpose of such a clause is to enhance a life insurance contract's value by providing assurances that its validity will not be questioned by the insurance company years after it was issued and has possibly given rise to a claim. It is important to understand that the incontestable clause applies to whether the contract is valid, not to whether the terms or conditions of the contract have been fulfilled. The clause was voluntarily adopted by insurance companies partly as a result of competitive pressures to overcome prejudices against the life insurance business created by contests based on technicalities, and to give an assurance to "persons doubtful of the utility of insurance, that neither they nor their families, after the lapse of a given time, shall be harassed with lawsuits when the evidence of the original transaction shall have become dim, or difficult of retention, or when, perhaps, the lips of him who best knew the facts are sealed by death."[2]

Example: ***Fraud and the Incontestable Clause***

Betsy was recently diagnosed as having colon cancer. She applied for life insurance and bribed the medical examiner and her physician to conceal her condition. The policy was issued, and 3 years later Betsy died of cancer, at which time the insurer discovered the fraud. The insurer is nevertheless obligated to pay the claim.

A typical incontestable clause reads as follows: "We will not contest the validity of this policy, except for nonpayment of premiums, after it has been in force during the insured's lifetime for two years from the Policy Date. This provision does not apply to any rider providing accidental death or disability benefits."[3]

The incontestable clause is a manifestation of the belief that a life insurance policy's beneficiaries should not be made to suffer for mistakes innocently made in the application. As will be shown, therefore, the beneficiary may be protected by the incontestable clause even if the error in the application is based on a fraudulent or material misrepresentation by the applicant or by a failure of a condition precedent to the existence of the contract. After the insured's death, it would be extremely difficult, if not impossible, for the beneficiary to disprove the allegations of the insurance company that irregularities were present in procuring the policy. If there were no time limit on the insurance company's right to question the accuracy of the information provided in the application, there would be no certainty during the life of the policy that the benefits promised by it would be payable at maturity. The honest policyowner needs assurance that at death the beneficiary will be the "recipient of a check and not of a lawsuit."[4] The incontestable clause provides that assurance. It is based on the theory that after the insurance company has had a reasonable opportunity to investigate the circumstances surrounding issuance of a life insurance policy, it should thereafter relinquish the right to question the validity of the contract.

Originally introduced in New York by voluntary action in 1864, the incontestable clause had become so firmly entrenched and was so obviously beneficial to all parties that the legislation that grew out of the Armstrong investigation in 1906 made the inclusion of the clause mandatory in life insurance policies. Other states followed New York's example so that, today, the clause is required by statute in all states. The laws of the various states differ as to the form of the clause prescribed, but no states permit a clause that would make the policy in general contestable for more than 2 years.

Effect of Fraud

It is generally agreed that the original purpose of the incontestable clause was to protect the beneficiary of a life insurance policy against the *innocent* misrepresentations or concealments of the insured. There was considerable doubt in the early years that the incontestable clause could operate to bar the denial of liability on the grounds of fraud. Basic tenets of contract law are that (1) fraud in the formation of a contract renders the contract voidable at the option of the innocent party, and (2) in general, parties to a contract are not permitted immunity from the consequences of their fraud. These two rules would seem to limit the applicability of the incontestable clause, therefore, to inadvertent misrepresentations or concealments. Nevertheless, over the years, judicial interpretation has firmly established the principle that the incontestable clause is also effective in cases involving fraud. Even more to the point, since no reputable life insurance company is likely to contest a policy under ordinary circumstances unless there is evidence of an intent to deceive, it may be concluded that the primary function, if not the purpose, of the incontestable clause is to protect the insured and the beneficiaries against the consequences of the insured's (or the policyowner's) fraudulent behavior or erroneous charges of fraud by the insurer.

Erroneous insurer charges of fraud are precluded by the clause for any policy in force beyond the contestable period. In holding that the expiration of the contestable period precludes a defense even on the grounds of fraud, the courts have been careful to emphasize that they are not condoning fraud. They justify their action on the grounds that the insurance company has a reasonable period of time in which to discover any fraud involved in procuring the policy and is obligated to seek redress within the permissible period of time. In line with this reasoning, one court stated as follows:

> This view does not exclude the consideration of fraud, but allows the parties to fix by stipulation the length of time which fraud of the insured can operate to deceive the insurer. It recognizes the right of the insurer, predicated upon a vast experience and profound knowledge in such matters, to agree that in a stipulated time, fixed by himself, he can unearth and drag to light any fraud committed by the insured, and protect himself from the consequences.... The incontestable clause is upheld in law, not for the purpose of upholding fraud, but for the purpose of shutting off harassing defenses based upon alleged fraud; and, in so doing, the law merely adopts the certificate of the insurer that within a given time he can expose and render innocuous any fraud in the preliminary statement of the insured...[5]

The incontestable clause has been described as a private contractual "statute of limitation" on fraud, prescribing a period shorter than that incorporated in the statutory enactment. This analogy with conventional statutes of limitations has been questioned by some critics,[6] but the basic purpose of the incontestable clause and statutes of limitation is the same: to bar the assertion of legal rights after the evidence concerning the cause of action has grown stale and key witnesses are no longer readily available.

The courts recognize that some unscrupulous persons are permitted to profit by their fraudulent action through the operation of the incontestable clause, but they proceed on the premise that the social advantages of the clause outweigh the undesirable consequences. "The view is that even though dishonest people are given advantages under incontestability clauses which any right-minded man is loath to see them get, still the sense of security given to the great mass of honest policyholders by the presence of the clause in their policies makes it worth the cost."[7]

Despite the courts' general adherence to the doctrine that the incontestable clause is a bar to a defense of fraud, there are some species of fraud so abhorrent that their nullification through the incontestable clause is regarded to be in contravention of public policy. For example, the incontestable clause has been held not to apply when a contract was negotiated with intent to murder the insured, even though the murderer was not the beneficiary.[8] In addition, in cases where the applicant lacks an insurable interest, it is the majority view that the courts will permit the insurer to deny liability beyond the contestable period.[9] Likewise, in cases where someone, presumably a healthier person and usually the beneficiary, has impersonated the applicant for purposes of undergoing the medical

---

Situations Not Protected by the Incontestable Clause

- The policyowner/applicant lacks an insurable interest.
- The physical examination was taken by a person other than the intended insured.
- There was no manifestation of mutual assent between the insurer and the applicant.
- The policy was obtained with the intent to murder the insured.

---

examination and answering the questions pertaining to the applicant's health, the courts have uniformly held the purported contract to be null and void because there has been "no real meeting of minds."[10] While the term "no real meeting of minds" has been replaced by the better term "no manifestation of mutual assent," it is nevertheless quite correct to state that the purported contract never came into existence. Since the incontestable clause is a part of the contract, it cannot be enforceable if the contract is void. Finally, in a few cases, the courts have recognized execution for a crime as legitimate ground for denial of liability,[11] although in other cases, the company has been held liable.[12]

Meaning of a Contest

A policy can be prevented from becoming incontestable only by appropriate legal action by the company during the contestable period or, under one type of incontestable clause (to be described later), by the death of the insured during the contestable period. The courts hold that there must be a "contest" during the contestable period, and it becomes a matter of interpretation as to what constitutes a contest within the meaning of the clause.

In some jurisdictions a notice of rescission accompanied by a return of the premium is deemed to constitute a contest. The majority of the courts, however, have held that there must be a court action that challenges the validity of the policy as a contract. Thus under the majority rule, the requirement of a contest can be satisfied only by a suit in equity for rescission before a court of competent jurisdiction or by a defense to a judicial (at law) proceeding seeking to enforce the contract. In the first instance, the company would be seeking rescission by a suit in equity; in the second case, it would be defending against an action at law instituted by the beneficiary in an attempt to collect the proceeds. A suit for rescission is permitted only when there is no adequate remedy at law, and in most jurisdictions, defense against a beneficiary's action is regarded as an adequate remedy. Equity proceedings, however, are always available to the company while the insured is alive during the contestable period and, as is

---

What Is a Contest of a Policy? (Majority of Courts)

- suit by insurer to rescind policy in a court of appropriate jurisdiction

or

- defense by insurer in a court proceeding seeking to enforce the contract

---

pointed out below, are usually available after the death of the insured only under certain types of incontestable clause.

Example: *Meaning of a Contest*

Gregg applied for a life insurance policy and successfully concealed from the insurer the fact that he had three previous convictions for driving under the influence of alcohol. He paid the annual premium, and the policy was issued with a 2-year incontestable clause. Twenty-three months later, the insurance agent learned of the convictions and notified the insurer. The insurer wrote to Gregg stating that, because of its standard underwriting requirements about drunk driving, it would no longer continue the coverage or accept the next renewal premium. Gregg died during the grace period in a DUI auto accident. The insurer will be required to pay the claim because its notification to Gregg did *not* constitute a contest of the policy in that jurisdiction.

Detailed rules of legal procedure have evolved to establish the precise moment at which a contest has materialized. Once the contest has been initiated, the contestable period stops running, and regardless of the outcome of the initial contest, the incontestable clause cannot be invoked to forestall any other proceeding. Thus if a contest is initiated with the insured during the contestable period, the beneficiary may be made a party to the proceedings after the expiration of the period specified in the incontestable clause.

The interpretation of the term contest is also important in another respect. Broadly interpreted, the incontestable clause could prohibit the denial of any type of claim after the contestable period has expired. It could force the company to pay a type of claim that was never envisioned under the contract. Fortunately, the majority of the courts do not interpret the clause in that manner. They make a distinction between contests that question the validity or existence of a contract and those that seek to clarify the terms of the contract or to enforce the contract's terms. In one widely cited case, the court stated as shown in the following example.

Example: It must be clear that every resistance by an insurer against the demands of the beneficiary is in one sense a contest, but it is not a contest of the policy; that is, not a contest against the terms of the policy but a contest for or in favor of the terms of the policy. In other words, there are two classes of contests; one to enforce the policy, the other to destroy it. Undoubtedly the term "incontestable" as used in a life insurance policy means a contest, the purpose of which is to destroy the validity of the policy, and not a contest, the purpose of which is to demand its enforcement.[13]

The significance of this distinction will be brought out in the discussion of the incontestable clause's application to other contract provisions.

Inception of the Contestable Period

Where the *operative date* of a life insurance policy coincides with the *effective date,* there is little question about when the contestable period starts to run. It begins the day following the date on the policy.[14] When the effective date of protection precedes the date of the policy, however, some courts have made the beginning of the contestable period coincide with the commencement of insurance coverage, regardless of the date of the policy. This would be the normal case when conditional receipts are used. On the other hand, when the policy has been antedated so that the date of the policy is earlier than the effective date of coverage, the courts, applying the rule of construction most favorable to the insured, have usually held that the contestable period begins with the date of the policy. This would be applicable when a policy has been backdated to obtain a younger insurable age. This is true whether the clause provides that the policy will be incontestable after a specified period from the "date of the policy" or the "date of issue." When the policy makes it clear that the contestable period starts to run only from the time the policy actually becomes effective, however, there is no reason to apply the rule of construction most favorable to the insured, and the courts will give effect to the contract as written.

Potential Dates for Inception of Contestable Period

- policy date
- effective date of coverage

TYPES OF INCONTESTABLE CLAUSES

As the incontestable clause went through a period of evolution, there were various changes in wording from time to time, usually to nullify the unfavorable interpretations developed out of litigation. The earliest forms of the clause were quite simple, and one that became involved in a precedent-making court decision read as follows: "After two years, this policy shall be noncontestable except for the nonpayment of premiums as stipulated...." It was the insurers' expectation that if the insured died during the 2 years, the

Monahan decision

policy would never become incontestable. This clause served satisfactorily for many years until the celebrated *Monahan decision* impaired its usefulness to insurance companies.[15]

In that case the insured died within the 2-year period, and the company denied liability, alleging a breach of warranty. The beneficiary waited until the 2-year contestable period had expired and then brought suit against the company. The company defended on the grounds of breach of warranty. The beneficiary asserted that since the 2-year period for contesting the policy had expired, the insurance carrier was precluded from raising the breach of warranty as a defense. The Supreme Court of Illinois, agreeing with the beneficiary, held that the policy was incontestable and found for the beneficiary. This decision, which was accepted as a precedent in virtually all jurisdictions, established the far-reaching principle that the contestable period was not ended by the insured's death but continued to run until the specified time had elapsed.

The practical effect of the *Monahan* decision was that, if a policyowner died within the contestable period, the company was forced to go into court during the contestable period to seek a rescission if it wanted to deny liability for any reason. If no action was brought before the period expired, the company was estopped from erecting any defense other than lapse from nonpayment of premiums. Much litigation was thus thrust upon insurance companies to avert claims that they regarded to be unwarranted—to their detriment in the public esteem.

In an effort to avoid the undesirable consequences of the *Monahan* case, many companies adopted a clause that provided that the policy would be incontestable after it had been *in force* for a specified period. It was believed that with such a clause, the death of the insured would stop the period from running since the policy would no longer be in force. When the clause was tested in the courts, however, the decisions (with some exceptions) held that a policy does not terminate with the death of the insured but continues "in force" for the benefit of the beneficiary. In other words, the contract still has to be performed. Thus this clause had the same weakness as the incontestable clause litigated in the *Monahan* case. Despite this disadvantage, some companies have continued to use this wording in the clause or to simply omit the words "during the lifetime of the insured," since this permits suits in equity, which are usually tried without a jury.[16]

Those companies that were willing to give up the advantage of suits in equity modified their incontestable clause to make the policy incontestable after it has been in force *during the lifetime of the insured* for a specified period. The courts have uniformly agreed that under this clause, the death of the insured during the contestable period suspends the operation of the clause and fixes the rights of the parties as of the date of death. Under such a clause, if the insured dies during the specified period, the policy never becomes incontestable, and the claimant cannot gain any advantage by postponing notification of the claim until the specified period has expired. However, since a legal remedy is available—that is, a defense against a suit instituted by the beneficiary—the company cannot avoid a jury trial and obtain rescission of the policy by a suit in equity except during the lifetime of the insured.

A final type of clause typically provides (with certain exceptions, to be noted), "This policy shall be incontestable after one year from its date of issue unless the insured dies in such year, in which event it shall be incontestable after 2 years from its date of issue." This clause does not solve the problem created by the *Monahan* decision since the death of the insured during the first year does not suspend the running of the period. However, should the insured die during the first year, the company will have a *minimum* of one year in which to investigate the circumstances of the case and, if desired, to institute a suit for rescission. Under all of the other types of clauses except the one requiring survivorship of the insured, it is possible for the company to have only a few days in which to investigate a suspicious death. In fact, it is quite likely that in many cases, the company would receive no notice of the insured's death until the contestable period had expired. The clause described in this paragraph is more favorable to the insured than the usual clauses because, if he or she survives the first year, the policy becomes incontestable at that time, and if he or she does not, the company's rights are no greater than they would have been under the typical clause. Note, however, that some companies limit the contestability of their policies to one year, whether or not the insured survives the period.

Contestable Period

- time for insurer to investigate and rescind policy
- maximum duration 2 years (unless insured dies within that period)
- duration of only one year under some policies
- may delay claim settlement if insured dies during the contestable period

---

MATTERS EXCLUDED FROM INCONTESTABLE CLAUSES

Nonpayment of Premiums

The original incontestable clause excluded nonpayment of premiums from its operation, and the practice has continued to the present. This exception is not only superfluous today, but it has also created confusion as to the applicability of the clause to matters not specifically excluded. Payment of the first premium, or the first installment of the first premium, is a consideration for the life insurance contract and is usually made a condition precedent. Unless this requirement is satisfied, there is no contract and hence no incontestable clause. If subsequent premiums are not paid, the contract does not fail as of its inception and may, in fact, continue in force under the nonforfeiture provisions.

This has not always been the case, however, and there was probably some justification to include the exception in the original clause. Early policies contained no surrender values, and default in premium, even years after a policy's issue, resulted in avoidance of the contract from its inception. It is clear, though, that the termination or modification of a modern policy through nonpayment of premiums is not a contest of the policy. When an insurer denies a claim based on nonpayment of premiums it is, in fact, declaring the insurance contract valid, and attempting to enforce one of the contract's terms—specifically the contract's requirement that the insurer's obligation to pay is conditioned on the policyowner's payment of premiums. Nevertheless, the historical precedent and the requirements of state statutes have made the exception a fixture.

expressio unius est exclusio alterius

The express exclusion of nonpayment of premium (and a few other conditions) from the operation of the incontestable clause has caused a minority of courts to apply the doctrine of *expressio unius est exclusio alterius*[17] to a company's attempts to avoid liability under other provisions of the policy. Under such a doctrine, if a particular hazard is not specifically excluded from the operation of the clause, a claim arising from that hazard cannot be avoided beyond the contestable period. This view arises from the idea that the incontestable clause precludes the insurer from disputing the *obligations* under the valid contract as well as disputing the contract's validity.

For example, assume that the policy contains an incontestable clause that says, "This policy shall be incontestable after it has been in force during the lifetime of the insured, for a period of 2 years from the issue date, except for nonpayment of premiums." Assume that the policy also contains a war hazard exclusion clause. Since the incontestable clause refers to nonpayment of premiums as a permissible reason for contesting the policy but does not refer to the war hazard clause, a minority of courts prohibit the insurer from applying the war hazard exclusion if the insured dies after the time limit prescribed in the incontestable clause.

Disability and Accidental Death Benefits

Sometimes an insurer may wish to exclude policy provisions or policy riders relating to disability and accidental death benefits from the operation of the incontestable clause. A typical clause containing these exclusions might read as follows: "This policy shall be incontestable after it shall have been in force for 2 years from its date of issue except for nonpayment of premiums and except as to provisions relating to benefits payable in the event of total and permanent disability and provisions that grant additional insurance specifically against death by accident."

If the courts could be relied upon to interpret the incontestable clause in accordance with its basic objective of protecting third-party beneficiaries, it would be unnecessary to specifically exclude disability and accidental death benefits from its scope. Unfortunately, the courts have had some difficulty in distinguishing between a contest involving the validity of the policy and one relating to the coverage of an admittedly valid policy. The distinction is a critical one in connection with disability and accidental death provisions since it is frequently difficult to determine whether a claim filed under one of these provisions is valid. In order to avoid any possible conflict with the incontestable clause in adjudicating such claims, some companies keep the provisions entirely outside the operation of the clause. Under the type of clause cited above, the *validity* of the provisions relating to disability and double indemnity can be attacked at any time, even after the expiration of the contestable period.

The general rule is that unless there is a specific exception in the policy's incontestable clause, the disability and accidental death provisions are included within the incontestable clause. However, insurers may draft policy language that excludes those provisions from the scope of the incontestable clause. If such an exclusion exists, a majority of courts have upheld it, although many other courts have held otherwise.

The exclusion of disability benefits from the protection of the incontestable clause is not in conflict with the intent of the clause. The purpose of the clause is to forestall a contest over the contract's validity after the insured is dead and cannot defend the representations he or she made in the application for insurance. Disability claims are filed during the lifetime of the insured, who can defend his or her actions, both at the time the policy was applied for and at the time of the claim.

RELATIONSHIP TO OTHER POLICY PROVISIONS

Excepted Hazards

At one time it was the view of the courts and the state insurance departments that once the contestable period had expired, no denial of liability based on lack of coverage could be sustained unless the hazard involved in the litigation was specifically excluded in the incontestable clause itself. Moreover, no hazard could be excluded from the scope of the incontestable clause unless the exclusion was recognized in the statute governing the clause. This is still the case.

This doctrine was attacked when the superintendent of insurance of the state of New York refused to approve a proposed aviation exclusion in a

Metropolitan Life Insurance Company policy on the ground that the exclusion was in conflict with the New York statute prescribing the substance of the incontestable clause. The superintendent's decision was appealed to the courts, and the issue was resolved in the *Conway decision*. The New York Court of Appeals ruled that there was nothing in the law that prohibited the issuance of such a restricted policy. The decision declared that the New York statute requiring an incontestable clause "is not a mandate as to coverage, a definition of hazards to be borne by the insurer. It means only this, that within the limits of the coverage, the policy shall stand, unaffected by any defense that it was invalid in its inception, or thereafter became invalid by reason of a condition broken…[Where] there has been no assumption of risk, there can be no liability...."[18]

Conway decision

Following the *Conway* decision, the various insurance commissioners reversed their rulings on the inclusion of aviation riders. Today it is the accepted view that a company may exclude any hazard that it does not wish to cover.

In general, the right to limit coverage has been invoked only with respect to aeronautical activities, military and naval service in time of war, and suicide. With advances in aeronautics, the aviation exclusion has lost most of its significance, and with few exceptions war clauses are not currently being added to policies. However, some insurers insert war clauses in new policies being sold to persons likely to be involved in a military action, such as the joint effort in Iraq. Once policies have been issued with such an exclusion, the clause remains part of the contract as long as it is kept in force. Limitations on the coverage of suicide, however, are contained in all policies.

Since the *Conway* decision, insurance companies could undoubtedly exclude death from suicide throughout the duration of the contract unless prohibited by statute. They feel, however, that it is a risk that they should properly assume, and their only concern is that they not be exposed to the risk of issuing policies to persons contemplating suicide. Consequently, they exclude death from suicide, whether the insured be sane or insane, for the first year or two after issue of the policy, with the risk thereafter being assumed in its entirety by the company. If the insured does commit suicide during the period of restricted coverage, the company's liability is limited to a refund of the premiums paid.

While the suicide exclusion is normally of the same duration as the contestable period, the suicide clause is independent of the incontestable clause. Since most suicide exclusions are of 2 years' duration, and some policies are contestable for only one year, a conflict could develop if the insured commits suicide during the second year of the contract. With few exceptions, the courts have upheld the company's right to deny coverage of suicide beyond the contestable period.

Conditions Precedent

The incontestable clause is a part of the policy and cannot become effective until the policy has gone into force. There must be a contract before there can be an incontestable clause. Therefore the incontestable clause does not bar a defense that the policy was never approved by the insurance company.[19]

On principle, it would seem that if a policy provides that it will not become effective until certain conditions have been fulfilled, there would be no contract at all until those conditions had been satisfied. Hence the incontestable clause itself, as part of the contract, would not be operative. This would suggest that the incontestable clause should not prevent the insurer from denying liability on the grounds that the applicant was not in good health at the time the policy was delivered or that some other condition precedent was not fulfilled. However, most of the courts have reached the conclusion that the delivery-in-good-health requirement and other such conditions precedent should be accorded the same treatment as representations. Since the incontestable clause was designed to deal with misrepresentations, it follows that the clause should bar suits based on nonfulfillment of conditions precedent if, at any time, both parties had treated the policy as having been operative.[20] This is the rule in most jurisdictions.

Misstatement of Age or Sex

Most life insurance policies contain a provision that stipulates that in the event of a misstatement of age or sex, the amount payable under the policy will be such as would have been purchased at the correct age (or sex) by the premium actually paid. For flexible premium policies, such as universal life, this would involve a retrospective recalculation of the mortality charges.

misstatement-of-age (or sex) provision

Most states have a statute requiring a *misstatement-of-age (or sex) provision*. In jurisdictions where the provision is mandatory, no conflict with the incontestable clause can arise. Even where the clause is not a matter of statute, the company's right to reduce the amount of insurance (even after the contestable period has expired) has seldom been questioned. This is undoubtedly due to the fact that the misstatement-of-age (or sex) adjustment was firmly established before any controversy developed over the right of a company to limit the coverage of a policy beyond the contestable period. If it had been held that misstatement-of-age (or sex) adjustments were subject to the incontestable clause, insurance companies would probably have found it necessary to require proof of age (or sex) before issuing a policy.

A misstatement of age that contravenes a company's underwriting rules may, at the company's option, serve as a basis for rescission. It has been held, however, that such action has to be taken during the contestable period.[21] If the misstatement is discovered beyond the contestable period, it can still be dealt with in the conventional manner.

Reformation

It sometimes happens that a life insurance policy in the form issued by the company does not represent the actual agreement between the company and the applicant. This may be due to simple clerical errors, such as a misspelled name or an incorrect date, or to more substantial mistakes, such as an incorrect premium, wrong face amount, inappropriate set of surrender values, or incorrect set of settlement options. The mistake may favor either the insured or the company. The overwhelming majority of such mistakes are rectified without any controversy or litigation. From time to time, however, a policyowner will oppose the correction of a mistake in his or her favor. In one such case, the policy actually applied for and issued was an ordinary life contract, but through a printer's error, the surrender values shown in the contract were those for a 20-year endowment insurance policy.[22] The company discovered the error 2 months after the policy was issued but had to resort to legal action to rewrite the contract.

suit for reformation of the contract

The appropriate legal action in such circumstances is a *suit for reformation of the contract.* This is an equitable remedy under which the written instrument is made to conform to the intention of the parties.[23] The party seeking relief must establish that there was either a mutual mistake in drafting the written instrument[24] or a mistake on one side and fraud on the other.

The remedy of reformation is clearly available to an insurance company during the contestable period. Moreover, it has long been the rule that reformation to correct a clerical error is not barred by the incontestable clause. A suit to rectify a mistake "is not a contest of the policy but a prayer to make a written instrument speak the real agreement of the parties."[25]

Reinstatement

All life insurance policies contain a provision permitting reinstatement in the event of lapse, subject to certain conditions. One of the conditions is usually evidence of insurability satisfactory to the company. Reinstatement will almost always necessitate a statement by the insured as to the current status of his or her health and will frequently involve a complete medical examination. It will also involve aspects of insurability other than health, just as at the time of original issue. A question arises about the legal effect of a misrepresentation or concealment in the reinstatement application not discovered until after the policy has been reinstated. Specifically, can a reinstated policy be rescinded after the original contestable period has expired?

If the incontestable clause specifically refers to a reinstatement of the policy, the language of the clause will control. For example, assume the clause provides that "this policy shall be incontestable after it has been in force during the lifetime of the insured, for a period of 2 years from the issue date or the date of its last reinstatement." In this event, the contract's reinstatement should begin a new 2-year contestable period. The insurer's renewed right to contest is applicable only to information provided in the reinstatement application.

When the incontestability clause does not refer to a reinstatement, there are conflicting views. One view, greatly in the minority, holds that the concept of incontestability does not apply to the reinstatement process.[26] Under this view, a suit for rescission or a defense against a claim is subject only to the conventional statute of limitations on fraud—which begins to run only *after the fraud has been discovered.*

At the other extreme, and also in the minority, is the view that the reinstatement is subject to the original incontestable clause.[27] If the original period of contestability has expired before the application for reinstatement is submitted, the reinstated policy is incontestable from the date of reinstatement. If a policy is reinstated during the original period of contestability, the reinstated policy can be contested during the remaining portion of the contestable period.

The majority opinion adopts a middle ground and holds that a reinstated policy is contestable for the same period of time as is prescribed in the original incontestable clause.[28] If the policy was originally contestable for a period of 2 years, the reinstated policy is again contestable for the same length of time. This is true even when the policy is lapsed and reinstated before the original period of contestability has expired. The reasoning is that the company needs the same period of time in which to detect any fraud in the application for reinstatement as it needed in connection with the original issue. It is hardly necessary to add that the policy becomes contestable again only with respect to the information supplied in the reinstatement process. In other words, after reinstatement the company does not have the right to question the validity of the contract on the grounds of irregularities in the original application.

Contestability of Reinstated Policy

- (majority) new contestable period, of same duration as original, applicable only to statements in reinstatement application
- (minority) only subject to the original contestable period
- (minority) reinstated policy not protected by incontestable clause

---

CHAPTER REVIEW

Answers to the review questions and the self-test questions can be found in the Supplement.

Key Terms

incontestable clause
Monahan decision
expressio unius est exclusio alterius

Conway decision
Misstatement-of-age (or sex) provision
suit for reformation of the contract

Review Questions

1. What is the purpose of the incontestable clause?

2. Explain how, and against what, the incontestable clause may protect the beneficiary of a life insurance policy.

3. Describe how state statutes currently influence both the use and the form of the incontestable clause.

4. State the general principle firmly established by judicial interpretation regarding whether the incontestable clause applies to cases involving fraud, and explain the grounds on which the courts have justified their actions.

5. List the types of cases involving fraud in which the courts have held that the incontestable clause does not bar the insurance company from its efforts to avoid liability.

6. Suppose that when Bill Hampton purchased life insurance on his own life, he lied on the application about whether he had seen a doctor during the past 5 years. In fact, just before Bill applied for the policy, a doctor had told him he had cancer. When Bill died after the policy had been in force for 5 years, would the insurance company be able to deny payment of the death claim on the ground of fraudulent misrepresentation of a material fact in the application? Explain.

7. In what ways can a life insurance policy be prevented from becoming incontestable?

8. What constitutes a contest of a life insurance policy in most jurisdictions?

9. Describe the two types of proceedings that can be used to satisfy the requirement of a contest under the majority rule, and indicate under what circumstances each is available to the insurance company.

10. Distinguish between the types of contests to which the majority of courts hold the incontestable clause does and does not apply.

11. Describe the rules generally applied by the courts in interpreting the date from which a policy's contestable period starts to run.

12. Describe the different types of incontestable clauses, and explain the effect, if any, that the insured's death during the contestable period has on the insurance company's rights to contest the contract.

13. Matt Smith purchased a life insurance policy on his own life and named his wife, Amy, as beneficiary. In completing the application, Matt misrepresented a material fact with intent to deceive the insurance company. The policy contained an incontestable clause that makes it incontestable after it has been in force during the lifetime of the insured for 2 years from the date of issue. If Matt died 22 months after the policy was issued but Amy did not notify the company of Matt's death until 4 months later, could the policy still be contested by the insurance company after it received notice of Matt's death?

14. Explain why nonpayment of premiums is excluded from the operation of the incontestable clause even if a specific exception is not included in the clause.

15. State the rules generally applied by the courts in determining whether the incontestable clause applies to contests involving disability and accidental death benefit provisions.

16. Explain what effect, if any, the operation of a policy's incontestable clause has on each of the following:

    a. the insurer's denial of liability on the ground that a policy provision excludes a particular hazard from coverage by the policy
    b. the insurer's denial of liability on the ground of nonfulfillment of the delivery-in-good-health requirement or another such condition precedent
    c. the right of the insurer to reduce the amount of insurance in accordance with the terms of the policy's misstatement-of-age (or sex) provision
    d. the right of the insurer to sue for reformation of the contract to correct a clerical error

17. For each of the following situations, explain what rights an insurer typically has to contest a reinstated policy on the grounds of misrepresentation or concealment after the original contestable period has expired:
    a. if the incontestable clause specifically refers to a reinstatement of the policy
    b. if the incontestable clause does not refer to a reinstatement of the policy

Self-Test Questions

T   F   1. The incontestable clause is no longer a source of frequent litigation.

T   F   2. If Joe Jones misrepresented a material fact when he purchased a life insurance policy on his own life, his policy would be incontestable when he died 10 years later.

T   F   3. In general, the incontestable clause applies to whether a contract is valid and not to whether the terms or conditions of the contract have been fulfilled.

T   F   4. Insurance companies originally included the incontestable clause in life insurance policies only after state statutes forced them to do so.

T   F   5. Generally, the beneficiary will not be protected by the incontestable clause if the error in the application is based on a fraudulent misrepresentation of the applicant.

T   F   6. The incontestable clause is based on the theory that after the insurance company has had a reasonable opportunity to investigate the circumstances surrounding the issuance of a life insurance policy, it should thereafter relinquish the right to question the validity of the contract.

T   F   7. In holding that the expiration of the contestable period precludes a defense even on the ground of fraud, the courts have been careful to emphasize that they are not condoning fraud.

T   F   8. In cases where the applicant lacks an insurable interest when the policy is issued, most courts will not permit the insurer to deny liability beyond the contestable period.

T   F   9. The only way a life insurance policy can be prevented from becoming incontestable is by appropriate legal action by the insurer during the contestable period.

T   F   10. The majority of courts have held that a notice of rescission accompanied by a return of premium are deemed to constitute a contest within the meaning of the incontestable clause.

T   F   11. To contest a policy, an insurer always has a choice between bringing a suit at equity for rescission of the contract or defending against a judicial (at law) proceeding that seeks to enforce the contract.

T   F   12. In interpreting the applicability of the incontestable clause, the majority of courts make a distinction between contests that question the validity or existence of a contract, and contests that seek to clarify or enforce the contract's terms.

T   F   13. Where the operative date of a life insurance policy coincides with the effective date, the contestable period begins the day following the date on the policy.

T   F   14. If a life insurance policy's incontestable clause provides that the policy will be incontestable after it has been in force during the lifetime of the insured for 2 years from the date of issue, and the insured dies 23 months after the policy was issued, the policy never becomes incontestable.

T F   15. Nonpayment of premiums after the first generally gives rise to a contest of the validity of the contract that is subject to the provisions of the incontestable clause.

T F   16. The accidental death benefit provision is no longer viewed by the courts as being included within the scope of the incontestable clause.

T F   17. For policies that are contestable for only one year and contain a suicide exclusion of 2 years' duration, the courts generally have upheld the company's right to deny coverage of suicide beyond the contestable period.

T F   18. Most courts have held that the incontestable clause bars suits based on nonfulfillment of the delivery-in-good-health requirement and other such conditions precedent if, at any time, both of the parties had treated the policy as having been operative.

T F   19. A misstatement of age that contravenes a company's underwriting rules may, at the company's option, serve as a basis for rescission of the contract.

T F   20. The remedy of reformation is available to an insurance company only during the contestable period.

T F   21. When the incontestable clause does not refer to a reinstatement, the courts generally hold that a reinstated policy is again contestable for the same length of time as prescribed in the original incontestable clause.

NOTES

1. H. M. Horne and D. B. Mansfield, *The Life Insurance Contract,* 2d ed. (New York: Life Office Management Association, 1948), p. 181.
2. *Kansas Mutual Life Insurance Co. v. Whitehead,* 123 Ky. 21, 26, 93 S.W. 609, 610 (1906).
3. Muriel L. Crawford and William T. Beadles, *Law and the Life Insurance Contract,* 6th ed. (Homewood, IL: Irwin Professional Publishing, 1989), p. 419.
4. Horne and Mansfield, *The Life Insurance Contract,* p. 181.
5. *Kansas Mutual Life Insurance Co. v. Whitehead,* 123 Ky. 21, 26, 93 S.W. 609, 610 (1906).
6. Critics of this analogy point out that (1) the usual statute of limitations begins to run from the time the fraud is discovered, whereas under the incontestable clause, the period runs from the beginning of the contract, and (2) the typical statute of limitations applies to actions and not to defenses such as those invoked by life insurance companies during the period of contestability. See Benjamin L. Holland, "The Incontestable Clause," in Harry Krueger and Leland T. Waggoner (eds.), *The Life Insurance Policy Contract* (Boston: Little, Brown & Co., 1953), p. 58. These critics are content to identify the incontestable clause as a constituent part of the contract and peculiar to a life insurance policy.
7. *Maslin v. Columbian National Life Insurance Co.,* 3 F. Supp. 368, 369 (S.D.N.Y. 1932).
8. *Columbian Mutual Life Insurance Co. v. Martin,* 175 Tenn. 517, 136 S.W. 2d 52 (1940).

9. See Holland, "The Incontestable Clause," p. 68, n. 27, for citations.

10. *Ibid.,* p. 69 and citations in n. 31.

11. *Scarborough v. American National Insurance Co.,* 171 N.C. 353, 88 S.E. 482 (1916); *Murphy v. Metropolitan Life Insurance Co.,* 152 Ga. 393, 110 S.E. 178 (1921).

12. *Afro-American Life Insurance Co. v. Jones,* 113 Fla. 158, 151 So. 405 (1933).

13. *Stean v. Occidental Life Insurance Co.,* 24 N.M. 346, 350, 171 Pac. 786, 787 (1918).

14. There is some case law to the effect that the last day when a contest can be made is, in the case of a 2-year contestable provision, the second anniversary of the date of issue, rather than the day thereafter. These rulings were made with respect to policies that state that the policy is contestable for 2 years after the date of issue.

15. *Monahan v. Metropolitan Life Insurance Co.,* 283 Ill. 136, 119 N.E. 68 (1918).

16. *Massachusetts Mutual Life Insurance Co. v. Goodelman,* 160 F. Supp. 510 (E.D.N.Y. 1958).

17. "The enumeration of some is the exclusion of others," usually paraphrased as "enumeration implies exclusion."

18. *Metropolitan Life Insurance Co. v. Conway,* 252 N.Y. 449, 452, 169 N.E. 642 (1930).

19. *McDonald v. Mutual Life Insurance Co. of New York,* 108 F. 2d 32 (6th Cir. 1939); *Harris v. Travelers Insurance Co.,* 80 F. (2d) 127 (5th Cir. 1935).

20. See Holland, "The Incontestable Clause", p. 64, n. 10, for citations.

21. *Kelly v. Prudential Insurance Co.,* 334 Pa. 143, 6 A. 2d 55 (1939).

22. *Columbian National Life Insurance Co. v. Black,* 35 F. 2d 571 (10th Cir. 1929).

23. The introduction of oral testimony is permitted in such cases, notwithstanding the fact that in so doing, the terms of the written instrument are changed. This is an exception to the parol evidence rule.

24. In this connection, it is held that knowledge by one party of the other's mistake is equivalent to a mutual mistake.

25. *Columbian National Life Insurance Co. v. Black,* 35 F. 2d 571, 577 (10th Cir. 1929). There are numerous later cases, 7 ALR 2d 504 (1949).

26. *Acacia Mutual Life Assn. v. Kaul,* 114 N.J. Eq. 491, 169 Atl. 36 (Ch. 1933); *Chuz v. Columbian National Life Insurance Co.,* 10 N.J. Misc. 1145, 162 Atl. 395 (Cir. Ct. 1932).

27. See Holland, "The Incontestable Clause," p. 78, n. 2, for citations. See also *Chavis v. Southern Ins. Co.,* 318 N.C. 259, 347 S.E. 2d 425 (1986).

28. *Ibid.,* p. 78, n. 3. *Sellwood v. Equitable Life Insurance Co. of Iowa,* 230 Minn. 529, 42 N.W. 2d 346 (1950).

8

Policy Provisions

Burke A. Christensen

Learning Objectives

An understanding of the material in this chapter should enable the student to

8-1.   Understand why a life insurance contract is a contract of adhesion.

8-2.   Identify the types of information generally included on the face page of a policy.

8-3.   Discuss the background and purpose of standard policy provision laws.

8-4.   Describe why a grace-period clause is included in a policy and how it is distinguished from a late remittance offer.

8-5.   Understand the distinction between a loan, a policy loan, and an advancement.

8-6.   Discuss the incontestable clause, the divisible surplus provision, and reinstatement provisions.

8-7.   Explain why the misstatement-of-age-or-sex clauses, nonforfeiture provisions, and settlement options are included in policies.

8-8.   Explain the entire-contract concept.

8-9.   Review the provisions that are generally prohibited from appearing in policies.

8-10. Describe the optional provisions that are permitted but not required to be included in policies.

8-11. Distinguish between the concepts of waiver and estoppel.

8-12. Identify certain common provisions appearing in policies.

Chapter Outline

contract of adhesion: a contract whose wording is not negotiated. It is drafted entirely by one party. The other party to the contract is not permitted to alter the terms of the contract but may only accept or reject the contract. Because the drafting party has the freedom to choose the words of the contract, the law requires that party to abide by the words it has chosen. This means that any ambiguities are interpreted in favor of the other party.

A life insurance contract is a contract of adhesion. This means that the policyowner and the insurer do not negotiate the terms of the contract. The prospective policyowner performs only these two functions in the creation of a life insurance contract:

- He or she applies for the policy (the contract) by filling out the application and supplying any medical information required by the insurer. This is not a negotiation. The applicant is merely specifying what type of contract he or she would like to be offered. Based on this information, the insurer will make an offer by issuing a policy.
- The applicant is then asked to accept or reject the contract as offered by the insurer. The applicant accepts the offer by paying the initial premium. If a partial premium has been paid and a premium receipt has been issued by the insurer's agent, only temporary coverage under the terms of the receipt is in effect. The contract is accepted by the applicant and binding on the insurer under the particular terms of the

receipt and the policy.[1] The applicant rejects the offered contract by refusing delivery of the policy. Even after the applicant accepts the insurer's offer of coverage and a contract is binding on the insurer, the policyowner may, in effect, reject the contract and get a full refund based on the 10-day free-look provision (which is explained later in this chapter). New York and about half of the other states require this provision, so it is now included in most contracts.

Because the prospective policyowner can only accept or reject the contract offered by the insurer, the contract-of-adhesion rules provide that all ambiguities in the contract of insurance will be resolved in favor of the policyowner and against the insurer. This rule of law is not entirely fair to insurance companies because there are substantial limitations on the insurer's freedom to draft the insurance contract as it wishes. Insurers are required by law to include many types of provisions and in some cases are required to use or not use certain words. Thus it is not entirely correct to state that because the insurers are free to select the contract language, they have to give the benefit of ambiguity to the applicant.

Many states require that the contract avoid complex sentences and arcane legal terminology. The goal is to make the contracts easier for the consumer to read and understand. This goal, while laudable, conflicts with the goal of lawyers to be certain that a contract is interpreted exactly as the drafter intended. Over many years, courts have given certain legal terms specific meanings upon which lawyers have come to rely in drafting contracts. This "legalese" may be hard for the uninitiated to understand, but it offers a certainty that lawyers prefer. Nevertheless, it has become the policy of this country to prefer less technical language over the certainty of interpretation. Lawyers will have to rely on current and future cases developing that certainty as the simplified language of modern contracts is interpreted by the courts.

There are a number of required, prohibited, and optional provisions that are controlled by state law. Before a policy may be sold in a particular jurisdiction, its provisions must be filed with that state's insurance department for approval.

POLICY FACE PAGE

Although the placement of the provisions may vary from company to company, the face pages of most life insurance contracts are quite similar. The face page of the contract usually has the following information:

- the name of the insurance company
- some specific details for that policy—for example, the name of the insured and the name of the policyowner, the face amount of the

policy, the policy number, and the policy date or issue date (some include both dates)

- a general description of the type of insurance provided by that policy contract. For example, the face page of a traditional participating whole life policy might read as follows:

> Whole Life—Level Face Amount Plan. Insurance payable upon death. Premiums payable for life. Policy participates in dividends. Dividends, dividend credits, and policy loans may be used to help pay premiums.

free-look provision

- statement about the policy's *free-look provision.* This is a provision that gives the policyowner a period of time, usually 10 days, to return the policy after acceptance. The following is an example of such a provision:

> Not later than 10 days after you get this contract, you may return it to us. All you have to do is take it or mail it to one of our offices or to the agent who sold it to you. The contract will be canceled from the start, and a full premium refund will be made promptly.

- the insurer's promise to pay. This is the heart of the insurance contract. Three different but typical statements read as follows:

> We will pay the beneficiary the sum insured under this contract promptly if we receive due proof that the insured died while this policy was in force. We make this promise subject to all the provisions of this contract.

> •   •   •

> We will pay the benefits of this policy in accordance with its provisions.

> •   •   •

> We agree to pay the death benefits of this policy to the beneficiary upon receiving proof of the insured's death; and to provide you with the other rights and benefits of this policy.

- the signatures of the officers (usually the president and the secretary) of the company, which binds the company to the terms of the contract

The remainder of the required and optional provisions are not usually included on the face page.

STANDARD POLICY PROVISIONS

The standard policy provisions laws of the various states require that life insurance policies include certain provisions but allow the insurance companies to select the actual wording. However, the wording must be submitted to and approved by the state insurance department. The standard provisions laws do not apply to group life insurance. For some insurance contracts, such as term, single premium, and nonparticipating policies, some of the standard provisions may not be applicable. To that extent, those contracts are excused from compliance with the law.

Prior to 1900, life insurance contracts were not regulated as they are today. After the Armstrong Investigation of 1905 in New York, the number of restrictions on the language and form of life insurance contracts was drastically increased. In fact, the state of New York enacted statutes that prescribed exactly how term life, ordinary life, and endowment contracts could be written. This inflexible statutory solution proved to be impractical almost immediately, and it was soon repealed. In its place, New York enacted legislation that merely required that certain kinds of provisions be included in the contract. Insurers were permitted to draft their own contractual language for these provisions. The language the insurers selected was subject to state approval, which would be granted so long as (1) the minimum intent of the required statutory provision was obtained or (2) the insurer's language was more favorable to the policyowner than the statutory intent.

The state insurance codes generally impose a requirement that unless specifically exempted from the law, all life insurance policies delivered or issued for delivery in the state must contain language substantially the same as certain specified provisions. Insurers are also generally given the option to insert different provisions than those specified in the statute if the language in the insurer's provisions is more favorable to policyowners. The insurance department determines whether an alternative provision is more favorable to consumers.

REQUIRED PROVISIONS

Grace Period

grace period

The *grace period* clause grants the policyowner an additional period of time to pay any premium after it has become due. While the clause is now required by law, it was a common practice among insurers before the existence of laws compelling the inclusion of the provision in the contract. Because of the provision, a policy that would have lapsed for nonpayment of premiums continues in force during the grace period. The premium remains due, however, and if the insured dies during the grace period, the insurer may deduct one month's premium from the death benefit. A contractual provision granting the insurer that right might read, "If the insured dies during the grace period, we will reduce the proceeds by an amount equal to one month's premium."

Note that although insurers could charge interest on the unpaid premium for the late period, they do not normally do so. If the insured survives the grace period but the premium remains unpaid, the policy lapses (except for any nonforfeiture options).

As with all renewal premiums, the policyowner has no obligation to pay the premium for the insurance coverage provided under the grace period provision. Thus it might be said that the insured has received "free" insurance during that time. This is an accurate conclusion only if the insured does not die within the grace period.

The standard length of the grace period is 31 days. If the last day of the grace period falls on a nonbusiness day, the period is normally extended to the next business day. A sample grace period provision reads as follows:

> We allow 31 days from the due date for payment of a premium. Your insurance coverage continues during this grace period.

Example: ***Operation of the Grace Period***

The renewal premium of $910 on Stan's $250,000 life insurance policy was due on April 8. Stan was severely ill in the hospital at the time, however, and the premium wasn't paid. Stan died there on April 27. The insurer will pay Stan's beneficiary $249,090—that is, $250,000 − $910.

Late Remittance Offers

late remittance offer

It is important to make a distinction between the grace period rules and a *late remittance offer*: they are not the same. There is usually no provision in the contract concerning late remittance offers. Such offers are made solely at the insurer's option. The late remittance offer is not a right of the policyowner or an obligation of the insurer that is included in the insurance contract under the requirements of the law. Late remittance offers are also different from reinstatement (discussed later in this chapter).

Some insurers will make a late remittance offer to a policyowner whose coverage has lapsed after the grace period has expired. This is not an extension of the grace period, and coverage is not continued as a result of the offer. Late remittance offers are intended to encourage the policyowner to reinstate the policy; they do *not* extend coverage. The inducement from the insurer is that coverage can be reinstated without having to provide evidence of insurability. The policyowner accepts the late remittance offer by paying the premiums that are due and meeting any other conditions imposed by the insurer. The most common condition is that the insured must have been alive when the late premium payment was made.

Policy Loans

The law requires that the insurance contract permit policy loans if the policy generates a cash value. To understand this requirement it is necessary to make a distinction between advancement, loan, and policy loan.

advancement

advancement: money or other property transferred to someone prior to the anticipated time of payment or delivery

loan: a transfer of money (or other property) with an obligation to repay the money plus interest (or to return the asset transferred) at a certain time

policy loan

policy loan: an advance of money available to the policy-owner from a policy's cash values. Interest is accrued on the amount borrowed from the policy. Although there is no fixed time for repayment of the money to the insurer, the amount of the loan plus any unpaid interest will be deducted from any policy values payable under the policy.

From the definitions above it can be seen that the term *policy loan* is a misnomer. A policy loan is actually an advancement against the policy's cash surrender value or death benefit. It is not technically a loan because the policyowner assumes no obligation to repay the money taken from the policy. Thus it is not technically correct to say that the policyowner borrows from the insurer and the loan is secured by the policy cash values. It is more accurate to say that the policyowner makes an advance withdrawal of cash values otherwise available when the policy is surrendered or when the insured dies. However, this distinction is really only of academic interest because the universal practice is to call it a *loan*.

One might ask, if it is not a loan, why is the insurer permitted to assess an interest rate against the amount borrowed? The policyowner is expected to pay interest on the "loan" because he or she has withdrawn assets from the insurer that were intended to support the level premium concept. If the policyowner withdraws those assets, it is fair to expect him or her to pay an interest rate that would approximate what the insurer would earn if the money was left with the insurer to invest.

Automatic premium loans are another type of policy loan. These loans are advances that the insurer makes from policy cash values to pay any unpaid premiums.

Incontestable Clause

incontestable clause

The National Association of Insurance Commissioners Standard Policy Provisions Model Act and the laws based upon it require that the policy contain an *incontestable clause* that makes the life insurance policy incontestable by the insurer after it has been in force for a certain time period. This provision was originally introduced in New York in 1864 by the voluntary action of insurers. By 1906, the clause had become so firmly entrenched and was so obviously beneficial to the public that it was made mandatory by New York law. Other states followed New York's example, and now the clause is required by statute in all states. The laws of the states differ as to the form of the clause prescribed, but no state permits a clause that would make the policy contestable for more than 2 years.

The following is a sample incontestable clause:

> Except for nonpayment of premium, we will not contest this contract after it has been in force during the lifetime of the insured for 2 years from the date of issue.

After a policy has been in effect for the period of time prescribed by the incontestable clause (normally 2 years), the insurance company cannot have the policy declared invalid. The courts have generally recognized three exceptions to this rule. If there was no insurable interest at the inception of the policy, if the policy was purchased with the intent to murder the insured, or if there was a fraudulent impersonation of the insured by another person (for example, for purposes of taking the medical exam), then the incontestable clause is deemed not to apply because the contract, which includes the incontestable clause, was void from its inception.

Flaws That Prevent Policy Creation

- lack of insurable interest at inception of the policy
- policy purchased with intent to murder the insured
- medical exam taken by someone other than the intended insured

---

Divisible Surplus

divisible surplus

The *divisible surplus* provision applies only to participating policies that may pay policyowner dividends. It requires the insurer to determine and apportion any divisible surplus among the insurer's participating policies at frequent intervals.

A typical divisible surplus provision from an insurance contract reads as follows:

> While this policy is in force, except as extended term insurance, it will be entitled to the share, if any, of the divisible surplus that we shall annually determine and apportion to it. This share is payable as a dividend on the policy anniversary.

In addition, some contracts provide that payment of a dividend is conditioned upon payment of all premiums then due. The provision in most contracts notes that a dividend is not likely to be paid before the second anniversary of the policy.

Entire Contract

Ordinarily we expect that a contract of any type include all the provisions that are binding on the parties. However, this is not always the case. Sometimes one contract will include the terms of another document without actually including that second document in the contract. This is done by referring to the other document and incorporating it into the contract by that reference. This is known as *incorporation by reference*. Entire contract

incorporation by reference

statutes grew out of an attempt to prohibit insurers' use of incorporation by reference and to make life insurance contracts more understandable by consumers. One goal was to assure that the policyowner was given a copy of all documents that constitute the contract. Another was to preclude any changes in the contract after it had been issued.

The various state statutes impose different requirements. Some states require a provision disclosing that the contract and the application constitute the entire contract; other states simply provide that the contract and the application are the contract regardless of what the policy may say.

A sample provision is as follows:

> This policy and any attached copy of an application form the entire contract. We assume that all statements in an application are made to the best of the knowledge and belief of the persons who make them; in the absence of fraud, they are deemed to be representations and not warranties. We rely on those statements when we issue the contract. We will not use any statement, unless made in an application, to try to void the contract, to contest a change, or to deny a claim.

Reinstatement

The *reinstatement provision* allows a policyowner to reacquire coverage under a policy that has lapsed. This right is valuable to both the policyowner and the insurer. The various state laws and the insurance contracts impose certain requirements that the policyowner must meet to reinstate the policy. New York law requires that life insurance policies contain a provision granting the policyowner the right to reinstate the policy ". . . at any time within three years from the date of default, unless the cash surrender value has been exhausted or the period of extended term insurance has expired, if the policyholder makes application, provides evidence of insurability, including good health, satisfactory to the insurer, pays all overdue premiums with interest at a rate not exceeding six per centum per annum compounded annually, and pays or reinstates any other policy indebtedness with interest at a rate not exceeding the applicable policy loan rate or rates determined in accordance with the policy's provisions. This provision shall be required only if the policy provides for termination or lapse in the event of a default in making a regularly scheduled premium payment."[2]

A typical reinstatement provision might provide the following:

> This policy may be reinstated within 3 years after the due date of the first unpaid premium, unless the policy has been surrendered for its cash value. The conditions for reinstatement are that (1) you must provide evidence of insurability satisfactory to us, (2) you must pay all overdue premiums plus interest at 6% per year, and (3) you must repay or reinstate any policy loan outstanding when the policy lapsed, plus interest.

Normally, insurers do not permit reinstatement of a policy that has been surrendered for its cash value, and this prohibition is often included in the contractual definition of the requirements for reinstatement.

Common Reinstatement Requirements

- Provide evidence of insurability.
- Pay all overdue premiums plus interest.
- Repay or reinstate any outstanding policy loans.
- Policy must not have been surrendered for its cash value.

Misstatement of Age or Sex

The age and sex of the insured are fundamentally important factors in the evaluation of the risk the life insurance company assumes. Inaccurate statements about the insured's age or sex are material misrepresentations. Rather than voiding the contract based on such misrepresentations, the practice after discovering the inaccuracy is to adjust the policy's premium or benefits to reflect the truth. Adjustments in the policy's premiums or benefits based on misstatements of age or sex are not precluded by the incontestability clause. This is because incontestability clauses preclude contests of the *validity* of the policy. If a misstatement of age or sex clause appears in the contract, an adjustment based on that clause would be an attempt to enforce the terms of the contract, not invalidate it.

A sample provision might read as follows:

If the age or sex of the insured has been misstated, we will adjust all benefits payable under this policy to that which the premium paid would have purchased at the correct age or sex.

Note that if the insured is still alive when it is discovered that the insured's age or sex has been misrepresented, it may be that the parties will elect to adjust the premium to the correct amount rather than to adjust the benefits.

The New York insurance code requires insurance contracts to contain a provision stipulating that if the age of the insured has been misstated, any amount payable or benefit accruing under the policy will be what the premium would have purchased at the correct age.[3] A majority of states have a similar provision. A minority of states have a provision requiring a reference to misstatement of sex.

Example: ***Operation of the Misstatement of Age or Sex Clause***

Larry misstated his age on a life insurance application as 40, when in fact he was 45. The premium at age 40 was $350, sufficient to purchase a $500,000 yearly renewable term policy. Larry died 7 months later, at which time his correct age of 45 was discovered. A $350 premium for a 45-year-old male would have purchased only $410,000 of yearly renewable term insurance from this insurer. Therefore, the insurer will pay Larry's beneficiary only $410,000.

Nonforfeiture Provisions

When insurers developed the concept of level premium insurance policies, the goal was to make life insurance more affordable to older policyowners. This was accomplished by charging a lifetime level premium. In the earlier years of the policy this level premium was higher than necessary to cover the mortality costs. The excess portion of the premium in the policy's early years (and the interest it earned) built up a cash reserve that was used to pay the mortality costs at older ages, which then exceeded the level premium being charged. A question soon arose concerning who was entitled to those reserves when a policy lapsed in the early years. Initially, these reserves were forfeited by the policyowner and kept by the insurer. This was clearly inequitable, and the practice was soon modified. Today that question has been answered by the nonforfeiture laws.

nonforfeiture laws

The states require that insurers assure policyowners who voluntarily terminate their contracts a fair return of the value built up inside some policies. These laws are known as the *nonforfeiture laws*. As late as the middle of the 19th century, insurance policies in the United States made no provision for refunds of excess premiums paid on cash value policies upon the policyowner's termination of the policy before maturity. However, in 1861 Massachusetts recognized that the policyowner had a right to at least a portion of those funds, and the first nonforfeiture law was enacted in that state. By 1948 that idea had evolved into the Standard Nonforfeiture Law, and subsequent versions of the law have become effective in all jurisdictions. Policies issued since that date have provided at least the minimum surrender values prescribed by the version of the law in effect when the policy was put in force. Modifications of the Standard Nonforfeiture Law do not apply retroactively to insurance policies that are already in force when the new law is adopted.

The Standard Nonforfeiture Law does not require specific surrender values. The only requirement is that surrender values are at least as large as those that would be produced by the method the law prescribes. In addition, each policy must contain a statement of the method used to find the surrender values and benefits provided under the policy at durations not specifically shown. This permits life insurance companies to use alternate formulas by describing them in their policies.

These laws require that after a cash value policy has been in effect for a minimum number of years—usually 3—the insurer must use part of the reserved excess premium to create a guaranteed minimum cash value. In addition, the insurer must make that value available to the policyowner in cash as a surrender value and must give the policyowner a choice of two nonforfeiture options: (1) extended term insurance for the net face amount of the policy or (2) paid-up insurance at a reduced death benefit amount. If the policyowner has not elected between them, the policy must provide that one of these two options will be effective automatically if the policy lapses.

Settlement Options

The standard policy provisions of the various states require that a life insurance policy must include certain settlement option tables if the settlement options include installment payments or annuities. These tables must show the amounts of the applicable installment or annuity payments.

PROHIBITED PROVISIONS

Although the state laws are not uniform, most states prohibit insurers from including certain provisions in their policies. For various reasons, courts or state legislatures have determined that these prohibited contract provisions violate public policy. There are five generally prohibited provisions:

- The insurance producer, who is the agent of the insurance company, cannot be made the agent of the insured for purposes of filling out the application for insurance. If the producer could be made the insured's agent rather than the company's agent, then the insurance company could not be charged with knowing facts presented to the agent but not communicated to the insurance company by the agent. Note that this restriction against making the producer the agent of the insured is confined to taking the application. As more completely described in chapter 16, the producer is sometimes held to be the agent of the insured for other purposes.

- Nonpayment of a loan cannot cause a forfeiture. The state laws generally provide that so long as the cash value of the policy exceeds the total indebtedness on the policy, the policyowner's failure to repay the loan or to pay interest on the loan cannot cause a forfeiture of the policy.

- Less value statutes preclude an insurer from promising something on the face of the policy and taking it away in the fine print. These laws are called less value statutes because the insurer is prohibited from providing a settlement option of less value than the death benefit of the policy.

statutes of limitation

- There are limitations on the time for filing lawsuits against the insurer. All states have *statutes of limitation* that control how long a person may wait before bringing a lawsuit of any type against another party. These statutes are designed to force people to sue in a timely fashion rather than waiting in the hope that evidence favorable to the other side will be lost. Once the time period specified in the statute has expired without filing a claim in the courts, the courts will not allow the lawsuit.

- The statutes of limitation have different lengths for different types of lawsuits. Ordinarily, the time period during which a lawsuit based on a contract must be brought is quite long; 10 years is not an unusual length. Sometimes the parties to a contract will agree to a shorter time period for initiating a lawsuit (based on a breach of that contract) than the period prescribed by the state law. The insurance codes of several states prohibit insurers from issuing policies that greatly reduce the length of the statute of limitations on contract actions. These statutes permit insurers to shorten the period to a reasonable length but not to eliminate it entirely. The permissibly shorter periods range from one to 6 years. Some states do not permit insurers to reduce the statute of limitations period at all. These laws protect the interests of the insurers and the public. Insurers are protected because the laws allow them to impose shorter limitation periods than otherwise permitted in the state. This benefits insurers because it requires plaintiffs to sue while information relevant to the insurance policy is still easy to obtain. The public is protected because the statutes do not allow insurers to shorten the limitation period so much that the public does not have sufficient time to determine whether a lawsuit is worthwhile.

- No lengthy backdating to save age is allowed. Backdating a policy means issuing the policy as if it had been purchased when the insured was younger. This practice has an advantage and a disadvantage. The advantage is that the insured will pay lower annual premiums for each increment of the policy because the premium will be based on the younger age. The disadvantage is that the insured must pay the premium applicable to the length of the backdating. This means that the insured will have paid for insurance protection during a period of time before the policy was issued when no coverage was provided. The statutes generally limit backdating to no more than 6 months.

OPTIONAL PROVISIONS

In addition to the required provisions and the prohibited provisions, there are numerous other provisions that are neither required nor prohibited:

suicide provision

- *suicide provision*. An insurer may elect to include suicide as a covered risk from the day the policy is issued. However, this is not normally the case, and as a general rule most insurance contracts do not provide coverage for a death by suicide within the first one or 2 years after the policy is issued. If the policy does not contain a suicide exclusion provision, then a death by suicide is covered by the policy and the death benefit is payable to the beneficiary regardless of when the suicide occurs.

The following is a typical insurance contract suicide provision:

> Suicide of the insured, while sane or insane, within 2 years of the issue date, is not covered by this policy. In that event, we will pay only the premiums paid to us less any unpaid policy loans.

- **ownership provision.** Ordinarily the insured is the applicant and owner of the policy. The ownership provision in the life insurance contract describes some of the rights of the owner. The typical ownership provision stipulates that the owner of the policy is the insured unless the application states otherwise. The provision also usually states that the policyowner may change the beneficiary, assign the policy to another party, and exercise other ownership rights. If these powers are described, the provision will also define how such powers are to be exercised in order to be recognized by the insurance company.

- **assignment provision.** As with most contracts and most interests in property, the policyowner has, as a matter of law, the right to transfer some or all of his or her rights to another person. In contract law this is generally known as the *right to assign.* The act of transferring a property right is an assignment. The right to assign an ownership interest in an insurance policy exists even without an assignment provision in the contract. However, most contracts include an assignment clause because it sets out clearly the conditions upon which an assignment can be made. If the policy contains a provision prohibiting an assignment, any attempted assignment by the policyowner will not be binding on the insurer. If the policy sets conditions for an assignment, the policyowner must comply with these restrictions. A sample assignment clause might provide the following:

right to assign

> You may assign this policy if we agree. We will not be bound by an assignment unless it has been received by us in writing at our home office. Your rights and the rights of any other person referred to in this policy will be subject to the assignment. We assume no responsibility for the validity of an assignment. An absolute assignment will be the same as a change of ownership to the assignee.

- **plan change.** This provision simply asserts that the parties may agree to change the terms of the contract. It does not add anything that does not already exist under the law. A sample contract change provision might read as follows:

> Subject to our rules at the time of a change, you may change this policy for another plan of insurance, you may add riders to this policy, or you may make other changes if we agree.

- accelerated benefits. As a result of the AIDS epidemic and public concern about other terminal illnesses, some insurers have added a provision that permits the insured to withdraw policy death benefits under certain circumstances. These accelerated benefits or living benefits provisions state that if the insured develops a medical condition that renders the insured terminally ill, then he or she may withdraw a portion of the policy's death benefit.

The 1990 NAIC Accelerated Benefits Model Regulation was designed to regulate accelerated benefit provisions of individual and group life insurance policies and to provide required standards of disclosure. (See Section 1 below of the model regulation.)

accelerated benefits
Accelerated benefits are defined as benefits payable during the lifetime of the insured under a life insurance contract to a policyowner (or certificate holder for group insurance) upon the occurrence of life-threatening or catastrophic conditions that are specified in the policy. To qualify as accelerated benefits, the lifetime payments must reduce the death benefit otherwise payable under the contract.

The model regulation prescribes that the condition that permits the payment of the accelerated benefits must be a medical condition that drastically limits the insured's normal life span expectation (for example, to 2 years or less). The regulation also lists several diseases as examples of a qualifying medical condition: acute coronary artery disease, a permanent neurological deficit resulting from a cerebral vascular accident, end-stage renal failure, AIDS, or such other medical condition as the commissioner may approve.

Twenty-five states have adopted regulations or statutes similar to the NAIC model. The first two sections of the model regulation are as follows:[4]

Section 1. Purpose

The purpose of this regulation is to regulate accelerated benefit provisions of individual and group life insurance policies and to provide required standards of disclosure. This regulation shall apply to all accelerated benefits provisions of individual and group life insurance policies except those subject to the Long-Term Care Insurance Model Act, issued or delivered in this state, on or after the effective date of this regulation.

Section 2.   Definitions

A.   "Accelerated benefits" covered under this regulation are benefits payable under a life insurance contract:

   (1) To a policyowner or certificateholder, during the lifetime of the insured, in anticipation of death or upon the occurrence of specified life-threatening or catastrophic conditions as defined by the policy or rider; and

   (2) Which reduce the death benefit otherwise payable under the life insurance contract; and

   (3) Which are payable upon the occurrence of a single qualifying event which results in the payment of a benefit amount fixed at the time of acceleration.

B.   "Qualifying event" shall mean one or more of the following:

   (1) A medical condition which would result in a drastically limited life span as specified in the contract, for example, twenty-four (24) months or less; or

   (2) A medical condition which has required or requires extraordinary medical intervention, such as, but not limited to, major organ transplant or continuous artificial life support, without which the insured would die; or

   (3) Any condition which usually requires continuous confinement in an eligible institution as defined in the contract if the insured is expected to remain there for the rest of his or her life; or

   (4) A medical condition which would, in the absence of extensive or extraordinary medical treatment, result in a drastically limited life span. Such conditions may include, BUT ARE NOT LIMITED TO, one or more of the following:

      (a) Coronary artery disease resulting in an acute infarction or requiring surgery;

      (b) Permanent neurological deficit resulting from cerebral vascular accident;

      (c) End stage renal failure;

      (d) Acquired Immune Deficiency Syndrome; or

      (e) Other medical conditions which the commissioner shall approve for any particular filing; or

   (5) Other qualifying events which the commissioner shall approve for any particular filing.

WAIVER AND ESTOPPEL

The concepts of waiver and estoppel are quite similar and easy to confuse. Some courts treat waiver and estoppel as two parts of the same theory.

> *waiver*: the voluntary and intentional surrender of a known right. By a waiver, a party relinquishes a right. For example, if an insurer issues a policy even though the medical questionnaire has not been completed and was not signed by the applicant, the insurer will have waived the right to have that information.

Nevertheless, the law is clear that some waivers are forbidden. No party to an insurance contract may waive a right that also partly benefits the general public. For example, the insurable interest requirement benefits the public as well as the insurer; thus an insurer may not waive its right to demand that the applicant have an insurable interest in the life of the insured at the time the policy is applied for. Similarly, a policyowner may not waive his or her rights to nonforfeiture values or premium notices.

Granting a waiver is not necessarily permanent. An insurer may elect to waive a particular right for one time and one purpose only. If so, the waiver will have no effect on future actions between the parties. If a party has repeatedly waived a contractual right in the past, it can reclaim that right simply by notifying the other party that it intends to reassert that right in the future.

> *estoppel*: the loss of the ability to assert a defense because the party has acted in a manner inconsistent with that defense. For example, if an insurer has repeatedly accepted payment of late premiums after the end of the grace period without requiring the insured to comply with the reinstatement process, the insurer may be prohibited (estopped) from requiring a reinstatement for future late premiums. This may be the result even if the prior late premiums were accepted by mistake and without recognizing that they were late.

There is a fine distinction between the example above and the rule that the concept of estoppel may not be used to create coverage or to extend coverage beyond that assumed by the insurer in the contract. A classic case is *Pierce v. Homesteaders Life Association.*[5] The policy in that case provided that the death benefit was payable only if the insured died before age 60. The policyowner paid and the insurer accepted premium payment through the end of September of the year in which the insured turned 60. The insured's 60th birthday was on March 3, and she died on March 11. The insured's beneficiary filed a claim for the death benefit asserting that because the insurer had accepted a premium payment for a period beyond the insured's 60th birthday, the insurance company had waived that contractual limitation and should therefore be estopped from denying coverage. The court held for the insurer and asserted that coverage cannot be created by waiver.

The essence of the distinction between the example and the case is narrow but clear. In the case, no coverage was to be provided after the insured reached age 60. Estoppel could not be invoked to create something that never existed. In the example, coverage existed for the insured subject to the condition that premiums be paid on time. The insurance company's actions were inconsistent with the existence of that timely premium payment condition; thus the insurance company was estopped from asserting it.

ADDITIONAL COMMON PROVISIONS

Other common policy provisions are those concerning accidental death benefits, the guaranteed purchase option (also known as the guaranteed insurability option), and the waiver of premium in the event of the insured's disability.

Accidental Death Benefits

rider

double-indemnity provision

This optional policy provision is added to some insurance contracts in the form of a *rider*, or amendment, to the policy. It is also known as the *double-indemnity provision* because it normally doubles the standard death benefit if the insured dies accidentally.

Since this benefit is payable only in the event of the insured's *accidental* death, that term requires definition. In the absence of a specific definition in the rider, the word *accident* means an unintentional event that is sudden and unexpected. An *accidental death* is one that is caused by an accident. This statement seems quite clear, but it is not always easy to apply. There have been cases where an insured has been mortally injured in an accident, but the actual cause of death is a disease. Is the accidental death benefit payable? The answer is yes only if the accident was the cause of death. If the insured is in an automobile accident but dies from a heart attack, the accidental death benefit will be payable only if the accident can be proven to have triggered the heart attack.

The problems caused by cases in which there is potentially more than one cause of death are mitigated somewhat by the standard practice of putting a time limit in the accidental death benefit provision. In the most common type the death must occur within 90 days of the accident that is said to have caused the injury.

These basic definitions preclude coverage for any death that is the natural and probable result of a voluntary act. It is an unchallenged principle of law that people are presumed to expect and intend the probable or foreseeable consequences of their actions. This concept is sometimes described by the term *assumption of the risk.* If one plays Russian roulette, jumps off buildings, or runs with the bulls in Pamplona, Spain, his or her death as a result of those activities cannot be described as accidental.

assumption of the risk

accidental result

accidental means

There are two types of accidental death clauses: (1) the *accidental result* type and (2) the *accidental means* type. A sample accidental result death benefit provision is as follows:

> We will pay this benefit to the beneficiary when we have proof that the Insured's death was the result, directly and apart from any other cause, of accidental bodily injury, and that death occurred within one year after that injury and while this rider was in effect.

An accidental means death benefit provision would be only slightly different:

> We will pay this benefit to the beneficiary when we have proof that the Insured's death was caused directly, and apart from any other cause, by accidental means, and that death occurred within one year after that injury and while this rider was in effect.

The most common type of provision that insurers use is the accidental result type. This is because the accidental result clause is more favorable to the consumer. It is also because most courts have recognized that the difference between the two clauses is too difficult for many consumers to understand and have therefore ceased to recognize a distinction between the two types of clauses.

The distinction can be explained as follows: Under an accidental means clause both the cause (means) of the death and the result must be unintentional. Under an accidental result clause, only the result must be unintentional. For example, assume that an insured is participating in an obstacle course race at a family reunion, and the race requires the racers to dive over a barrel, do a somersault, and run to the next event. The insured breaks her neck and is killed doing the somersault. Since she was doing exactly what she intended to do, the means was not accidental although the result was certainly an accident. The accidental means clause would not require the payment of the benefit, but the accidental result clause would.

There is another factor that has made accidental means clauses less attractive to insureds and thus less frequently used by insurers. This is the provision requiring that, in addition to being accidental, the means (cause) of death must also be violent and caused by an external agency. Courts have been liberal in their interpretation of these limitations in favor of the public.

Most accidental death benefit clauses do not provide coverage in the event of the insured's death by suicide. If suicide of the insured (whether sane or insane) is excluded, then an examination of the insured's mental state at the time of the suicide is avoided. If the insured is sane at the time of the suicide, then it is an intentional act that would not qualify as an accident. If the insured is insane, the suicide might be classified as unintentional because the insured may be presumed not to have been able to intend the consequences of his or her act.

Guaranteed Purchase Option

guaranteed purchase option
guaranteed insurability option

Another popular policy provision is the *guaranteed purchase option,* which is also called the *guaranteed insurability option.* Although it is quite common now, this is a relatively new option for insureds. It was developed during the 1950s, but it did not become widely available for many years.

This provision helps policyowners protect themselves against the possibility that they might become uninsurable. Under the typical provision, the insured may purchase the right to acquire additional insurance in specified amounts at specified times or ages. Typically this provision allows additional purchases every 3 years and after the birth of a child, provided the events occur before the insured reaches the specified maximum age (often 45). This right to purchase additional insurance may be very valuable because the insured does not have to provide evidence of insurability in order to exercise the option. Another benefit of the guaranteed purchase option is that the new coverage is normally not subject to a new suicide provision or a new incontestability clause.

There is a ceiling on the maximum amount of insurance available under the guaranteed purchase option and a maximum age at which the option may be exercised. Once the insured passes an age or event that triggers the right to purchase additional insurance but he or she does not exercise that option, the option lapses.

Waiver of Premium

waiver-of-premium provision

A *waiver-of-premium provision* in the event of the insured's disability is another extremely valuable coverage.

According to a typical waiver-of-premium provision, if the insured becomes totally disabled as defined in the life insurance contract, the insurance company will waive payment of premiums on the policy during the continuance of the insured's disability.

The disability waiver of premium has some limitations. For example, the waiver will not be granted if the insured's disability begins after a specified age. In addition, the provision in the sample below will not waive premiums if the disability is self-inflicted or the result of an act of war. As with all contracts, it is important to pay close attention to the language used. Seemingly small differences in the language of the provision can make large differences in the obligations the insurer incurs.

The following is a sample disability waiver-of-premium rider:

Disability Waiver-of-Premium Rider

Waiver of Premiums. We will start to waive the premiums for this policy when proof is furnished that the Insured's total disability, as defined in this rider, has gone on for at least 6 months in a row.

If a total disability starts on or prior to the anniversary on which the Insured is age 60, we will waive all of the premiums that fall due during that total disability. If it goes on until the anniversary on which the Insured is age 65, we will make the policy fully paid-up as of that date, with no more premiums due.

If a total disability starts after the anniversary on which the Insured is age 60, we will waive only those premiums that fall due during that total disability and prior to the anniversary on which the Insured is age 65.

Premiums are waived at the interval of payment in effect when the total disability started. While we waive premiums, all insurance goes on as if they had been paid. We will not deduct a waived premium from the policy proceeds.

total disability   **Definition of Total Disability.** *Total disability* means that, because of disease or bodily injury, the Insured cannot do any of the essential acts and duties of his or her job, or of any other job for which he or she is suited based on schooling, training, or experience. If the Insured can do some but not all of these acts and duties, disability is not total and premiums will not be waived. If the Insured is a minor and is required by law to go to school, "Total Disability" means that, because of disease or bodily injury, he or she is not able to go to school.

"Total Disability" also means the Insured's total loss, starting while this rider is in effect, of the sight of both eyes or the use of both hands, both feet, or one hand and one foot.

Total Disabilities for Which Premiums Not Waived. We will not waive premiums in connection with any of these total disabilities.

1. Those that start prior to the fifth birthday of the Insured, or start at a time when this rider is not in effect.
2. Those that are caused by an injury that is self-inflicted on purpose.
3. Those that are caused by any kind of war, declared or not, or by any act incident to a war or to an armed forces of one or more countries while the Insured is a member of those armed forces.

Proof of Total Disability. Written notice and proof of this condition must be given to us, while the Insured is living and totally disabled, or as soon as it can reasonably be done. As long as we waive premiums, we may require proof from time to time. After we have waived premiums for 2 years in a row, we will not need to have this proof more than once each year. As part of the proof, we may have the Insured examined by doctors we approve.

Payment of Premiums. Premiums must be paid when due, until we approve a claim under this rider. If a total disability starts during a grace period, the overdue premium must be paid before we will approve any claim.

Refunds of Premiums. If a total disability starts after a premium has been paid, and if it goes on for at least 6 months in a row, we will refund the part of that premium paid for the period after the policy month when the disability started. Any other premium paid and then waived will be refunded in full.

Values. This rider does not have cash or loan values.

Contract. This rider, when paid for, is made a part of the policy, based on the application for the rider.

Incontestability of Rider. We have no right to contest this rider after it has been in force during the lifetime of the Insured for 2 years from its date of issue, unless the Insured is totally disabled at some time within 2 years of the date of issue.

Dates and Amounts. When this rider is issued at the same time as the policy, we show the rider premium amount on the front page of the policy. The rider and the policy have the same date of issue. When this rider is added to a policy which is already in force, we also put in an add-on-rider. The add-on-rider shows the date of issue. The rider premium amount is shown in a new Premium Schedule for the policy.

When Rider Ends. You can cancel this rider as of the due date of a premium. To do this, you must send the policy and your signed notice to us within 31 days of that date. If this rider is still in effect on the anniversary on which the Insured is age 65, it will end on that date.

This rider ends if the policy ends or is surrendered. Also, this rider will not be in effect if the policy lapses or is in force as extended or paid-up insurance.

Policy Filing and Approval

It is the rule that if a policy is sold in a state but does not include a required provision or has not been filed with the state for approval, the courts will treat the policy as if it did include all the required provisions under the law of that jurisdiction. The policyowner or beneficiary will be permitted to enforce the policy against the insurer as if it complied in all respects with the applicable state law. The state insurance commissioners are charged with the responsibility to see that the insurance companies doing business in their state are complying with that state's law regarding the permitted and prohibited policy provisions. To enable the insurance department to do its job, a policy may not be issued or delivered in a state until it has been approved by the department. In some states, the insurer may assume that the policy has been approved if it has not been advised otherwise within a fixed period of time, such as 30 days, after it has been submitted to the state insurance department. In other states, the insurer may not issue the policy until it has received notice of approval from the department.

If an insurer issues a policy that has not been approved by the insurance department, the policyowner may seek a refund of premiums paid or seek to enforce the policy. If suit is brought, the courts will enforce the unapproved contract against the insurer on behalf of the beneficiary. If the unapproved policy does not include a provision that would have been required for approval, the policy will be treated by the courts as if it does contain such a provision. Furthermore, if a required provision is more favorable to the policyowner than one actually included in the contract, the courts will treat the contract as if it included the more favorable provision. The insurer that violates the laws requiring filing of the policy and approval of its provisions by the state will also be subject to fines or other penalties (such as revocation of the insurer's right to do business in that state).

CHAPTER REVIEW

Answers to the review questions and the self-test questions can be found in the Supplement.

Key Terms

free-look provision	advancement
grace period	policy loan
late remittance offer	incontestable clause

divisible surplus
incorporation by reference
reinstatement provision
nonforfeiture laws
statutes of limitation
suicide provision
right to assign
accelerated benefits
    rider

double-indemnity provision
assumption of the risk
accidental result
accidental means
guaranteed purchase (guaranteed
    insurability) option
waiver-of-premium provision
total disability

Review Questions

1. Why is a life insurance contract called a contract of adhesion?

2. What information is usually contained on the face page of a life insurance policy?

3. What is the grace-period clause, and how does it benefit the policyholder?

4. What is a late remittance offer?

5. Distinguish between the following terms in the context of a life insurance contract:
   a. loan
   b. policy loan
   c. advancement

6. What are the three exceptions to the incontestable clause?

7. What is a divisible surplus provision, and how does it relate to the payment of dividends?

8. Explain what entire-contract statutes are.

9. What is the purpose of reinstatement provisions?

10. Roger is a strong believer in a strict regimen of daily exercise and adherence to health food diets. He prides himself on being mistaken for a man much younger than his actual age of 45 years. When Roger applied for an insurance policy on his life, he stated that he was 35 years old in order to reduce the amount of his premium payments. What steps is the insurance company likely to take when it discovers that Roger misrepresented his age?

11. Explain what nonforfeiture laws are intended to accomplish.

12. What types of provisions are insurers usually prohibited from including in their life insurance policies?

13. Describe the following optional provisions that may be included in a life insurance contract:
    a. suicide provision
    b. ownership provision
    c. assignment provision
    d. plan change
    e. accelerated benefits

14. Explain the concepts of waiver and estoppel in the context of life insurance.

15. For several years Martin was under a cardiologist's care. After suffering a heart attack 2 years ago, Martin underwent a successful quadruple bypass. Although he was in good shape physically after the surgery, Martin was involved in a multi-vehicle car crash recently and died from a heart attack shortly after this accident. Martin was the owner of a life insurance policy on his life that included an accidental death benefits clause. Is the accidental death benefit payable in this situation?

16. Describe the two types of accidental death clauses:

    a. accidental result type
    b. accidental means type

17. How does the guaranteed purchase (guaranteed insurability) option benefit an insured?

18. What is the effect of a waiver-of-premium provision in a life insurance contract?

Self-Test Questions

T   F   1. In a life insurance contract, the policyowner and the insurer do not negotiate the contract terms.

T   F   2. Since life insurance contracts are contracts of adhesion, any ambiguities in the contract are resolved in favor of the insurer.

T   F   3. Before a life insurance policy may be sold by an insurer in a particular state, its provisions have to be filed with the insurance department of the state for approval.

T   F   4. The free-look provision grants the insurance company a period of time, usually 30 days, during which it can investigate the information the applicant has supplied on the application form.

T   F   5. The standard provisions laws do not apply to group life insurance.

T   F   6.   Although a policyowner has a grace period in which to pay a premium that is past due, if the policyowner dies during the grace period, the insurer is relieved of its obligation to pay death benefits under the contract.

T   F   7.   If a policy contains a grace-period clause, it must also include a late remittance offer.

T   F   8.   The term *policy loan* is a misnomer because a policy loan is actually an advancement against the policy's cash surrender value or death benefit.

T   F   9.   Only a few states have not enacted statutes requiring all life insurance policies to include an incontestable clause.

T   F   10.   Most states require that the incontestable period stated in a policy be for a minimum of 2 years.

T   F   11.   The insurance codes of most states encourage insurers to incorporate several documents by reference into a life insurance contract so that the policyowner knows all the facts concerning his or her policy.

T   F   12.   Although reinstatement provisions allow a policyowner to reobtain coverage under a lapsed policy, the policyowner must meet certain requirements prior to reinstatement.

T   F   13.   Adjustments in a policy's premium or benefits due to a misstatement of age or sex are not prohibited by the incontestability clause because the incontestability clause concerns a policy's validity rather than misstatements.

T   F   14.   The Standard Nonforfeiture Law requires that specific surrender values be stated in every cash value policy a policyowner purchases.

T   F   15.   The primary purpose of statutes of limitation is to force individuals to bring potential lawsuits in a timely manner.

T   F   16.   A disadvantage of backdating is that the insured must pay the insurer for insurance protection during a period of time before the policy was issued when no coverage was provided.

T   F   17.   If a policy does not include a suicide exclusion clause, the insured's suicide is covered and the death benefit is payable regardless of when the suicide took place.

T   F   18.   There does not have to be an assignment clause in a life insurance contract for the policyowner to have a right to assign the ownership interest in the policy to another person.

T   F   19.   The main goal of an accelerated death benefit provision is for a policyowner with a terminal disease to receive the full death benefit under the policy at a time when he or she needs it most.

T   F   20. By signing a consent form, a policyowner is able to waive his or her right to receive premium notices.

T   F   21. In order for an accidental death provision to apply, an insured's death must have occurred within the period of time following the accident that is stated in the provision.

T   F   22. Under the majority of guaranteed purchase option provisions, the amount of additional insurance the insured may purchase is not restricted.

T   F   23. Generally, under a waiver-of-premium provision, an insured who becomes disabled according to the terms of the life insurance contract is released from paying premiums during the period of disability.

T   F   24. When a policy is sold without including a provision that is required under the applicable state law, the courts will hold that the policy included the omitted provision.

NOTES

1. If a partial premium has been paid but no premium receipt has been issued, the general rule is that no coverage is in effect until the policy has been issued by the insurer and accepted by the policyowner.
2. N.Y. Ins. Law Sec. 3203(a)(10) McKinney 1985.
3. N.Y. Ins. Law Sec. 3203(a)(5).
4. Accelerated Benefits Model Regulation. Copyright NAIC 2005.
5. *Pierce v. Homesteaders Life Association,* 272 N.W. 543 (Iowa 1937).

9

Premiums

Burke A. Christensen

Learning Objectives

An understanding of the material in this chapter should enable the student to

9-1. Explain the rights of policyowners and other parties to pay life insurance premiums.

9-2. Describe the rights derived by nonpolicyowners as a result of paying policy premiums.

9-3. Describe the special rights derived by collateral assignees who pay premiums to keep the assigned policy in force.

9-4. Explain the important legal distinction between initial premiums and renewal premiums.

9-5. Explain the importance of timely premium payments.

9-6. Describe the general determinant of premium due dates.

9-7. Explain the importance of premium notices and grace periods.

9-8. Describe the various acceptable methods of premium payment.

9-9. Explain the importance and ramification of conditionally accepting checks and notes for premium payment.

9-10. Describe automatic premium loans, and indicate the advantages and disadvantages of paying premiums by this method.

9-11. Describe the obligation of the insurance company with regard to unearned premiums.

Chapter Outline

Submitting an application for life insurance and payment of the initial premium for the insurance policy are the fundamental acts required of the policyowner to create a life insurance contract. In legal terms, these acts constitute the consideration paid by the applicant/policyowner in exchange for the insurer's promise to pay the benefits described in the contract. Without this consideration, a life insurance contract cannot exist. The face page of one insurer's policy recognizes this requirement very explicitly: "The consideration for this policy is the application and payment of the total initial premium on or before policy delivery."

In addition to this policy provision, the consideration requirement is recognized in the language printed on the application forms of many life insurance companies in different ways. The following are several examples.

Example 1:   The insurance provided for in this application shall not take effect until this application has been approved by us, and the policy has been delivered to and accepted by you, and the full first premium has been paid while the insured is alive and while the health and insurability of the insured have not changed from that as described in the application.

Example 2:   You agree that the application is the basis for issuing the policy and that, except as provided in the conditional receipt, insurance does not take effect until you pay the full first premium and the policy is delivered while the insured is insurable under our underwriting rules.

Example 3:   I agree that except as provided in the receipt, the insurance applied for never takes effect unless, during the lifetime of the insured, the policy has been issued, delivered to and accepted by me, and the required first premium has been paid while the health and habits of the insured remain as stated in the application.

Example 4:   If a conditional life insurance agreement was delivered in consideration of the payment of the first premium and is in effect, its provisions and terms will apply. Otherwise, this policy will take effect and coverage will begin on the issue date specified in the policy, if the full first premium is paid and the insured is living, and the answers and statements in the application continue to be true at the time of delivery of the policy

PAYMENT OF PREMIUMS

Remember, a life insurance policy is a unilateral contract. This means that one party to the life contract (the insurer) makes a promise (to pay the policy benefits) that is conditioned upon the performance of an act (payment of the premium) by the other party (usually the policyowner). Since payment of the initial premium is a condition that must be fulfilled before the contract comes into existence, we will examine that requirement in detail.

Payment by Someone Other Than Policyowner

For the vast majority of life insurance policies, the premiums are normally paid by the policyowner. (Several different methods of premium payment are available to policyowners. These methods—for example, cash,

Common Payment Methods

- cash
- check
- automatic transfer

check, and automatic transfer—are discussed later in this chapter.) When the premiums are paid by someone other than the policyowner, however, a few special questions arise.

By the Insured

If the insured and the policyowner are not the same person, payment of the premiums by the insured does not give the insured any rights in the insurance contract whatever. The insured is the object of the insurance contract and is vital to its creation and continuation, but he or she is *not* a party to the contract.

Depending on the relationship between the insured and the policyowner, if the insured pays the premiums, there may be gift or income tax consequences to consider. If the insured is a sole proprietor and the policyowner is an employee of the insured, the payment of premiums by the insured may be treated as compensation to the insured. If there is no employment relationship between the two parties, payment of the premiums may be a gift from the insured to the policyowner subject to federal gift taxation.

By a Revocable Beneficiary

Payment of insurance premiums by a revocable beneficiary does not give that beneficiary any additional rights in the contract beyond those accorded by designating that person as a beneficiary. Since the policyowner can change a revocable designation at any time, it is described as a defeasible interest (also known as a mere expectancy). However, if the beneficiary can produce evidence indicating a promise by the policyowner to pay all or a portion of the insurance proceeds to the beneficiary in exchange for the beneficiary's payment of the premiums, the courts will enforce such an agreement. In such a case, the courts will direct the insurer to pay the proceeds to the beneficiary even if the policyowner has changed the beneficiary designation to another person.

By a Trustee

If a trustee is both owner and beneficiary of a life insurance policy that has been transferred to or purchased by the trust, the trust document will normally have a provision either requiring or permitting the trustee to pay the premiums on the policy. This gives the trustee a fiduciary responsibility to see that the premiums are paid. If the trustee is not the owner of the policy but is merely designated as beneficiary of the policy in trust, there is usually no duty imposed on the trustee to see that premiums are paid.

This is clearly the case if the trustee is merely a revocable beneficiary of the policy. Nevertheless, the terms of the trust define the trustee's responsibilities with respect to all property interests the trustee possesses on behalf of the trust.

By an Irrevocable Beneficiary

If a person is designated as an irrevocable beneficiary, payment of the premiums on the policy for the policyowner still does not increase that person's interest in the policy beyond that granted by the beneficiary designation. To the extent that payment of premiums by an irrevocable beneficiary continues the policy in force, however, the irrevocable beneficiary has acted to protect the rights acquired under the beneficiary designation. Individuals may elect to pay premiums or not as their own self-interest dictates. Trustees must act in accordance with the provisions of the trust and with state law governing their management of trust assets.

By an Assignee

Life insurance policies are frequently assigned by their owners to other persons for various purposes. The assignment may be as collateral for a loan, or it may be an absolute assignment. Payment of premiums by an assignee has different consequences, depending on which type of assignment has been made. If the policy has been assigned as collateral, the terms of the collateral assignment document define whether the assignee has any duty to pay premiums. The standard American Bankers Association (ABA) collateral assignment form does not give the assignee any duty to pay premiums. It provides as follows:

> The Assignee shall be under no obligation to pay any premium, or the principal of or interest on any loans or advances on the Policy whether or not obtained by the Assignee, or any other charges on the Policy, but any such amounts so paid by the Assignee from its own funds shall become a part of the Liabilities hereby secured, shall be due immediately, and shall draw interest at a rate fixed by the Assignee from time to time not exceeding 6% per annum.

A person who receives an insurance policy as the result of an absolute assignment becomes the owner of the policy. Thus an absolute assignee, like the initial policyowner who assigned the contract, has no duty to pay any premiums because the life insurance policy is a unilateral contract. Of course, if the premiums on the policy are not paid after the assignment, the policy will be likely to lapse.

Presumption of Payment

At one time it was common for insurance companies to acknowledge receipt of the initial premium by automatically inserting language to that effect in the insurance contract. This is no longer the case because of statutes and court decisions adverse to the insurers. Insurance companies used to print that language in the contract because they assumed that the policy would not be issued unless they had, in fact, received the initial premium. However, circumstances frequently arose where companies issued policies without first receiving the initial premium and insurance agents delivered the policies without collecting the initial premium. Usually the premium was collected in short order, and the policy was treated by all parties as a contract for insurance. But in some of these cases, the insured died before the initial premium was collected. Because the premium had not been paid, the insurance companies denied the ensuing claim for the death benefit on the logical ground that the contract did not exist because the applicant had not provided the full consideration (application and premium). Some courts held, however, that by delivering the policy, the insurers had waived their right to demand payment prior to delivery. Thus the contract was in effect.

Conclusive Presumption

Today, a majority of the states have established a rule of law that if an insurance policy with such a provision has been delivered to the policyowner, there is a *conclusive* presumption that the policy is in effect, even if the available evidence suggests that the initial premium has not been paid. It is important to understand that the presumption is conclusive only as to the fact that the policy is in effect, not that the premium has actually been paid. In most jurisdictions, the insurer will be permitted to establish that the premium has not been paid and be allowed to collect the premium due (by deducting it from the death benefit, for example), but the insurer will not be permitted to challenge the validity of the contract.

Rebuttable Presumption

Modern insurance contracts do not contain this language. Thus it is clear that an insurance contract is an evolving document. Its terms change in response to adverse court decisions, new legislation, and competitive pressures. With respect to the relationship between premium payment and the insurer's obligation to pay policy benefits, language such as the following two examples is common.

Example 1:   We will pay the life insurance proceeds to the beneficiary promptly when we have proof that the insured died, if premiums have been paid as called for in this contract.

Example 2:   We will pay the policy benefits only if premiums have been paid as called for by this policy.

For policies with these types of provisions, possession of the policy by the owner or beneficiary will still create a presumption that the initial premium has been paid. However, that presumption is *rebuttable*—meaning that if the insurer can provide evidence that the initial premium has not been paid, the presumption will be overcome and the policy will be void.

conclusive presumption

conclusive presumption: a fact that is deemed to be true and that cannot be rebutted by contrary evidence

rebuttable presumption

rebuttable presumption: a fact that is assumed to be true unless convincing evidence to the contrary is available

Limitation Provisions

The terms of the application and the insurance contract governing the payment of the initial premium will be binding on the policyowner and the insurer. However, the insurer in some circumstances may be held to have waived the requirements of those documents. For example, as explained above with respect to the presumption that the initial premium has been paid, the acts of the insurer or its agent may be interpreted as a waiver by the insurance company of the requirements for timely payment of the initial premium. This might happen if the agent delivers a policy, does not collect the initial premium and advises the policyowner that a later payment of the initial premium will be acceptable. In such a case, the insurer may find itself bound by a contract (and obligated to pay a death benefit) even though it has not yet received the initial premium.

One solution to this problem is to avoid contract language acknowledging receipt of the initial premium. To further avoid this possibility, both the insurance application and the policy now usually have a provision limiting the agent's authority to alter the terms of the contract. Such language is contained in the application so that the policyowner will be put on notice prior to the delivery of the policy that the agent's power is limited.

In the Application. A typical limitation provision in the *application* states as follows:

> It is agreed that the policy issued based upon this application cannot be modified except in a writing signed by an authorized officer of the Company and that the agent has no authority to make any promise or representation regarding coverage or to waive the terms of any application or policy.

In the Policy. A typical limitation provision in the *policy* stipulates as follows:

> Only our president or one of our vice presidents can modify this contract or waive any of our rights or requirements under it. The person making these changes must put them in writing and sign them.

These provisions are designed to put the applicant on notice that the agent does not have the authority to waive the timely payment of the initial premium or to change any other requirement in either document. If these provisions had existed in the application and policy referred to in the above example, the insurance company would probably not have been bound by the contract. This result would be appropriate because the initial premium (part of the required consideration for the contract) was not paid at the time of delivery. If both the application and policy had contained a notice to the applicant and the policyowner that the agent did not have the authority to waive that requirement, it is likely that the courts would enforce the contract language as written in those documents and deny the claim for coverage.

Common Limitations on Powers of Agents

- not permitted to alter the requirement for timely payment of premiums
- not permitted to alter any provision in the application
- not permitted to alter any provision in the policy

RENEWAL PREMIUMS

renewal premiums   *Renewal premiums* have a different impact on the life insurance contract than the initial premium. Since the life insurance policy is a unilateral contract, the policyowner has no obligation to pay renewal premiums. After the insurance contract is in effect, it will exist according to its terms for a certain period of time even if no renewal premiums are paid. While renewal premiums are unrelated to the creation of the contract, they are vital to the continuation of the contract.

According to most courts, the payment of renewal premiums is a condition precedent to the performance of the insurer's obligations under the contract. In effect, the payment of each renewal premium continues the insurer's obligation to perform for an additional period of time. A minority of courts have held that the failure to pay renewal premiums is a condition subsequent that will terminate the contract. While the distinction between the two views is important, the condition subsequent theory is *not* the trend in the law.

Contractual Provisions

As it can with the initial premium, the insurance company can set the requirements for payment of the renewal premiums. The provisions controlling the policyowner's payment of the renewal premiums are usually contained only in the policy. The provisions governing the payment of the initial premium are found in the application and often in the policy as well. This difference is because notice to the policyowner about the payment of renewal premiums is not relevant to the creation of the contract.

Because the insurer's promise to pay policy benefits is conditioned upon payment of the policy's premiums, the contractual provisions governing how and when the renewal premiums are to be paid are very specific. The contractual language governing renewal premiums typically requires that premiums for any particular period of time are due in advance on or before the due date specified in the contract.

Sample contractual provisions on renewal premiums read as follows.

Example 1:   Each premium is payable, while the insured is living, on or before its due date as shown in the premium schedule on the policy data page. Premiums are payable at our home office or at one of our service offices. Any payment to us by check or money order must be made payable to (name of insurer).

Example 2:   The premium period, which we show on the first page, starts on the contract date. Each premium is to be paid by its due date. It may be paid at our home office or to any of our authorized agents.

Example 3:   Each premium after the first is payable in advance at the home office. Payment may also be made to a company agent in exchange for a receipt signed by the President or Secretary of the company and countersigned by the agent.

Note that although these provisions identify both a date and a recipient for proper payment of the premium, all insurers accept payment of the renewal premiums by mail as a matter of standard business practice. Consequently, if the available evidence establishes that the policyowner mailed a properly addressed renewal premium payment to the insurer sufficiently in advance of the due date that he or she could reasonably expect the post office to deliver the premium on time, the premium will be deemed paid on time even if the mail is delivered late or not at all. This is known in the law as the *mailbox rule.*

Nonpayment of Premium

During the 1860s, many policyowners in the United States were unable to pay insurance premiums due to the American Civil War. The consequence of that excuse for nonpayment of premiums has varied somewhat over the years. Some cases held that the policy lapsed for nonpayment of premiums. Other cases held that the policy was suspended during the war, and after the war's conclusion, the contract was revived by payment of back premiums. In 1876 the United States Supreme Court held in *New York Life Insurance Company v. Statham*, 93 U.S. 24, that the policy could be terminated by the insurer but that the policyowner was entitled to the reserve value of the contract.

This case is probably not generally applicable today, however. The Treaty of Versailles, which concluded World War I, created an option for policyowners to surrender the policy as of the date during the war when the policy lapsed for nonpayment of premiums or to reinstate the policy by paying the unpaid premiums. No similar provisions were instituted after World War II. However, the modern requirement that insurance policies contain the standard nonforfeiture provisions should resolve these issues today.

The contract may also contain a rider, such as a waiver of premium in the event of disability. If so, the terms of that rider govern if the premium is not paid due to a disability. Similarly, the terms of the dividend election (discussed later in this chapter) control if the policyowner has selected the option that applies dividends to reduce the premium. Finally, the automatic premium loan provision's terms (also discussed later) are applied if that contractual benefit is available to pay policy premiums. Because the payment of renewal premiums is required to keep the policy in force and the contractual language is so specific, a policyowner who fails to pay a premium when it is due (and not paid by a rider or dividend election) has very few excuses that will prevent the insurer from lapsing the policy.

There are a few cases where policyowners have tried to pay premiums, but the insurer's agent has refused to accept the payment, or where the insurer's agent had a responsibility to collect premiums but did not fulfill that responsibility, thereby preventing a policyowner from paying premiums. In these cases, the insurers were precluded from lapsing the policy because the policyowner had an acceptable excuse for failing to pay the premium.

Waivers of Payment

As it can with the initial premium, the insurance company may waive any of the requirements for payment of renewal premiums. An example of such a waiver is the extension of time for payment of a premium (also known as a late remittance offer) that companies sometimes make at their discretion after the grace period has expired. Beyond this offer, companies do not normally waive these requirements. (This practice is discussed later in this chapter.) The offer by the insurer to reinstate a policy after lapse may also be viewed as a form of waiver since the insurer gives up its right to lapse the policy if the policyowner complies with the conditions of the reinstatement offer. (Reinstatement is discussed in chapter 8.)

Insurance companies do not want the actions of their agents to be treated as a waiver of those premium payment requirements. Consequently, the provisions discussed that limit an agent's power to modify the terms and conditions of the contract are also applicable to reduce the chance that an insurance agent's actions may inadvertently waive one of those renewal premium requirements.

Making Premium Payments

To Authorized Agent

When payment of a renewal premium is made to an agent who is authorized to receive the payment, no problems are likely as long as the agent promptly forwards the payment to the insurer. As far as the policyowner is concerned, payment to an authorized agent of the insurer is the same as payment to the insurer directly. If the agent retains the premium, the problem of collection lies between the insurer and its agent.

To Unauthorized Agent

Payment of premiums to an insurance agent who is not authorized by the insurer to receive premium payments may or may not be an effective payment of the premium. If the agent delivers the policyowner's payment to the insurance company prior to the due date, the agent's lack of authority will not cause a problem. If the unauthorized agent of the insurer does not properly deliver the policyowner's premium payment, the efficacy of the payment will depend on whether the unauthorized agent had the *apparent authority* to accept the premium payment. Apparent authority is governed by the law of agency and is based on the reasonable belief of a third party (in this case, the policyowner) arising from the conduct of the principal (the insurer). Apparent authority can exist even if there has not been a grant of actual authority. (See chapter 16 for a complete discussion of actual and apparent agency authority.)

To Policyowner's Agent

It should be clear that payment of a premium to an agent of the policyowner (as opposed to an agent of the insurer) does not constitute payment to the insurance company. A transfer from a principal to the principal's agent is not a transfer at all so far as third parties are concerned. In the life insurance industry, this is somewhat complicated by the imprecise usage of the term *agent*. An insurance producer is rarely the agent of the client. Although there are statutory distinctions in the state insurance codes between agents and brokers, those distinctions are not always recognized by the courts. (See chapter 16 for an explanation of agency law as applied to life insurance producers.)

Fixed Premium Payment Dates

Remember that the payment of renewal premiums is a condition precedent to the insurer's obligation to pay the policy benefits. If it were not for the grace period provisions and the nonforfeiture benefits, an unpaid renewal premium would release the insurer from the obligation to pay any benefits under the contract. This raises the issue of what date is applicable for the payment of renewal premiums—the issue date or the policy date.

Issue Date

issue date

The *issue date* is the date on which the contract is prepared by the insurer and sent to the agent for delivery.

Policy Date

If the applicant has paid an advance premium and been given a premium receipt, the policy may be dated as of the date of the premium receipt. This will, of course, be an earlier date than the issue date. The policy date may also be earlier than the issue date if the applicant has asked that the policy be backdated. A policy is backdated, when permitted by state law, to treat the insured as if he or she had purchased the policy at a younger age. It is done to give the insured the benefit of the lower annual premium appropriate to the lower age. State law and insurance company practice often limit the length of time allowed for backdating a policy. Normally, a policy cannot be backdated for more than 6 months before the application date.

When the policy date is used to provide life insurance coverage under a premium receipt, the insured receives a full year's protection for a full year's premium. The insurance protection begins with the date of the premium and receipt and continues until the renewal date. This is not the case with backdated policies, because the applicant pays for insurance protection during the period prior to issuance of the policy when no coverage was provided. Thus the first year's premium does not buy a full year's coverage under a backdated policy.

Example: ***Backdating and the Premium Due Date***

On October 18, 2002, Ajax Insurance Company issued and sent to its agent for delivery an annual premium life insurance policy on the life of John Sloan. To obtain the benefit of a lower premium, John and the agent agreed to have the policy backdated to August 3, 2002. When will the first renewal annual premium be due? August 3, 2003. Note that John paid for 2 1/2 months of coverage (August 3 – October 18, 2002) that he didn't have.

When backdating or premium receipts are not involved and the premium period is measured by the issue date of the policy, there will also be a slight shortage in the length of coverage provided in the first year. This is because the insurance coverage will not be effective from the issue date; it will begin only when the policy has been delivered and the initial premium has been paid. However, the premium payment period will begin to run on the issue date. Some companies have tried to resolve this problem by dating the policy as of a few days after it has been issued to allow time for delivery.

Regardless of which of the above methods is selected, the courts have uniformly supported the insurer's ability to set forth in the contract the due date for the payment of renewal premiums. The necessity for a clearly defined date, which is to be used for calculation of premiums, loan values, paid-up insurance, and nonforfeiture benefits, outweighs the relatively minor

---

Renewal Premium Due Dates

- Due dates are generally set forth in the policy.
- If the date is ambiguous, courts resolve the due date in favor of the policyowner or beneficiary.

---

loss of a few days of coverage. Where there has been any ambiguity in the selection of the appropriate measuring date, the courts have resolved the matter in favor of the policyowner or beneficiary.

Due-Date Provisions

Modern insurance contracts universally provide for the date for payment of renewal premiums. This is defined in the policy, not in the application. The following are some sample policy provisions.

Example 1: The first policy premium is due in advance on the policy date. Thereafter, renewal policy premiums are due at the end of the time interval paid for by the prior premium.

Example 2: The first premium is due on or before delivery of the policy. Subsequent premiums are due on January 1, 200X (the anniversary of the date of issue) and every 12 months thereafter during the premium period in accordance with the above premium table.

Example 3: Premium due dates fall on the same day of the month as the contract date. They occur only while the insured is living. The premium period, which we show on the first page, starts on the contract date. Each premium is to be paid by its due date.

When renewal premiums are not paid, the policyowner is in default on the contract and the policy is in danger of lapsing—which is usually not in the best interests of the insurer, the beneficiary, or the policyowner. Consequently, insurers try to help their policyowners avoid a lapse whenever possible. As briefly mentioned earlier in this chapter, two methods used to avoid lapses are premium payment grace periods and extensions of time for payment of the premium after expiration of the grace period. If these two methods fail to keep the policy in force, insurers normally offer the policyowner the chance to reinstate the policy. (Reinstatement is covered in chapter 8.)

Flexible Premium Policy Due Dates

Universal life and variable universal life policies have flexible renewal premiums with no set amount or date applicable to any single payment. The policy will remain in force as long as the policy cash value (less any potentially applicable surrender charge) is sufficient to cover 2 months of policy charges. Failure to satisfy that condition amounts to a default and starts the grace period. Notices from the insurer will set the default date.

Universal life and variable universal life policies with a target or suggested premium and a no-lapse guarantee do impose a more rigid schedule for premiums. If any of the renewal premium payments are for less than the target premium amount, the no-lapse guarantee expires. In a similar manner, if the renewal premiums are not paid on the schedule anticipated, the guarantee expires. The policy may still be in force if the cash value is adequate to support it but the no-lapse guarantee will be lost.

PREMIUM NOTICES

A few states impose an obligation on the insurer to send premium notices to policyowners in that state. In these states, if an insurer has failed to send the required notice, the policyowner has an additional period of time (as much as 6 months) to pay the premium before the insurer may lapse the policy. During this time, the statutes require the insurer to keep the policy in force.

There is considerable variety in the types of notice statutes, but they generally require that the notice must

- identify the amount of the premium due, the due date, and where it is to be paid
- be sent no less than 15 days and no more than 45 days prior to the due date

Most insurers have established a custom and practice of sending premium notices to their policyowners (even in those states where it is not required by statute). If an insurer ends this practice without notice to the policyowners, a majority of the states will not permit the insurer to lapse a policy for nonpayment of the premiums until after the policyowner has had a chance to adjust to the new practice. If, however, the insurer ends the practice of sending premium notices only after it has informed all policyowners in advance, it will not be precluded from lapsing a policy for nonpayment of premiums after giving the notice.

A few insurers provide in their insurance contracts or other documents that they will send premium notices to their policyowners. If so, they are obligated to give such notice and may not lapse a policy for failure to pay premiums if they have not given the required notice. The following is an example of such a notice for a flexible-premium adjustable life policy.

Example: The first day of the grace period is called the date of default. We will send a notice to your last known address, or to the person named by you to receive this notice, not later than the date of default. The notice will state the due date and the amount of premium due to keep the policy in force.

An insurance company's dealings with a particular policyowner may create an express or implied agreement between the two that the insurer will send a premium notice to that policyowner or will not lapse the policy until after it has sent that policyowner a notice that the premium is unpaid after the due date. If the policyowner can establish the existence of such an express or implied agreement, and that he or she relied upon it, the insurer will be estopped from lapsing the policy until after such notice has been given. However, a policyowner cannot be required to pay a premium on time if he or she does not know the amount that is payable to the insurer. This would be the case for policies where dividends are being used to reduce the premium or for graduated premium policies, to cite two examples.

Grace Period

To avoid lapses, insurance companies will accept a late payment of renewal premiums for a certain number of days after the premium is due. This is known as a *grace period*. Such a provision is generally required by the various state insurance codes, and as a practical matter it is included in most insurance contracts. There is no such thing as a grace period for the initial premium. If the initial premium is not paid on time, the contract does not exist. Three typical grace period provisions are as follows.

Example 1:   There is a grace period of 31 days for you to pay each premium after the first. Insurance will continue during the grace period.

Example 2:   While your policy is in full force, there is a 31-day grace period for the payment of the renewal premium. This means a renewal premium not paid by its due date may be paid in the next 31 days. During the grace period, the policy will stay in full force. If the policy renewal premium is not paid by the end of the grace period, your policy lapses and is no longer in full force as of the due date.

Example 3:   We grant 31 days of grace for paying each premium except the first one. If a premium has not been paid by its due date, the contract will stay in force during its days of grace. If a premium has not been paid when its days of grace are over, the contract will end and have no value, except as we state under Contract Value Options.

Payment of premiums during the grace period can usually be made at any time up until midnight of the 31st day of the grace period. If the 31st day is a nonbusiness day, it is the normal practice to extend the grace period to the next business day.

Extensions of Time

Frequently, insurers will grant an additional period of time for payment of premiums after the grace period has expired. Such an offer is an extremely valuable benefit to the policyowner because the offer is usually not contingent on the insured's providing new evidence of insurability. Because of the risk of adverse selection, granting an extension of time to pay premiums is an entirely discretionary matter with the insurance company. Nevertheless, insurers generally prefer to grant extensions rather than suffer a policy lapse.

Life insurance contracts and applications do not contain a provision granting such an extension of time. In fact, insurers do not even indicate that this possibility exists. As a result, the policyowner does not have a contractual right to the extension or even an expectation that he or she might receive such an offer. Insurers want to avoid the possibility that a policyowner will expect that an extension, once granted, will always be granted, because this may appear to give the policyowner a right to the extension. When an extension is granted and the insurer waives the right to demand new evidence of insurability, the offer will usually advise the policyowner specifically that the waiver being granted at this time does not apply to any future premium.

Typically, a late remittance offer imposes these conditions on the policyowner:

- The policyowner must submit payment of all past-due premiums no later than the date specified in the offer.

- Since the policyowner does not have a contractual right to the extension, there is no grace period following the expiration of the extension.
- The insured must be alive when the policyowner makes the payment.
- Payment must be complete before the offer expires and before the insured dies. This means that payment by check is conditionally accepted, and payment is not complete unless the check is honored by the policyowner's bank.

When the insurer elects to grant an extension, the extension period granted is commonly 2 weeks from the end of the grace period.

METHOD OF PREMIUM PAYMENT

The insurance company is entitled to receive the premium payment in cash, but it may agree to accept any valuable property in lieu of cash, unless prohibited by state law. The payment of premiums by any method other than cash, check, credit, or policy loans is generally prohibited.

The insurance application and contract can prescribe the acceptable methods for payment of the premiums. Usually, however, these documents do not prescribe any particular method. Currently, the most common method is by cash or check.

Payment by an Exchange of Services

At one time it was not unusual for premiums to be paid by an exchange of services. Because this too easily lends itself to rebating, however, some states have prohibited this form of premium payment, and it is no longer a generally accepted practice. (By placing an excessive value on the services rendered, an insurance company could in effect refund a portion of the premium due, thereby providing a rebate.)

Payment on Credit

Promissory notes, which are based on the policyowner's creditworthiness, were once an acceptable form of premium payment for both initial and renewal premiums, but this is no longer an accepted practice. The use of promissory notes to pay the initial premium raised a question of law about the existence of the contract if the promissory note was not honored at its maturity. Some court decisions held that the insurer's unconditional acceptance of the promissory note meant that the premium had been paid even if the policyowner later defaulted on the note. Despite the default, the insurer was not permitted to declare the policy void from inception for nonpayment of the premium. The insurer's only remedy then was to sue the policyowner for payment based on the promissory note. As a result, insurers were unwilling to accept a promissory note unconditionally as payment of a premium.

Today, few insurers will accept a promissory note to pay the initial premium, and it is rare for an insurer to accept a promissory note to pay a renewal premium. If an insurer accepts a promissory note at all, it will accept it only on the condition that the note must be paid when it comes due. If it is not paid at that time, the insurer can treat the premium as unpaid. If the note was taken for the initial premium, the insurer can declare the policy void. If the note was taken for a renewal premium, the default will permit the insurer to lapse the policy for nonpayment of premium.

College Student Financing Plans

Insurance companies used to promote the sale of insurance through financing programs targeted toward college seniors and graduate school students. In effect, the policyowner would borrow money from the insurance company (but not via a policy loan) to purchase insurance from the company. Since it was expected that the policyowner would soon finish his or her education, the loan would be repaid out of the student's anticipated much higher income upon graduation. A key to the success of these college student financing plans was the federal income tax deduction for the interest incurred on the loans. When that deduction was eliminated in a revision to the federal tax law, these plans stopped being attractive to most people and were discontinued even though the financing plans are still permissible by law.

Insurance companies do not usually extend forms of credit to policyowners other than those discussed here. The provisions in the application and the policy that limit the agent's power to amend the contract or to bind the insurer also prevent the agent from extending credit on behalf of the insurance company. It sometimes happens, however, that the insurance agent will pay the premium and extend credit to an applicant or policyowner. In this event, the policy will be in effect and the agent will have a right of action against the policyowner or applicant if the debt to the agent is not paid.

Payment by Cash or Check

Currently, the most common method of premium payment is by check from an individual or a business. (Payment of the premium by cash is common for debit insurance, although that form of insurance is not of great significance today.) Although checks for insurance premiums are readily accepted by insurance companies, they are technically accepted only as conditional payment (somewhat like a promissory note). This means that the actual crediting of the premium payment is conditioned on whether the bank upon which the check is drawn honors the check when it is returned for payment. If the check is not honored by the bank for any reason, the insurance company will treat the premium as being unpaid. Depending on the terms of the contract and the policyowner's payment history, this may result in an automatic premium loan, a reduction in the cash accumulation account, or a lapse of the policy that releases the insurer from its obligations under the contract.

Preauthorized Check Plans

preauthorized check plans

Payment by preauthorized check is a form of payment that is only slightly different from the regular check payment process. *Preauthorized check plans* have been in use for many years. Under these arrangements, the policyowner gives the insurance company the right to order the withdrawal of the premium payment (usually on a monthly basis) directly from the policyowner's checking account. The policyowner also authorizes his or her bank to pay the insurance premiums upon receipt of the insurer's order. (To induce the banks to participate in these plans, there has to be an agreement between the bank and the insurer that obligates the insurer to indemnify the bank for any liability it might incur when making a withdrawal from an account pursuant to an insurer's order.)

Except that the premium is paid without the policyowner's direct participation in each payment, payments by preauthorized check plans are treated just like regular check payments—that is, they are conditional upon actual payment. If the insurer's order under a preauthorized check plan is not honored by the bank, the premium has not been paid.

A company may decide to accept a check as an unconditional payment of the premium. While this rarely occurs, it could result if the company issued a premium receipt in exchange for the policyowner's check that expressly provided that the receipt of the check constituted payment. If the issuing bank subsequently dishonored the check, the insurer could not treat the premium as being unpaid but would have to assert its rights to payment of the debt based on the terms of the unconditional premium receipt. However, the presumption is that acceptance of a check is conditioned upon the check's being cashed. Moreover, most premium receipts are conditional and do not permit this consequence. The language in this premium receipt for the initial premium completely avoids the problem:

> This receipt will provide no life insurance protection of any type and the premium will be refunded to the applicant … if any check or draft used to pay the required premium is not honored when first presented for payment.

When a check is offered in payment of a premium, the insurer has an obligation to promptly deposit the check. If the bank does not honor the check, the insurance company has an obligation to promptly advise the policyowner and to return the dishonored check. This is in the best interests of both the insurer and the policyowner because it gives the policyowner a chance to make a proper premium payment before the grace period and any extensions of time for payment expiration. If a premium check is given to the insurer before the due date, but is dishonored after the grace period has expired because of the insurer's delay in presenting it for payment, the insurer may be required to give additional time for payment or to perform its obligations under the contract if the insured dies.

Electronic Transfers

An electronic funds transfer is a form of payment that shares some of the characteristics of both a cash and a check payment. In some cases, a policyowner may use a telephone or computer modem connection to authorize a transfer of funds to his or her insurer for each premium payment as the premium comes due. In other situations, the policyowner might sign an authorization form directing the bank to automatically transfer the funds to the insurer at specified intervals (usually monthly). This latter method is similar to the preauthorized check plan that is discussed above. Regardless of whether a preauthorization form is signed, this method also has the characteristics of a cash transaction: If the money is available in the policyowner's account to be electronically transferred on the specified date, the transaction is complete and the premium paid. If the money is not available, the premium has not been paid and there is no question of a conditional payment before a check clears.

Payment by Automatic Premium Loan

As a protection to the insurer and the policyowner against an inadvertent lapse of the policy, most cash value life insurance policy contracts have an automatic premium loan provision. Some provisions are short and simple, as shown in the first example below; others are not, as shown in the second example.

Example 1:   Any premium not paid by the end of its grace period will be paid by charging it as a policy loan if you requested it in writing and the maximum loan value is sufficient to cover the premium.

Example 2:   If you so elect, premiums will be paid automatically by policy loans. Any original election is in the application. If you have not elected in the application to have automatic premium loans, then you may so elect by writing to us at any time prior to the end of the grace period of any premium in default. You may revoke this election at any time by writing to us. We will send you a written notice of any automatic premium loan with the policy loan interest rate. This notice will be sent within 45 days of the date of such loan. We make these loans only if there is sufficient loan value to pay at least a quarterly premium, plus interest. The loan is made on the last day of the grace period. Interest is charged from the premium due date.

Because it keeps the policy in force, the automatic premium loan also retains any riders, such as accidental death and disability. If the policy were to lapse, such riders would not be continued in force under the nonforfeiture options. This provision is also better for the policyowner than attempting to reinstate a lapsed policy because the automatic premium loan does not require new evidence of insurability. On the other hand, like policy loans in general, the automatic premium loan reduces the policy's cash values and increases the cost of maintaining the policy by the amount of the additional interest owed to the insurer. This reduction in policy value may cause the policy to terminate early.

Other features of the automatic premium loan provision are well summarized as follows:

The automatic premium loan provision is valid and indeed is required to be offered in at least one state (Rhode Island). It is not in conflict with the nonforfeiture statutes. The provision applies only if the loan value of the policy equals or exceeds the premium then due. The insurer is not required to change the method of payment to another method such as quarterly or monthly, in which case the amount due would be less. The automatic premium loan provision, once elected, continues in effect even though the policy is assigned and even though the assignee has no notice of the premium due. The assignee cannot complain if the effect of the loan is to reduce the net cash value available on surrender. The Bankruptcy Reform Act of 1978 recognizes the right of the insurer to continue to deduct premiums under the automatic premium loan provision even after the insured [policyowner] is declared a bankrupt.[1]

Payment by Dividends

Life insurance policies that pay dividends offer the policyowner a variety of options for the use of that dividend. The application for participating policies has a section where the applicant is asked to select the dividend option he or she desires. The four basic dividend options are to

- purchase paid-up additions
- reduce the premium
- pay to the policyowner in cash
- accumulate by the insurer at interest

If the policyowner elects the second dividend option, the insurer will use the dividend to pay all or a portion of the premium and send the policyowner a premium notice for any balance due. Some companies do not offer all of these options. These companies generally give the policyowner the choice between taking the dividend in cash or using it to purchase paid-up additional insurance. Regardless of the number of options, if the policyowner does not choose one, the insurer will select one by default. Most insurers will not select the option that uses the dividend to pay premiums but will apply dividends to the purchase of paid-up additions.

Many insurance companies offer a fifth dividend option, which applies the dividend to purchase one-year term insurance in varying amounts (for example, equal to the policy cash value, the face amount of the policy, or the total premium). Any dividend amount left over after being used for the fifth dividend option is applied as directed by the policyowner under one of the first four dividend options. The alternatives under the fifth dividend option were created to maintain the death benefit when it was expected that the policyowner would be using policy loans to finance the policy and thereby reducing the death benefit by the amount of the policy loans.

The policyowner may change the dividend election under whatever terms the insurance company prescribes in the policy. Companies generally require only that the policyowner sign and deliver a written notice of the desired change to the insurer's home office.

The dividend election gives the policyowner a contractual right that the insurance company is obligated to respect once that right has been exercised. This means that if the policyowner has made a dividend election (for example, has told the insurer to send the dividends on his or her policy to the policyowner in cash), the insurance company cannot elect to use a dividend to pay premiums even if the grace period is about to expire for nonpayment of premium. This is so even if the dividend would be more than sufficient to pay the premium and keep the policy in force. If the policyowner has not selected a dividend option, however, and the insurer has dividends sufficient to pay the past-due premium, it has been held that the insurer must apply those dividends to the premium to prevent a forfeiture.

Even if the insurer may (or must) use the dividends to pay a premium, the insurer is not obligated to make a partial payment on the premium due unless it has previously agreed to do so. In these circumstances, if the dividend available for premium payment is sufficient to pay the premium under the mode then in effect (monthly, quarterly, or annually), it will be used for that purpose. If it is insufficient to meet the payment due under the current mode, the insurer is under no obligation to change the mode to match the available dividend.

Prepaid Premiums

Under some circumstances policyowners want to pay two or more annual premiums in advance of the date on which they are due. While insurers are willing to accept such advance premium payments, some limitations are imposed and several issues arise that must be resolved.

The normal industry practice is to accept prepaid premiums for up to 20 years in advance. The first issue to resolve is the amount of the discount to give for the premiums paid in advance of the due date. The discounted prepaid premium payable will be defined in the receipt from the insurer and will represent the present value (at an interest rate the insurer selects) of the stream of premium payments scheduled to be paid under the policy. The company will usually specify the interest rate to be paid on the prepaid funds, the tax consequences to the policyowner, when and how any of the money may be withdrawn, and what happens to the money if the policy is surrendered or if the insured dies during the period for which premiums were prepaid.

RETURN OF UNEARNED PREMIUMS

It can happen that an insurer may be in possession of premium payments that it is not entitled to keep. The general rules are quite clear:

- If an insurer has assumed the risk under the contract, the entire annual premium is earned and may be retained.
- If the insurer has not assumed the risk, it is not entitled to retain any portion of the premium.

There are no exceptions to the first rule; there are numerous exceptions to the second rule.

The first exception to the general rule is for marketing purposes. Although the insurer is entitled to a full annual premium in advance for assuming the risk, most policyowners do not pay an annual premium. It is far more common for policyowners to pay premiums on a quarterly or monthly basis. When a policyowner is making monthly premium payments and the insured dies early in a policy year, it is sometimes hard for the beneficiary to understand why the insurer is entitled to reduce the death benefit by the remaining amount of that year's unpaid premiums. Consequently, many insurance companies no longer exercise that right. (This concession is related to the circumstance in which a policy is purchased and two or more annual premiums are paid in advance.)

It is sometimes the case, when a life insurance policy is purchased on an infant, that as many as 20 annual premiums are paid in advance. Premiums paid in advance of the year in which they are due are unearned by the insurance company. Thus if the insured dies before those premiums have been earned, the insurer must return the premiums. Similarly, when premiums are paid after the insured has died, those premiums are unearned and must be returned.

The remaining exceptions are as follows:

- Most life insurance contracts include a *free-look* provision, which gives the policyowner a certain number of days (usually 10, but sometimes 20) to examine the contract. If the policy is returned within that time period, the insurer will refund all premiums paid.
- If the insured commits suicide during the exclusion period, the premiums paid by the policyowner will be returned. The insurer will have the right to reduce the refund by the amount of any policy loans plus interest outstanding at the insured's death.
- If the contract is rescinded based on a misrepresentation by the policyowner/insured, the premiums paid to that time will be refunded. As with the suicide refund, the insurer has the right to reduce the refund by the amount of any outstanding policy loans plus interest.
- If the policy was purchased by a minor, the applicable state law may give him or her the right to disaffirm the contract and have the premiums refunded. In some jurisdictions, the insurance company has the right to retain the cost of the coverage provided to the minor prior to the date the contract is disaffirmed.

Note that a revocable beneficiary who pays premiums (based on a promise from the policyowner that he or she will receive the proceeds) may be entitled to a portion of the death benefit equal to the premiums paid, even if the policyowner names someone else as beneficiary. This is not a refund of premiums in the same sense as the other exceptions discussed in this chapter. It is more accurately described as a redirection of the death benefit.

A collateral assignee is also entitled, under most collateral assignment agreements, to a portion of the death benefit equal to any premiums paid. This should not be confused with a refund of premiums either. It is also better described as a redirection of the death benefit.

CHAPTER REVIEW

Answers to the review questions and the self-test questions can be found in the Supplement.

Key Terms

conclusive presumption   issue date
rebuttable presumption   preauthorized check
renewal premiums   plans

Review Questions

1. What fundamental acts by the applicant-policyowner are required to create a life insurance policy?

2. Describe the conditional nature (with respect to premiums) of the insurer's promise to pay the policy benefits.

3. Describe the rights created by payment of premiums by someone other than the policyowner when the payor is

    a. the insured
    b. a revocable beneficiary
    c. a trustee
    d. an irrevocable beneficiary
    e. an assignee

4. Describe the factors that determine whether a trustee is responsible for paying premiums on a policy.

5. Explain why current life insurance policies do not include a provision acknowledging receipt of the initial premium payment.

6. Describe what steps life insurers have taken to inform purchasers that life insurance agents do not have authority to alter the terms of the contract.

7. Explain the difference between the majority and minority courts with regard to conditionality of renewal premiums.

8. Describe the mailbox rule regarding renewal premiums.

9. Indicate three ways that policyowners may be able to keep coverage from lapsing without paying renewal premiums with out-of-pocket funds.

10. Discuss the effectiveness of making premiums payments to
    a. an authorized agent
    b. an unauthorized agent
    c. the policyowner's agent

11. Explain why the policy date may be different from the issue date.

12. What determines the due date of renewal premiums?

13. Identify two methods insurers use to help policyowners avoid lapses.

14. Describe the general requirements found in the few state statutes that mandate that insurers send premium notices.

15. What are the consequences of ending a practice of sending premium notices without prior notice of the changed procedure being sent to policyowners?

16. What is the normal practice if the last day of the grace period falls on a nonbusiness day?

17. Indicate why insurers may grant extensions of time for payment of premiums and what that usually implies about evidence of insurability.

18. Indicate the conditions typically imposed by a late premium extension offer.

19. Explain why insurers are reluctant to accept promissory notes for renewal premium payments.

20. Why have college student financing plans been discontinued by most life insurers?

21. Why are checks accepted as conditional payment of premiums?

22. Indicate the similarities and the differences between preauthorized check plans and electronic fund transfers.

23. Describe premium payment by automatic premium loans, and indicate the limitations thereby imposed on coverage.

24. Describe the different ways policyowners can direct that policy dividends be used.

25. Indicate how failure to select a dividend option changes the insurance company's responsibility for applying policy dividends to keep the policy in force.

26. Indicate the general rules regarding whether an insurance company is entitled to keep premium payments.

Self-Test Questions

T F 1. If the insured and the policyowner are not the same person, payment of the premiums by the insured does not give the insured any rights in the insurance contract whatever.

T F 2. The payment of premiums by an insured on a policy owned by someone else cannot trigger gift or income taxes.

T F 3. If the trustee does not own the policy and is merely a revocable beneficiary of the policy in trust, there is usually a duty imposed on the trustee to pay the premiums.

T F 4. The terms of the trust define the trustee's responsibilities with respect to all property interests the trustee possesses on behalf of the trust.

T F 5. Policyowners rarely assign life insurance policies.

T F 6. The assignee of a life insurance policy has no duty or obligation to pay premiums.

T F 7. Assignees under the ABA collateral assignment form cannot recover any premium payments paid by the assignee to keep the policy in force.

T F 8. If a life insurance policy contains language acknowledging receipt of the first premium, there is a conclusive presumption that the premium has actually been paid.

T F 9. A policy that acknowledges receipt of the initial premium will bar the insurance company from showing that the premium has not been paid.

T F 10. Renewal premium payments mailed to the insurer sufficiently in advance of the due date will be deemed paid on time even if the mail is delivered late.

T F 11. Payment of a premium to an agent of the policyowner (as opposed to an agent of the insurer) does not constitute payment to the insurance company.

T F 12. A policyowner cannot be required to pay a premium on time if the amount payable is unknown.

T F 13. The grace period does not apply to the initial premium.

T F 14. There is no legal requirement that life insurance policies contain a grace period provision.

T F 15. Policyowners have a contractual right to make late premium payments after the end of the grace period.

T F 16. The payment of premiums by any method other than cash, check, credit, dividends, or policy loans is generally prohibited.

T   F   17. Some states prohibit exchange of services as an acceptable form of premium payment.

T   F   18. The most common method of premium payment is by check.

T   F   19. Unconditional acceptance of a check for premium payment prevents the insurer from treating the premium as unpaid if the bank dishonors the check.

T   F   20. If a premium check is given to the insurer before the due date, but is dishonored after the grace period has expired because of the insurer's delay in presenting it for payment, the insurer will be able to treat the premium as unpaid.

T   F   21. Paying premiums by use of automatic premium loans increases the cost of maintaining the policy.

T   F   22. When dividends are being applied to pay premiums and the dividend amount is adequate to cover only a monthly premium even though the premium mode is annual, the insurer must change the premium mode to match the available dividend.

T   F   23. Premiums paid after the insured has died must be returned by the life insurance company.

NOTE

1. Buist M. Anderson, *Anderson on Life Insurance* (Boston: Little Brown and Company, 1991), pp. 296–297.

10

Rights and Remedies

Burke A. Christensen

Learning Objectives

An understanding of the material in this chapter should enable the student to

10-1. Discuss the common meaning and the legal meaning of *property*.

10-2. Distinguish real property law from personal property law.

10-3. Discuss the effect of marriage and divorce on property rights in common law states.

10-4. Discuss the effect of marriage and divorce on property rights in community-property-law states.

10-5. Explain the management of marital property in community-property jurisdictions.

10-6. Describe the ownership of life insurance in community-property jurisdictions.

10-7. Explain the effect of exoneration statutes in community-property jurisdictions.

10-8. Discuss the ownership interests of policyowners' creditors.

10-9. Describe the beneficial ownership interest resulting from the wrongful killing of the insured.

10-10. Understand the difference between remedies at law and equitable remedies.

10-11. Discuss the different types of equitable remedies.

Chapter Outline

The first section of this chapter covers property rights in life insurance contracts. The second section deals with remedies available at law and at equity for the violation of a party's rights in a life insurance contract.

PROPERTY RIGHTS IN LIFE INSURANCE

The term *property* is familiar to us all. We define things as being "your property" or "my property." As we shall see in this chapter, the term property has both a common meaning and a specialized legal meaning. The common definition of the term generally refers to tangible things such as land, cars, money, or securities. The legal definition, which includes the common usage, gives a broader meaning to the term. It focuses on whether one possesses the right to use tangible and intangible things.

property

> *property:* the exclusive right of ownership; the right to possess, enjoy, transfer, or dispose of a thing or an interest

It is easy to demonstrate why the common definition of property is insufficient even for everyday use. For example, a stock certificate is a tangible thing and can be described as a piece of property. Nevertheless, if it is lost or destroyed, the ownership interest in the corporation that the stock certificate represents is unaffected. This is because the ownership interest in the corporation is an intangible property right that is independent of the existence of the stock certificate.

Consider a stock option as another example. One can possess a stock option, and the option is clearly a property right that can be owned or transferred. Since it exists independently of the document that describes it, an option is an intangible property right. One may also possess a property right as the result of an oral contract. In this case there might not be any tangible evidence of the existence of the property right. Nevertheless, this lack of physical evidence does not eliminate the right possessed.

Is a life insurance policy a piece of property? Or is the life insurance contract merely tangible written evidence of an intangible right to property? Of course, the answer is that the life insurance policy is both. The contract is a piece of property, and it is also evidence of intangible property rights.

We have already indicated that a basic understanding of the laws concerning contracts in general is fundamental to an understanding of the unique characteristics of life insurance contracts. The same is true for the laws governing property. To clearly understand the unique property rights various parties hold in life insurance policies, it is necessary to understand the basic rules of property law. The starting point is the basic principle of property law, that the term property does not refer only to things that we can see and touch. In the language of the law, "property" refers to the collection of ownership rights that permit people, corporations, and trusts to use both tangible and intangible things.

The law of property is divided into two major subdivisions: the law of real property and the law of personal property.

Real Property Law

real property

The law of *real property*, or real estate, is concerned with the land and those things that are a part of or attached to the land. Natural resources such as minerals, crops, and forests are a part of the land. Houses, dams, factories, and bridges are attached to the land. As long as these items of property are a part of or attached to the land, they are subject to the real property laws. When any property is separated from the land, it becomes *personal property*.

personal property

An item of personal property can become subject to the real property laws. For example, when it is in the factory, a furnace is an item of personal property. When it has been installed in someone's home, it is described as a fixture and is assumed to be part of the real estate. As long as it is attached to the land as a fixture or has not been legally removed from the land, it passes with the title to the land.

Personal Property Law

Personal property is any property that is not land or not attached to the land. There are two types of personal property, and these two divisions recognize the difference between tangible personal property and intangible personal property. There are no such distinctions in real property law.

Tangible personal property is sometimes referred to in the law as a *chose ("show-zee") in possession*. The word "chose" is French for "thing," and the term is used to describe all of those types of tangible personal property that a person may physically possess—computers, clothes, tennis rackets, and photographs, for example.

chose in action

Intangible personal property is sometimes referred to in the law as a *chose in action*. Since this type of property is intangible, it is not really a thing. It is instead a right of action that exists only in the law. An "action" is another word for a lawsuit; therefore a chose in action is a right to do something, usually evidenced by a legal document and enforceable by the law. Mortgages, notes, deeds, and all types of contracts represent intangible personal property rights and are included within the term "chose in action."

A life insurance policy is a chose in action and represents the intangible personal property rights that are described in the policy. The insuring clause on the face page of life insurance contracts, as in the following three different examples, sets forth a broad statement of those rights.

Example 1:   We (the insurance company) agree with you (the policyowner) to pay the benefits of this policy according to its provisions.

Example 2:   The XYZ Insurance Company agrees, subject to the conditions and provisions of this policy, to pay the sum insured to the beneficiary if the insured's death occurs while this policy is in full force, and to provide the other benefits, rights, and privileges of the policy.

Example 3:   ABC Life Assurance Company agrees, in accordance with the provisions of this policy, to pay to the beneficiary the death proceeds upon receipt at the principal office of due proof of the insured's death prior to the maturity date. Further, the company agrees to pay the surrender value to the owner if the insured is alive on the maturity date.

These general provisions and the more specific provisions within the policy language define the intangible personal property rights of the policyowner and the beneficiary. Some property rights are inherent in the law and do not need to be conferred by the policy. Transferability of property is one of these. Unless parties agree to the contrary, the law assumes that a person may freely assign or transfer any property interest that he or she possesses. Therefore, as with most items of real or personal property, the owner may transfer the life insurance contract by sale, absolute assignment, or gift. To protect the rights of the insurer, the transferee, and the policyowner, the contract will prescribe the methods by which such transfers must be effected.

Life Insurance Ownership May Be Transferred By

- sale
- absolute assignment
- gift

There are at least two other special circumstances when ownership rights in an insurance policy may be transferred. The first is as a result of a divorce. Life insurance protection on either ex-spouse is a valuable asset for the benefit of the children of the marriage or to ensure the continuation of support payments beyond the death of the payor spouse. Thus insurance policies are frequently transferred as a part of a divorce settlement. The second circumstance occurs when the insured is not the policyowner and the policyowner predeceases the insured. This can happen when a parent owns a policy on a minor child or when policies are owned by business partners on each other's lives for the purpose of a cross-purchase buy-sell agreement. In either case, when the policyowner dies, the policy generally passes to another person pursuant to the applicable intestacy laws or under the provisions of the deceased policyowner's will. It is also possible that a contingent or successor owner will have been designated in the policy by the initial policyowner. If so, such a designation will take precedence and the policy will pass to the successor owner.

A policy beneficiary usually has no ownership or property rights in a life insurance policy because the beneficiary is not a party to the contract. A revocable beneficiary has nothing more than an expectancy that he or she might receive the death benefits if the beneficiary designation is unchanged and the policy remains in force until the insured's death. If that expectancy comes to pass, then the property right that the beneficiary possesses *at the insured's death* is a perfect example of a chose in action. The beneficiary then possesses a right to the proceeds that is enforceable by a court in an action at law.

An irrevocable beneficiary has some limited additional rights prior to the insured's death, but his or her right to the death benefit is still only an expectancy that will be extinguished if the policy is lapsed. In some jurisdictions an irrevocable beneficiary's consent must be obtained before a policy loan may be obtained, or the policy may be surrendered.

Among the many rights that the life insurance contract specifically confers upon the policyowner are the right to surrender the policy, to assign it to a third party as collateral for a loan, to designate and change the beneficiary, to obtain policy loans (if the policy has a cash value or cash accumulation account), to select and change dividend options (for participating policies), to select and change investment options (for variable policies), and to select settlement options. In some jurisdictions and for some policies, policyowners are now permitted to claim a portion of the death benefit in advance of the date of death if the insured is diagnosed as terminally ill and is expected to die within a short period of time (2 years or less).

In most circumstances, the language of the life insurance contract and the general principles of contract or property law determine the extent of a

---

Life Insurance Policyowner Rights

- Surrender the policy.
- Assign the policy.
- Designate and change the beneficiary.
- Obtain a policy loan (if policy has cash value).
- Select and change dividend options (if policy is participating).
- Select and change investment options (if policy is variable).
- Select settlement options.

---

person's ownership interest in a life insurance policy. However, there are three circumstances that may permit persons who are not parties to the contract to acquire an ownership interest in the policy benefits. The first two relate to the marital status and financial condition of the policyowner. The third arises when the named beneficiary murders the insured and another person acquires the murderer's interest in the policy proceeds.

Effect of Marriage and Divorce on Ownership Interests

With respect to property law, the 50 states of the United States and the District of Columbia are divided into two quite different systems of law: *community property* and *common law property*. The common law system is the general rule in the United States. It is based on the common law as it was brought to this country from England. The common law was developed over the centuries as cases were decided by the courts of England.

The community-property law system was brought to this country from France and Spain. Since the English common law is the basis of our country's legal system, community-property laws exist only where they have been enacted into law by the state legislatures.

Nine states are considered community-property states. Eight of them form a line along the southern and western border of the United States. From east to west, they are Louisiana, Texas, New Mexico, Arizona, California, Nevada, Washington, and Idaho (note that Oregon is not a community-property state). In addition, Wisconsin has enacted a form of community-property law known as marital property. Although it has not been enacted in any other state, the National Conference of Commissioners on Uniform State Laws has created a model law known as the Uniform Marital Property Act.

Common Law System

common law system

The *common law system* is the law in the 41 other states and in the District of Columbia. Under the common law system, a policyowner's marital status generally has no direct or automatic effect upon the ownership interests in an insurance policy. A policyowner may marry or divorce, and unless some specific affirmative action is taken with respect to the policy, it will remain the sole property of the policyowner. The marriage does not give the other spouse any interest in the ownership rights of the policy, and it does not give him or her any interest in the proceeds. Furthermore, if a policyowner in a common law jurisdiction designates "my husband, Robert" as the beneficiary of a life insurance policy on her life, it is the general, but not unanimous, rule that Robert will remain her beneficiary even if the parties are subsequently divorced. In one state, Michigan, if the divorce decree does not change a beneficiary designation from the ex-spouse to someone else, then the statute mandates that the policy is payable to the estate of the insured until the policyowner designates a new beneficiary.

Community-Property Law System

community-property law system

The *community-property law system* is quite different from the common law system. And, in fact, the differences among the community-property states are almost as wide as the difference between the common law jurisdictions and community-property law jurisdictions. Be cautious in applying the community-property rules discussed in this chapter, because some community-property states apply rules that are not consistent with the general rules described herein. Thus, students of life insurance as it is affected by the community-property laws need to examine the law of the appropriate state closely. A survey of the general principles of community-property law is not sufficient.

The impact of the community-property legal system, though adopted by a minority of jurisdictions, has been considerable on the entire country. For example, the estate tax marital deduction and the income tax joint return arose from a necessity to equalize treatment of income and property between common law jurisdiction taxpayers and community-property jurisdiction taxpayers.

The community-property laws are applicable to all residents of community-property jurisdictions. If a married couple resides in a common law jurisdiction and acquires personal property while visiting a community-property state, the community-property laws are inapplicable. Similarly, if a married couple residing in a common law jurisdiction acquires realty in a community-property law jurisdiction, it does not normally become community property. Title to that property will be held in whatever manner the parties desire, just as if the property was located in a common law state.

Ours is a very mobile society, and married couples may move their residences from community-property jurisdictions to common law jurisdictions and back during their marriage. The effect of these moves between jurisdictions is beyond the scope of this discussion. Life underwriters, however, need to be aware of the potential complications such relocations can cause and must be able to assist their clients in obtaining competent advice.

The fundamental principle of community property is that each spouse has an undivided one-half interest in all property acquired by the husband and wife during the marriage. Like all fundamental rules, there are some exceptions. The basic exception is that property acquired by one of the spouses by gift, under the laws of intestacy, or as a beneficiary of someone's will, is the separate property of the acquiring spouse and does not become part of the community property.

Note that any property acquired before the marriage or after the divorce by either spouse is not considered to be community property. Separate property brought into the marriage generally retains its status as separate property during the marriage. The general rule is also that property acquired with separate property funds is separate property. Similarly, property acquired with community funds is normally community property regardless of whether title is taken only in one spouse's name. Finally, property acquired by a mixture of community and separate property funds is usually treated as if it is partially community property and partially separate property in the same ratio as the mixed funds that were used to acquire the property.

Termination of the Marriage

If the marriage ends by either divorce or annulment, the marital community is dissolved and the marital property acquired by the spouses will be divided by the court if the parties cannot reach an amicable agreement between themselves. This division of property will include the community-property life insurance policies. The general rule is that the cash value of community-property life insurance policies is a community asset and is subject to division between the parties during a divorce.

In non-community-property jurisdictions, divorce does not have an automatic impact on specific items of property such as a life insurance policy. The marital estate will be divided between the parties as they may agree or as a court may direct. Generally, the divorce does not change any beneficiary designations, unless the divorce decree or property settlement agreement so provides. Divorce decrees frequently require one spouse to maintain a life insurance policy for the benefit of the other spouse or the children of the marriage.

Sometimes the spouse will violate the terms of the divorce decree or agreement and designate someone else as the beneficiary of the policy's proceeds. If this happens, two parties will assert a claim to the death benefits. If the insurer pays the claim of the party appropriately designated by the policyowner without knowledge of the mandate of the divorce decree, the insurer will almost certainly be protected against a later claim from the other party. If the insurer receives both claims prior to making any payment, it is not the insurer's responsibility to determine who has the better claim. In this circumstance, the insurer will pay the claim to the proper court clerk and file an interpleader action asking the court to determine who is to be paid.

The death of a spouse also terminates the community-property relationship. Since the spouses each possessed an undivided one-half interest in the marital estate, the surviving spouse is entitled to one-half of all the community property. While he or she is not entitled to any specific community-property asset, the surviving spouse is entitled to receive property equal in value to one-half of the community property. The other half of the community property passes under the deceased spouse's will or, if there is no will, under the state's intestacy laws. If the deceased spouse owned any separate property, that property does not automatically pass to the surviving spouse. Just as in a common law state, separate property passes under the deceased's will or by intestacy.

Death of the spouse in a common law state terminates the marriage, and the property of the deceased spouse passes by will or intestacy. Assets held by the couple in some form of joint ownership (joint tenancy or tenancy by the entireties) pass by operation of law to the surviving tenant, or if held as tenancy in common, pass to the heirs and beneficiaries of the deceased spouse.

Management of Community Property

Under the English common law it was once said that, "in marriage the husband and wife were one; and the husband was that one." That is, of course, no longer the law or the practice. Under the community-property law, there was a similar principle that in marriage the husband and wife created a marital community and the husband had the right to manage that community. With only a few exceptions, he did not have to obtain the consent of his wife to use or dispose of the marital property. That, too, is no longer the case, although it lasted much longer in the community-property legal system than it did under the common law.

The general rule in the community-property jurisdictions today is that each spouse has the right and power to manage or dispose of the marital property. This right is not unlimited. For example, one spouse may not make a gift of community property to a third party without the consent of the other spouse. Also, a spouse may not act in a manner intended to defraud the other spouse of his or her interest in the community property. These rules have a direct impact on life insurance policies, because they preclude a spouse from designating a third party as the beneficiary of a community-property life insurance policy without the consent of the other spouse.

New statutes in the community-property jurisdictions impose a high degree of care for each other upon the spouses as they deal with their community-property assets. These laws, where enacted, now require each spouse to act as a fiduciary for the other when managing the marital property.

Life Insurance Community Property

A life insurance policy or its proceeds, like any other asset, may be either community or separate property. In the normal case, the ownership status of an item of property as either community or separate is clearly determined when it is acquired, and that status usually does not change over time. That is not always the case with a life insurance policy. To further complicate the matter, most insurance contracts appear on their face to be the sole property of the owner identified on the policy and the application. The impact of the community-property laws is such that a policy that seems to the insurer to be the sole property of one person may actually be the community property of a married couple. If so, a person who is not identified on the policy or the application as an owner is entitled to exercise ownership rights in the policy. Furthermore, a person who is identified as the sole owner on the application and the policy will not be entitled to freely exercise those ownership rights because of the spouse's community-property interest. Finally, a policy that started out as solely separate or community property may over time acquire the characteristics of the other type of property. Let's examine how the community-property laws affect life insurance policies.

If the policy is acquired before the marriage, it is separate property. However, the community-property states do not have a uniform rule on whether it remains separate property after the marriage. If, after the marriage, premiums are paid entirely with separate funds, the policy will remain the separate property of the acquiring spouse. In some jurisdictions, the policy will remain the separate property of the acquiring spouse even if the premiums are paid out of community funds after the marriage. In other jurisdictions, as community funds are used to pay the premiums, the policy becomes a mixed community and separate asset in proportion to the ratio of community and separate funds used to purchase the policy.

If a policy is acquired during the marriage but is paid for entirely with separate funds, the general rule is that it will be held as separate property. If it is acquired during the marriage and paid for with community funds, it will normally be the community property of both spouses.

Example: ***Separate and Community Property***

Eric owns a $250,000 annual premium life insurance policy on his own life with his mother designated as beneficiary. Now Eric marries Nancy and moves into her home in a community-property state. Eric and Nancy divorce soon thereafter, and Nancy claims that half of the cash value of the policy belongs to her. Is she correct? Maybe, depending on how the premiums were paid after the marriage. If from Eric's separate property funds, Nancy is probably out of luck. But if they were paid with community-property funds, Nancy may have a valid case.

If a policy is the community property of both spouses, and one spouse takes an action that transfers that property to a third party, the nontransferring spouse is entitled to recover his or her interest in that property. This principle of community-property law can cause difficulties for insurance companies if a community-property policy is assigned, its cash values withdrawn, or its beneficiary designation changed without the cooperation of both spouses.

To protect themselves from having to pay policy values twice, insurance contracts contain language such as this excerpt from a provision governing policy assignments: "Any rights created by the assignment will be subject to any payments made or actions taken by [the insurer] before the change is recorded. [The insurer] will not be responsible for the validity of any assignment." The purpose of this language is to permit the insurer to take actions with respect to the policy as directed by the policyowner named in the application. Similar language exists in the provision governing beneficiary changes.

Exoneration Statutes

exoneration statutes

State laws known as *exoneration statutes* give insurers further protection. These statutes, which are unique to community-property jurisdictions, are a necessity to permit policyowners in community-property states and insurers to take action efficiently on insurance contracts. Exoneration statutes state that if an insurer pays insurance proceeds or other policy benefits in accordance with the terms of the contract (including the application), the insurer will not be held liable if an unknown party asserts a community-property interest in the policy of which the insurer had no prior knowledge. This means that if the recorded owner of a policy in a community-property state changes the beneficiary, assigns the policy, obtains a policy loan, or takes any other action with respect to the policy, the insurer is entitled to assume that the owner has the full and complete authority to take the action.

Of course, if the insurer has been given actual notice that the policy is the community property of two people, the exoneration statute will provide no protection if the insurer acts on the direction of only the recorded owner. Without the protection of exoneration statutes, insurers would always require both spouses to consent to any action taken with respect to any policy if the insurer thought that there was a possibility of the spouse's later asserting a community-property interest in the policy.

Ownership Interests of Creditors

Under the law, a general creditor acquires no interest in any specific property of the debtor. This includes life insurance policy values and death benefits. A secured creditor is one who has an interest in a specific piece of property that the creditor may claim if the debt is not paid. Life insurance is a valuable piece of property that may become the security for a loan.

A policy loan is an example of a secured interest. The policyowner is permitted to borrow money from the insurance company in any amount up to a fixed percentage of the policy's cash value. The policy cash values themselves are not borrowed but serve as the policyowner's collateral for the loan.

With considerable variation in the law from state to state, life insurance policy values and proceeds receive differing levels of protection from general creditors in the event of the insured's bankruptcy.

Ownership Interest Due to Wrongful Killing of the Insured

The final circumstance in which a third party may acquire an interest in an insurance policy outside of the terms of the application and contract is when the insured is killed by the named beneficiary. The law is universally clear that a beneficiary who kills the insured will not be permitted to obtain the policy's death benefits. This prohibition extends beyond the killer to apply also to those who could claim the proceeds through him or her (for example, those who would take the killer's place under the intestacy laws).

Not every type of killing of the insured by a beneficiary will initiate the exclusion. The general rule is that the killing must be both wrongful and intentional or the beneficiary's claim will not be denied. Thus, the rule would not disqualify a beneficiary who is insane when he or she kills the insured. This is because our legal system assumes that the insane are incapable of forming the necessary intent. Similarly, a killing that is accidental or involuntary will not cause a disqualification if it can be established that the killing was not intentional. A killing in self-defense will not give rise to the exclusion because, even though the beneficiary may have intended to kill the insured at the time, such killings are not wrongful.

Example: ***Insured Killed by Beneficiary***

Gene carries $500,000 of insurance on his own life with Claire, his "significant other," as the beneficiary. One night, in a drunken rage, Gene begins to beat Claire fiercely. In self-defense, Claire stabs Gene and kills him. Although she killed the insured, she is entitled to the policy proceeds.

Although the U.S. Constitution gives everyone the right to a speedy trial, frequently there can be considerable delay between killing an insured and the ultimate determination of whether the beneficiary is guilty of a wrongful and intentional killing. To effect payment, the insurer will attempt to get a release from the accused beneficiary. If this is not possible, the insurer will normally pay the proceeds to an appropriate court and file an interpleader action asking the court to determine the identity of the proper beneficiary.

If the primary beneficiary is precluded from receiving the proceeds of the policy, the insurer must decide on another recipient. If the policyowner has designated a contingent or secondary beneficiary, the majority rule is that the contingent beneficiary is entitled to the proceeds. Some states have enacted statutes to support this rule of law. These statutes also generally provide that if there is no contingent beneficiary, the proceeds are payable to the insured's estate or to the insured's heirs. Case law in a few states ignores the designation of a contingent beneficiary and awards the proceeds to the insured's estate.

REMEDIES

When a person believes that he or she has been injured by another person, our court system gives the injured party an opportunity to seek a recovery for the damages incurred. The courts also permit lawsuits designed to force people to do something. Under the common law of England (which is the source of most of our law) there were two separate ways for this to be done: through the courts of law or through the courts of equity. Today these two separate court systems have been merged into one system, but the separate remedies remain.

remedy at law

action at law

Remedy at Law

The first legal solution was to file an *action at law*. Using this method, an aggrieved party would claim that a person was bound by a contract to do a certain thing that had not been done. The plaintiff would ask the court to

action in equity

require the other party to pay money damages for his or her failure to perform the required duties under the contract. If the court concluded that the plaintiff was right, the defendant would have to pay a specific sum of money to make the plaintiff whole. Sometimes, however, money damages were an inadequate solution to the problem. This led to an *action in equity*, where the plaintiff's goal was not to obtain money damages but to put the parties in the position they were in before the contract was breached or the injustice committed. To accomplish these goals the courts of equity created new remedies designed to make the parties fix what was broken, rather than pay for the damage.

equitable remedy

Equitable Remedy

The most important equitable remedies for our purposes are declaratory judgment, interpleader, reformation, and rescission. (Each is discussed in detail shortly.) It is important to understand that these equitable remedies are not available to a plaintiff unless he or she can meet the three basic requirements of the law of equity. Before an equitable remedy may be sought, a judge (not a jury) will decide whether the plaintiff has met the requirements of entering a plea in equity.

Those three requirements are as follows:

- *no adequate remedy at law.* Equitable remedies are available only when there is no adequate remedy at law. Equity forces people to do things they do not wish to do. In civil actions, courts do not like to use the law to impose a form of involuntary servitude when a less onerous remedy is available. Consequently, if the plaintiff can be made whole simply by requiring the defendant to pay an amount of money, the courts will not force the defendant to take an action (for example, transfer real estate, deliver or accept delivery of merchandise, or accept a job) that he or she does not wish to take.

clean hands

- *clean hands.* A person who seeks equitable relief from the courts must have "clean hands." Equity is based on the concept that the law is inadequate to do the right thing in certain circumstances. A person who seeks equitable relief therefore is asking the court to take a very flexible look at the problems between the parties and then craft a solution that doesn't necessarily attempt to enforce the agreement between the parties but instead will do what is right. This requirement means that the courts of equity will not aid a person in an attempt to defraud or cheat another person. In fact, equity will not be available at all to a person who has not acted fairly and honestly with the other party.

- *no unnecessary delay.* For all actions there are statutes of limitation that require a party to bring his or her problem to court before a certain date or the case will not be heard at all. For actions at law a potential plaintiff may wait until the last day of the statutory period before filing the lawsuit; as long as it is filed before the period expires, the courts will hear and decide the case. Equity adds a more stringent requirement. To gain access to the various forms of equitable relief, a plaintiff must bring his or her problem to court quickly. If a party delays seeking relief for too long, the equitable remedies may be denied. This is especially true if the delay results in harm to the other party. We say that a person has been guilty of *laches* when there has been an unreasonable delay in seeking relief which results in harm to the other party.

laches

DECLARATORY JUDGMENT

declaratory judgment

Declaratory judgment is a useful equitable remedy when the relative rights and duties of various parties in a contract or other legal relationship are in doubt. An equitable action seeking a declaratory judgment asks a court to review the facts and legal relationships of the concerned parties and define for the parties their obligations and rights. The parties can then move forward without question as to who owes what duties to whom. Note that a declaratory judgment does not require any party to pay any damages because this is an equitable action, not an action at law. In fact, unlike other equitable actions, the declaratory judgment does not require a party to do anything. It merely defines the parties' duties and responsibilities.

Interpleader

interpleader

An *interpleader* is an equitable proceeding that a party uses when he or she holds (but does not claim to own) property that is claimed by two or more other parties. (Note that the party seeking the interpleader remedy may not assert a claim to the property in dispute.) An interpleader action may be brought in a state court, or if the parties are from different states, the interpleader may be brought in federal court. An interpleader is permitted only when multiple parties claim the same item of property that is held by a disinterested person or entity.

The mechanics of an interpleader action are relatively simple. If the insurer is presented with conflicting claims for the same proceeds, it will file a *bill of interpleader* with the proper court and name the conflicting claimants as the defendants. The insurer normally will then pay the proceeds to the court, and since the insurer is asserting no claim to the proceeds, it will often be dismissed from the case. Sometimes, however, the insurer is sued by one of the claimants before it can file a bill of interpleader or before it knows that there are conflicting claimants. In that case, the insurer will respond to the plaintiff's complaint by filing a bill of interpleader as its answer to the complaint. The action will then proceed as outlined above.

It is easy to see that when two or more parties assert conflicting claims to the death benefits of a life insurance policy, an interpleader action is a proper solution for the insurer. The insurer concedes that it has no claim to the proceeds. Thus it pays the proceeds to the appropriate court and asks it to determine which of the claimants is entitled to the proceeds. In this way the insurer avoids multiple lawsuits because all claimants are present at one time. By adjudicating all claims at one time, the insurer also eliminates the possibility of having to pay policy benefits more than once, which could happen if the insurer is sued by conflicting claimants for the same proceeds in the courts of two or more different states.

Elements of Interpleader Action

- Two or more parties claim the same death benefits.
- The insurer has no claim on the proceeds.
- The insurer pays benefits to the court and asks the court to determine the rightful recipient.

Reformation

Assume that an agreement is reached between two or more parties. Then one of the parties asserts that the agreement does not express what he or she believed was the actual intent of the agreement. In an action at law, the court would not look behind the agreement to determine the intent of the parties. The court would either enforce the agreement as written or require one party to pay damages to the other for breaching the contract. This legal remedy could sometimes lead to an unfair result if the contract as written did not reflect the intent of the parties. It would be especially unfair if the difference was due to the mutual mistake of the parties or fraud by one party. **reformation** *Reformation* is an equitable remedy that looks behind the written contract, discovers the intent of the parties, and rewrites or reforms the agreement.

Reformation is not an easy remedy to obtain. It is a wise and important principle of law to start from the assumption that a signed contract represents the intent of the parties. Thus the first goal of the law is to enforce written agreements. If a party wants a court to change a written agreement by reformation, he or she must present clear and convincing evidence that the agreement does not reflect what the parties intended.

beyond a reasonable doubt standard of proof
preponderance of the evidence standard of proof
clear and convincing standard of proof

There are three possible levels of proof required in our courts. The highest level, *beyond a reasonable doubt standard of proof,* is reserved for proving guilt in criminal trials. The lowest level, a *preponderance of the evidence standard of proof,* is applicable to civil disputes. In between these two is the *clear and convincing standard of proof* required to reform a contract.

There are only two grounds for reformation of a contract: mistake and misrepresentation. Both must occur at or before the time the contract is executed (although the mistake or misrepresentation will not be discovered until after the agreement has been signed).

mutual mistake

Mistake. There are two kinds of mistake that will permit a court to reform the contract. The first is a *mutual mistake.* This occurs when there is a difference between the parties' intent and the written agreement at the time it is executed, but neither party is aware of the mistake. When the mistake is discovered, the agreement will be reformed to correct the mistake because equity will not permit one party to profit from the mistake at the expense of the other party. This is fair since neither party intended for the mistaken language to appear in the contract. Consequently, equity is merely doing what is right and restructuring the agreement to give the parties what they bargained for.

unilateral mistake

Sometimes an agreement is reached, and when the written contract is executed, one party is aware that there is a mistake in the written document. If the other party is not aware of the mistake and signs the agreement, this is known as a *unilateral mistake.* If the mistake favors the party who is aware of the mistake, he or she may sign the agreement, intending that the mistaken language is now part of the agreement. Again, the courts of equity will not permit one party to take advantage of the other in this fashion. Since the written agreement does not represent the intent of the parties (because of the unilateral mistake of the party who did not discover the error), the courts will reform the contract to correct the mistake.

Misrepresentation. This can occur, for example, when one person agrees to purchase a 1975 Volkswagen Super Beetle from another person and signs the seller's agreement of sale that describes a 1972 Volkswagen Beetle as the item to be purchased. Whether the misrepresentation is intentional or not, the result is the same—the agreement does not represent the intent of the parties. If the plaintiff can give clear and convincing evidence to prove that the written agreement misrepresents the intent of the parties, the court will reform the contract.

Rescission

Rescission means to abrogate or cancel the contract. Like a reformation, the grounds for a rescission are mistake and misrepresentation. Also, like a reformation, the mistake or misrepresentation must have occurred at or before the execution of the contract. Because the remedy's consequences are so severe, rescission is available only if the mistake or misrepresentation is based on a fact that is material to the contract's existence.

Generally, if the misrepresentation is material, it does not matter that it may have been unintentional. In a few states, however, the misrepresentation must be both material and fraudulent to justify a rescission. For less serious mistakes or misrepresentations the appropriate equitable remedy is reformation of the contract. The test of whether something is material is fairly clear: If the truth had been known, is it reasonable to believe that the party would still have entered into the contract? If the answer is no, the fact is material.

It is the general rule that if the insured dies before the expiration of the contestability period and the insurer discovers that there is a material misrepresentation in the application, the insurer may sue to rescind the contract, even if the cause of death is unrelated to the misrepresentation. There are exceptions to this rule, which permit rescission only if the misrepresentation was related to the cause of death. Under the exception, if an insured was killed in an automobile accident but had concealed the fact that he or she had AIDS, the insurer would be obligated to pay the claim even though the company would not have issued the policy had it known the truth. In the majority of jurisdictions, however, the policy would be rescinded on the basis of the concealment.

There are a few states that permit rescission by insurers if the misrepresentation is intentional, regardless of its materiality. However, the general rule is that, to constitute fraud sufficient to permit the insurer to rescind the contract, an intentional misrepresentation must be of a material fact.

This is a very important equitable remedy for insurance companies when there has been a misrepresentation of the insured's underwriting status that the insurer discovers before the expiration of the contestable period. The result of a rescission is that the contract is void from its inception and is treated as if it had never been created. This means that the court will return the parties to the positions they were in prior to signing the contract. In the life insurance context this means that the insurer will return the policyowner's premiums and will be released from its obligations to pay policy benefits.

Court action is not required for a rescission to be accomplished. The parties may voluntarily agree that it is in the best interests of both to rescind the agreement. In a similar fashion, one party may decide to rescind the contract and return to the other party any property received. If the second party takes no action to continue the contract, the rescission will be effective.

Because of the requirements of the insurance contract's incontestability clauses, the second method described above is unavailable to life insurers. A typical incontestability clause requires that the insurer must "contest" the contract within 2 years. Simply declaring a rescission and returning the policyowner's premium payments is not a contest of the policy. Thus, in order to effect a rescission, the insurer must obtain the policyowner's consent or it must obtain a court order rescinding the policy.

CHAPTER REVIEW

Answers to the review questions and the self-test questions can be found in the Supplement.

Key Terms

property	laches
real property	declaratory judgment
personal property	interpleader
chose in action	reformation
common law system	beyond a reasonable doubt standard
community-property law system	of proof
exoneration statutes	preponderance of the evidence
remedy at law	standard of proof
action at law	clear and convincing standard of
action in equity	proof
equitable remedy	mutual mistake
clean hands	unilateral mistake

Review Questions

1. How is the common definition of property different from the legal definition of property?

2. What types of property constitute real property?

3. What are the two types of personal property?

4. What are the classifications of the following properties?
   a. construction contract
   b. diamond ring
   c. apple orchard
   d. mobile home
   e. common stock certificates

5. Identify some of the property rights represented by life insurance contracts.

6. What effect does a policyowner's marital status generally have on his or her ownership interest in a policy within a common law jurisdiction?

7. Describe how community-property-law jurisdictions differ from common law jurisdictions.

8. Under what circumstances does property acquired during marriage in a community-property state remain the separate property of one spouse?

9. How do divorce and death affect the property rights of spouses in a common law jurisdiction and in a community-property jurisdiction?

10. Although the general community-property rule is that each spouse has the right and power to manage or dispose of the marital property, what restrictions apply to this right?

11. Explain why a married person who is identified as the sole owner on the application may not be entitled to freely exercise his or her ownership rights concerning the policy in a community-property jurisdiction.

12. How do exoneration statutes protect insurers in community-property jurisdictions?

13. Jerry and Jane are brother and sister. Both are divorced, and neither has any children. They both own their own homes and live only a few streets away from each other in the same small town. Jerry is the beneficiary of his sister's life insurance policy, and Jane is the beneficiary of Jerry's life insurance policy. Recently, when Jerry was very late for a doctor's appointment, he quickly backed his car out of the garage. Unknown to Jerry, Jane had just walked over to borrow some coffee and was bent down in his driveway, searching for a fallen earring. Tragically, Jerry ran over Jane, and Jane died. Referring to this case, discuss the circumstances under which a beneficiary is and is not entitled to receive the proceeds of an insured's life insurance policy when the beneficiary is responsible for the death of the insured.

14. What is the fundamental difference between remedies at law and equitable remedies?

15. What are the three requirements that a plaintiff entering a plea in equity must meet?

16. What is the purpose of a declaratory judgment?

17. As part of Marsha and George's divorce decree, the court required George to maintain a life insurance policy for the benefit of Marsha and the children. A number of years later, George married Karen and changed the beneficiary designation to Karen, in violation of the divorce decree. When George died, both Marsha and Karen filed claims with the insurance company for the

death proceeds from the policy. The insurer was unaware of the divorce decree requirement and is uncertain about the appropriate beneficiary. What should the insurer do?

18. Reformation of a contract may occur only in certain limited situations. Explain the following reasons for reforming a contract:
    a. mutual mistake
    b. unilateral mistake
    c. misrepresentation

19. Even when Adam was a relatively young man, he started to experience severe cardiac symptoms. Knowing that numerous members of his extended family had died as a result of heart problems and wanting to protect his family financially, Adam misrepresented his medical condition on the application for a large insurance policy on his life. Eight months after obtaining the life insurance coverage, Adam died from his heart problem, and the insurer discovered that he had concealed his medical condition. What can the insurance company do? Explain.

Self-Test Questions

T   F   1. A personal property item may become subject to the law that governs real property.

T   F   2. An orange blossom is intangible real property that will become tangible real property when it grows into an orange.

T   F   3. A life insurance policy represents intangible personal property rights.

T   F   4. There are at least three parties to every life insurance contract—the policy-owner, the insurer, and the beneficiary.

T   F   5. In some situations, a policyowner/insured is permitted to claim a portion of the death benefit in advance of his or her death.

T   F   6. Individuals who are not parties to the contract may be able to acquire an ownership interest in the policy benefits.

T   F   7. The common property law system is the law used in 31 states.

T   F   8. Generally, in a common law state, if a husband designates his wife as the beneficiary of his life insurance policy and they later divorce, the wife remains the beneficiary in the absence of a designation change.

T   F   9. In a community-property state, a car purchased after a marriage with money earned by the wife prior to the marriage is considered community property if the husband is the sole driver of the car.

T   F   10. In a community-property state, a deceased spouse's share of community property remains community property until the surviving spouse's death.

T   F   11. One spouse may make a gift of community property to a third person if the other spouse agrees to the gift.

T   F   12. Exoneration statutes are used in both common law states and community-property states to protect insurers.

T   F   13. A secured creditor has the right to claim a specific piece of property if the debtor defaults on the debt.

T   F   14. If a beneficiary intentionally kills the insured and the beneficiary refuses to release the insurance company from paying the death benefit to him or her, the insurance company will probably pay the proceeds to the court.

T   F   15. The common law of England is the source of remedies at law, while France and Spain are the source of remedies in equity.

T   F   16. When a plaintiff's objective in a lawsuit for breach of contract is to obtain money from the defendant, the plaintiff files an action at law.

T   F   17. Before a plaintiff may enter a plea in equity, a jury must meet to determine whether the plaintiff has met three requirements.

T   F   18. If X, one of the parties to a contract, has committed wrongs to Y, the other party to the contract, the courts of equity will not be available to X even though Y's wrongs to X were of much greater significance than X's wrongs to Y.

T   F   19. A declaratory judgment is an equitable remedy used to establish the rights, duties, and legal relationships of the parties to a contract.

T   F   20. A bill of interpleader is an invoice a life insurance company submits to the beneficiary for any legal fees the company incurred regarding the policy benefiting the beneficiary.

T   F   21. If a party to a contract is seeking reformation of the contract, he or she must present proof beyond a reasonable doubt that the contract does not reflect what the parties originally intended.

T   F   22. In order for a court of equity to rescind a contract, there must have been a mistake or misrepresentation at or before the time the contract was executed.

Performance of the Contract by the Insurer

Burke A. Christensen

Learning Objectives

An understanding of the material in this chapter should enable the student to

11-1. Explain which elements add to the death benefit amount.

11-2. Explain which elements reduce the death benefit amounts.

11-3. Understand what type of postclaim underwriting is acceptable.

11-4. Identify circumstances under which the insurer will return premiums rather than pay a death benefit.

11-5. Indicate the information necessary to establish that a death benefit is payable and to whom it is payable.

11-6. Identify the criteria necessary to establish a presumption of death after the insured has disappeared.

11-7. Describe problems associated with benefit claims arising from the disappearance of the insured.

11-8. Explain the complications of settling death claims when the beneficiary has killed the insured.

11-9. Indicate the role of the reasonable expectations doctrine, releases, and compromise settlements in settling death benefit claims.

Chapter Outline

A life insurance contract is performed when the insurer fulfills the promises it makes in that contract. Because an insurance contract is unilateral, the policyowner (normally the insured) makes no promises in it; the only party with promises to fulfill is the insurer. The basic promise is, of course, to pay a death benefit, but the insurer also makes promises with respect to the amount and availability of cash values, the election of settlement options, and so forth.

COMPUTATION OF DEATH BENEFIT AMOUNT

Although every life insurance policy has a death benefit, the calculation of the amount payable to the beneficiary at the insured's death begins, not ends, with that amount. A sample contract provision governing the amount of the death benefit provides as follows:

> The insurance benefits we will pay upon the death of the insured include the following amounts: the face amount of the policy, plus any death benefits due from any riders to this policy, plus any amount due from dividends paid under this policy, plus or minus any adjustments for the last premium, minus any loan (and any unpaid loan interest) on the policy. To this amount we will add interest from the date of death to the date we pay the death benefit.

Depending on how the policyowner has used the benefits and options available in an insurance policy, the actual amount payable may be quite different from the face amount printed on the policy. In fact, if the policy is providing coverage under the nonforfeiture option—which provides a reduced amount of paid-up insurance—then the policy's face amount is not relevant to the calculation of the death benefit at all. The death benefit payable under the reduced paid-up insurance option depends on the policy cash value when the nonforfeiture option is elected. Furthermore, under variable, variable universal, or universal life insurance policies, there may be a changing death benefit based upon the provisions of those contracts and the investment performance of the cash accumulation account.

Adjustments to Death Benefit Amount

After any changes have been made to the death benefit as described above, there is the possibility of the following additional adjustments:

postclaim underwriting

- The first adjustment may be as a result of *postclaim underwriting*. If it is discovered that the insured's age or sex has been misstated, the contract is likely to require that the policy's death benefit be adjusted to the amount that the premium paid would have purchased at the accurate age or sex.

- It is also possible that an adjustment will result in the elimination of the death benefit entirely. In these circumstances, the company will refund the premiums paid, usually without interest. This would be the case if the insured dies within the policy's contestable period and the insurer discovers a material misstatement in the application. This would also be the case in the event of a suicide within the time period before the policy's suicide exclusion clause expires. If the policy contains an exclusion for death as a result of war or aviation, the insured's beneficiary in these circumstances will not receive the normal death benefit but may be entitled to receive the larger of (1) a refund of premiums paid or (2) the net cash value.

- The insurer then adds any additional death benefits purchased by the policyowner under the terms of the contract. These include any paid-up additions, accidental death benefits, or other riders.

premium adjustments

- This is followed by any *premium adjustments* provided under the contract or by state law. For example, premiums paid for insurance coverage after the month in which the insured died may be refundable based upon a policy provision or state law. There may also be premium adjustments that reduce the death benefit. These include any premiums due but unpaid at the insured's date of death as well as any unpaid premium loans plus any unpaid interest on those loans. If the insured dies while coverage is being provided under a premium receipt, premiums paid in advance for periods after the date of the insured's death will also be added to the death benefit.

- The death benefit may also be reduced by any benefit amounts previously withdrawn from the policy. These include the amount of any unpaid policy loans plus any unpaid interest on those loans. If the policy permits cash withdrawals in a nonloan format—as is possible with universal life, variable life, and variable universal life policies—these also reduce the amount of the death benefit. If the insured has withdrawn policy values under a policy provision that permits the payment of any accelerated death benefits, the death benefit is reduced by the amount of such benefits already paid out.

- Some insurers may include termination dividends for policyowners whose policies have been in effect for specified periods of time. Dividends accumulated by the insurer at interest will also be payable with the death benefit.
- Finally, a policy provision or state law may require that the insurer add interest to the death benefit for the period between the insured's death and payment to the beneficiary.

Table 11-1 shows the formula for calculating the death benefit.

TABLE 11-1
Formula for Calculating Death Benefit

The net death benefit payable by the insurance company is calculated by starting with the policy's face amount or the reduced paid-up amount (if the policy is exercising the nonforfeiture option) and making these adjustments:

Start	Face amount of the policy (or reduced paid-up amount)
Plus or minus	Adjustments for misstatement of age or sex
Plus	Amount of paid-up additions, accidental death benefits, or other riders
Plus	Refund of any premiums paid in advance
Plus	Any accumulated dividends and termination dividends
Equals	Gross death benefit
Less	Any unpaid policy loans (including any due and unpaid interest)
Less	Any due and unpaid premiums
Plus	Interest on net death benefit
Equals	from date of death to payment date
	Net death benefit payable to the beneficiary

ESTABLISHING NEED TO PAY DEATH BENEFIT

proof of the insured's death

Before a death benefit is payable by a life insurance company, the beneficiary must provide *proof of the insured's death.* A typical life insurance policy contractual provision imposing this requirement states, "We will pay the proceeds of this life insurance policy to the beneficiary promptly upon receipt of proof that the insured has died, if premiums have been paid as required by this policy."

In the usual case, the beneficiary, the policyowner, or sometimes the executor of the insured's estate will advise the insurer of the insured's death. Upon receipt of the death certificate or other evidence of death, the insurer will investigate the death claim to determine its validity. The insurer will seek answers to questions such as the following:

- What were the date and cause of the insured's death?
- Was the policy in effect on the date of the insured's death? (For example, had the policy premiums been paid to the date of death? If the policy was for term insurance, had the term expired?)
- Was the cause of death excluded from the coverage provided by the policy? (For example, was the death a suicide within the exclusion period? Was there an aviation or war exclusion clause?)
- Is the policy contestable, and if so, is there a reason to contest the claim? (Was the insured's age, sex, or medical history misrepresented, for example?)

Example: ***Some Adjustments to Death Benefit Amount***

At the time of her death, Pauline's $50,000 face amount whole life policy had a $3,500 outstanding policy loan, plus interest of $425. Dividends had been used to purchase a total of $1,300 of paid-up additions to the policy. State law requires the insurer to pay the beneficiary interest on the net proceeds at a 5 percent annual rate for the 36 days between Pauline's death and the payment of the proceeds. How much will Pauline's beneficiary receive from the insurer?

	Face amount	$50,000
+	Paid-up additions	1,300
−	Policy loan	3,500
−	Loan interest	425
=	Subtotal	$47,375
+	Interest on proceeds	
	(36/360 x .05 x $47,375)	237
=	Amount payable	$47,612

Disappearance of the Insured

In the typical situation, there is clear evidence that the insured has died. In such cases, the date and cause of death are known, and there is normally no difficulty in determining whether and when the death benefit is payable. However, there are exceptions. Sometimes there is no clear evidence about the cause of death or even that the insured has died. Such a case is known in the law as a *mysterious disappearance*.

mysterious disappearance

If an insured disappears and the policy remains in force, at what point does the insurance company become obligated to pay the policy's death benefit? The common law answer to this question was to establish a rebuttable presumption of death if a person was absent from his or her usual residence without explanation or communication for 7 continuous years.

There are some qualifications to this general statement. In some jurisdictions, the period of absence is 5 years.[1] Some jurisdictions do not specifically refer to the absence of communication from the missing person as a requirement, and some permit a shorter period of absence if the missing person was known to have been exposed to a specific peril at the time of his or her disappearance.

Some authorities have criticized the common law rule as being "arbitrary, unpractical, anachronistic, and obstructive. The circumstances of each case," critics contend, "should be the basis for decision, and there should be no fixed or uniform rule."[2] A few states have agreed with this view and have responded by enacting the Uniform Absence as Evidence of Death and Absentee's Property Act. This act abolishes any presumptions of death, and states that a jury will decide in each instance when and if death has occurred based on the facts appropriate to that case.

The common law rule has been codified by many states. These state laws generally establish a set of criteria to determine whether death will be deemed to have occurred. Under these laws, a person may be presumed dead if four criteria are met. Once the presumption of death has been established by a court, the person will be declared dead and his or her property may be distributed based on that presumption.

The four criteria that must be met to establish a presumption of death are as follows:

- The person must have been continuously missing from his or her normal place of residence for a fixed period of time, traditionally 7 years.
- There must be no reasonable explanation for the absence. If a reasonable explanation for the disappearance can be established, there can be no presumption of death. For example, there may be evidence that the person has simply run away or is in hiding. This is known as a *purposeful disappearance*, and it precludes a presumption of death based upon the disappearance. A purposeful disappearance may be deemed to exist if there is evidence that the missing person is a fugitive

purposeful disappearance

from the law or may be trying to avoid creditors or obligations of support.

- There must be a total absence of communication from the missing person to those who would reasonably be expected to have heard from the person if he or she were still alive. Of course, if there is credible evidence of any communication from the missing person to anyone during the specified time period, there can be no presumption of death.

- It must be established that a diligent and unsuccessful search has been conducted for the missing person.

Reappearance of the Missing Person

It sometimes happens that a person who has been declared dead is later discovered to be alive. If the insurance company has paid the full death benefit based upon the presumption of death, the majority rule is that the insurance company can recover the policy proceeds from the beneficiary plus interest.[3] This rule does not apply, however, if the insurance company and the beneficiary settle the beneficiary's claim for an amount less than the full proceeds. In this circumstance, the courts have held that there has been a compromise settlement of the beneficiary's claim. The agreement signed by the parties as evidence of that settlement is a contract that precludes a recovery of the amount paid by the insurance company if the insured later reappears.[4]

Example: | ***Reappearance of a Missing Person***

Steve's father, who has a serious case of Alzheimer's disease, wandered away one day from the nursing home where he had been living. He totally disappeared and, despite extensive searches by the police and others, could not be found. After 3 years, Steve reached a compromise settlement of $300,000 with the insurer of a $500,000 policy on the father's life with Steve as the beneficiary. A few month later, Steve's father was found living in a home for the indigent several hundred miles away from his nursing home. In this situation, Steve keeps the $300,000 and receives nothing more from the insurer when his father dies.

It is important to note that the presumption of death under common law and under state statutes is a rebuttable presumption. This means that anyone can present evidence at any time that the missing person is still alive. If this occurs, a court will be required to weigh the evidence and determine whether there is sufficient credible evidence to overcome the presumption of death.

Disappearance Attributed to Common Disaster

If a person is missing as a result of a common disaster or specific peril such as an explosion, airplane crash, flood, or earthquake, there may be no need to wait until the time period for the presumption-of-death rules to elapse. In these cases, if there is sufficient circumstantial evidence to establish that the missing person was killed in a common disaster or other specific peril, he or she may be declared dead at an earlier date. If a person is seen clinging to a raft that is swept over Niagara Falls or is a passenger on an airplane that explodes in midair, the fact and date of death may be established by circumstantial evidence without waiting for a lengthy period of time to pass.

The common law rule and the statutes do not generally prescribe any particular date (during the period of absence) on which the missing person is presumed to have died. They simply prescribe that at the end of the applicable period it is presumed that the missing person has died. There is a minority view that the missing person is presumed to have died on the last day of the applicable period. There is, however, no reason to prefer that date over any other date, and in fact, a date at the beginning of the period is more likely to be accurate.

As can be readily seen, the date selected can make a significant difference for many purposes, such as remarriage, payment of pension benefits, inheritance, and the payment of life insurance premiums. If the actual date of death is important, the interested parties may introduce whatever evidence they have to support their claim of a specific date, and the court will make a determination.

Beneficiary's Filing of Death Claim

When an insured person disappears under circumstances that suggest that he or she has died, the beneficiary will usually file a death claim with the insurer. If the insurer is not satisfied that the information provides due proof of death and denies the claim, the beneficiary has the following options:

- He or she can petition a court to declare the missing person dead.
- The beneficiary may sue the insurer for payment of the death benefit.

If neither of these options is successful, the beneficiary must await the passage of time and the arrival of the presumption of death under the appropriate statute or under that jurisdiction's common law rule. During this period, the beneficiary or policyowner must decide whether to continue paying premiums on the policy. If there is sufficient equity in the policy, there are several options. The beneficiary may elect to (1) let the policy cash values pay the premiums, (2) take a reduced paid-up policy, or (3) take extended term insurance.

If the policy terminates before the presumption-of-death period expires, the policy's beneficiary may still obtain benefits under the policy. However, this can be done only if he or she can establish that the insured died while the policy was in force. This is usually an extremely difficult goal to accomplish. Consequently, it is usually in the beneficiary's best interest to keep the policy in force until the statutory period of time has elapsed. If it should later be discovered that the insured actually died years earlier, the beneficiary will be entitled to a refund of premiums paid after the actual date of death and, in many cases, interest on the proceeds from the actual date of death to the date of benefit payment.

WHO GETS THE PROCEEDS?

Once it has been established that the insured has died and the policy death benefits are payable, the next question is, who is entitled to the policy benefits? This, of course, is controlled by the beneficiary designation. If there is a properly executed beneficiary designation, the party named therein will be entitled to the policy proceeds as long as he or she survives the insured.

With respect to the requirement that the named beneficiary must survive the insured, some insurance policies contain a provision such as the following:

> If, before we receive proof of the insured's death, any beneficiary dies at the same time as, or within 15 days after, the insured, we will pay the proceeds as if that beneficiary died before the insured.

These provisions are similar to the simultaneous death provisions that are sometimes included in a person's will. The purpose of the requirement that the beneficiary survive the insured by a specified time period is to avoid the possibility that the insurance proceeds will have to pass through two estates in the event that the insured and his or her beneficiary die in a common disaster.

A legal entity such as a trust, a partnership, a charity, or a corporation may also be designated as a policy beneficiary. If so, that entity must also be in existence at the insured's death. If the proceeds are to be paid to a trust, the insurance company usually will require that a copy of the deed of trust and the trustee's acceptance of that position be filed with the company. Similarly, before insurance proceeds will be paid to the administrator or executor of an estate, the insurer will require copies of the official documents that appoint those persons to those positions.

When No Beneficiary Is Designated

It sometimes happens that there is no designated beneficiary to receive the policy proceeds. This can occur if all named beneficiaries have predeceased the insured or, in the rarer case, if there has been no valid designation of a beneficiary. The policy usually has a contractual provision for resolving this problem.

One policy provides this solution:

> If no designated beneficiary is living at the death of the insured, we will pay the policy proceeds to the insured's surviving children in equal shares, or if none, to the insured's estate.

This is not the only contractual solution. Another policy provides as follows:

> If there is no surviving beneficiary for all or a portion of the policy proceeds, the right to such proceeds will pass to the owner of the policy. If the owner is the insured, this right will pass to the insured's estate.

Assigning Proceeds to a Third Party

An interest in the policy proceeds may be permanently or temporarily assigned by the owner of the policy to a third party. This is frequently done when the policy is serving as collateral for a loan. Such collateral assignments are also frequently made in split-dollar life insurance. The following is a sample insurance policy provision covering the rights of assignees:

> During the lifetime of the insured, you may assign this policy or any interest in it. If you do, all other interests in this policy, except those retained by you, will be subject to the interests of the assignee. An assignment is not effective until we have recorded it, and the assignment will be subject to any payment we make or any action we take before we record the assignment.

We are not responsible for the validity of any assignment. The assignee may not change the owner or beneficiary of this policy. Any policy proceeds payable to an assignee must be paid in one lump sum.

Consequences of the Beneficiary Killing the Insured

It is clearly the public policy of all jurisdictions in the United States that people should not be permitted to profit from their wrongful acts. Consequently, it is also public policy in the United States that a beneficiary should not be allowed to receive the proceeds of an insurance policy if the beneficiary kills the insured. When this public policy is converted into law, however, numerous complications arise. Whether a beneficiary is entitled to the proceeds after killing the insured is controlled by state statutes and state court decisions interpreting those statutes. Since state statutes are not identical and the courts of one state are not bound by another state's courts, the law is not uniform throughout the United States. Nevertheless, the general rule is that killing the insured must be wrongful and intentional to preclude the beneficiary from receiving the death benefits.

As an example, state A's statute stipulates that the beneficiary may not receive the insurance proceeds if he or she is convicted of murdering the insured. State B's statute precludes the beneficiary from receiving the proceeds if he or she causes the wrongful death of the insured. Assume Sally intends to kill Mary, her husband's mistress. However, her aim is poor and she shoots and kills her husband by mistake. She is likely to be convicted of something but probably not murder. In state A, if Sally has not been convicted of murder, she would not be precluded from receiving the insurance proceeds even if she is convicted of a lesser crime. In state B, Sally would be denied the proceeds because she caused the wrongful death of the insured.

Under the law of some states, the beneficiary may be acquitted of a crime involving the death of the insured, yet still be denied the proceeds of the insurance policy. This can result if, after the acquittal, the insurance company denies the beneficiary's claim for the death benefits. When this happens, the beneficiary can sue the insurance company, which will be a civil action, not a criminal trial. The standard of proof in a criminal action is proof beyond a reasonable doubt. The standard in a civil action is merely proof by a preponderance of the evidence. This means that while there may not be enough evidence to establish "beyond a reasonable doubt" that the beneficiary wrongfully and intentionally killed the insured, there may be enough facts to establish proof by a "preponderance of the evidence."

There are other defenses available to a beneficiary who has killed the insured. The killing must be both wrongful and intentional to preclude the insured from obtaining the proceeds. If the beneficiary can show that he or she acted in self-defense or in the defense of another person, the killing is not wrongful. If the beneficiary was insane (or otherwise incapable of forming an intent to kill) or the killing was accidental, then the killing was not intentional.

REASONABLE EXPECTATIONS DOCTRINE

An insurance policy is a contract that attempts to set out in writing the agreement of the parties as to their respective rights and responsibilities. When the parties disagree about what the terms of their contract mean, they may look to the courts to resolve the dispute.

Some types of contracts, known as *contracts of adhesion*, receive special treatment by the courts. Contracts of adhesion are prepared solely by one party to the agreement. The other party cannot negotiate the terms; he or she may only accept or reject the contract as written by the other side. Since one side has the advantage of selecting the language used in the contract, the courts assume that the words that are used are exactly the words that the drafting party wanted to use. Therefore any ambiguity in the contract will be construed against the drafter and in favor of the other party.

The majority of courts will enforce the contract as written when the language is clear and give the benefit of any ambiguity to the nondrafting party when the language is not clear. A minority of jurisdictions have court-made law that gives even greater advantage to the nondrafting party. When faced with a provision of a contract—particularly an insurance contract—that conflicts with that court's view of the way the contract should have read, the court "will find ambiguity in policy language where most other courts will say that the policy is perfectly clear. These courts are accused of employing 'constructive ambiguity' in their effort to impose liability on the insurer."[5]

reasonable expectations doctrine

An even smaller minority of jurisdictions employ a philosophy that has come to be known as the *reasonable expectations doctrine*. This is an interpretation of contract law that has not acquired a significant following since it was first proposed in 1970. The essence of this view is that the reasonable expectations of the nondrafting party in a contract of adhesion will control even if the language of the contract is contrary and unambiguous. This is clearly contrary to the traditional view that it is the intentions of *both* parties that control contract interpretation. While this philosophy gained some credence in the past, it now seems to have passed its prime.

On occasion there is a dispute between the insurer and a beneficiary about the amount of proceeds that should be paid to the beneficiary or even about whether the person asserting the claim is in fact eligible to be a beneficiary. To protect the rights of the public in settling these disputes, the National Association of Insurance Commissioners (NAIC) developed the Unfair Claims Settlement Practices Model Act in 1990. Almost all of the states have enacted laws similar to this model act. These laws require insurers to investigate all claims promptly and to settle those claims as soon as the insurer's liability has become reasonably clear. The model act contains a list of unfair practices that are prohibited. In addition, the NAIC has prepared the Unfair Life, Accident and Health Claims Settlement Practices Model Regulation, listing actions that are required of insurers in settling claims. About half of the states have adopted regulations similar to those in the model.

RELEASES AND COMPROMISE SETTLEMENTS

When a claim is filed with an insurer, only the five results that follow are possible:

- The insurer pays the claim in full.
- The insurer denies the claim, and the claimant accepts that decision.
- The insurer denies the claim, and the parties submit the matter to a court for trial.
- The insurer admits liability as to the amount of the claim but asks a court to determine the proper recipient. This is known as an *interpleader*, which is the method used when a party (such as a life insurance company) holds disputed property but does not claim an interest in the property. (See chapter 10 for a more complete discussion of interpleader.) If two or more persons assert a claim to insurance proceeds held by an insurer after the death of the insured, the insurer will pay the proceeds to a court and ask the court to determine which party has the lawful claim. Such disputes often arise if an attempted change of beneficiary is incomplete or if a completed change of beneficiary is contrary to a court order or other restrictions on the policyowner's rights to change the beneficiary.
- The insurer denies the claim, but the parties reach a compromise settlement and part of the claim is paid.

Resolving the parties' rights is quite simple if one of the first four options occurs because the parties, in one way or another, are simply enforcing the terms of the contract. If, however, the claim is settled under the fifth alternative, the terms of the insurance contract do not resolve the issue. In this event the parties must execute a release or enter into a compromise settlement.

Releases

release

A *release* is the intentional giving up of a right to do or have something. For the release to be enforceable, usually there must be an exchange of consideration. This means that the releasing party must receive something in exchange for giving up the right he or she possessed before the release. Assume that Fred dies owing John $100. Since the debt is acknowledged, John possesses a right to claim that amount from Fred's estate. If Fred's estate has insufficient funds to pay the debt, it may offer John $50 if he will release the estate from the debt. If John accepts the $50, he will sign a release, which will terminate his right to receive the remaining $50. Similarly, life insurers will require a release from the beneficiary as part of any negotiated settlement of a death claim.

Compromise Settlements

compromise
settlement

Do not confuse a release with a *compromise settlement* (also known as an *accord and satisfaction*), which is applicable when the existence of a right is in dispute. Assume that at Jane's death, Elaine asserts a claim against Jane's estate for $100. Jane's executor disputes the validity of the debt but decides to settle. She offers Elaine $50 as a compromise settlement. If Elaine accepts, there will be an accord (or agreement) to accept the $50 in settlement of Elaine's disputed claim. The estate's payment of the money to Elaine will satisfy her claim. Life insurers sometimes make compromise settlements in cases where the insured has disappeared but there is no proof of death and the requirements of a presumption of death have not yet been fully satisfied.

CHAPTER REVIEW

Answers to the review questions and the self-test questions can be found in the Supplement.

Key Terms

postclaim underwriting
premium adjustments
proof of the insured's death
mysterious disappearance
purposeful disappearance

reasonable expectations
   doctrine
release
compromise settlement

Review Questions

1. Explain why the death benefit amount may be different from the amount stated on the face page of the policy.

2. Indicate what determines the death benefit payable under the reduced paid-up nonforfeiture option.

3. Indicate those items that will increase the amount of the death benefit payable.

4. Indicate those items that will reduce the death benefit payable.

5. Indicate which types of policies have changing death benefit amounts.

6. Indicate the two factors that may result in postclaim underwriting and how they would be adjusted.

7. Describe the two most likely reasons the insurer would return premiums paid instead of paying the death benefit if the insured dies.

8. Describe the benefit payable by the insurer if the insured dies in a manner excluded from coverage.

9. Indicate how paid-up additions and accidental death benefits may alter the amount of the death benefit.

10. Explain how outstanding policy loans and interest accrued thereon affect the death benefit amount.

11. Explain how termination dividends and dividends accumulated at interest will modify the amount of the death benefit payable.

12. Indicate the type of proof the insurer usually requires to establish that the insured has died.

13. Indicate the usual questions that must be answered to establish that a death benefit is payable under a life insurance policy.

14. Describe the four criteria usually necessary to establish a presumption of death.

15. How long after an insured has disappeared will the beneficiary or policyowner need to keep the policy in force in order to assure the beneficiary of death-benefit eligibility?

16. Explain how the reappearance of the missing insured affects the insurance company's rights if a death claim has already been paid.

17. Explain how disappearance attributed to a common disaster may modify the requirements to establish the death of the missing person.

18. Indicate three possible ways to keep a policy in force during the insured's disappearance without continuing premium payments in cash.

19. Explain how it is possible for a life insurance policy to mature into a death benefit with no designated beneficiary.

20. What is the general rule regarding public policy in cases where the beneficiary kills the insured?

21. Explain how a beneficiary can be acquitted for murdering the insured and still be denied the life insurance proceeds.

22. Describe the reasonable expectations doctrine.

23. Distinguish between a release and a compromise settlement.

Self-Test Questions

T F 1. The only party to a life insurance policy with promises to fulfill is the insurance company.

T F 2. The only enforceable promise the life insurer makes is the promise to pay a death benefit.

T F 3. Adjustments for the last premium can either increase or decrease the death benefit payable.

T F 4. Death benefit amounts include interest from the date of the insured's death until the actual date of payment.

T F 5. Life insurers are strictly forbidden from doing any form of postclaim underwriting.

T F 6. Life insurance policies may contain exclusions for war or aviation.

T F 7. Benefits withdrawn under an accelerated death benefit provision will reduce the benefit amount payable at the insured's death.

T F 8. Cash withdrawals from a policy in a non-loan format may reduce the death benefit payable.

T F 9. The contestability of a life insurance policy at the time of death will not affect the claims process.

T F 10. The Uniform Absence as Evidence of Death and Absentee's Property Act establishes a presumption of death after 7 years' absence.

T F 11. Purposeful disappearance precludes a presumption of death based on the disappearance.

T F 12. Courts can declare that a person is dead even though no remains of the body have been found.

T F 13. The courts generally agree that the appropriate date of death is the last day of the applicable period of disappearance.

T F 14. The insurance company is the only party permitted to rebut a presumption of death.

T F 15. A partnership cannot be named as beneficiary of a life insurance policy.

T   F   16. Life insurers generally require a copy of the deed of trust before paying proceeds to a trust.

T   F   17. Life insurers generally require a copy of the trustee's acceptance of that position before paying proceeds to a trustee.

T   F   18. An interest in the policy proceeds may be permanently or temporarily assigned by the owner of the policy to a third party.

T   F   19. The majority of courts are guided by the reasonable expectations doctrine.

T   F   20. Almost all states have enacted laws similar to the Unfair Claims Settlement Practices Model Act (which was developed by the NAIC in 1990).

T   F   21. Life insurers are prohibited from making compromise settlements for policies involving disappearance of the insured.

NOTES

1. Under federal law a member of the U.S. military forces may be declared dead under certain circumstances for purposes of military pay and dependent benefits after an absence of only 1 year. See 37 U.S. Code Secs. 555–556.
2. *Wigmore on Evidence*, Sec. 2513b, at 614 (Chadbourne 1981).
3. *Alexander Hamilton Life Ins. Co. v. Lewis*, 550 S.W.2d 558 (Ky. 1977).
4. *Southern Farm Bureau Life Ins. Co. v. Burney*, 590 F.Supp. 1016 (E.D. Ark. 1984).
5. Buist M. Anderson, *Anderson on Life Insurance* (Boston: Little, Brown & Company, 1991) p. 183.

The Beneficiary:
Part 1

Dan M. McGill
Revised by Burke A. Christensen

Learning Objectives

An understanding of the material in this chapter should enable the student to

12-1. Identify the key types of life insurance beneficiaries.

12-2. Explain the rights of the beneficiaries and the rights of the policyowner under various types of beneficiary designations.

Chapter Outline

beneficiary

The *beneficiary* is the person, trust, charity, or other entity named in the life insurance contract to receive all or a portion of the proceeds payable at maturity. The section of the contract dealing with the designation and rights of the beneficiary is in many respects the most significant one in the entire contract. It reflects the insured's decisions concerning the disposition of his or her human life value. It is the means by which the insured provides family financial security after he or she dies. In a well-planned estate, the beneficiary designations will be integrated with the election of a settlement option in the most effective way to carry out the insured's objectives.

There are many facets to a study of the beneficiary in life insurance, and the starting point is a description of the various categories of beneficiaries and beneficiary designations. Emphasis is placed on customary situations and policy provisions, and the student is cautioned that any particular case is decided on the basis of its own facts and the policy wording involved.

TYPES OF BENEFICIARIES

Beneficiaries can be classified from various points of view. For the purposes of this discussion, they will be classified as to

- nature of the interest
- manner of identification
- priority of entitlement
- revocability of the designation

Nature of the Interest

From the standpoint of the interest involved, beneficiaries fall into two broad categories:

- the estate of the *insured*
- a *third-party beneficiary*—an entity or person or persons other than the insured (the policyowner and the insurance company are the first and second parties to the contract)

The Estate of the Insured

The insured is normally designated as the person to receive the proceeds of an endowment insurance policy or a retirement income policy because those policies are designed primarily to provide benefits to the policyowner. The insured may designate someone else to receive the proceeds in the event of his or her death, or may specify that the proceeds be payable to his or her estate. Proceeds are usually made payable to the estate only for a purpose associated with the settlement of the estate, such as the payment of last-illness and funeral expenses, debts, mortgages, and taxes. If any proceeds remain after the claims against the estate have been satisfied, they are distributed in accordance with the decedent's will or the appropriate intestate law.

Payment to the insured's estate is generally unwise because it exposes the proceeds to transfer costs and taxes that can otherwise be avoided. It is also considered highly undesirable to have the policy proceeds payable to the insured's estate when it is intended that they should go to certain specific individuals. The proceeds will be subject to estate administration and may be reduced through probate costs, taxes, and the claims of creditors. Moreover, distribution to the intended beneficiaries will be delayed until settlement of the estate has been completed.

When it is intended that the proceeds be paid to the insured's estate and be subject to the control of the executor or administrator, as the case may be, the proper designation is "the executors or administrators of the insured." If the policy involved is an endowment or a retirement income policy and the proceeds are to be paid to the insured if he or she survives to the date of maturity and to his or her estate if the insured does not survive, the proper designation is "insured, if living; otherwise to his or her executors or administrators." The simple designation "insured's estate" is effective, but such terms as "heirs," "legal heirs," or "family" are not because when those terms are used, the proceeds do not become part of the probate estate. The appropriate intestate law is followed in determining the legal heirs, who receive the proceeds directly, being treated as named beneficiaries, rather than heirs. In other words, the proceeds pass outside the probate estate.

When the insured is the applicant and designates himself or herself as beneficiary, the insured can exercise all rights under the policy without the consent of any other person. The policy is the insured's property and can be dealt with like any other property.

Third-Party Beneficiary

There are three general types of third-party beneficiaries:

- the owner-applicant
- a donee or gratuitous beneficiary
- a creditor or a person who has furnished valuable consideration in exchange for the designation

owner-applicant

When one person procures insurance on another person's life and becomes the owner of the policy, he or she is known as the *owner-applicant*. Ordinarily the owner will designate himself or herself as beneficiary, although it is not inconceivable that he or she would direct that the proceeds be paid to someone else, particularly in the event that he or she predeceases the insured. This type of arrangement is typically used with key person insurance and business-continuation agreements, but it is by no means confined to such situations. It may be used by a creditor to protect his or her interest or by a family group to provide estate liquidity and minimize death taxes.

From the standpoint of ownership rights, the third-party owner occupies the same position as the insured who designates himself or herself as beneficiary. There is a difference, but it is of no legal significance: The insured owns his or her policy because he or she is the only party involved, while a third-party owner has his or her rights established by an express provision in the contract. The third-party applicant, like every other applicant, must have an insurable interest in the insured at the inception of the contract. There need be no insurable interest at the date of the insured's death; the third-party owner, or the beneficiary of his or her choice, is entitled to retain the full amount of the proceeds.

donee or gratuitous beneficiary

The second type of third-party beneficiary is the person who has furnished no consideration. Technically, this person is known as the *donee or gratuitous beneficiary*. In typical situations the insured designates a member of his or her family as beneficiary for no consideration other than "love and affection." It is not necessary for the donee beneficiary to have an insurable interest, although he or she usually does. Unless a specific notation is made to the contrary, the discussion in the succeeding pages is directed at the donee beneficiary.

The third type of third-party beneficiary is the person who has furnished a valuable consideration in exchange for the designation. A creditor may be designated as beneficiary under a policy on his or her debtor's life, although it is much more common for the policy to be collaterally assigned to the creditor. In either event, the creditor is permitted to retain only that portion of the proceeds equal to his or her interest at the time of the debtor's death. During the insured's lifetime, the creditor can exercise no rights in the policy without the insured's consent or joinder. Occasionally, the ex-spouse is designated as beneficiary under a policy as part of a divorce settlement. The prior spouse's rights in the policy proceeds depend on the terms of the settlement if the insurer has notice of the settlement. The designation is usually irrevocable or, if revocable, can be changed only by an appropriate court order.

Manner of Identification

specific beneficiary

class beneficiary

Classified by identification, beneficiaries may be termed specific or class. A *specific beneficiary* is an individual or entity designated by name or in any other manner that clearly sets him or her apart from any other individual or entity. A *class beneficiary* is a person not mentioned by name who belongs to a clearly identifiable *group* of persons designated as beneficiaries.

Specific Designation

In making specific designations, it is customary to identify the person both by *name* and *relationship* to the insured if there is a legal or blood relationship. For example, a son would be designated "Charles William Doe, son of the insured." A wife would be designated "Mary Smith Doe, wife of the insured." Preferably the full name—first name, middle name, and surname—should be given. If the designated beneficiary is the insured's wife, her maiden name should also be included to prevent confusion and litigation in the event that there is an antecedent or subsequent wife with the same first name. It invites litigation to designate the insured's spouse simply as "husband" or "wife." If the insured has married more than once, there is likely to be controversy as to whether the designation refers to the person who was married to the insured at the time the designation was made or the spouse who was married to him or her at the time of the insured's death.

The relationship accompanying the name in a beneficiary designation is regarded as descriptive only and not as a statement of entitlement. If a beneficiary is identifiable by name or otherwise, he or she is still entitled to the policy proceeds even though the stated relationship to the insured is no longer applicable—or never was. For example, if a man purchases a policy prior to his marriage and designates his fiancée by name as beneficiary, describing her as his wife, his death prior to their marriage does not deprive his fiancée of the policy proceeds. Nor does an invalid marriage have any effect on the beneficiary's entitlement.

Class Designation

A class designation is appropriate whenever the insured desires that the proceeds be divided equally among the members of a particular group, the composition of which may not be definitely fixed at the time of designation. Examples of such groups are children, grandchildren, brothers, sisters, or heirs. Perhaps the most common class designation is "children of the insured." This type of class designation is especially favored for the designation of secondary or contingent beneficiaries. It may also be used in combination with a specific designation—for example, when the insured designates living children by name and then adds "and any other surviving children born of the marriage of the insured and John Doe, husband of the insured."

From the standpoint of the law, class designations are entirely proper. Courts have repeatedly sustained the validity of such designations. From a practical standpoint, however, class designations present the problem of identifying the members of the class. No class designation is entirely free of possible complications. Even the simplest designations can cause difficulties. For example, the designation "children of the insured" seems to circumscribe the class precisely enough to permit ready identification. In discharging its responsibilities under such a designation, however, the insurance company has to determine whether the insured was also survived by any illegitimate children, children by a previous marriage or marriages, or adopted children.

If the surviving children are adults, there is always the possibility that one of them has severed normal ties with the family. His or her whereabouts may be unknown to the other members of the family and perhaps even his or her existence denied or concealed by them.

Even the designation "children born of the marriage of the insured and Mary Smith Doe, wife of the insured," while quite precise, does not indicate whether adopted children of the marriage should be accorded the same status as natural children. For the sake of clarity and to avoid possible litigation, therefore, some designations include a statement that the word "children" will be construed to include adopted children.

Class Designation "Children of the Insured" Should Specify Whether It Includes

- adopted children
- stepchildren
- illegitimate children

Similarly, the use of the term "heirs" in a beneficiary designation makes it necessary for the insurance company to refer to previous court rulings as to the meaning of the term in the jurisdiction involved or, lacking these, to seek court interpretation. The company will then have to identify and locate the heirs. The perils to the company are so great that many companies will not even accept the designation "heirs."

When either the insured or the insured's spouse has children by a previous marriage, a class designation must be carefully worded to carry out the insured's intentions. The insured may wish to provide for all his or her children and those of his or her spouse by the spouse's former marriage, or the insured may want to confine his or her bounty to the children of the insured's current marriage. If the insured specifies that the proceeds are to be paid to "my children" or "children of the insured," the insured's children by any marriage would be included, but the children of the insured's spouse by a previous marriage would be excluded. On the other hand, by speaking, for example, of "my wife, Mary Smith Doe, and our children," the insured is not only excluding his wife's children by her former marriage but also any children he may have had by an earlier marriage and any he may have by a subsequent marriage.

Most companies today restrict the use of class designations. At best they lead to delays in settling death claims. At worst, they involve considerable trouble and expense for the company and possibly even multiple payment of some claims. Insurance companies, therefore, will not accept designations of a class whose relationship to the insured is remote or whose composition will be difficult to determine. Moreover, when the class is acceptable, it must be described as precisely as possible. All insurance companies, for example, permit the designation of children as a class. This protects the interests of unborn children. Otherwise, many children would be deprived of insurance protection through failure of the insured to revise his or her settlement plan after the birth of an additional child or children.

Class Designations Force the Insurer To

- determine all potential members of the class
- verify the prior deaths of class members who predeceased the insured
- delay settlement until the appropriate beneficiaries can be determined
- search for class members no longer in communication with other class or family members

---

Priority of Entitlement

Primary and Contingent Beneficiaries

primary beneficiary

With respect to priority of entitlement, beneficiaries may be classified as primary and contingent. A *primary beneficiary* has the first claim to the insurance policy proceeds if the conditions on which they are payable are fulfilled. There may be two or more primary beneficiaries, in which event they will share the proceeds in the proportion specified by the policyowner. It is not implicit in such an arrangement that the beneficiaries share equally in the proceeds, except as to the members of a class. Class beneficiaries do share equally in the proceeds since, without mentioning names, it is impracticable to provide disproportionate shares. Any one of a group of primary beneficiaries, whether specifically named or designated as a class, therefore, enjoys rights in the policy equal to those of any other beneficiary.

contingent
beneficiary

The *contingent beneficiary*, frequently called the *secondary* beneficiary, has a claim to the proceeds that ripens only on the death or removal of the primary beneficiary. A contingent beneficiary is a person or organization that takes the place of the primary beneficiary if the primary beneficiary predeceases the insured or loses his or her entitlement in some other manner before receiving any proceeds. With the increased use of installment settlement plans, however, the contingent beneficiary has assumed importance in another role—namely, to receive the benefits under an installment option payable beyond the death of the primary beneficiary. In this role, the contingent beneficiary can become entitled to benefits even though the primary beneficiary survives the insured. This function is important in connection with the interest option, installment time option, installment amount option, and guaranteed installments under life income options.

The two functions of the contingent beneficiary are quite distinctive, and his or her rights thereunder are quite different. Under the original concept, the contingent beneficiary becomes the primary beneficiary on the death of the primary beneficiary during the insured's lifetime—subject, of course, to being divested of that position by the policyowner. The contingent beneficiary thus succeeds to all the rights of the original primary beneficiary, including those arising under the provisions for optional settlement. Upon the death of the insured, he or she is regarded as a *first-taker beneficiary*, with all that this status implies under company settlement option practices. He or she might be given the right to take the proceeds in a lump sum, to elect a settlement option, or to designate contingent beneficiaries to receive any benefits unpaid at the time of his or her death.

first-taker beneficiary

At the death of the insured, proceeds payable in a lump sum vest immediately in the primary beneficiary (in the absence of a delay clause), and the interest of the contingent beneficiary or beneficiaries is terminated. If the primary beneficiary dies after the insured but before receiving a check from the insurance company, the proceeds go to the primary beneficiary's estate, not to the contingent beneficiary. If the proceeds are payable under an installment option, the contingent beneficiary becomes entitled to the benefits at the primary beneficiary's death. The contingent beneficiary is a *second-taker beneficiary*, however, and under the practices of most companies has to take the proceeds under the distribution pattern prescribed for the primary beneficiary. In other words, a second-taker contingent beneficiary is not usually permitted to commute the unpaid installments or to elect to have them paid out under a settlement arrangement different from that in effect for the primary beneficiary.

second-taker beneficiary

There may be, and usually are, two or more contingent beneficiaries. The typical insured designates his or her spouse as primary beneficiary and his or her children, by name or as a class, as contingent beneficiaries. For a lump-sum distribution, the designation might read, "Mary Smith Doe, wife of the insured, if she survives the insured; otherwise in equal shares to the surviving children of the insured." If the proceeds are to be distributed under an installment option, a more complex designation is necessary.

Example: ***Functions of a Contingent Beneficiary***

Adam, the policyowner and insured, names Barbara as primary beneficiary and Claire as contingent beneficiary. Proceeds are to be paid under a 10-year fixed-period settlement option.

- If Barbara dies before Adam, Claire receives the entire proceeds.
- If Barbara dies one year after Adam, Claire receives 9 years of installment payments from the proceeds.

Levels of Contingent Beneficiaries

There may be various degrees of contingent beneficiaries, each successive level having a lower order of entitlement to the proceeds. Thus, there may be first contingent, second contingent, and third contingent beneficiaries.[1] Two levels of contingent beneficiaries are provided for in the following designation: "Mary Smith Doe, wife of the insured, if she survives the insured; otherwise in equal shares to the surviving children, if any, of the insured; otherwise to Harry Doe, father of the insured, if he survives the insured." If the proceeds are to be paid out under an installment option, the agreement usually specifies that any installments remaining unpaid at the death of the last surviving contingent beneficiary will be paid in a lump sum to that beneficiary's estate. This obviates the necessity of reopening the insured's estate to receive the unpaid installments, which—if one or two levels of contingent beneficiaries have died—might precipitate a series of estate reopenings, with considerable expense and little benefit. Many persons designate an educational institution, hospital, charity, or religious organization as the last contingent or ultimate contingent beneficiary. This minimizes the likelihood that the benefits will be payable to an estate because all beneficiaries predeceased the insured.

Right of Revocation

revocable beneficiary

irrevocable beneficiary

Under modern practice, the identification of a beneficiary in the policy application may be unilaterally changed by the policyowner. If so, the designation is referred to as *revocable* and the designee as the *revocable beneficiary.* In some situations, the beneficiary designation may be changed, but only with the beneficiary's consent. If the insured does not have the unilateral right to change the beneficiary, the designation is properly described as *irrevocable* and the designee as the *irrevocable beneficiary.* This distinction is so significant that a word on the historical development of the concept of revocability seems warranted. Note, however, that the right to change the beneficiary must be included in the application or in the policy. Otherwise the initial designation is irrevocable.

Historical Development

Early life insurance contracts in the United States made no provision for a change of beneficiary. The insured simply entered into a contract with the insurance company that upon his or her death, the company would pay a specified sum of money to the person designated as beneficiary—usually the insured's spouse. Since there were no surrender values or other prematurity rights of significance to the insured, the person entitled to receive the death proceeds was regarded to be the owner of the policy. One of the early students of American insurance law had the following to say about the interest of the beneficiary:

> We apprehend the general rule to be that a policy, and the money to become due under it, belong the moment it is issued to the person or persons named in it as the beneficiary or beneficiaries, and that there is no power in the person procuring the insurance by any act of his or hers, by deed or by will, to transfer to any other person the interest of the person named.[2]

In 1888, the United States Supreme Court defined the interest of the beneficiary in substantially the same terms.[3]

In consonance with this concept of policy ownership by the beneficiary, the majority of the early court decisions held that the death of the beneficiary before the insured did not terminate the beneficiary's interest.[4] That is, the insured was not permitted to designate a substitute beneficiary; at his or her death, the proceeds were payable to the estate of the beneficiary originally named in the policy.

Around the turn of the century (1901), some of the larger companies adopted the practice of including a provision in their policies that permitted the insured to substitute a new beneficiary even during the original beneficiary's lifetime, provided that the policyowner had specifically reserved the right. Moreover, the change could be effected without the consent of the beneficiary. There was some doubt as to the validity of this practice until the standard forms that grew out of the Armstrong investigation of 1905 and 1906—and became statutory (or compulsory) in New York on January 1, 1907—included a change of beneficiary clause. This clause was supplemented shortly thereafter by another that stipulated that the beneficiary's interest, whether revocable or irrevocable, would terminate upon his or her death during the insured's lifetime, with such interest reverting to the insured. The designation of a contingent beneficiary to succeed to the interest of a deceased primary beneficiary was the next logical development.

Status of the Revocable Beneficiary

**defeasible vested
interest concept**

For some time after the validity of a reserved right to change the beneficiary had become well recognized, the revocable beneficiary was generally regarded to have a vested interest in the policy that could be defeated only by the exercise of the insured's right to revoke the designation. This view became known as the *defeasible vested interest concept*. Under that concept, it was believed that the beneficiary's consent was necessary to the exercise of any policy rights by the insured other than the right to change the beneficiary. For example, the insured could not surrender or assign the policy, make a policy loan, or elect a settlement option without the consent of the beneficiary. Yet there was nothing to prevent the insured from revoking the beneficiary designation and then exercising the various policy rights and privileges.

During the last quarter century, court after court have rejected the defeasible vested interest theory in favor of a more practical rule that considerably simplifies the administration of policy rights. The modern rule holds that a revocable beneficiary's interest is at most a mere expectancy that is subject to every other interest created by the insured and to every policy right or privilege exercisable by the policyowner alone. Under this concept, the beneficiary's consent is not needed for the policyowner's exercise of any policy right or privilege.

The interest of a revocable beneficiary, such as it is, terminates upon his or her death during the insured's lifetime because of the reversionary clause referred to above. This is true even though there is no contingent beneficiary and the insured has failed to appoint a successor beneficiary. Thus the nature of the revocable beneficiary's interest comes into sharper focus. A revocable beneficiary has no enforceable rights in the policy prior to maturity, and cannot interfere in any way with the exercise by the policyowner of his or her rights in the policy. The revocable beneficiary has an "expectancy" in the proceeds that will materialize only if *all* of the following conditions are fulfilled:

- The policy remains in force until the death of the insured.
- The beneficiary designation remains unchanged.
- The policy is not assigned.
- The beneficiary outlives the insured.

Despite the fulfillment of these conditions, the beneficiary's interest can be greatly impaired through policy loans negotiated by the policyowner.

On the positive side, the policyowner's right to revoke a beneficiary designation is extinguished at the insured's death, and the interest of the revocable beneficiary vests absolutely at that point. The beneficiary's interest in the proceeds is, of course, subject to any operative deferred settlement agreement.

There are circumstances under which an insured who has reserved the right to change the beneficiary will not be permitted to exercise that right. This would be the case, for example, if the policy were subject to a collateral assignment agreement. Similarly, when a spouse is designated beneficiary of a policy under an agreement made in contemplation of divorce, or when—by court order—an insured is directed to designate his or her divorced spouse as beneficiary of a policy intended to serve as security for alimony payments or in lieu of such payments, the right to change the beneficiary is relinquished.[5] In all such circumstances, the insurance company would permit a change of beneficiary if it had received no notice of the limitation on the insured's right.

Status of the Irrevocable Beneficiary

It is well settled that whenever the insured designates a particular person as the irrevocable beneficiary of a policy, the beneficiary acquires a vested interest in the contract. The exact nature of the interest depends on the terms of the contract.

At one time, an irrevocable beneficiary designation could equal co-ownership of the policy. If there were no conditions under which the beneficiary could be deprived of the right to receive the full amount of proceeds payable under the terms of the policy, that interest would be vested absolutely or unconditionally, and the beneficiary would be regarded as the sole owner of the policy. He or she could exercise all policy rights without the joinder of the insured and would even have the right to pay premiums to keep the policy in force. The insured would have no rights in the policy. Consequently, the insured could do nothing with the contract without the beneficiary's consent that would in any way diminish or adversely affect the beneficiary's right to receive, at the insured's death, the full amount of insurance provided by the policy. If the beneficiary predeceased the insured, his or her interest in the policy would become a part of the beneficiary's estate, and his or her heirs would be entitled to the proceeds upon the policy's maturity.

Such absolute vesting is not common in modern policies. Most policies today provide that the interest of a beneficiary, even one irrevocably designated, terminates if the beneficiary's death occurs during the lifetime of the insured. In that event, all rights to the policy proceeds revert to the policyowner. This is sometimes called a *reversionary irrevocable designation*. Under this type of designation, the interest of the irrevocable beneficiary is only conditionally vested. There is a condition—namely, the beneficiary's death before maturity of the policy—that can destroy his or her interest.

Since the insured can reacquire ownership rights in the contract's death benefit through the death of the beneficiary during his or her lifetime, the

reversionary irrevocable designation

insured possesses a contingent interest in the policy's death benefit from the beginning. Thus in the usual circumstances, neither the policyowner nor the irrevocable beneficiary can exercise any policy rights or dispose of the policy without the consent of the other. For all intents and purposes, the policyowner and the beneficiary are regarded as joint owners of the policy when the beneficiary designation is irrevocable.

It is possible for an insured to procure a policy under which he or she does not reserve the right to change the beneficiary but does retain all other normal policy privileges.[6] In this case, even though the insured can diminish the beneficiary's interest in such a policy or destroy it completely by surrender, the insured cannot revoke the beneficiary's interest, such as it may be, and give it to another without the beneficiary's consent. As courts have pointed out, the terms and conditions of the policy determine the rights of the insured and the interest of the beneficiary. In the majority of policies issued today, however, there are no specific conditions that would permit the policyowner to impair or destroy the interest of an irrevocably designated beneficiary.

Example: ***Status of an Irrevocable Beneficiary***

Which of the following is a policyowner allowed to do without the consent of the irrevocable beneficiary?

- Take out a policy loan? No.
- Change the dividend option? No.
- Collaterally assign the policy? No.
- Change the contingent beneficiary? No.
- Collect the proceeds if the beneficiary predeceases the insured? Yes. If the irrevocable designated beneficiary predeceases the insured, all of that beneficiary's rights in the policy are extinguished. The policyowner can then designate anyone to collect the proceeds at the insured's death.

Irrevocable beneficiary designations are not widely used. An irrevocable beneficiary designation does offer the advantage of protecting the beneficiary's interest in the proceeds during his or her lifetime, and automatically vesting complete ownership rights in the insured in the event that he or she survives the beneficiary. But the same result can be achieved by an absolute assignment or an appropriately worded ownership clause.

SUCCESSION IN INTEREST

Whenever there is only one beneficiary in a beneficiary classification (primary, first contingent, and so forth), the interest of any beneficiary who predeceases the insured passes in the manner and according to the rules described in the preceding pages, unless the contract provides otherwise. Whenever there is more than one beneficiary in a beneficiary classification, however, a question arises as to the disposition of the interest of any beneficiary who dies before his or her interest materializes. The problem has frequently arisen with class designations, such as "my children," but it is equally relevant to multiple specific designations.

To pinpoint the problem, assume that A, the insured, names A's three children, B, C, and D, as primary beneficiaries of A's insurance, share and share alike, without designating any contingent beneficiaries and without specifying what the disposition should be of the share of any child who fails to survive him. Assume further that D predeceases A, leaving three children, E, F, and G. Who is entitled to D's share? (See figure 12-1.)

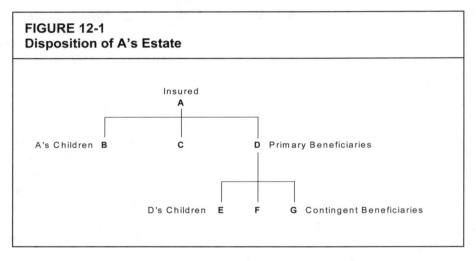

FIGURE 12-1
Disposition of A's Estate

A policy provision on this point is controlling, but in the absence of a pertinent policy provision, D's interest might conceivably be disposed of in one of three ways. It might pass to A's estate, on the theory that where there are multiple designations, the interest of each beneficiary is severable and is contingent on the beneficiary's surviving the insured. The share might pass to B and C, on the theory that the designation of multiple beneficiaries creates a form of undivided interest, analogous to a joint tenancy, with right of survivorship. Finally, the share might pass to D's children, E, F, and G, on the theory that a primary beneficiary has a vested interest in the proceeds that cannot be defeated by his or her failure to survive the insured.

The New York Rule and the Connecticut Rule

In the litigation that has developed around this question, there has been no support for the view that a deceased beneficiary's interest should revert to the insured's estate, despite the fact that this would have been the outcome had the deceased beneficiary been the sole primary beneficiary. The majority of the decisions have followed the rule that the surviving beneficiaries of the classification to which the deceased beneficiary belonged are entitled to take the deceased beneficiary's share. In the example, therefore, B and C would be entitled to the full amount of proceeds. This doctrine is known as the *New York Rule*, because it was first espoused by the New York courts. From a practical standpoint, much can be said in favor of the rule. Most of the cases involve children, which means that if the deceased child's share were to revert to the insured's estate, it would ultimately be distributed to the surviving children—the other beneficiaries—reduced by its share of administration expenses and bequests to other persons, including the widow.

A substantial minority of the courts have followed the *Connecticut Rule,* which holds that the heirs of the deceased beneficiary are entitled to his or her share. In the above example, E, F, and G, therefore, would receive the proceeds to which D would have been entitled had D survived A. Each of D's children would receive one-ninth of the total proceeds; B and C would receive one-third each. This rule conflicts with the prevailing view of a beneficiary's interest in a life insurance policy, but it reflects the desire of the jurists involved to carry out what they believe to be the insured's wishes.

New York Rule *(margin note)*

Connecticut Rule *(margin note)*

Succession-in-Interest Clauses

Anticipating this problem, many companies have incorporated a provision in their policies that—in the absence of contrary instructions from the insured—will control the disposition of the interest of any beneficiary who dies before becoming entitled to payment of his or her share of proceeds. This provision, commonly known as the *succession-in-interest clause,* is applicable to both primary and contingent beneficiaries and to beneficiaries designated irrevocably or revocably. A typical clause might appear as follows:

succession-in-interest clause *(margin note)*

Succession in Interest of Beneficiaries

The proceeds of this policy, whether payable in one sum or under a settlement option, shall be payable in equal shares to such direct beneficiaries as survive to receive payment. The share of any direct beneficiary who dies before receiving payments due or to become due shall be payable in equal shares to such direct beneficiaries as survive to receive payment.

At the death of the last surviving direct beneficiary, payments due or to become due shall be payable in equal shares to such contingent beneficiaries as survive to receive payment. The share of any contingent beneficiary who dies before receiving payments due or to become due shall be payable in equal shares to such contingent beneficiaries as survive to receive payment.

At the death of the last to survive of the direct and contingent beneficiaries:

(a) if no settlement option is in effect, any remaining proceeds shall be paid to the owner or to the executors, administrators, successors, or transferees of the owner; or

(b) if a settlement option is in effect, the withdrawal value of payments due or to become due shall be paid in one sum to the executors or administrators of the last to survive of the direct and contingent beneficiaries.

A direct or contingent beneficiary succeeding to an interest in a settlement option shall continue under such option, subject to its terms as stated in this policy, with the rights of transfer between options and of withdrawal under options as provided in this policy.

Note that this clause applies not only to the situations in which either a primary or a contingent beneficiary fails to survive the *insured,* but also to cases in which a contingent beneficiary fails to survive a *primary beneficiary.* The latter is important when proceeds are being paid out on an installment basis. If the proceeds are to be paid in a lump sum, specifying in the beneficiary designation that the proceeds will be paid only to those beneficiaries who survive the insured will solve the problem, provided this solution is in accord with the insured's wishes.

Per Stirpes

per stirpes

The disposition of deceased beneficiaries' interest envisioned by the succession-in-interest clause does not represent the desires of all policyowners. In designating their children as beneficiaries, many insureds want the share of a deceased beneficiary to go to the beneficiary's children, the insured's grandchildren. This can be accomplished by directing that the proceeds be distributed *per stirpes,* a Latin expression meaning "by the trunk." For example, in designating her husband as primary beneficiary and her children as contingent beneficiaries, an insured could use the following wording: "John Doe, husband of the insured, if he survives the insured; otherwise in equal shares to the surviving children of the insured, and to the surviving children of any deceased children of the insured, per stirpes." The expression "per stirpes" means that the deceased person's issue or lineal descendants take the share (of an estate or of the insurance proceeds) that the deceased would have taken had he or she survived. It is used in wills and trusts, as well as in insurance policies. The children represent the parents, and grandchildren represent the children, and so on down the "trunk." The words "by representation" are sometimes used in lieu of "per stirpes." The Connecticut Rule, referred to earlier, embodies the per stirpes concept.

per capita

Per Capita

Sometimes, however, an insured wants the children of a deceased beneficiary to share equally with the surviving members of the original beneficiary group. In the example used earlier, A might have wanted D's children to share equally with B and C, each taking one-fifth of the proceeds. A could have achieved this objective by specifying that the proceeds should go "in equal shares to such of B, C, and D, children of the insured, as may survive the insured, and to the surviving children of such said children as may be deceased, per capita."

In all these matters, the insurance company accedes to the wishes of the insured, requiring only that his or her desires be clearly expressed in the designation.

OWNERSHIP RIGHTS

Life insurance policies issued today offer many valuable rights and privileges in addition to the company's basic obligation to pay the face amount of the policy upon maturity. Most of these rights—such as surrender options, dividend options, policy loans, assignments, and change of beneficiaries—can

prematurity rights

be exercised during the insured's lifetime and are referred to as *prematurity rights.* It is essential, therefore, that the ownership of the various rights be clearly established and known to all parties concerned.

When a person applies for insurance on his or her own life and designates himself or herself, or his or her estate, as beneficiary, all ownership rights in the policy are vested in that person. The same is true if an insured designates another person as beneficiary but reserves the right to revoke the designation. The interest of such a third-party beneficiary is usually regarded as a "mere expectancy," so tenuous as not to interfere with the exercise of the insured's prematurity rights. In the rare case when a person applies for insurance on his own life and designates another person as beneficiary without reserving the right to revoke the designation (as is normal in most policies), the insured and the beneficiary are considered to be joint owners of the policy, and neither can exercise any prematurity rights without the consent of the other. Note that in none of these situations is the beneficiary considered to be the sole owner of the policy.

In today's complex world of business and finance, there are more and more situations in which it is desirable—or even essential—that the beneficiary (or some other party) be the absolute owner of the policy. For example, if the insured wants to keep the proceeds out of his or her gross estate for federal estate tax purposes, the insured must divest himself or herself of all incidents of ownership. A creditor wants all ownership rights in a policy taken out on the debtor to secure a loan. Partners need to be absolute owners of policies on the lives of fellow partners used to finance business continuation agreements. Employers must be the owners of policies on the lives of key employees.

Sole and complete ownership of a policy can be vested in a person other than the insured in one of three ways, discussed briefly below. The first is through procurement of the policy by the prospective beneficiary or trust. The intended owner applies for the insurance with the consent of the insured and designates himself or herself as owner of the policy, and designates the appropriate beneficiary.

The second method is the *transfer* of ownership rights in a policy originally issued to the insured by means of an endorsement on the policy. The insured directs the company to vest all of his or her rights, privileges, and options in the new owner, and the policy designates the appropriate beneficiary.

The third method is identical with the second, except that it involves the use of an absolute assignment form. This is the oldest procedure and one that is still preferred by many.

The owner of a policy, whether procured on his or her own application or by transfer from the insured, can designate a person other than himself or herself to receive the proceeds of the policy and can reserve the right to revoke the designation. He or she may also transfer ownership to another person, provided the transfer takes effect at the time it is made. Likewise, it is generally agreed that an insured—in transferring ownership of the policy to another person—may nominate a successor to take ownership in the event that the original transferee should die before the insured.

CHAPTER REVIEW

Answers to the review questions and the self-test questions can be found in the Supplement.

Key Terms

beneficiary	donee or gratuitous beneficiary
owner-applicant	specific beneficiary

class beneficiary
primary beneficiary
contingent beneficiary
first-taker beneficiary
second-taker beneficiary
revocable beneficiary
irrevocable beneficiary
defeasible vested interest concept

reversionary irrevocable designation
New York rule
Connecticut rule
succession-in-interest clause
per stirpes
per capita
prematurity rights

Review Questions

1. List and describe the types of beneficiaries from the standpoint of the nature of the interest involved.

2. Explain why it is generally unwise to designate the insured's estate as the primary beneficiary, especially when it is intended that the policy proceeds should go to certain specific individuals.

3. When it is intended that the proceeds go to the insured's estate, explain why designations such as "heirs" or "family" are not effective, and identify what designations are effective for accomplishing this objective.

4. Explain the difference between a specific and a class beneficiary, and give an example of each.

5. Explain why designating one's spouse as simply "husband" or "wife" can cause problems, and what steps can be taken to minimize such problems by specifically designating a spouse.

6. While married to Beth, Bob Hamilton took out a life insurance policy on his life and designated the beneficiary as "Beth Hamilton, wife of the insured." Subsequently, Beth and Bob were divorced and he married Tammy. He kept the policy in force but did not change the beneficiary designation. When he later died, who would be entitled to the policy's death proceeds—Beth or Tammy—and why?

7. Explain under what circumstances class designations are appropriate and what practical problems are often encountered in using them.

8. When his first child, Anne Marie, was born, John Livingston took out a life insurance policy on his life. After his second child, Adam, was born, John forgot to change the beneficiary designation in the policy. For each of the following beneficiary designations, indicate whether Adam would be entitled to share in the proceeds of the policy upon his father's death if that was the designation made by John at the time he bought the policy:
   a. Anne Marie Livingston, daughter of the insured
   b. children of the insured

9. When a policy has more than one primary beneficiary, explain how the primary beneficiaries share in the proceeds.

10. Describe the two functions of the contingent beneficiary.

11. Tom Jones purchased a life insurance policy covering his own life. Tom named his wife, Tasha, as primary beneficiary and his daughter, Catherine, as contingent beneficiary. When Tom died, Tasha elected a life income option with 20 years, certain that it guaranteed to provide monthly income payments for as long as she lived, and at least 20 years' worth of payments even if she died before the end of 20 years. If Tasha died 5 years after Tom, what role, if any, would Catherine play?

12. Contrast the nature of the interests of revocable and irrevocable beneficiaries today, and explain how these interests influence the ability of the policyowner to exercise policy rights during the lifetime of the insured.

13. Under what circumstances will a policyowner who has reserved the right to change the beneficiary not be permitted to exercise that right?

14. Under each of the following sets of circumstances, explain how the two living children of a primary beneficiary who predeceased the insured would share, if at all, in the policy proceeds with the other primary beneficiaries who were still living at the time the insured died:
    a. if no pertinent policy provision and the courts applied the New York rule
    b. if there was no pertinent policy provision and the courts applied the Connecticut rule
    c. if the policy contained a typical succession-in-interest clause
    d. if the beneficiary designation also directed that the proceeds be distributed to the surviving children of any deceased primary beneficiaries, per stirpes
    e. if the beneficiary designation also directed that the proceeds be distributed to the surviving children of any deceased primary beneficiaries, per capita

15. Describe the three ways the sole and complete ownership of a life insurance policy can be vested in a person other than the insured, and what rights such owners have with respect to designating and changing the beneficiary.

Self-Test Questions

T   F   1. A trust or business corporation can be a beneficiary.

T   F   2. It is generally wise to name the insured's estate as primary beneficiary of a life insurance policy.

T F 3. When the insured is the applicant and designates himself or herself as beneficiary, the insured can exercise all rights under the policy without the consent of any other person.

T F 4. If a creditor is designated as beneficiary under a policy on the debtor's life, the creditor is a donee beneficiary.

T F 5. In making specific designations, it is customary to identify the person both by name and by relationship to the insured if there is a blood or legal relationship.

T F 6. If at the time of his death the beneficiary designation in John Smith's policy was "Jane Smith, wife of the insured," she would generally be entitled to the proceeds of her former husband's policy even though they had been divorced for many years.

T F 7. With a class beneficiary designation, the individual beneficiaries are mentioned by name, but all belong to a clearly identifiable group.

T F 8. When a class designation is used, proceeds are divided equally among only those individuals who were members of the particular group at the time the designation was made.

T F 9. Because class designations present practical problems for insurers, most companies place certain restrictions on their use.

T F 10. A specific beneficiary always has a claim to policy proceeds prior to that of a class beneficiary.

T F 11. If the primary beneficiary dies before the insured, the contingent beneficiary succeeds to all the rights of the original primary beneficiary.

T F 12. The contingent beneficiary always becomes a second-taker beneficiary in cases where the primary beneficiary dies after the insured.

T F 13. If the proceeds are to be paid out under an installment option, the agreement usually specifies that any installments remaining unpaid at the death of the last surviving contingent beneficiary will be paid in a lump sum to the insured's estate.

T F 14. Today, a revocable beneficiary is generally regarded to have a defeasible vested interest in the life insurance contract.

T F 15. A revocable beneficiary has no enforceable rights in the policy prior to maturity.

T F 16. There are circumstances under which a policyowner who has reserved the right to change the beneficiary will not be permitted to exercise that right.

T   F   17. Most policies today provide that an irrevocable beneficiary has an absolute vested interest in the contract and thus is regarded as sole owner of the policy.

T   F   18. When the beneficiary is designated irrevocably, the policyowner must obtain the consent of the irrevocable beneficiary in order to exercise any policy rights or dispose of the policy.

T   F   19. The living children of a primary beneficiary who predeceased the insured would not share in the policy proceeds with the other surviving primary beneficiaries if the court applied the New York Rule, or if the policy contained a typical succession-in-interest clause.

T   F   20. The living children of a primary beneficiary who predeceased the insured would take the share of the proceeds the deceased beneficiary would have taken had he or she survived, if the beneficiary designation provided for a distribution to them per capita.

T   F   21. Prematurity rights of a life insurance policy can never be exercised solely by the beneficiary.

NOTES

1. In setting up successive classes of contingent beneficiaries, the insured must be careful not to violate the rule against perpetuities or statutory prohibitions against the unlawful accumulation of income.
2. George Bliss, *The Law of Life Insurance* (1871).
3. *Central National Bank v. Hume,* 128 U.S. 195 (1888).
4. *Couch Cyclopedia of Insurance Law,* 2d ed. rev. (Rochester, NY: The Lawyers Cooperative Publishing Co., 1993), vol. 4, secs. 27.130–27.136.
5. *Mutual Life Insurance Co. of New York v. Franck,* 9 Cal. App. 2d 528, 50 P. 2d 480 (1935).
6. *Morse v. Commissioner,* 100 F.2d 593 (7th Civ. 1938).

The Beneficiary:
Part 2

Dan M. McGill
Revised by Burke A. Christensen

Learning Objectives

An understanding of the material in this chapter should enable the student to

---

13-1. Describe the problems commonly encountered in attempting to carry out the policyowner's wishes through the use of beneficiary designations and the steps that can be taken to avoid or minimize such problems.

13-2. Describe the procedures prescribed by insurers for effecting a change of beneficiary.

Chapter Outline

It should now be clear that the rights of various parties can be vitally affected by the question of whether the primary beneficiary survives the insured, or *vice versa*. Under normal circumstances, this is a question of fact that can be easily and conclusively established. If, however, the insured and the beneficiary are killed in a common disaster, such as an automobile accident, an airplane crash, an explosion, or other tragic circumstance, it may well be impossible to determine who survived the other.

SIMULTANEOUS DEATH

**Uniform Simultaneous
Death Act**

In an attempt to avoid litigation to establish survivorship and provide an equitable basis for disposing of the property of the parties involved, 49 states and the District of Columbia have adopted the *Uniform Simultaneous Death Act*, which applies to all types of property and property rights. The underlying theory of the act is that in the absence of evidence to the contrary, each person is presumed to be the survivor as to his or her own property. In the case of jointly held property, each party is presumed to be the survivor as to his or her share of the property. The act makes specific references to life insurance, stating that when the insured and the beneficiary have died and there is no sufficient evidence that they died otherwise than simultaneously, the policy proceeds will be distributed as if the insured had survived the beneficiary. This is a conclusive presumption, and it applies whether the beneficiary is designated revocably or irrevocably.

The objectives of the Uniform Simultaneous Death Act can be achieved through the inclusion of a *common disaster clause* in the policy. With language similar or even identical to that of the Act, this clause states that when the insured and beneficiary perish in a common accident, the insured will be presumed to have survived the beneficiary.

SHORT-TERM SURVIVORSHIP

The Uniform Simultaneous Death Act settles the question of survivorship when there is not sufficient evidence as to whether the insured or the beneficiary survived, but it does not eliminate the possibility of legal action by a personal representative of the beneficiary claiming that the beneficiary survived the insured. Moreover, it is not effective when it can be proved that the beneficiary, in fact, did survive the insured, even by a moment. In the absence of contrary instructions in the policy, the proceeds would, under such circumstances, go to the beneficiary's estate.

When there are contingent beneficiaries and the proceeds are held under the interest option or are payable in installments (other than a life income), the primary beneficiary's short-term survivorship creates no particular problems. The primary beneficiary's estate would be entitled to one monthly payment at most, and the remainder of the proceeds would go to the contingent beneficiaries. Under all other circumstances, however, the survival of the beneficiary for only a short period is generally considered to be an unfavorable event.

If the proceeds are payable to the primary beneficiary under a life income option, there is likely to be a substantial forfeiture of proceeds even though there are surviving contingent beneficiaries. If there are no refund features in the option, the company's obligation would be discharged completely by the payment of one monthly installment to the beneficiary's estate. If the payments are guaranteed for a specified number of years, some forfeiture would still be inevitable—the extent, of course, varying inversely with the length of the period. There would be no forfeiture, other than loss of interest, under the cash refund or installment refund form of the life income option.

The problem of short-term survivorship is made clear if the proceeds are payable in a lump sum and the surviving spouse was the primary beneficiary. After probate, the proceeds of both estates pass under the surviving spouse's will or (if there was no will) to his or her heirs in intestacy. This may be a result the insured did not intend. Even if the results were acceptable, the proceeds would reach the beneficiaries only after going through estate administration and suffering some shrinkage. The cost consequences would be the same had the insured survived the beneficiary and died shortly thereafter, unless contingent beneficiaries had been named to take the proceeds in that event.

Delayed-Payment Clause

In an effort to avoid the undesirable consequences of short-term survivorship of the beneficiary (which is a far more common occurrence than simultaneous death), a few companies stipulate that the life insurance policy proceeds will be payable to the beneficiary only if he or she is alive at the time of payment. Other companies use a provision that states that the proceeds will be payable to a designated beneficiary only if the beneficiary survives the insured by a specified period of time, such as 10, 14, or 30 days. Insurers are understandably reluctant to delay payment for a protracted period, but some have been willing to defer payment up to 180 days. Such clauses solve the short-term survival problem effectively, although no reasonable period would be long enough to cover every case that might arise.

The delayed-payment clause has one disadvantage for the policyowner who anticipates a federal estate tax liability. The policyowner would normally want the proceeds of the life insurance policies to qualify for the marital deduction, which is allowed for all property passing outright to the decedent's spouse. The vesting of insurance proceeds, or any property includible in the decedent's gross estate, can be delayed up to 6 months without jeopardizing their qualification for the marital deduction, provided the spouse survives the period and obtains complete dominion over the proceeds. But if the spouse does not survive the period, the proceeds do not qualify.

There are several solutions to this problem. One is the use of trusts. The insured could also elect payment of the proceeds under an interest option and then designate contingent beneficiaries. If the primary beneficiary is given the unlimited right of withdrawal, the proceeds will qualify for the marital

---

Example: ***The Delayed-Payment Clause Problem***

Joseph is the owner and insured under a life insurance policy with Jennifer, his wife, as the beneficiary. The policy contains a 14-day delayed-payment clause. Joseph and Jennifer die in an auto accident in which she outlived him by 2 days. The death proceeds are in the estate of Joseph, the policyowner, for estate tax purposes. They do not qualify for the marital deduction because Jennifer didn't live long enough to be entitled to the proceeds. If she had outlived him by 14 days or more, the proceeds would have qualified for the marital deduction and thus would have escaped taxation in Joseph's estate. Of course, they would then be a part of Jennifer's estate.

---

deduction even though the surviving spouse never has an opportunity to exercise the right. If the beneficiary-spouse dies in a common disaster with the insured or dies from any cause shortly after the insured, the proceeds will pass to the contingent beneficiaries. In the event that the beneficiary survives the insured by an extended period, he or she will be permitted under the practices of most companies to elect a liquidation option at contract rates within a specified period, such as one or 2 years after the insured's death. The portion of proceeds passing to others at the primary beneficiary's death will be includible in the primary beneficiary's gross estate for federal estate tax purposes, but if he or she dies within a specified period after the insured, the law allows a credit for any taxes paid on the same property in the insured's estate.

Approaches to Short-Term Survivorship

- delay clause for beneficiary
- interest-only option with contingent beneficiaries
- use of trusts to take full advantage of marital deductions

Reverse Common Disaster Clause

reverse common disaster clause

Another method of assuring the availability of the marital deduction when there is no evidence of survivorship is through the use of a *reverse common disaster clause* in the insurance policy. This clause makes the presumption that the *beneficiary* survives. Obviously, the clause should be used only when it is compatible with the insured's overall estate plan.

Example:

Common Disaster and Reverse Common Disaster Clause

Clark is the owner and insured under a life insurance policy of which his brother, Kent, is the beneficiary. No contingent beneficiary is named. Both Clark and Kent are killed when Clark's private plane crashes.

- If the policy contains a common disaster clause, the proceeds go to Clark's estate.
- If the policy contains a reverse common disaster clause, the proceeds go to Kent's estate.
- But if there is any evidence that one of the two brothers outlived the other by even a very short time, neither type of clause applies.

Installment Option

It should be emphasized that a perfectly satisfactory method of dealing with the short-term survivorship hazard is through the use of installment options (except life income options) with contingent beneficiaries. Neither the simultaneous deaths of the insured and the beneficiary, nor the beneficiary's short-term survivorship, present any problems when the proceeds are to be distributed under the installment time or installment amount options, or when they are to be held under the interest option with contingent beneficiaries to succeed to the primary beneficiary's interest. Again, an installment option should be used only if it meets the insured's distribution objectives.

EFFECTING A CHANGE OF BENEFICIARY

The owner of a life insurance policy normally retains the right to change the beneficiary. If so, he or she can remove not only the original beneficiary but also any successor beneficiaries that have been appointed. The policyowner may relinquish this right by a policy endorsement or by a collateral assignment of the policy. The right to change the beneficiary is a matter of contract, and the insurance company cannot refuse to assent to a change of beneficiary on the ground that the prospective beneficiary has no insurable interest, or on any other ground. On the other hand, the company can—and does—prescribe the procedure the policyowner must follow to effect a change of beneficiary. Following the procedure is also a condition of the contract.

All insurers require written notice of a change of beneficiary, and a few specify that the change must be endorsed on the policy. Most insurers, however, merely require that the policyowner's written request be received and filed by the insurer. Filing is preferred over the endorsement method because occasionally there are situations in which the insured is not able to produce the policy for endorsement. It may have been lost, or it may be in the possession of a person who refuses to release it—an estranged or divorced spouse, for example. In such cases, the company may recognize the change of beneficiary despite the lack of formal compliance with the procedural requirements, but it would probably do so only if the insurer were satisfied that there is no danger of the prior beneficiary establishing a claim. The courts have consistently held that the policy provisions concerning a change of beneficiary are for the protection of the company and can be waived under proper circumstances.

Divorce between the insured and the beneficiary deserves special mention. The general rule in all states except Michigan is that divorce in itself does not terminate the beneficiary's interest. This is based on the doctrine that the interest of a named beneficiary is a personal one, not dependent on the relationship to the insured that may have been stated in the designation. Thus a beneficiary designation that reads, "to my wife, Emily," remains payable to Emily even after a divorce and the husband-insured's remarriage to another woman. In Michigan, a statute provides that a spouse's interest is automatically terminated by divorce, regardless of whether the spouse was revocably or irrevocably designated. Unless the court decree specifies otherwise, the insured's estate then becomes the beneficiary.

Change of Beneficiary Issues

- Irrevocable beneficiaries must agree to the change.
- The change request must be in writing and communicated to the insurer.
- Collateral assignment may limit the ability to change some rights and parties.
- Divorce situations should prompt a reevaluation of beneficiary designation.
- A divorce decree may limit or prohibit changes (insurer should be notified in writing).
- Michigan divorces automatically terminate the spouse's rights in the policy.

A MINOR AS BENEFICIARY

The designation of a minor as beneficiary creates problems that are not ordinarily encountered with an adult beneficiary. Perhaps the most obvious complication arises when an insured designates a minor as beneficiary without reserving the right to revoke the designation. This would now be a rare occurrence since most policies today routinely provide that the policyowner reserves the right to change a beneficiary designation. However, if the policy does not reserve the right, and the insured wants to change the beneficiary, assign the policy as collateral for a loan, make a policy loan, or surrender the policy for its cash value, he or she could do so only with the minor's consent—which the minor does not have legal capacity to give. The insured might seek to have a guardian appointed for the minor, but it is highly unlikely that a court would permit the guardian to waive the minor's rights.

There will almost certainly be problems if the policy matures while the beneficiary is still a minor. The insurance company cannot safely make payments directly to the minor since he or she is not legally competent to receive payment and release the insurer. Upon attaining majority, the minor might repudiate the release in the receipt and demand payment of the proceeds once again. To protect itself, the company would have to insist on the appointment of a guardian, which involves expense to the minor's estate. In some states, insurance companies are authorized by special statutes to waive the guardianship requirement and make payment on behalf of the minor to an adult, usually a parent or someone standing in place of a parent. However, the amounts that can be distributed under these statutes tend to be nominal; the usual limit is less than $500, although a few states permit amounts up to $1,500 to be paid in this manner.

Minor Beneficiaries

- cannot give insurer binding release
- will have to have a guardian appointed to facilitate receipt of death proceeds
- cannot give release to change irrevocable designation

Statutes in 44 states provide that persons who have attained the age of 18 years have reached the age of majority and thus are competent to receive and give full acquittance and discharge for any amount. Some of the remaining states give minors between the ages of 18 and 21 special capacity for limited amounts, ranging from $2,000 to $3,000, in any one year in the form of benefits payable upon the death of the insured, as long as the insurance policy or the policy settlement agreement specifically provides for direct payments to such minor. In some states the statute applies only to periodic payments that do not exceed the specified maximum in any one year.

Statutes in a few states also embrace benefits payable under annuity contracts. Some statutes permit either a lump-sum payment or periodic payments not exceeding the stipulated amount in any one year. For example, a New York statute permits the payment of $3,000 to a minor, either in a lump sum or in periodic payments not exceeding $3,000 per year. The New York statute also pertains to benefits payable upon the maturity of a policy as an endowment.

Difficulties also exist with respect to the election of settlement options by a minor or a guardian acting on the minor's behalf. The statutes above authorize installment payments directly to minors only when the settlement option was elected by the insured or other owner of the policy. They do not authorize the minor to elect a settlement option. Because it is quite clear that a minor lacks the legal capacity to elect a settlement option, most companies are not willing to run the risk of the minor's later repudiation of the contract unless the amounts involved are small. However, if the beneficiary is within one or 2 years of attaining his majority, an insurer may agree to a settlement involving the payment of interest only, with a provision for payment of principal to the minor beneficiary at his or her majority or to his or her estate in the event of death.

THE TRUSTEE AS BENEFICIARY

There are circumstances under which it is advisable to have life insurance proceeds administered by a trustee. A trust can serve many useful purposes, but it is especially desirable when there is a need for great flexibility in the administration of the proceeds or when some of the beneficiaries are minors. It is a common practice for a parent to designate his or her spouse as primary beneficiary and to designate a trustee as contingent beneficiary to administer proceeds for the benefit of minor children. The trustee may be a natural person or a corporation, and the designation may be revocable or irrevocable.

It is essential that a trust agreement exists at the time the trustee is the designated beneficiary. If the insured should die before instructions have been provided to the trustee, the trust would undoubtedly be dissolved as unenforceable. In such cases the courts have held that, since there is nothing to guide the trustee as to the purpose or manner of distribution of the trust estate, the funds must be paid over to the person or persons presumably entitled to them. If the distributees were children, the proceeds would be paid to duly appointed guardians.

When a trustee is designated as beneficiary, it is usually intended that the trustee will collect the proceeds in one sum and administer them in accordance with the terms of the trust agreement. There are occasions, however, when the trustee deems it advantageous to make use of the insurance company's deferred-settlement options. Under these circumstances, it becomes important to determine whether the trustee has the right to select such options.

Trustees as a class first developed a real interest in insurance policy settlement options in the 1930s, when the going interest rate on new investments dropped below the rate of return guaranteed in insurance company settlement options. Many companies, feeling that trustees were attempting to shift their investment responsibilities (for which they were compensated) to the life insurance industry, and having other reservations about the practice, refused to honor settlement option elections by trustees. When litigation in 1939[1] established the right of a trustee to elect a settlement option unless that right is denied in the insurance policy, many insurers inserted a prohibition in their policies against the use of settlement options by trustees. Today, however, few insurers continue that practice. Some policies stipulate that the power of all beneficiaries to select settlement options is subject to the insurer's consent. Others do not limit the rights of natural persons to select settlement options but reserve the right to deny the selection of settlement options to nonnatural persons (trusts and corporations).

In the absence of express permission in the trust instrument, there is a serious question whether a trustee has the legal right to use settlement options, even though the insurance company makes them available. It is standard practice therefore to include proper language in the trust agreement giving trustees the right to exercise ownership powers over life insurance policies. Absent such a clause, the issue hinges on whether or not a life insurance settlement option is a legal investment for a trustee. When the investment statute is the "prudent man" type, a strong argument can be made in favor of the legality of the practice. Many legal experts have concluded, however, that a trustee has an unquestioned right to elect a settlement option only when (1) the trust instrument expressly confers the right, and (2) the insurance policy does not deny the right.

CHAPTER REVIEW

Answers to the review questions and the self-test questions can be found in the Supplement.

Key Terms

Uniform Simultaneous Death Act   reverse common disaster clause

Review Questions

1. Albert Polk purchased a life insurance policy on his own life and named his wife, Nancy, as primary beneficiary, and his daughter, Shirley, as contingent beneficiary. Albert and Nancy both died as a result of a plane crash. Explain how the state's Uniform Simultaneous Death Act would affect the distribution of policy proceeds in each of the following situations:
   a. if there was no sufficient evidence that Albert and Nancy did not die simultaneously
   b. if it can be proved that Nancy survived Albert even for a very short time

2. Describe the consequences of short-term survivorship of the primary beneficiary under each of the following circumstances:
   a. when there are contingent beneficiaries, and the proceeds are held under the interest option or are payable in installments (other than life income)
   b. when there are contingent beneficiaries, and the proceeds are payable to the primary beneficiary under a life income option
   c. when there are contingent beneficiaries, and the proceeds are payable to the primary beneficiary in a lump sum

3. Describe one possible advantage and one possible disadvantage of including a delayed-payment clause in a life insurance policy, and explain the methods available for overcoming the disadvantage.

4. Describe the various procedures prescribed by insurance companies that a policyowner must follow to effect a change of beneficiary.

5. Describe the problems created by the designation of a minor as a beneficiary that are not ordinarily encountered with an adult beneficiary, and explain how policyowners, insurance companies, and the state legislatures have attempted to deal with the problems.

6. Explain why it is essential that there be a trust agreement at the time a trustee is designated as the beneficiary of a life insurance policy.

7. Explain what factors must be considered in determining whether a trustee designated as a beneficiary has the right to select settlement options.

Self-Test Questions

T   F   1. The Uniform Simultaneous Death Act provides that if the primary beneficiary survives the insured for only a very short period following a common accident, life insurance proceeds payable as a lump sum will be distributed to the contingent beneficiary.

T   F   2. When the insured and the primary beneficiary die as a result of a common accident, and there is no evidence that they died otherwise than simultaneously, the policy proceeds will generally be distributed as if the primary beneficiary survived the insured.

T   F   3. The delayed-payment clause provides that the proceeds of the life insurance policy will be paid to the designated beneficiary only if the beneficiary survives the insured by a specified period of time.

T   F   4. Use of a delayed-payment clause can result in life insurance policy proceeds not qualifying for the marital deduction.

T   F   5. All life insurers require written notice of a change of beneficiary and specify that the change must be endorsed on the policy.

T   F   6. The courts have consistently held that the policy provisions concerning change of beneficiary are for the protection of the insured and thus cannot be waived by the insurance company.

T   F   7. Most states have enacted statutes that permit payments of life insurance proceeds directly to minors.

T   F   8. Minors lack the legal capacity to elect settlement options.

T   F   9. A trust agreement must exist at the time a trustee is designated beneficiary of a life insurance policy.

T   F   10. A trustee designated as beneficiary clearly has a right to elect a settlement option when the trust agreement expressly confers the right and the insurance policy does not deny the right.

NOTE

1. *First Trust Co. of St. Paul v. Northwestern Mutual Life Insurance Co.,* 204 Minn. 244, 283 N.W. 236 (1939).

Assignment of Life Insurance Contracts

Dan M. McGill
Revised by Burke A. Christensen

Learning Objectives

An understanding of the material in this chapter should enable the student to

14-1.   Explain the basic concept of assignment, and distinguish between absolute and collateral assignments.

14-2.   Describe the rights of a policyowner and a beneficiary to assign their interests in a life insurance policy.

14-3.   Explain the effects that absolute and collateral assignments have on a beneficiary's rights and on the ownership rights in a life insurance policy.

14-4.   Explain the insurance company's role in the assignment process with respect to notice of an assignment, payment of proceeds when there are multiple assignees and other types of conflicting claims, and responsibility for the validity of an assignment.

Chapter Outline

The life insurance contract, with its valuable prematurity rights and promise to pay a specified sum of money upon maturity, is an ideal form of collateral for credit transactions. Hence it is not surprising that the practice of assigning life insurance policies as collateral security has reached large proportions. Policies are, in addition, frequently assigned as a means of transferring ownership rights to another person or organization. It is important to note the circumstances under which a life insurance contract can be assigned and the manner in which the rights of the various parties involved are affected by the assignment.

RIGHT OF ASSIGNMENT

assignment

absolute assignment

partial assignment

collateral assignment

assignment: the transfer of some or all of a person's (the assignor's) ownership rights in property to another (the assignee). An *absolute assignment* is a transfer to the assignee by sale or gift of all the assignor's rights. A *partial assignment* transfers less than all the assignor's rights. A *collateral assignment* is a transfer of some of a property owner's interests to provide security for a loan. The collateral assignment terminates when the loan is repaid.

Assignment by the Insured or Owner of the Policy

It is a settled rule of law that anyone having an interest in a life insurance contract can transfer that interest, with or without consideration, to another person. Hence the contract need not (but frequently does) contain a provision expressly authorizing the owner to transfer his or her interest; it is an inherent right that can be restricted only by contract. Industrial life insurance policies contain limitations on the right of assignment, but ordinary insurance policies are generally free from restrictions other than requiring notice and making assignments subordinate to policy loans.

Consideration is a legal term that refers to something of value that is exchanged between two parties to a transaction. Anything that has value can serve as consideration. In a life insurance contract, the consideration exchanged is the policyowner's money and the insurer's promise to pay. A

gift

transfer without reciprocal consideration is a *gift*.

incidents of ownership

In the usual situation all ownership rights in a policy are vested in the policyowner (normally the insured). Among the incidents of ownership is the right to assign the policy. In addition to its contract law implications, the term *incidents of ownership* is extremely important for purposes of the federal tax law. According to IRC Sec. 2042, if the insured had any incidents of ownership in the policy during the 3 years prior to death, the policy's death proceeds are included in the insured's estate for federal estate tax purposes. The right to assign the policy carries with it the power to transfer all rights and interests in the policy to another person. When someone other than the insured is the owner of the policy, it is customary for the policy to restrict the right of assignment to the owner. This is not a restriction on the assignability of the policy as such; it merely identifies the person who has the right to assign it.

The following are three sample assignment provisions:

> We will not be deemed to know of an assignment unless we receive it, or a copy of it, at our Home Office. We are not obligated to see that an assignment is valid or sufficient.

•   •   •

> You may assign this policy as collateral security, subject to policy loans. Beneficiaries' interests and methods chosen for the payment of proceeds are subordinate to such an assignment.

•   •   •

> Your interest in this policy may be assigned without the consent of any revocable Beneficiary. Your interest, any interest of the insured, and any interest of any revocable beneficiary shall be subject to the terms of the assignment. We will not be on notice of any assignment unless it is in writing; nor will we be on notice until a duplicate of the original assignment has been filed at our Home Office. We assume no responsibility for the validity or sufficiency of any assignment.

The person assigning the policy cannot transfer any interest greater than he or she possesses; nor can the obligation of the insurer be enlarged by an assignment. This means that the assignor of the contract cannot, by the unilateral action of assigning the contract, impair or defeat the *vested* interest of another party to the contract. In the typical case only one other party can be adversely affected by the assignment, and that is the beneficiary. But is the beneficiary's interest entitled to protection against infringement? The answer depends on whether the beneficiary designation is revocable or irrevocable.

Revocable or Irrevocable Beneficiary Designation

If the beneficiary designation is revocable, the majority rule is that the policyowner can assign the policy without the consent of the beneficiary and without complying with the formalities for changing the beneficiary designation. In some jurisdictions an absolute assignment is held to automatically extinguish a revocable beneficiary's interest to the extent of the assignee's interest. In other jurisdictions the revocable beneficiary's interest is unaffected unless changed by the assignee. As might be expected, the majority rule reflects the decision of those courts that the interest of the revocable beneficiary is not vested but is a mere expectancy. The minority view is that the beneficiary has a vested interest in the policy, but that the beneficiary's interest may be extinguished or terminated by the policyowner. This is known in the law as a *defeasible vested interest.* Courts that adhere to the defeasible vested interest theory hold that the policyowner cannot give the assignee an interest in the policy proceeds without obtaining the beneficiary's consent or revoking the beneficiary designation.

Example: ***Effect of Assignment on a Beneficiary***

Manuel was the owner and insured under a $100,000 life insurance policy in which Maurice is designated as the revocable beneficiary. Manuel executed a collateral assignment of the policy, without Maurice's knowledge or consent, to John to secure a $55,000 loan. When Manuel died, $43,800 of principal was still owned to John, plus $3,700 of interest. Therefore, the death proceeds will be divided, with $47,500 belonging to John and $52,500 belonging to Maurice.

It is the rule in all states, however, that when the beneficiary designation is irrevocable, the policy cannot be assigned without the beneficiary's consent.

Assignment by the Beneficiary

In the absence of a provision to the contrary, the beneficiary can assign his or her interest, both before and after maturity of the policy. Prior to the policy's maturity, the beneficiary's interest is virtually worthless because the insured has the right to change the beneficiary. If the insured does not reserve that right or if the designation of a beneficiary is irrevocable, there is something of substance to be transferred. However, even that irrevocable interest is contingent upon the original beneficiary's survival of the insured, unless the beneficiary's estate is designated (as contingent beneficiary) to receive the proceeds if he or she predeceases the insured.

Upon maturity of the policy, proceeds payable in a lump sum vest in the beneficiary and can be assigned by him or her. When the proceeds are held by the insurer under a deferred-settlement agreement, the beneficiary's right of assignment is subject to the rights of the contingent beneficiaries, if any, and to restrictive provisions in the policy or settlement agreement. A common restriction for a policy or settlement agreement to contain is a **spendthrift clause** *spendthrift clause,* which denies the beneficiary the right to commute, alienate, or assign his or her interest in the proceeds. Furthermore, in a few states the laws that protect insurance proceeds from the claims of the beneficiary's creditors prohibit an assignment of the beneficiary's interest.

EFFECT OF AN ASSIGNMENT ON A BENEFICIARY'S RIGHTS

The effect of an assignment on the rights of the beneficiary depends not only on the type of beneficiary designation but also on the type of assignment involved: an absolute assignment or a collateral assignment.

The absolute assignment divests the policyowner of all incidents of ownership and transfers all rights and interests in the policy absolutely and permanently to the assignee. It is designed for situations (such as a gift or a sale) in which the assignor's clear intent is to make the assignee the new owner of the policy. The collateral assignment, on the other hand, transfers to the assignee those rights—and only those rights—needed to protect a loan from the assignee to the assignor. It resembles a mortgage of land or a pledge of marketable securities. The arrangement is intended to be temporary; upon repayment of the loan, the assignment terminates, and all assigned rights revert to the previous owner. The assignee's interest in the policy is limited to the amount of the indebtedness and unpaid interest, plus any premiums paid by the assignee to keep the policy in force.

For reasons explained later in this chapter, absolute assignments have frequently been used when only a security arrangement was intended. In such cases the assignment is treated as a collateral one and is released upon satisfaction of the assignor's obligation to the assignee. In fact, the courts will enforce such a result if the assignor can prove that a collateral assignment between the assignor and assignee was intended.

If assignment of a policy is absolute in form and the parties intended the assignment to be absolute in substance as well, the beneficiary's interest is completely extinguished, provided the designation was revocable, or if irrevocable, that the beneficiary joined in the assignment. If an assignment is collateral in substance, irrespective of its form, the beneficiary's interest will be extinguished to the extent of the assignee's interest, which is limited in the manner described above. If the policyowner attempts to assign the policy without the consent of the beneficiary when such consent is necessary, a valid transfer of the policyowner's interest takes place, but the beneficiary's interest is not affected. If the assignment affects a revocable beneficiary in a jurisdiction that sees a defeasible vested interest, the designation remains in effect until a change has been accomplished in the prescribed manner. If the assignment involves an irrevocable beneficiary, the designation is unaffected and the assignee can exercise no contract rights and privileges without the irrevocable beneficiary's consent.

With regard to whether the interest of a third-party beneficiary is subordinate to that of the assignee without a formal change of beneficiary, courts in general have based their rulings purely on the intent of the parties. Most of the litigation involved collateral assignments; in such cases, there is usually a clear intent to subordinate the beneficiary's interest to that of the creditor-assignee.

In absolute assignments the courts recognize this intent to subordinate the beneficiary's interest to that of the assignee in two ways. First, if the assignee can perfect his or her claim by observing the formalities of a change of beneficiary, the courts are willing to spare the assignee the trouble of doing so. Thus in cases involving absolute assignments that are not incidental to a credit transaction, some courts have concluded that a formal assignment with notice to the insurance company substantially conforms to the requirements for a change of beneficiary and operates as such. (This rationale is patently inappropriate for collateral assignments, however, since the beneficiary of record receives the proceeds in excess of the claims of the assignment.) Second, an absolute assignment of policy ownership does not operate to change the preexisting beneficiary designation. Consent of the beneficiary to the assignment is therefore regarded in all jurisdictions as conclusive evidence of intent to give a preferred status to the rights and claims of the assignee (the new owner), who must act in accordance with the policy provisions to name a new beneficiary.

Revocable Beneficiary Subordinate To

- change of beneficiary
- collateral assignment
- absolute assignment

In all states it is held that whenever the beneficiary of a policy is the insured or the insured's estate, the claims of the assignee will prevail over those of the executor or administrator of the insured's estate.[1] This is true whether the assignment is absolute or collateral in form. Accordingly, it is the current practice to use collateral assignment forms that require the beneficiary's signature. In the execution of assignments incidental to policy loans, insurers *require* this procedure unless the wording of the policy makes it unnecessary (as is the case with current policies). A sample provision reads as follows:

> The interest of any revocable beneficiary in this policy and any settlement option elected shall be subordinate to any assignment made either before or after the beneficiary designation or settlement option election.

The effectiveness of this type of provision has been upheld[2] even under the laws of New Jersey, which historically has been one of the states requiring the consent of a revocable beneficiary to an assignment of the policy. Nevertheless, it would seem that an assignee who wants to avoid any possible legal complications upon the death of the insured would be well advised to designate himself or herself as beneficiary. There could then be no doubt as to the assignee's right to receive the proceeds.

EFFECT OF ASSIGNMENT ON OWNERSHIP RIGHTS

Concept of Ownership

There are two sets of rights in a life insurance policy: those that exist during the insured's lifetime and those that arise after the insured's death. The first set is known, quite logically, as prematurity rights, and the second set as *maturity rights*. The most important of the prematurity rights are the

maturity rights

rights to surrender the policy for cash or paid-up insurance, to borrow against the policy, to designate and change the beneficiary, and to assign the policy. Among the lesser—but still significant—prematurity rights are the rights to elect settlement options, to elect dividend options, to reinstate the policy, to convert or exchange the policy for another, and to take advantage of the automatic premium loan feature. The maturity rights include the rights to receive the proceeds, to elect settlement options (unless usurped by the insured or owner), and to designate direct and contingent beneficiaries (only under certain circumstances).

The concept of ownership of these rights has undergone dramatic development during the last century. The original concept was that all prematurity and maturity rights were vested in the beneficiary and his or her estate. In other words, the beneficiary was regarded as the absolute owner of the policy. Once the insured's right to change the beneficiary was recognized, the insured and the beneficiary were considered to be joint owners of the prematurity rights and the beneficiary the sole owner of the maturity rights—

Ownership Rights before Death of Insured

- surrender policy for cash value
- request policy loans
- elect nonforfeiture option
- assign the policy
- designate primary and contingent beneficiaries
- elect dividend options (if participating)
- elect settlement options
- exchange the policy for another
- reinstate the policy after lapse
- utilize automatic premium loan

Ownership Rights after Death of Insured

- beneficiary to receive proceeds
- beneficiary to elect settlement options (unless made irrevocably by owner before death)
- beneficiary to designate direct and contingent beneficiaries (if applicable)
- collateral assignee to receive proceeds

subject, however, to the right of the insured, if reserved, to divest the beneficiary of all interests in the policy and the proceeds. Over the years this concept has been modified, and today, in the absence of a contrary ownership arrangement, the insured/policyowner is regarded to be the absolute owner of the prematurity rights and the possessor of the power to dispose of the maturity rights. If the policyowner has designated a third person as an irrevocable beneficiary, such beneficiary is considered to be the sole owner of the proceeds (when due at maturity), subject to the policyowner's reversionary interest, and the policyowner and beneficiary are looked upon as the joint owners of all prematurity rights.

Ever since the concept of a beneficiary change was recognized around the turn of the century, the insured has been identified with ownership rights, either as sole or as joint owner. The most recent development is the insured's complete dissociation or disattachment from ownership rights in the policy. This development received its impetus from the growth of business insurance, juvenile insurance, and insurance for estate-transfer purposes, where there is a distinct need to have ownership of the policy in a person other than the insured, but it was also motivated by insurers' desire to clarify the ownership status of the various rights in the contract.

Dissociation is accomplished by specifying on the face of the policy that a particular person or firm is the owner of the policy and restricting the exercise of the various policy rights and privileges to the owner. In most cases the insured is designated as owner, but the insured, as such, has no rights in the policy. All prematurity rights are vested in the owner, including the right to control the disposition of the maturity rights. The owner is given express authority to designate and change primary and contingent beneficiaries. Furthermore, during the lifetime of the insured, the owner can exercise all the rights and privileges in the policy without the beneficiary's consent. The application for the policy makes no reference to the question of whether the applicant does or does not reserve the right to change the beneficiary. If the applicant wishes to create a joint ownership of the policy by the policyowner and the beneficiary, he or she can designate them as joint owners, with whatever survivorship provisions might be appropriate or desired.

The owner is given the sole right to assign the policy, and the interest of any beneficiary is made subject to the assignment. The assignee, however, does not necessarily become the owner of the policy. The policy may stipulate the manner in which a transfer of ownership is to be accomplished, and some policies state that ownership of the policy can be transferred only by a written instrument, satisfactory to the company, endorsed on the policy.

It can be seen therefore that a minimum of *five* parties other than the insurance company may be associated with a life insurance policy: the applicant, the insured, the owner, the beneficiary, and the assignee. In the great majority of cases, the applicant, insured, and owner are one and the same person. Nevertheless, the ownership of all rights and privileges is crystal clear, irrespective of the number of parties or interests involved. The next problem is to determine what happens to these rights and privileges when the policy is assigned.

Collateral Assignments

A collateral assignment is nothing more than a pledge, subject to the general rules of law governing such a transaction. A pledgor is entitled to get his or her property back upon paying the debt when due and after tendering the correct amount at the proper time, may recover the property in a legal proceeding. On the other hand, if the debt is not paid when due, the pledgee may, under authority of a court obtained in a suit for that purpose—or more commonly under the authority of the pledge agreement itself—have the property sold to satisfy the claim, including expenses of the sale. The sale can be private if the agreement gives the pledgee that alternative. The surplus remaining after the pledgee has been satisfied belongs to the pledgor.

Pledging a life insurance policy as collateral for a debt raises some additional issues. Since the pledgee is not the absolute owner of the policy, he or she cannot surrender the policy in the absence of a specific agreement to that effect. If the pledgor of an insurance policy dies before paying the debt for which the policy is security, the pledgee has a claim against the policy proceeds and may enforce that claim to the extent of the debt and other related charges. However, since the collection of the proceeds is not a sale, the pledgee does not have the power, in the absence of an express stipulation, to collect the full amount of the proceeds, holding the excess for the pledgor's representatives.

It was not customary before the development of the *American Bankers Association (ABA) assignment form* for collateral assignment forms to confer specific rights and powers in the policy on the assignee. When the assignee attempted to surrender a pledged policy or to take other action concerning it, most companies insisted that the owner of the policy join in the action. Furthermore, upon maturity of the policy, the assignee was permitted to collect only the amount of the outstanding indebtedness, unpaid interest, premiums paid on the policy, and other expenses incurred in connection with the loan. The remaining portion of the proceeds, if any, was paid to the beneficiary of record.

Many creditors resented having to prove the extent of their interest to the insurance company, preferring to receive the entire amount of proceeds and to account to the beneficiary for the excess over their claims, as they computed them. To make matters worse, the collateral notes (not the collateral assignment form) used by some banks proved to be defective, in that they failed to give the bank the unquestioned right to pay premiums on the policy in the event of the owner's default and to add the sums thus paid to the principal of the indebtedness. The bank's only recourse in some circumstances was to obtain title to the policy through foreclosure proceedings, thus establishing its right to pay premiums and to bring these payments under the protection of the collateral assignment. To obviate such difficulties, the ABA assignment form contains a provision that specifically authorizes the assignee to pay premiums and to add them to the amount of the indebtedness.

Example: ***An Assignee's Rights under ABA Assignment Form***

Ken, the policyowner and insured, named "my children" as revocable beneficiaries. He collaterally assigned the policy to Local Bank as security for a loan. Ken died before the loan was repaid. Local Bank has two options under the ABA form:

- Collect the full death proceeds, take what is owed to it, become a "resulting trustee" for the excess, and determine who is to receive the proceeds as a member of the class designation "my children."
- Collect only the amount of its interest in the proceeds from the insurer and let the insurer sort out who gets the remainder, perhaps with the help of the courts if there is a dispute as to who makes up the group "my children."

Whatever the impact of a collateral assignment on ownership rights, it is intended to be temporary in nature. As stated earlier, once the loan is repaid by the assignor, the assignment is released and all ownership rights revert to their status before the assignment. An irrevocable beneficiary, for example, in joining in a collateral assignment, does not relinquish any vested rights in a policy; he or she merely agrees to subordinate his or her interest to that of the assignee during the time the assignment is in force. Once the assignment is terminated, the former status of all rights is restored. Repayment of the loan cancels the assignment, even though there may not be a formal release of the encumbrance.

Absolute Assignments

An absolute assignment conveys all the title, rights, and interests possessed by the assignor to the assignee. If the assignor owned all the rights in the policy, or if all persons having an interest in the policy joined in the assignment, the assignee becomes the new owner of the policy and can exercise all the rights therein without the consent of any other person. The transfer is intended to be permanent.

This was the conventional way of transferring ownership of a policy to another person. It was used, for example, when the insured wanted to make a gift of the policy or, on rare occasions, to sell the policy. It was the approved method of divesting the owner of all incidents of ownership in a policy, to the end that the proceeds would not be includible in his or her gross estate for federal estate tax purposes. Transferring ownership rights by means of an *ownership endorsement* is also used. Under this method and as specifically stated in the policy, ownership in the full legal sense can be transferred only by means of a written instrument, acceptable to the company, endorsed on the policy.

ownership endorsement

In the days when an absolute assignment was universally regarded as a full and complete transfer of ownership rights, many creditors—particularly banks—turned to it as a more effective method than collateral assignments of safeguarding their interests. They began to insist on an absolute assignment when a policy was being pledged as security for a loan. In this way, they hoped to avoid the restrictions that were frequently imposed on them in connection with collateral assignments. They wanted the right, without the consent of the insured, to surrender the policy for cash, to borrow the loan value, to elect paid-up insurance, and to exercise any of the other rights and privileges that might protect their interests. They also wanted the right to receive the full proceeds upon maturity of the policy, from which they would deduct amounts due them and pay over the excess to the beneficiary. In so doing, of course, they would deprive the beneficiary of the privilege of utilizing the policy's settlement options. In most cases, because of the smallness of the sums involved, this was not a serious disadvantage to the beneficiaries. When the sums involved were substantial and the options were favorable, however, this practice was a potential source of great loss to the beneficiaries.

In many cases, perhaps, the absolute assignment form worked out exactly as the banks and other creditors had hoped it would. In other cases, however, the insurance company, realizing that the intent was that the policy had been assigned only as collateral, refused to recognize the assignee as sole owner of the policy and insisted upon the policyowner's joinder in the exercise of the various policy rights. Insurers based their refusal on the failure of the assignment form to mention the specific rights conferred upon the assignee.

Dissatisfaction of both creditors and debtors with the absolute assignment form eventually led to the development of a form especially designed for the assignment of life insurance policies. It was developed by the Bank Management Commission of the American Bankers Association with the collaboration of the Association of Life Insurance Counsel. The official name of the form is "Assignment of Life Insurance Policy as Collateral," but it is popularly known as the ABA assignment form.

ABA Assignment Form

The essence of the ABA assignment form is that it sets forth clearly and specifically the rights that are transferred to the assignee and the rights that are not transferred and are presumably retained by the assignor. The assignment is absolute and unqualified in the sense that the rights vested in the assignee can be exercised without the consent of any other party. It is collateral in that the assignee's rights are limited to his or her interest, with all rights reverting to the assignor upon termination of the assignee's interest.

The form states that the following rights will pass to the assignee, to be exercised by him or her alone:

- the right to collect from the insurance company the net proceeds of the policy when it matures by death or as an endowment
- the right to surrender the policy for its cash value
- the right to assign or pledge the policy as security for loans or advances from the insurance company or other persons
- the right to collect and receive all distributions of surplus to which the policy may become entitled during the time the assignment is in force, as well as all dividend deposits and paid-up additions credited to the policy as of the date of the assignment, provided appropriate notice is given to the insurance company by the assignee
- the right to exercise all surrender options and to receive the benefits and advantages therefrom

The form stipulates that the following rights will not pass to the assignee, unless the policy has been surrendered:

- the right to collect from the insurance company any disability benefit payable in cash that does not reduce the amount of insurance (The so-called *maturity type* of permanent and total disability income provision found in some of the older policies provides for the deduction of each monthly payment from the face amount of the policy.)
- the right to designate and change the beneficiary, subject to the assignment
- the right to elect settlement options, likewise subject to the assignment

In consideration of the rights vested in him or her the assignee agrees

- to pay over "to the person entitled thereto under the terms of the Policy had this assignment not been executed" any sums remaining after the liabilities, matured or unmatured, to the assignee are satisfied
- not to surrender the policy or borrow upon it except for the purpose of premium payment, unless there has been a default in the obligations to the assignee or a failure to pay premiums when due, and in any event, not until 20 days after the assignee mails to the assignor notice of his or her intention to exercise such right
- upon request, and without unreasonable delay, to forward the policy to the insurance company for endorsement of any designation or change of beneficiary or any election of a settlement option

The insurance company is authorized to make payment to the assignee without investigating the reason for any action taken by the assignee, the validity or amount of the assignee's claims, or the existence of any default on the assignor's part. Upon surrender or maturity of the policy, the assignee is entitled to all the monies due but may, at his or her option, request a smaller sum. From the standpoint of the assignee, the right to receive the full proceeds eliminates one of the objections to the collateral assignment, but the assignee may also permit the proceeds in excess of his or her claims to be paid under the settlement plan selected by the owner. If the assignee requests the payment of a greater sum than the amount of the assignee's interest, he or she becomes what **resulting trustee** in law is known as a *resulting trustee* for the excess and must account under the principles of trusteeship to the owner or beneficiary, as the case may be, for such sum. In this connection, it is pertinent to observe that bank assignees tend to be reluctant to invoke their right under the ABA assignment form to collect more than their claim upon maturity of the policy. They prefer to avoid the responsibility of determining who under the policy language is entitled to the remainder of the proceeds.

The assignee is relieved of the obligations to pay premiums and policy loan principal or interest. If the assignee does pay any such items out of his or her own funds, the amounts so paid become part of the liabilities secured by the assignment, are due immediately, and draw interest at a rate not exceeding 6 percent annually until paid.

Other provisions of the form establish the superiority of the assignment instrument in case of conflict with any provisions of the note for which it is security, grant administrative discretion to the assignee in handling a claim, and certify that the assignor has no bankruptcy proceedings pending against him or her and has not made an assignment for creditors.

Until recently, the ABA form was the most widely used of all such forms. It no longer enjoys such popularity because differing requirements in various states make the ABA form inappropriate in some jurisdictions. In its place some insurers have prepared their own collateral assignment forms that are tailored to the varying state requirements. Policyowners should always seek the advice of competent local counsel when they intend to make a collateral assignment of a life insurance policy.

Notice to the Company of Assignment

If the interest of an assignee is to be protected, the insurance company must be notified of the assignment, preferably as soon as the assignment has been executed. A life insurance policy is not a negotiable instrument; a transfer of rights in the policy, to be effective, must be recorded with the party who is under obligation to perform. If, without notice of an assignment, a life insurance company, upon maturity of a policy, pays the proceeds to the beneficiary of record, it will be absolved under the general rules of law from any further liability or obligation under the policy, even though a valid assignment of the policy was in effect at the date of the insured's death. To implement the law and to put all parties on notice, insurers incorporate a statement in their policies that no assignment will be binding on the company unless it is in writing and filed in the home office. This provision has no effect on the *validity* of an assignment, but it has a material bearing on the enforcement of the rights transferred to the assignee.

Multiple Assignees

The issue is broader than the rights of the beneficiary and the assignee. At the maturity of the policy, there may be more than one valid assignment of the policy in effect, and the relative rights of the assignees must be resolved. This can happen when one of the assignees failed to demand delivery of the policy with the assignment or when the owner obtained a duplicate copy or copies of the policy by alleging that the original had been lost. Although it is conceivable that an insured could innocently or inadvertently assign a policy while a valid assignment of the policy was still outstanding, in most such cases the owner is guilty of fraudulent behavior.

English rule

Definite rules of law have evolved to settle disputes arising over multiple assignments of the same interest. The *English rule*, adopted in a minority of American jurisdictions, holds that the assignee who first gives notice to the insurance company has prior claim to the proceeds, provided that such assignee, at the time the policy was assigned to him or her, had no notice of a prior assignment.[3] If the assignee did know of an earlier unrecorded assignment still in effect, he or she would, of course, have been guilty of fraud in accepting a second assignment of the same interest.

American rule

The *American rule*—or prevailing rule—is that the assignee who is first in point of time will be preferred, regardless of notice to the company.[4] This rule is subject to the important exception that if the prior assignee fails to require delivery of the policy and thus permits a subsequent assignee to obtain delivery of the policy with no notation of the prior assignment, the subsequent assignee's claim will be superior to that of the original assignee.

A third general rule, applicable under either the English or American rule, is that an assignee not guilty of fraud will be permitted to retain any proceeds that may have been paid to him or her. Thus an assignee with a preferred claim will lose his or her priority in any jurisdiction if that assignee fails to notify the insurer of the claim before the company has paid another assignee of record. In jurisdictions applying the American rule, the assignee first in point of time will have his or her interest protected even under the general rule as long as the assignee records the assignment with the insurance company at any time prior to payment by the company.

Example: ***Multiple Assignees***

Zachary, who is getting a bit forgetful in his old age, makes an absolute assignment as a gift of a $50,000 policy on Zachary's life to Annie, who is his favorite daughter. Some time later he gives away the same policy by an absolute assignment to his church, which promptly notifies the insurer. When Zachary dies, who gets the proceeds, Annie or the church?

- English rule: the church, if it had no knowledge of the earlier assignment because Annie apparently didn't notify the insurer
- American rule: Annie, the first assignee in point of time, unless she failed to require delivery of the policy to her

Policy loans or advances made by the insurer are subject to the foregoing rules. Since assignments involving policy loans or advances are automatically recorded with the company, no difficulties are likely to develop around them. The only time that an insurer would find its lien against the cash value and proceeds subordinate to that of another assignee would be if—with notice of another valid assignment and without the consent of the assignee—it went ahead and made a policy loan. Presumably, this would happen only through inadvertence. If a valid assignment of the policy had been executed prior to the policy loan but with no notice to the insurer, the company would be protected under the exception to the American rule.[5]

Bill of Interpleader

bill of interpleader

Whenever there are conflicting claims for insurance proceeds or other benefits, whether the claimants are assignees or beneficiaries, the insurance company generally seeks the assistance of the courts. To do otherwise would be to invite the possibility of having to pay the benefits more than once. In such circumstances, the insurer files a *bill of interpleader,* an equitable device, and pays the proceeds into court. In taking such action, it admits its obligation to pay and petitions the court to adjudicate the conflicting claims and determine who is entitled to receive the money. The insurer discharges its responsibility by paying the disputed sum over to the court. This is an extremely important legal remedy for insurance companies.[6]

OTHER MATTERS RELATING TO ASSIGNMENT

Company Not Responsible for Validity of Assignment

The policy provision pertaining to assignment almost invariably contains a statement that the company is not responsible for the validity of any assignment of the policy. Some policies broaden the statement to include the word *effect* as well as *validity*. This provision is intended to protect the company against suits by a beneficiary or some other person alleging that the assignment was invalid because of the owner's incompetence or because the assignment was tainted with fraud or executed under duress. In the leading case,[7] an insured and his wife, who was the beneficiary of the policy, executed an assignment at a time when both were of advanced age and lacking in mental capacity. Upon the death of the insured, the company, having no knowledge of the incompetence of the insured and beneficiary, paid the proceeds to the assignee. Subsequently, the wife's guardian sued the company to recover the proceeds on the ground that the assignment was void. The court refused to hold the company liable for a second payment of the proceeds, giving as one of its reasons the exculpatory statement in the assignment provision. The court noted, however, that this clause protects the company only when it has no knowledge of a defect in the assignment instrument or of any irregularity in the circumstances surrounding the assignment.

Insurable Interest

The right of an owner to assign the policy to anyone of his or her choice, whether or not such person has an insurable interest in the life of the insured, is recognized in all jurisdictions when no financial consideration is involved. Such donee-assignees have been regarded to be in the same class as donee-beneficiaries as far as insurable interest is concerned. The position of the courts is that it is immaterial whether the insured designates the payee of the policy within the contract itself (a conventional beneficiary designation) or by means of a separate instrument (an assignment). If the applicant for insurance has an insurable interest in the life of the insured at the inception of the contract, an insurable interest on the part of the assignee is not required, either at the inception of the contract or at the time of the insured's death. Of course, if the insured were induced by the assignee to take out the policy, the assignee would have to have an insurable interest since in effect the assignee would be the applicant.

The situation is different when an assignment is made for a consideration. If the policy is assigned to a creditor as security for a debt, the assignee is permitted to retain only the amount of his or her interest, even though the assignment was absolute in form. Thus a creditor-assignee must have an insurable interest in the life of the insured at the maturity of the contract. If the creditor-assignee's interest is extinguished prior to maturity of the policy, the assignment terminates. While it is clear that a creditor has an insurable interest in the life of his or her debtor, the amount is not limited to the amount of the debt, and there is no clear rule as to how much more than the debt is acceptable public policy.

On the other hand, an assignment to a purchaser for value is valid in the federal courts and in all but four states, regardless of the question of insurable interest. In other words, in most jurisdictions a policy can be sold to a person who has no insurable interest in the life of the insured. In 1911 Mr. Justice Holmes explained the rationale of this doctrine:[8]

> Life insurance has become in our days one of the best recognized forms of investment and self-compelled saving. So far as reasonable safety permits, it is desirable to give to life policies the ordinary characteristics of property. . . . To deny the right to sell . . . is to diminish appreciably the value of the contract in the owner's hands.

Briefly, the argument is that there should be a free market for life insurance policies when a person in poor health can obtain the true value of his or her policy. The minimum price at which a policy should sell is the cash value, but the real value of a policy on the life of a person in poor health is somewhere between the cash value and the face amount of the policy, depending on the individual's chances of survival. If a person is ill and needs money for medical treatment, it is argued, he or she should be permitted to sell his or her policy to the highest bidder, without regard to insurable interest. The chances of murder are thought to be remote; in any case, the danger is probably not greater than when the insured designates a beneficiary who has no insurable interest.

Four states—Alabama, Kansas, Kentucky, and Pennsylvania—do not follow the majority rule. These states require the assignee to have an insurable interest when the policy is assigned for value. In these states such an assignment is permitted only up to an amount equal to the value paid by the assignee.

CHAPTER REVIEW

Answers to the review questions and the self-test questions can be found in the Supplement.

Key Terms

assignment	partial assignment
absolute assignment	collateral assignment

gift	ownership
incidents of ownership	endorsement
spendthrift clause	resulting trustee
maturity rights	English rule
American Bankers Association	American rule
(ABA) assignment form	bill of interpleader

Review Questions

1. Describe the nature of the policyowner's right to assign a life insurance policy, and explain how that right may be affected by whether the policy's beneficiary designation is revocable or irrevocable.

2. Describe the nature of the beneficiary's right to assign his or her interest in a life insurance contract in each of the following situations:
    a.   before maturity of the policy
    b.   after maturity of the policy

3. Compare an absolute assignment and a collateral assignment with respect to each of the following:
    a.   the nature and extent of the rights that are transferred
    b.   the intended duration of the transfer
    c.   the extent of assignee's interest
    d.   the typical use(s) in connection with life insurance policies

4. How have the courts tended to treat absolute assignments that have been used when only a security arrangement was intended by the parties involved?

5. Describe what effects, if any, the assignment of a life insurance policy has on the beneficiary's rights in each of the following situations:
    a.   when the assignment is absolute in substance as well as in form
    b.   when the assignment is collateral in substance, irrespective of its form

6. List the rights in a life insurance policy that

    a.   exist during the insured's lifetime
    b.   arise after the insured's death

7. Describe how the concept of ownership of the rights in a life insurance policy has evolved over the last century.

8. When a life insurance policy is pledged as collateral for a debt, what rights and/or obligations does the assignee have with respect to surrendering the policy for its cash value under each of the following circumstances:
    a.   in the absence of any specific agreement indicating that the policy can be surrendered by the assignee
    b.   when the policy was assigned using the ABA assignment form

9. When a life insurance policy is pledged as collateral for a debt and the policy matures by death, what rights and/or obligations does the assignee have with respect to collecting the proceeds under each of the following circumstances:
   a. in the absence of any express stipulation that the assignee may collect the full amount of the proceeds
   b. when the policy was assigned using the ABA assignment form

10. Explain in what sense the ABA assignment form is absolute and in what sense it is collateral.

11. Joe Jones purchased a $100,000 life insurance policy on his life and named his wife, Sherri, as primary beneficiary. Several years later, Joe assigned the policy to Sam Smith as security for a $50,000 loan, but the insurance company was never notified of the assignment. When Joe died, the insurance company paid $100,000 to Sherri upon receiving proof of death. What obligation would the insurance company have to Sam, the assignee?

12. Explain the rules applied in resolving the relative rights of the assignees when there is more than one valid assignment in effect for a life insurance policy.

13. Describe the legal remedy commonly used by insurance companies in cases where there are conflicting claims by assignees or beneficiaries for insurance proceeds or other benefits.

14. Explain why insurance companies commonly include a provision in life insurance policies stating that the company is not responsible for the validity of any assignment of the policy.

14-15. Explain whether the assignee must have an insurable interest in the life of the insured in order to have a valid assignment under each of the following circumstances:
   a. when no financial consideration is involved in the assignment
   b. when an assignment is made for a consideration

Self-Test Questions

T   F   1. Assignment involves the transfer of some or all of a person's ownership rights in property to another.

T   F   2. A life insurance policy can be assigned by the policyowner only if the policy contains a provision expressly authorizing such a transfer.

T   F   3. When someone other than the insured is the owner of a life insurance policy, it is customary for the policy to restrict the right of assignment to the owner.

T   F   4. A majority of courts hold that when the beneficiary designation is revocable, the policyowner must revoke the existing beneficiary designation before assigning the policy.

T   F   5. A beneficiary cannot assign his or her interest before a policy matures.

T   F   6. If an assignment is collateral in substance, the beneficiary's interest is completely extinguished, provided the designation was revocable, or if irrevocable, provided the beneficiary joined in the assignment.

T   F   7. With collateral assignments, the interest of a third-party beneficiary has usually been viewed by the courts as being subordinate to that of the assignee.

T   F   8. With dissociation, all prematurity rights in a life insurance policy, including the right to control the disposition of the maturity rights, are vested in the insured.

T   F   9. When a life insurance policy is pledged as security for a debt, the pledgee can neither surrender the policy nor collect the full amount of the proceeds at maturity if they exceed the amount of the pledgee's interest unless there is a specific agreement that confers such rights on the pledgee.

T   F   10. With a collateral assignment, once the loan is repaid by the assignor, the assignment is released and all ownership rights revert to their status before the assignment.

T   F   11. If a collateral assignment was made using the ABA assignment form, the assignee would need the policyowner's consent to surrender the policy for its cash value or to collect death proceeds in excess of his or her interest.

T   F   12. If, under the terms of the ABA assignment form, the assignee requests payment of a greater sum than the amount of the assignee's interest, he or she becomes a resulting trustee for the excess and must account under principles of trusteeship to the owner or beneficiary, as the case may be, for that sum.

T   F   13. If, without notice of an assignment, a life insurance company paid the policy proceeds to the beneficiary of record after the insured died, it would generally be required also to pay the assignee the value of his or her interest if a valid assignment of the policy was in effect at the time of the insured's death.

T   F   14. If there are multiple assignments in effect for a life insurance policy, the prevailing (American) rule is that the assignee who is first in point of time will always be preferred, regardless of notice to the company.

T   F   15. When there are conflicting claims for insurance proceeds among assignees or beneficiaries, often an insurer will petition the court to adjudicate the conflicting claims by filing a bill of interpleader and paying the proceeds over to the court.

T   F   16. Generally the policy provision pertaining to assignment contains a statement that the company is not responsible for the validity of any assignment of the policy.

T   F   17. The assignee must always have an insurable interest in the life of the insured in order for an assignment to be valid.

NOTES

1. See citations in Harry Krueger and Leland T. Waggoner (eds.), *The Life Insurance Policy Contract* (Boston: Little, Brown & Co., 1953), p. 89, n. 17.
2. *Phoenix Mutual Life Insurance Co. v. Connelly,* 188 F. 2d 462 (3d Cir. 1951), reversing, 92 F. Supp. 994 (D. N.J., 1950).
3. See Krueger and Waggoner, *The Life Insurance Policy Contract,* p. 69, n. 2, for a list of jurisdictions following the English rule. Such important insurance states as California, Connecticut, Ohio, and Pennsylvania follow this rule.
4. See *ibid.,* p. 70, n. 3, for a list of states following the American rule. New York is one.
5. *Patten v. Mutual Benefit Life Insurance Co.,* 192 S.C. 189, 6 S.E. (2d) 26 (1939).
6. Strictly speaking, a *bill of interpleader* requires that the insurance company be entirely disinterested in the outcome of the litigation. Under various state statutes and the Federal Interpleader Statute, the company can file a *bill in the nature of a bill of interpleader* when it does have an interest in the outcome—for example, when the representatives of the insured and the beneficiary killed in a common accident are claiming the proceeds, and the settlement agreement calls for the payment of the proceeds to the beneficiary under a life income option. If the beneficiary is held to have survived, the company may be able to discharge its obligations with one monthly payment. A more common example of the use of a bill in the nature of a bill of interpleader is when a company admits a death claim but denies liability for accidental death benefits.
7. *New York Life Insurance Co. v. Federal National Bank,* 151 F. 2d 537 (10th Cir. 1945), reversing 53 F. Supp. 924 (W.D. Okla. 1944), certiorari denied, 327 U.S. 778 (1946), rehearing denied, 327 U.S. 816 (1946).
8. *Grigsby v. Russell,* 222 U.S. 149, 156 (1911).

15

Protection against Creditors

Dan M. McGill
Revised by Burke A. Christensen

Learning Objectives

An understanding of the material in this chapter should enable the student to

---

15-1. Explain what protection is afforded life insurance in the absence of that specially provided by the state exemption statutes.

15-2. Describe the effects of the Bankruptcy Reform Act of 1978 and the Federal Tax Lien Act of 1966 on the ability of creditors to enforce claims against life insurance policy cash values and maturity proceeds.

15-3. Identify the various types of state exemption statutes, and describe the protection they typically provide for life insurance.

Chapter Outline

The protection enjoyed by life insurance against creditors' claims is a vast and complex subject, and it can be dealt with here in only the most cursory fashion. Emphasis will be on guiding principles with a minimum of substantiating detail. There are so many facets to the subject that a rather detailed outline is necessary. The most basic dichotomy distinguishes between protection available in the absence of special legislation and that available under statutes specifically designed to give life insurance a preferred status.

A life insurance policy is a valuable property right, and thus a policyowner's creditors may attempt to acquire an interest in the policy's value. A creditor may acquire an interest by operation of the contract in the following ways:

- The creditor can become the owner of the policy insuring the life of the debtor.
- The creditor can become the collateral assignee of the policy to the extent permitted to secure the debt.
- The creditor can be designated the beneficiary of the policy.

NONSTATUTORY PROTECTION

The topic of nonstatutory protection can itself be broken down into various subtopics, but the most important distinction is between creditors of the insured and creditors of the beneficiary.

Creditors of the Insured

Creditors of the insured may seek to satisfy their claims out of the cash value of a policy still in force or out of the proceeds of a matured policy. The legal principles involved in these two types of action are so different that they must be dealt with separately.

Before Maturity of the Contract

If the policy is payable to the insured or to a *revocable* third-party beneficiary, the insured is the owner of the policy and is entitled to the cash value upon surrender of the policy. The cash value is an asset of the owner and is reflected as such in his or her financial statements. It would seem therefore that in the absence of special statutory rules, the cash value of such an insurance policy would be available to the creditors of the owner on the same basis as any other personal property. Such is not the case, however.

In theory, the insured's creditor is entitled to the cash value of a policy owned by the insured; in practice, the creditor is generally unable to enforce his or her rights because of procedural difficulties. The normal collection processes are not effective against the cash value because the insurance company is under no obligation to pay the money to anyone until the owner exercises his or her privilege of surrendering the policy. Moreover, the courts are loath to force the owner to exercise the right to surrender. Direct action against the company, in the form of a garnishment or distraint proceeding, has uniformly been unsuccessful, while attempts by judgment creditors to force the owner to surrender the policy have been successful in only a few jurisdictions.

If the creditor has no contractual rights in the policy, he or she may seek to satisfy the debt by securing a judgment against the policyowner. The creditor may try to execute the judgment by seizing the debtor's property—including the insurance policy. The creditor might seek to obtain the cash value of an unmatured policy or the policy proceeds if the insured-debtor has died.

Bankruptcy Reform Act of 1978

Bankruptcy Reform Act of 1978. Federal law and the laws of all 50 states permit creditors to protect themselves from defaulting debtors in this fashion. However, the states, as well as the federal government, create special protection from creditors for certain kinds of property. The applicable federal law is the *Bankruptcy Reform Act of 1978.* That law, like the state laws, exempts certain categories of property from creditors' claims. These exemptions were continued under the Federal Bankruptcy Law that become effective in October 2005. One category of property uniformly protected under these exemption laws is life insurance. This, like the tax advantages given to life insurance under the Internal Revenue Code, adds to the value of life insurance as the foundation of an individual's financial plan.

Under federal bankruptcy law, an individual filing bankruptcy may elect either the exemptions provided under the federal statute or those provided by the applicable state law. However, the federal Bankruptcy Reform Act of 1978 also permits states to "opt out" of the reach of the federal law. If a state passes such an opt-out statute, then its citizens are deprived of the federal alternative and may protect property from creditors only under that state's exemption statute. More than 75 percent of the states have enacted legislation to opt out of the federal bankruptcy system.

The situation is different when the policyowner is bankrupt and a trustee in bankruptcy has been appointed. The federal Bankruptcy Reform Act of 1978 provides that the trustee of the bankrupt's estate will be vested with the bankrupt's title, as of the date the petition in bankruptcy was filed, to all property that the bankrupt could have transferred by any means prior to filing the petition or that might have been levied upon and sold under any judicial process. Since a life insurance policy payable to the insured or to a revocable third-party beneficiary could have been transferred, title to it passes to the trustee in bankruptcy. The trustee, as owner of the policy, can then surrender it for its cash value. Policies without a cash value do not pass to the trustee in bankruptcy.

Note, however, that the interest of the trustee in bankruptcy is limited to the cash value of the insurance on the date the petition in bankruptcy was filed. Thus if the insured dies prior to adjudication of the bankruptcy and before the policy is surrendered, the excess of the proceeds over the cash value must be paid to the designated beneficiary, if any, or otherwise to the insured's estate. Under the federal law prior to the 1978 act, if the insured, within 30 days after the insurance company certified the amount of the cash value to the trustee, paid the trustee the sum of money so certified, the insured was entitled to recover his or her policy free from the claims of the creditors participating in the bankruptcy proceeding. (Funds borrowed for this purpose could have been repaid almost in full from the proceeds of a policy loan.) This provision was to prevent the hardship to the bankrupt's family if all his or her life insurance policies were to pass absolutely to the trustee in bankruptcy. Unfortunately, this provision, known as the *insurance proviso*, was not included in the Bankruptcy Reform Act of 1978.

Example: ***Federal vs. State Creditor Protection***

George is the bankrupt policyowner of a universal life policy. A trustee in bankruptcy has not yet been appointed, so George's creditors have no claim to the cash value under the Bankruptcy Reform Act of 1978.

However, George's home state has enacted an opt-out statute of the procedural type. Consequently, the protection provided by the federal law is inapplicable, and the cash values probably will be subject to the claims of George's creditors.

Federal Tax Lien Act of 1966

Federal Tax Lien Act of 1966. There are special rules for federal tax liens against a person's property. Under the *Federal Tax Lien Act of 1966*, the government's lien overrides state exemption laws. The federal government may require the insurance company to withdraw the policyowner's policy loan values up to the amount of the tax and pay that amount to the government within 90 days after notice.

The government's right to the policy loan values extends to the policy proceeds if the federal tax lien was attached prior to the insured's death. In this case, the beneficiary will be paid only if the policy proceeds exceed the amount of the government's lien. However, if the insured dies prior to the attempted attachment of the federal tax lien, the state exemption laws apply and the proceeds will be protected to the extent of the state law.

After Maturity of the Contract

When proceeds are payable to the insured or the insured's estate, they become available to estate creditors on the same basis as any other unrestricted assets in the estate. When they are payable to a third-party beneficiary, however, they vest in the beneficiary immediately at the insured's death, whether the beneficiary designation was revocable or irrevocable. In this case, the proceeds are free from the claims of the policyowner's creditors.

Creditors of the Beneficiary

The cash value of a life insurance policy cannot be levied upon by a creditor of a third-party beneficiary, whether the designation is revocable or irrevocable. When the designation is revocable, the policyowner (whether or not he or she is also the insured) is the sole and absolute owner of the policy. When the designation is irrevocable, the policyowner has rights that cannot be defeated by a creditor of another person regardless of his or her status as beneficiary. Once the policy has matured, however, the proceeds are the property of the beneficiary and can be freely levied upon by his or her creditors.

STATUTORY PROTECTION

All states have seen fit to enact legislation providing special protection to life insurance against the claims of creditors. This legislation has a long history, the oldest law going back to 1840. The laws are a manifestation of a long-standing public policy that sets a higher priority on people's obligations to their spouses and children than on their obligations to their creditors. Today, these laws are based on the public policy that creditors should not be permitted to make someone destitute and a potential ward of the state. Since the creditor has the right to select his or her debtor, these state exemption laws caution a creditor to be careful in extending credit. They reflect a philosophy that has led to laws exempting workers' compensation awards, veterans' benefits, and other similar payments from attachment by creditors.

The state exemption statutes are diverse in nature. The broadest among them exempt all types of life insurance benefits from attachment by all types of creditors. At the other extreme are laws exempting modest amounts of policy *proceeds* payable to the insured's surviving spouse and children from claims of the insured's creditors. Some of the laws apply to all types of life insurance, while others protect only a particular form, such as group insurance, pensions, disability income, annuity income, or fraternal insurance. Some protect only insurance taken out by a married woman on the life of her husband. There are statutes that protect the insurance against the creditors of the insured only, creditors of the beneficiary only, or any unsecured creditors other than the federal government. Finally, some laws protect only policy proceeds, while others protect all types of benefits, especially cash values. To make matters more confusing, some states have more than one type of statute.

Whether the policyowner's creditors can obtain insurance policy funds depends on whether the creditor is trying to claim the death proceeds or the policy's cash value. In some circumstances, the result depends on the identity of the policyowner, the beneficiary, or the creditor.

State Exemption Statutes

- vary significantly
- generally protect some or all of life insurance from some categories of creditors, especially creditors of the insured or policyowner
- do not exempt life insurance cash values from federal tax liens
- have an intent to protect life insurance proceeds payable to spouses and children from claims of most creditors
- may extend protection
  – to policy cash values, loans, and dividends
  – to nonfamily, third-party beneficiaries
  – against claims of beneficiary's creditors

The identity of the creditor changes the creditor's rights. The federal government can reach a policy's cash values via a tax lien, whereas a private citizen creditor cannot. The identity of the beneficiary is also important. As an example, see the New York exemption statute, which provides in part as follows:

> If any policy of insurance has been or shall be effected by any person on his own life *in favor of a third person beneficiary,* or made payable, by assignment, change of beneficiary or otherwise, to a third person, *such third person beneficiary,* assignee or payee *shall be entitled to the proceeds and avails* of such policy as against the creditors, personal representatives, trustees in bankruptcy and receivers in state and federal courts of the person effecting the insurance. (emphasis added)

Under this statute the policy's proceeds are not exempt from creditors' claims if the beneficiary is the insured, but they are exempt if a third person is the beneficiary.

The New York statute also provides special protection for certain policyowners as follows:

. . . if the person effecting such insurance . . . shall be the wife of the insured, she shall be entitled to the proceeds and avails of such policy as against *her* own creditors. . . . (emphasis added)

A comparison of the New York and Oklahoma statutes points out that some statutes provide more protection for the policy values than others. The Oklahoma exemption statute protects the insurance policy *proceeds* from creditors. The New York statute extends the protection to the *proceeds and avails* of the policy, and it defines that term to include the death benefit, cash surrender and loan values, premiums waived, and dividends.

Types of Statutes

At first blush, it seems impossible to classify such a hodgepodge of legislation. Closer inspection, however, reveals patterns that can serve as the basis for classification. The most apparent breakdown is between statutes of general applicability and those that apply to specialized forms of life insurance, such as group insurance, annuities, and so forth. The general statutes may, in turn, be classified into six groups.

Married Women's Statute

The first group embraces those statutes that pertain only to policies taken out by or for the benefit of married women on the lives of their husbands. Appropriately known as *married women's statutes*, these were the earliest laws of this type enacted.[1] The early laws protected only a small amount of insurance per married woman, but the amount of insurance exempted under the modern statute is unlimited. As a rule, the protection is effective only against creditors of the insured.

Distributive Statute

In time, the married women's type of statute was followed by the so-called *distribution* type of statute. These laws provide, in essence, that proceeds payable to the insured's estate will pass to his or her spouse and children free of the claims against the estate. It would be assumed that the very language of these statutes would rule out any protection during the insured's lifetime, but in Tennessee, by a court decision, and in Florida, by statute, cash values were also protected. These laws have seldom protected the policy against claims of the beneficiary's creditors, however.

Procedural Statute

A somewhat later type of statute can be called the *procedural* type. The common characteristic of these laws is that they were enacted not as a part of the insurance law but as one of the general exemptions from execution that are frequently found in civil practice or procedure codes. Since they were general exemption statutes, they usually provided immunity from all types of creditors, including those of the beneficiary. The amount of insurance exempted is usually quite limited, and the cash values are typically not protected. This is perhaps the most heterogeneous group of statutes dealing with the protection of insurance from creditors' claims.

New York Statute

The type of statute that has wielded the greatest influence was first enacted in the state of New York in 1927. It has served as a model for the statutes of 15 other states and has affected the course of legislation in many other jurisdictions. A majority of states now have statutes similar to New York's. Hence it can be described as the typical state exemption statute. Unless the context suggests otherwise, the use hereafter of the term *New York statute* refers to that statute as a generic type, rather than to the specific law of New York state.

The New York statute applies to all policies of life insurance payable to a person or organization other than the insured or the person applying for insurance if he or she is not also the insured. It protects both the cash value and the proceeds against the creditors of the insured and the person procuring the insurance. The protection is available whether the beneficiary designation is revocable or irrevocable, and a reversionary interest in the insured is expressly declared to be immaterial.

The New York statute does not protect anyone against claims of the beneficiary's creditors. However, there are statutes that provide an exemption for proceeds even after they have been distributed to the beneficiary. These statutes bar the creditors of the insured as well as the beneficiary. Normally this protection would not be available to policy values after receipt; thus dividends payable in cash would usually be subject to seizure.

Comprehensive Statute

The broadest protection is available under the so-called *comprehensive statutes*. This type of statute exempts, without limitation, all types of benefits associated with life insurance from the claims of the creditors of the insured, beneficiary, third-party owner, or any other person or organization.

Spendthrift Statute

Finally, there are the laws, called *spendthrift statutes* and found in most states, that are concerned solely with the protection of proceeds held under a settlement agreement against the claims of creditors of the *beneficiary*. The statutes are designed to protect the proceeds only while they are in the hands of the insurer and not after they have been received by the beneficiary. Unlike the other exemption statutes, these laws do not provide automatic protection; they are, instead, permissive in nature. They permit the insurance company and the insured to agree that the proceeds will not be subject to encumbrance, assignment, or alienation by the beneficiary, or to attachment by the beneficiary's creditors. Such an agreement must be embodied in either the policy or the settlement agreement, and the beneficiary must not be a party to it.

Functional Analysis of the Statutes

The minimum objective of state exemption statutes is to provide protection against the claims of the insured's creditors for all or a portion of the proceeds payable to the insured's spouse and children upon the policy's maturity. The maximum objective, typified by the comprehensive statutes, is to provide unlimited protection against creditors of every description to all types of insurance benefits payable to anyone. An intermediate goal, representing the public policy of most jurisdictions, is to protect—both during the lifetime of the insured and upon his or her death—the benefits of an insurance policy payable to anyone other than the insured's estate from the insured's creditors. This objective involves protecting the cash value of the policy; otherwise, the policy may be destroyed by creditors' seizure before it has had an opportunity of serving its basic function—namely, the support of the insured's spouse and children after the insured's death.

Many of the early statutes spoke only of proceeds. Some courts adopted a narrow construction of the term, but most gave it a broad enough interpretation to include cash values. To indicate that prematurity values are to be protected, many statutes use the language "proceeds and avails." A few actually use the words "cash value." The result is that practically all statutes, other than the distributive and procedural types, exempt—by specific language or court interpretation—both the cash value and the maturity value.

The word "proceeds" has had to undergo interpretation in another direction. Does it include paid-up additions, accumulated dividends, and prepaid or discounted premiums, or are proceeds limited to the original face amount? The usual interpretation is that proceeds include all amounts payable upon maturity of the policy.

Exemption of the cash value is of singular importance in connection with the Federal Bankruptcy Reform Act of 1978. If a state does not opt out, the act recognizes all exemptions from creditors' claims granted under the law of the state in which the bankrupt resides. Thus to the extent that a state law exempts cash values, the trustee in bankruptcy cannot take title to the life insurance

---

Protected Life Insurance Proceeds

- original face amount
- paid-up additions
- accumulated dividends
- prepaid premiums

(generally all amounts payable when the insured dies)

---

policies of a bankrupt policyowner. The revocability of the beneficiary designation does not affect the exemption. The bankrupt enjoys more protection under the typical state exemption statute than under case law.

As a matter of fact, the treatment of bankrupts under these laws has been the subject of severe criticism by creditor interests. These critics argue that all too often a person in financial difficulty places a substantial amount of assets in life insurance payable to his or her spouse and children, and then—after going through bankruptcy—uses the insurance to reestablish a business. Since most states permit a person who has become insolvent to maintain existing insurance or even acquire new insurance *for the protection of his or her family* without being in fraud of creditors, there is little that creditors can do to prevent abuse of an otherwise desirable relief provision. Admittedly, the law usually restricts the insurance that an insolvent debtor can acquire or maintain to a "reasonable" amount, but the courts tend to construe the limitation liberally.

The federal tax authorities, on the other hand, have not let state exemption statutes stand in the way of their collection of tax liens. This is true even under the broadest statutes. The government can obtain a policy's cash value through either forced surrender during the insured's lifetime or collection from the proceeds after death, provided a lien had been placed against the cash value before the taxpayer's death.

Among the general state exemption statutes, only those of the married women's and comprehensive types protect benefits payable to the insured or the third-party procurer of the insurance. Thus disability income and annuity payments are usually not exempt from attachment by creditors. In some states, however, these benefits are protected by special statutes.

Parties Entitled to Protection

Note that the intent of the exemption statutes is to protect third parties—not necessarily the policyowners—from the policyowner's creditors. Broadly speaking, state exemption statutes protect all third-party beneficiaries against the claims of the insured's creditors. The New York statute and those patterned after it also protect assignees and third-party owners. The comprehensive statutes protect all the above plus the insured. On the restrictive side, the married women's and distributive statutes protect only the insured's widow(er) and children. The clear trend therefore is toward increasing the number of parties who are given preference over the policyowner's creditors. A few statutes now permit exemption from the policyowner's creditors if the policy is paid to the insured's estate. Such statutes, however, are distinctly in the minority.

Consistent with the goal to subordinate the policyowner's creditors to those of third-party beneficiaries but not to the policyowner, the state exemption statutes do not protect the persons procuring the insurance from their own creditors. Thus with the exception of the comprehensive statutes, policyowners enjoy no protection under the exemption statutes against their own creditors. A policyowner cannot be compelled by his or her creditors to surrender a policy for cash and thus impair the rights of third parties, but if he or she voluntarily does so, the funds can be attached by creditors. Note that the cash value and death proceeds of an endowment policy are exempt in many jurisdictions, despite the fact that the insured is the beneficiary of the endowment proceeds. In a few states, proceeds of an endowment payable to the insured in the form of income are exempt up to the limits of monthly income stated in the law.

Nature of Limitations, If Any

As a rule, the statutes of broad application contain no limitations on the amount of insurance that will be protected thereunder. Several of the statutes, however, contain definite limitations, expressed in terms of either the face amount, a stated cash value, or the amount of annual premiums. For example, some states limit the exemption from creditors to $5,000 or $10,000 in proceeds payable only to a surviving spouse or minor child. The exemption in a few states is available against all creditors—the beneficiary's as well as the insured's. Several states exempt only such amounts of insurance as can be purchased with a maximum annual premium, such as $500, without specifying the plan of insurance. Some states exempt policy cash values only to certain limited amounts. When protection is afforded to disability and annuity payments, a limit such as $400 per month may be placed on the exempted amount of income.

Type of Creditors against Whom Protection Is Afforded

State exemption statutes as a class are concerned only with creditors of the insured. A sizable number of statutes also provide protection against the claims of *creditors of the beneficiary*. This is true of the comprehensive statutes, which tend to exempt all types of insurance benefits from all types of creditors. The procedural statutes, likewise, usually make no distinction between creditors of the insured and those of the beneficiary, but the exemption is typically available only for the amount of insurance that can be obtained with a specified premium, such as $500. The law in many states exempts the proceeds and avails of a policy purchased by a person on the life of his or her spouse against the claims of the purchaser's creditors. Several other states provide a limited amount of protection against the claims of a wife's creditors in connection with policies on her husband's life purchased by the wife with her own funds.

The most prevalent and significant form of statutory protection of insurance proceeds against the creditors of the beneficiary, however, is represented by those statutes that authorize the inclusion of spendthrift clauses in life insurance policies. This type of provision originated with personal trusts and had the dual purpose of protecting the trust income from the creditors of the trust beneficiary and preventing the beneficiary from alienating or disposing of his or her interest in the trust. The validity of such a restrictive provision was widely debated in this country during the latter half of the 19th century, but it was ultimately held to be valid in most jurisdictions, either by statute or by judicial decision.

Once the validity of a spendthrift clause in a trust agreement was well established, it was a logical development to introduce it into life insurance settlement agreements. At first its validity in this setting was very much in doubt, however, since life insurance companies did not segregate assets, accept discretionary powers, or otherwise conform to the trust pattern in the administration of proceeds under a deferred-settlement agreement. Now more than half of the states have enacted statutes stating that a spendthrift clause will be enforced if it is contained in either the life insurance policy or the settlement agreement, and the use of spendthrift clauses has become widespread. The following are two examples of spendthrift clauses:

> A beneficiary or contingent payee may not, at or after the insured's death, assign, transfer, or encumber any benefit payable. To the extent allowed by law, the benefits will not be subject to the claims of any creditor of any beneficiary or contingent payee.

> • • •

> The proceeds and any income payments under the policy will be exempt from the claims of creditors to the extent permitted by law. These proceeds and payments may not be assigned or withdrawn before becoming payable without our agreement.

SCOPE OF EXEMPTION STATUTES

There is considerable diversity in state law as to the length of time proceeds payable under a life insurance policy are exempt from creditors' claims and the amount of physical change proceeds can undergo without losing their exempt status. With respect to claims of the insured's creditors, proceeds are generally regarded to be exempt as long as they can be identified as such. For example, the courts have almost universally extended the exemption to cover the bank account into which the exempt proceeds have been deposited. Furthermore, it has been held that real estate purchased with exempt insurance proceeds is not subject to creditors' actions.

The law is similarly diverse with respect to claims of the beneficiary's creditors. Some statutes that extend their cloak of protection to such claims state specifically that life insurance policy proceeds are exempt from claims of creditors, whether of the insured or the beneficiary, both before and after receipt by the beneficiary. Other statutes do not state that the proceeds are exempt while in the hands of the beneficiary, and the question may be raised as to whether under such statutes proceeds are protected against the beneficiary's creditors after the beneficiary receives the proceeds, particularly as to debts created after receipt. Finally, it seems clear that the protection afforded the beneficiary under a spendthrift clause, even though sanctioned by statute, does not extend beyond the instant of receipt of the proceeds.

CHAPTER REVIEW

Answers to the review questions and the self-test questions can be found in the Supplement.

Key Terms

Bankruptcy Reform Act of 1978   Federal Tax Lien Act of 1966

Review Questions

1. List the three ways a creditor may acquire an interest in a life insurance policy's value by operation of the contract.

2. Explain why, even if there are no state exemption statutes, the creditors of policyowner-insureds are generally unable to enforce their rights against policy cash values.

3. Describe how federal bankruptcy law operates with respect to protecting life insurance from the claims of creditors.

4. Explain what rights the federal government has to the policy loan values and the death proceeds of a life insurance policy under a federal tax lien.

5. Explain whether, in the absence of state exemption statutes, life insurance proceeds would be subject to the claims of the policyowner-insured's creditors when the proceeds are payable to each of the following types of beneficiaries after the contract has matured:
   a. the insured or the insured's estate
   b. a third-party beneficiary

6. Explain whether life insurance cash values and death proceeds would be subject to the claims of the creditors of the beneficiary if there were no state exemption statutes.

7. List the six types of general exemption statutes, and describe the nature of the protection that each tends to provide for life insurance against the claims of creditors.

8. Describe the minimum objective, the maximum objective, and the prevailing intermediate goal of state exemption statutes.

9. What types of state exemption statutes exempt both cash values and maturity values from the claims of creditors, and what types typically exempt only maturity values?

10. Describe the parties who are likely to be protected and those who are likely not to be protected by the state exemption statutes.

11. What types of state exemption statutes provide protection against the claims of the beneficiary's creditors and of the insured's creditors, and what type of statute provides protection only against the claims of creditors of the beneficiary?

Self-Test Questions

T F 1. In the absence of state exemption statutes, the policyowner-insured's creditors are generally able to enforce their claims against the cash value of a policy owned by the insured.

T F 2. Under federal bankruptcy law, an individual filing bankruptcy may elect either the exemptions provided under the federal statute or those provided by the applicable state law as long as the state has not enacted legislation to "opt out" of the reach of the federal law.

T F 3. Under a federal tax lien, the federal government may require an insurance company to withdraw the policyowner's policy loan values up to the amount of the tax and pay that amount to the government within 90 days after notice.

T F 4. The cash value of a life insurance policy cannot be levied upon by a creditor of a third-party beneficiary, whether the designation is revocable or irrevocable.

T   F   5. Distributive, procedural, and New-York-type exemption statutes typically provide protection for cash values as well as for death proceeds.

T   F   6. Spendthrift statutes are concerned solely with the protection of proceeds held under a settlement agreement against the claims of the beneficiary's creditors.

T   F   7. The goal of state exemption statutes in most jurisdictions is to protect—both during the insured's lifetime and upon his or her death—the benefits of an insurance policy payable to anyone other than the insured's estate from the insured's creditors.

T   F   8. With the exception of the comprehensive statutes, policyowners enjoy no protection under the exemption statutes against their own creditors.

T   F   9. A sizable number of state exemption statutes provide protection against the claims of the beneficiary's creditors.

T   F   10. Under state exemption statutes, policy proceeds are generally regarded to be exempt from claims of the insured's creditors as long as they can be identified as proceeds.

NOTE

1. At the time these early laws were enacted, married women did not have legal capacity to own separate property.

16

Agents and Brokers

Burke A. Christensen

Learning Objectives

An understanding of the material in this chapter should enable the student to

16-1. Discuss the law of agency relationships.

16-2. Understand the terminology relevant to the agency relationships.

16-3. Distinguish between agents and brokers.

16-4. Explain the effect of producers' licenses.

16-5. Describe why it is difficult to effectively regulate the financial planning profession.

16-6. Understand the distinction in agency law between power and authority.

16-7. Distinguish actual authority and apparent authority in agency.

16-8. Explain the act of ratification in agency relationships.

16-9. Discuss the duties agents owe to principals and the consequences of breaching these duties.

16-10. Identify the rights and liabilities of principals and agents.

16-11. Explain the levels of a producer's duties to the insured.

16-12. Discuss the limitations on an agent's powers by insurers.

16-13. Describe the termination of an agent's authority.

Chapter Outline

Insurance is a business that is based on the law of agency. Thus the basics of this branch of the law are critical to understanding the insurance business.

Insurance companies conduct their business through two types of agents: employees and salespersons (or producers). The insurers are the principals for whom these two types of agents work and to whom they must account. Employees are accountable only to their employers, but as you will see, sometimes the insurance producer is also an agent of the insured.

The Latin term that is used in the law to explain the concept of agency is "Qui facit per alium facit per se." The translation: "He who acts through another acts for himself." Consequently one should be very careful when selecting an agent. Whatever that agent does in the performance of the duties delegated to him or her will be deemed to be the act of the principal, and the principal will be bound thereby.

LAW OF AGENCY

One of the first premises of the law of agency is that the agent is engaged in the business of the principal. Therefore the agent has a duty to act solely for the benefit of and in accord with the principal's directions. Under the rules of agency law, an agent is a fiduciary of the principal. Thus an agent occupies a special position of trust that imposes on the agent a duty of loyalty to the principal.

    agency: fiduciary relationship that results when there is a
    manifestation of consent by one person to a second person

that the second person shall act on the first person's behalf and be subject to the first person's control on the condition that the second person agrees to that relationship

The comprehensive and legalistic definition above can be stated less precisely, but more simply, by breaking it down into its several parts as follows:

- An agency exists between two persons when they both agree that one of them shall have the authority to act for the other.
- The person granting the agency authority is the principal; the person receiving the agency authority is the agent.
- Those who become agents or principals may be human beings, known as "natural persons," or they may be artificial persons, such as corporations, which exist only as legal entities.
- When the agent agrees to the agency relationship, he, she, or it becomes a fiduciary for the principal. Being a fiduciary means that the agent must act in the best interests of the principal.

Agency Relationships

There are many different kinds of principal and agent relationships. One type is referred to as master and servant. This term, once in common use, is now largely limited to defining relationships for purposes of determining personal injury liability. It is applicable, for example, when a person is injured or his or her property damaged by another person's employee.

For employment purposes, the more common terms are *employer and employee* or *employer and independent contractor.* However, the latter relationship is not really an agency relationship; it is actually a contractual arrangement between two independent contractors.

principal   *principal:* one who employs another to act for him, her, or it, subject to the principal's general control and instruction. The principal is the person or entity from whom the agent derives his or her authority.

agent: a person or entity who has been given the authority to act for another person or entity (the principal)

fiduciary   *fiduciary:* a person or entity who has an obligation to act in the best interests of another person. A fiduciary is required to exercise a high degree of trust and good faith in handling the affairs of another person or entity. A fiduciary has a duty of loyalty. An agent is a fiduciary for his or her principal.

There are only a few limitations on the principal's liability for the acts of his or her agent. For liability to attach to the principal, the agent's action must meet one of the following three criteria:

- It must have occurred while the agent was exercising the authority expressly granted by the principal.
- It must have been done while the agent was exercising the authority that the agent reasonably believed he or she had to perform duties necessary to those specifically delegated.
- The agent's actions must have related to all those duties that a third party reasonably believed the agent had authority to perform.

capacity

capacity: the legal qualifications, competency, power, or fitness to accept authority or responsibility

Capacity is a term with a specific definition in the law. If a person or entity has legal capacity, then he, she, or it is eligible to accept authority or responsibility to act for another.

Capacity is not the same as authority or permission. For example, a 21-year-old American citizen residing in Philadelphia has the capacity to vote in municipal elections. Until that person registers to vote, however, he or she does not have the right, permission, or authority to vote.

Legal capacity is required for persons or entities to act as principals or as agents. The capacity required to perform either role is different. Lesser capacity is required to be an agent than to be a principal.

Capacity to Be a Principal

Not every person or entity may be a principal. To be a principal one must have the capacity to execute a contract. Minors, incompetents, and other natural persons with limited contractual capacity may be restricted in their ability to be a principal or even prohibited entirely from becoming a principal. Adult persons of limited mental capacities or adults who are temporarily incapacitated (for example, while intoxicated) are not permitted to appoint agents freely. Under modern legal theory, minors have contractual capacity for necessities and thus may be principals and appoint agents for any item deemed to be necessary (food, shelter, and so on). This is complicated by the fact that there is no uniform definition of what falls within the term "necessary." Consequently the practical result is that very few people are willing to contract with minors for anything, and even fewer people will deal with the agent of a minor.

A corporation has contractual capacity and can be a principal. The corporation's ability to appoint an agent is limited to the scope of activities authorized in its articles of incorporation. This caused some problems in the past because lawyers used to draft the articles of incorporation to encompass only those activities contemplated by the incorporators (for example, to operate a railroad). However, since modern legal practice is to create a corporation with the ability to conduct any business the law allows, there are few limitations on a corporation's capacity to act as a principal.

Partnerships can usually act as principals, although there are two legal theories to explain how. Where state law does not treat a partnership as a legal entity, the partnership itself is not technically capable of being a principal. In these states, because the partnership lacks contractual capacity, the individual partners are deemed to be the principal and the partnership's agent is really the agent of the partners. In states where a partnership is a legal entity, this fiction need not be observed, and the partnership can act directly as a principal through its agents.

Capacity to Be an Agent

When an agent creates a contract on behalf of the agent's principal, the agent is not a party to that contract. A contract signed by an agent is the contract of the principal, not the agent. Thus the agent need not have contractual capacity in order to create binding contracts for his or her principal.

Since it is not necessary that an agent have contractual capacity, there are fewer limitations on who can serve as an agent. Minors and incompetent persons who do not have the capacity to act as principals and appoint agents still have the capacity to act as the agent for another as long as they are capable of understanding the assignments given to them and can transmit information.

Regardless of whether the agent has contractual capacity, it is also the general rule that an agent will not be personally liable to a third party on a contract entered into by him or her on behalf of a principal if the identity of the principal and the fact of the agency relationship are disclosed to the third party. In the context of an insurance agent's relationships with his or her clients this means that for an insured to recover against the insurance agent, the basis of the agent's liability must arise from something other than the terms of the insurance policy and the agency or brokerage contract. A producer is not likely to incur personal liability to an insured (under the law of agency) as long as the producer is clearly understood to be the agent of the insurer and stays within that role. However, the law of agency may operate to impose unexpected duties and liabilities on producers who are also found to be agents of the insured. (This will be more fully discussed below.)

Many businesses are regulated by government at various levels because of the impact they have on the general public. Agents may not be appointed to act in these businesses—examples are law, real estate, public accounting, and insurance—unless they meet the state licensing requirements. Insurance is a business that so manifestly affects the public welfare that it is subject to considerable governmental regulation—primarily at the state level. Thus the capacity to be an insurance agent and the capacity to appoint insurance agents are closely regulated. Only persons licensed by the state may act as insurance agents. Only those insurers approved by the state may act as principals and employ agents to offer their products for sale in the state. A person who wants to become an insurance agent must meet the state requirements to obtain and maintain the license to sell insurance. An insurance company that wants to appoint agents must meet the state requirements for being admitted to business in that state.

AGENCY LAW IN MARKETING LIFE INSURANCE[1]

Agent and Broker Defined

Insurance codes for many of the various states give separate definitions for the terms agent and broker. The National Association of Insurance Commissioners (NAIC) has adopted the Agents and Brokers Licensing Model Act to define those terms. Several states, however, do not have a provision for insurance broker.

The model act defines agent as "an individual, partnership, or corporation appointed by an insurer to solicit applications for a policy of insurance or to negotiate a policy of insurance on its behalf."[2] A *broker* is "any individual, partnership, or corporation who, for compensation, and not being a licensed agent for the company in which a policy of insurance is placed, acts or aids in any manner in negotiating contracts for insurance or placing risks or effecting insurance for a party other than himself or itself."[3]

broker

Producers' Licenses

The distinction of the broker relationship in these statutes is largely eliminated by insurance industry practice, which generally requires that, regardless of the producer's license, each producer must be separately licensed by each insurer that he or she represents as that company's agent.

The model act also defines the different relationships that, depending on whether the producer is an agent or broker, are created between producers, insureds, and insurers. The act provides as follows:

Every agent . . . who solicits or negotiates an application for
insurance of any kind shall, in any controversy between the insured

or his beneficiary and the insurer, be regarded as representing the insurer and not the insured or his beneficiary. This provision shall not affect the apparent authority of an agent.

Every insurance broker . . . who solicits an application for insurance of any kind shall, in any controversy between the insured or his beneficiary and the insurer issuing any policy upon such application, be regarded as representing the insured or his beneficiary and not the insurer.[4]

A few states—Texas, for example—have a special category of licenses that are generally referred to as insurance counselor licenses. These licenses normally permit people to give advice on life insurance products, to place insurance on behalf of applicants, and to charge fees for the services they render. Such licensees, however, are usually not permitted to accept commissions for the sale of insurance policies.

As you will see, these statutes are rarely determinative of agents' and brokers' rights and responsibilities. In American law the titles used by insurance producers are less important than the facts and circumstances surrounding their relations with their clients. Brokers are usually agents of the insurer for purposes of delivering the policy and collecting the first premium.

Regulation of Financial Planners

financial planner

Lawmakers and regulators have struggled for years to find an effective means to regulate financial planners. One of the key reasons for the problem is an acknowledged inability to define the term *financial planner*. It is difficult to regulate what cannot be defined. Therefore as a general rule, financial planners are regulated under the laws governing investment advisers, rather than as a separate profession.

Financial planners who meet the definition of investment adviser under the Investment Advisers Act of 1940 must register with the Securities and Exchange Commission. States have enacted similar requirements under their "blue sky" or securities laws. In addition, some states have expanded their definition of investment adviser to include those individuals who hold themselves out as financial planners.

holding-out provisions

These *holding-out provisions* can be problematic for two main reasons. First, they base regulation on title rather than function. Second, these provisions rarely define what is meant by either "financial planner" or "holding out." The end result is that individuals who are not performing any activities that fall under the authority of the regulator may be subject to regulation.

Holding-out provisions have caused special problems for life insurance agents who have earned a professional designation such as Chartered Financial Consultant (ChFC). The designation is evidence of education, not of business activities. However, if the state regulators take the position that use of the designation is "holding out," then the individual will be required to register as an investment adviser.

In light of the complicated approach to financial planning regulation, ChFCs should review the following to ensure compliance:

- the definition of investment adviser in the 1940 act to determine whether the definition applies
- SEC Release IA-1092. This states the Securities and Exchange Commission's position on the application of the 1940 act to financial planners.
- applicable state blue sky laws

ChFCs are also advised to check their state insurance or unfair trade practice laws to determine if these laws place any restrictions on use of the term "financial planner."

CREATION OF PRINCIPAL-AGENT RELATIONSHIP

Power and Authority

Note that agency is defined in terms of the agent's authority to act for the principal. In the law there is a difference between power and authority, although the terms are not always used by lay persons or lawyers with a clear understanding of the difference. For our purposes, power is the ability to affect the rights and duties of another. Power can be exercised with or without that other person's authority and consent.

Authority is the ability to affect another person's rights and duties with that person's actual or apparent consent. Authority can be exercised only when granted by that person, although in some cases authority to act may be presumed by a third party when the principal has permitted circumstances to exist that justify that assumption.

While agency is not necessarily a contractual relationship, in some cases a contract between the principal and the agent is executed to formalize the nature and scope of the agency being created or granted. This is, of course, the case for life insurance agency relationships. But a contract is not required to create agency, and as mentioned above, a person can create an agency with someone who does not have contractual capacity.

Since a contract is not required to create an agency, the formalities of contract law are also not required. For example, one essential element of the creation of a contract is the exchange of consideration between the parties. This is not true of agency; no consideration is required to appoint an agent. It follows then that absent an agreement to the contrary, compensation to the agent is also not necessary to create an agency relationship. The fact that a contract is not required to create an agency is recognized by our use of the term "appoint an agent," rather than "contract an agent."

Actual and Apparent Authority

An agency relationship is created only after some affirmative act by the principal. No one can make himself or herself the agent of another person without that person's actual or apparent consent. Consequently there are two basic types of agency authority: *actual authority* and *apparent authority* (see table 16-1[5] for a comparison of agency authority).

actual authority

> *actual authority:* the power of the agent to affect the legal relations of the principal by acts done in accordance with the principal's manifestation of consent to him[6]

Actual authority is further distinguished based on how that actual authority is granted to the agent. Actual authority is either express or implied. *Actual express authority* is created when the principal either orally or in writing affirmatively "expresses" his or her intent to appoint another party as an agent and that other party consents to the appointment. A principal may limit the scope of an agent's actual express authority, but if such limitations are to be binding on third parties, they must be clearly communicated to the agent and publicly made known. This is especially so if the limitations take away powers that the public or the agent would reasonably expect the agent to have.

actual express authority

If there is a dispute over the extent of the authority actually granted to the agent, the determination will be based on what the agent (not the principal) reasonably believed his or her scope of authority to be. Since a court cannot read minds, it is not important what the principal believed or intended to grant. The actions of the parties (primarily those of the principal) that manifested their intent will control. Since the principal (and not the agent or the third party) has the ability to expand or limit the scope of the agency granted, he or she bears the burden if any ambiguity arises over the scope of the agent's authority.

actual implied (incidental) authority

Actual implied authority is sometimes also called *incidental* authority. By whatever name it is called, actual implied authority is a derivative of actual express authority, and it does not exist in an agent unless there has

TABLE 16-1 Agency Authority		
Actual Authority	Apparent Authority	No Agency Authority
The authority intended to be given to an agent, actual authority is either express or implied.	This agency is based on the reasonable belief of a third party arising from the conduct of the principal. Apparent authority can exist even if there has not been a grant of actual authority.	*Unauthorized act:* any act done without an actual or apparent grant of agency. An unauthorized act is not binding on the principal.
Express: based on an oral or written grant of authority "expressed" by the principal and reasonably believed by the agent		*Ratification:* applies only to the acts of a purported agent. There can be no ratification if there was no claim of agency authority.
Implied: derived from express authority, the authority to do those acts that are incidental to the acts expressly authorized. Absent a grant of express authority, implied authority does not exist.		

been an express grant of authority to the agent by the principal. Implied authority is the authority to do all the actions that are necessary to carry out the grant of express authority.

> *apparent authority:* the power to affect the legal relations of another by virtue of that other's manifestations to a third party. Apparent authority must be derived primarily from the acts of the principal as observed by the third party; it cannot be based solely upon the statements, representations, or actions of the agent.[7]

The important distinction between apparent and actual authority is that apparent authority is determined by the reasonable perceptions of the third party. It is the agent's power as it is reasonably perceived by a person observing the agent. The key to apparent authority is the inducement to a third party to act derived from the acts of the principal that give the agent the appearance of authority to act.

Apparent authority is created when the principal allows conditions to exist that lead a third party (not the purported principal or agent) to reasonably believe that actual authority exists. Apparent authority may exist in addition to a grant of actual express authority, or it may exist when there has been no express grant of actual authority at all. Apparent authority is created when the principal permits its actual agent or an unauthorized person to have the indicia of authority that would lead a third person to believe that agency authority exists.

No one can unilaterally make himself or herself the agent of another person. Consequently those who deal with an agent have an obligation to exercise reasonable diligence and to act in good faith to discover whether the agency actually exists. Agency may not be presumed. However, the third party is not required to establish proof that the principal has conferred actual express authority. If actual authority exists, the principal will be bound by the agent's actions consistent with that authority. If the agent's actions are beyond the scope of the actual express grant of authority, the principal will be bound if there were actions by the principal to establish a reasonable belief by the agent that he or she had sufficient implied authority to act.

If no actual express or implied authority to do the act in question exists, apparent authority can be established to bind the principal. The third party

---

Elements of Apparent Authority

- Actions of the principal create the impression of authority granted to the agent.
- Apparent authority may exceed express authority.
- The extension of apparent authority beyond actual authority is based on reasonable expectations of the party dealing with the agent, having observed the agent's actions.
- The absence of actions by the principal to limit the actions of the agent may increase apparent authority.

---

needs to establish that the putative agent possessed sufficient indicia of authority that it was reasonable for the third party to believe that the agent had authority to bind the principal. Absent the ability to show that agency exists, everyone deals with an agent at his or her peril. It is the conduct of the principal, not the agent, that must be the basis for establishing the reasonable belief that the agency existed.

Note that the law presumes that the principal has control over its agents. Thus two important rules emerge: (1) The principal is liable if the agent's wrongful acts within the scope of the agency injure a third party, and (2) the knowledge of the agent is imputed to the principal. These are rules of law that the principal and agent cannot alter by contract. Therefore if an agent acts wrongfully to the detriment of either the principal or a third party and neither of them is at fault, the courts will normally assign the responsibility for that loss to the principal.

Example: ***Has Apparent Authority Been Created?***

Edwina opened an office, had business cards and stationery printed, and hung out a sign stating fraudulently that she was an agent of Farm and City Insurance Company. These actions were taken without any knowledge by the insurer. Soon thereafter, Edwina sold phony life insurance policies to a number of clients, kept the premiums, and disappeared 6 weeks later. One of her customers died, and the beneficiary filed a claim, at which time the fraud came to light. The beneficiary sued Farm and City, alleging that it was bound by Edwina's apparent authority as its agent. The court ruled in favor of Farm and City, stating that the insurer had done nothing to create apparent authority on Edwina's part. The beneficiary's only right of action, therefore, is against Edwina, if she can be found.

Ratification

A person's unauthorized actions on behalf of a purported principal may be acts beyond the scope of an actual grant of express or implied authority to an agent, acts done with or beyond the scope of apparent authority, or acts done with no authority whatever but in the name of the purported principal. In any of these circumstances, the principal may wish to accept the benefit of these acts and retroactively claim that person as his or her agent. To do so a *ratification* must occur.

ratification   *ratification:* the validation of an unauthorized act

Ratification is relevant only to unauthorized acts. If an agent's act is within the scope of the agent's authority, there is no need for the principal to ratify it.

Ratification requires the following steps:

- The unauthorized act must have been performed by a person claiming to act for another person as his or her agent. If there has been no representation of agency, there can be no ratification. The third party must reasonably believe that the actor was an agent of another person.
- Only the purported principal may ratify the act. This means that there can be no ratification by an undisclosed principal. If the third party

does not believe that the agent is acting as an agent for a particular party, he or she cannot be required to accept a deal with someone else.

- All material facts and circumstances about the transaction to be ratified must be disclosed to the principal prior to the ratification.

- There can be no partial ratification of the transaction. The principal must take the entire deal as negotiated by the agent or disclaim the entire deal. The principal may not ratify only the portion of the agreement that is favorable to the principal.

- The third party may withdraw from the transaction prior to the ratification but may not withdraw after the ratification has been communicated. Once the ratification has been made, a contract is in effect.

- The third party's consent to the ratification is not required to make the ratification effective. The third party has already negotiated an agreement with the principal through the purported agent. All that remains is for the principal to reject or ratify that agreement.

- Changed circumstances may preclude ratification. For example, the property subject to the agreement may be sold to someone else before the ratification.

- Ratification must occur within a reasonable time. The length of time that is considered reasonable varies with the type and purpose of the agreement.

Form of Ratification

If the original transaction must be in writing to be effective, then the ratification must also meet the same formalities. Absent a requirement for some formality, any act manifesting the principal's approval of the act is sufficient for the ratification. Thus in the same way that agency authority may be actual or apparent, so may the ratification.

Ratification may occur if the principal accepts the benefit (such as profits, services, publicity, and so forth) of the agent's unauthorized activities. Acceptance of the benefits will override the principal's claimed lack of intent to ratify the act. In addition, ratification may occur if the principal has full knowledge of the facts of the agent's unauthorized action and fails to repudiate it within a reasonable time.

Effects of Ratification

Ratification has the following results:

- Once effective, the ratification binds the principal to the same extent as if the agent had been given actual express authority to act.

- The ratification is effective as of the date of the agent's act, not the date of the principal's ratification.
- Ratification relieves the agent of liability to the principal for acting without authority.
- Ratification relieves the agent of liability to the third party for performance of any of the duties purportedly to be performed by the principal.
- Ratification entitles the agent to the compensation, if any, payable for the acts of an authorized agent.

Breach of Agency

An agent has these three basic duties to his or her principal:

- a duty of loyalty to his or her principal
- a duty to obey the principal's instructions
- a duty to exercise reasonable skill, care, and diligence in executing the principal's instructions

As a result of these duties, the agent may not divert the principal's business to benefit the agent or another party. Similarly, an agent must disclose to the principal any interests that the agent may have that are adverse to the principal's interests. Except in the rare case of dual agency, which is discussed below, an agent may not serve two principals whose interests are adverse unless both consent.

If the agent violates his or her duties to the principal, the law will hold the agent liable for damages caused by that breach of duty. The remedies available to a principal vary depending on the duty violated.

The wrongful acts of an agent toward a third party may result in a third-party lawsuit against the principal. Such an action could be based on a breach of contract by the agent or by an act of the agent that resulted in a personal injury to another party. If the principal is required by the court to pay damages to the third party, the principal may then recover the amount of the damages from the agent.

The principal may also have a direct action against the agent if the agent breaches the terms of the agency contract or violates a duty owed to the principal. If the agent has failed to perform his or her duties, the principal may terminate the agent's contract and refuse to pay the agent.

Common Duties of Principal

The agency relationship imposes some duties on the principal, and the principal can be held liable to the agent if these duties are not performed.

Note that the contract defining the agency relationship may specify otherwise. If there is a contract defining the agency relationship, the principal will be required to abide by the terms of that agreement.

A principal has a general obligation not to interfere with the agent's opportunity to conduct his or her duties. Unless their contract provides differently, a principal has a general obligation to compensate the agent reasonably and to reimburse the agent for expenses reasonably incurred on the principal's behalf. Both the principal and the agent have an obligation to keep accurate accounts of the money or other property that is the subject of the agency.

The principal's duties can be summarized as follows:

- Give the agent an opportunity to work.
- Provide goods for the agent to sell.
- Pay the agent for services rendered.
- Reimburse the agent for authorized expenses incurred.
- Indemnify the agent for liabilities incurred while acting for the principal within the scope of the agency.
- Keep accurate accounts of finances.

If the principal breaches the agency agreement, the agent is entitled to sue the principal for damages incurred as a result of that breach. The agent may also retain any of the principal's property that is lawfully in the agent's possession as security for any money that the principal owes to the agent.

Normally, neither the agent nor the principal will be able to sue the other party for specific performance of the agency agreement. This is because an agency agreement is a contract for the performance of personal services, and the law of this country will not require a person to perform personal services against his or her will. If someone refuses to perform personal services as required by a valid contract, the proper remedy is not specific performance but a lawsuit for damages incurred by the failure to perform.

Consequences of Agent-Principal Relationship

The agent's knowledge is imputed to the principal. It is a rule of agency law that any material knowledge the agent acquires about a transaction within the scope of the agency will be imputed to the principal. It does not matter if the agent does not, in fact, communicate his or her knowledge to the principal. (This rule does not apply if there has been collusion between the third party and the agent to perpetrate a fraud upon the principal.)

In the majority of states, if an insurance agent knowingly provides false information on an application for life insurance, the insurance company will

> *Example:*   ***Duty of an Agent to the Principal***
>
> In the process of completing a life insurance application, Wendy, the agent, told Stan, her client, that his mild heart attack 4 years ago need not be reported because it happened so long ago. The policy was issued, and Stan died a few months later, at which time the truth came to light. A court awarded the death proceeds to the beneficiary on the theory that knowledge of Wendy was knowledge of the insurer. The insurer then sued Wendy and was awarded a judgment against her in the amount of the death proceeds paid to Stan's beneficiary, plus interest.

not be charged with knowing that the information is false. Upon discovery of the material misstatement, the insurer can sue to rescind the policy. This reflects an exception to the general rule of agency law that the knowledge of the agent is the knowledge of the principal.

This exception to the general rule exists despite the fact that in a minority of jurisdictions, the insurer is charged with the agent's knowledge even in the case of the agent's participation in a fraud upon the insurer. In these few states, the general rule is strictly applied, and the insurer is bound by the contract even if it is issued in reliance on the false information and would not have been issued if the truth had been known.

There is an additional rule of agency law, however, that works to the benefit of insurers who are defrauded by their agents. This rule states that people who sign a contract are presumed to know the terms of the contract. A majority of jurisdictions have applied this rule to require applicants to read their policies upon receipt and to inform the insurer if there are any material misstatements. Consequently in the majority of jurisdictions, if an agent knowingly falsifies an application that induces an insurer to issue a policy and the applicant does not report the material misstatement to the insurer upon delivery, the insurer will be permitted to sue for rescission of the contract.

RIGHTS AND LIABILITIES

The Principal

Just as the principal is bound by a contract created by the principal's agent, the third party with whom the agent created the contract is also bound. The third party is bound either because he or she created an agreement with the principal's authorized agent or because the principal ratified an agreement between the third party and an agent acting with apparent authority. Furthermore, since a principal would have an action against his or her agent if that agent defrauded the principal, there would also be an action against the third party if that person induced or assisted the agent in violating his or her duties to the principal.

The Agent

An agent is not a party to the contract he or she negotiates between a third party and the principal. This means that he or she cannot sue either party based upon the contract. Any lawsuit by the agent against the third party would have to be based on a claim of a personal injury to the agent by the third party. Similarly, the third party cannot sue the agent based on the contract between the third party and the principal. The third party cannot sue the agent for breach of the agency agreement (if any) between the agent and the principal. Any action maintained by the third party against the agent has to be based on some misrepresentation or other personal injury caused by the agent.

Insurance producers, as agents or brokers, have duties to others in three specific categories:

- the states in which they are licensed to do business
- the insurance companies with whom they have agent or broker contracts
- the persons to whom they sell insurance[8]

Duties Owed to the State

The business of life insurance has its own set of laws for insurance companies and producers. These laws are primarily at the state level.

Duties Owed to the Insurer

The relationship between the producer and the insurer is controlled by the producer's agent or broker contract. An insurance agent or broker can become liable to an insurer by some improper conduct that causes loss or damage to the insurer. This could be a direct loss to the insurer such as negligent or intentional destruction of the insurer's property. It could be based on a claim against an insurer by an insured or a beneficiary because of the producer's actions. In either case, the insurance company may assert a claim against the producer to recover its losses.

According to *Responsibilities of Insurance Agents and Brokers,* "[t]he general principles in the relationship are simple enough. Agents, in the legal technical sense (1) have a duty of care to their principals, and (2) may not exceed their scope of authority and cause damage to their principals. Moreover, where a duty of care is owed someone, and there is a negligent breach of it to that one's detriment, an action for damages will lie. Lastly, the legal conception of honest and fair dealing applicable to parties generally must always be considered (footnotes omitted)."[9]

Duties Owed to the Insured

A producer's duties to the insured usually arise at one of these three levels:

generalist level

- *generalist level.* All producers have a duty to exercise reasonable skill, care, and diligence.

dual agency level

- *dual-agency level.* A producer's actions may create an agent-principal relationship between the producer and the client.

expert level

- *expert level.* A producer's representations of expertise may induce the client's reliance on that expertise.

Generalist Level

At the generalist level the basic level of responsibility has been clearly articulated as follows:

> One who holds himself out to the public as an insurance broker is required to have the degree of skill and knowledge requisite to the calling. When engaged by a member of the public to obtain insurance, the law holds him to the exercise of good faith and reasonable skill, care and diligence in the execution of the commission. He is expected to possess reasonable knowledge of the types of policies, their different terms and coverage available in the area in which his principal seeks to be protected. If he neglects to procure the insurance or if the policy is void or materially deficient or does not provide the coverage he undertook to supply, because of his failure to exercise the requisite skill or diligence, he becomes liable to his principal for the loss sustained thereby.[10]

Dual-Agency Level

As in any other agent-principal relationship, an insurance agent owes a fiduciary duty to his or her principal. Because of the nature of life insurance marketing, however, it is not always easy to answer the question, who is the principal?

Most people assume that the insurance producer is the agent of the insurance company with whom he or she has an agent's contract. Such an assumption is correct, but there are many exceptions to this rule. The result is that an insurance producer may be an agent of the insurer for some purposes and an agent of the insured for others. For example, an insurance producer is clearly the agent of the insurer for purposes of taking the application and accepting payment of premiums.

On the other hand, delivery of an insurance policy is an act where the producer's agency can shift between the insured and the insurer. For example, assume the policy has been issued and given to the agent for delivery to the insured without any further act to be performed by the insured. In that event, the producer acts as agent for the insured for delivery of the policy. A physical transfer from the producer to the insured is unnecessary for the policy to be in force. However, if the agent has been instructed to deliver the policy only after some condition is fulfilled (such as determining that the insured is in good health or obtaining payment of the first premium), then the producer remains the agent of the insurer for purposes of delivering the policy. In that event the insurance policy will be effective only upon fulfillment of the condition and the transfer of the policy.

In the usual context, an insurance *agent* is considered to be the representative of the insurer,[11] and an insurance *broker* is deemed to be the representative of the insured.[12] As indicated earlier, this is the presumption created by the statutes defining "agent" and "broker" that are based on the NAIC model act.

Statutory distinctions between agents and brokers are frequently overlooked by the courts when the issue is a producer's liability to his or her clients: "The courts do not draw any fine distinctions between agents and brokers in imposing liability. It is well recognized that many are both agents and brokers; that a broker often is acting as agent for the insurer; and that an agent may have direct obligations to the insured, whether he is licensed as a broker or not."[13]

Requiring (or at least recognizing) that an individual be the agent for two potentially adverse principals is at odds with normal agency law, but there are numerous cases where such a dual agency has been found.[14] For example, a broker is considered to be the agent of the insured for most purposes. Nevertheless, he or she becomes the agent of the insurer for purposes of taking the application and delivering the policy. A broker is also the agent of the insurer for purposes of accepting the first premium payment and delivering it to the insurer.[15]

Three factors further blur the agent-broker distinction. First, several states have statutes that impose certain agency duties upon brokers with respect to insurers. Second, several states have no statutory category at all for brokers. Third, even though a producer may be a "broker" with respect to his or her property/casualty business, in order to sell life insurance, the producer will have to be licensed as an "agent" of a life insurer.[16]

Those agents who state or imply that they purchase insurance for the client, that they select from among many different insurers on behalf of the client, and that they are acting for or in the best interests of the client help create an implied or apparent agency relationship between the producer and the insured. Although it is common for clients to refer to the producer as "my agent," and it is also common for the producer to tell the client, "I'm your agent," the consequences of comments like these can be the creation of an agency relationship between the producer and the insured.

Lazzarra v. Aetna Cas. & Sur. Co.[17] imposed a fiduciary duty on a broker in favor of the insured. Perhaps that duty would not have been imposed had the producer been an agent rather than a broker. However, even if a producer is not held to be an agent of the insured, the courts may find a way to impose duties upon the producer based upon the producer's representations of special expertise.

However, there are cases to the contrary. In *Lazovick v. Sun Life Ins. Co. of America*[18] the producer was held to be the insurer's agent, not the insured's. Thus the agent had no fiduciary duty to advise the insured. Under the facts of this case, the purchase of insurance is an arm's-length transaction involving no confidential or fiduciary relationship between the insured and the agent.

Expert Level

Chartered Life Underwriters and Chartered Financial Consultants have worked to build a reputation for professional expertise and credibility. "This heightened status of agents is not always an advantage, given our litigious society where the desire to redress harm frequently outstrips the need to uncover fault and where the search for justice seemingly has been replaced by the search for the deep pocket."[19]

It follows that the more credentials and expertise a person has or professes to have, the less tolerance others will exhibit toward real or perceived shortcomings in performance. In effect, the possession of such expertise may create an expectation that the possessor will act according to a higher standard. The law clearly recognizes if a person holds himself or herself out to have a special level of expertise, the public has a right to expect that the person will have the expertise professed and will exercise that expertise.

An example of the higher standard imposed upon experts is *Hardt v. Brink*.[20] Here, a property/casualty agent was found liable to the insured on the basis of the agent's failure to exercise the degree of expertise he held himself out to possess. In an attempt to escape, or at least spread the liability, the insurance broker argued that the insured's lawyer was the party responsible for the improper coverage. The court responded that although the lawyer may also be responsible for the accuracy of a client's legal affairs, that did not relieve a skilled insurance consultant of his responsibilities and liabilities.

Does this impose a standard of care equal to that of a lawyer? Probably not, but the standard is certainly far in excess of the "reasonable skill, care and diligence standard for one who merely claims to take applications for insurance. The law here involved is not particularly startling; nor is it necessarily an extension over previous cases. This is an age of specialists and as more occupations divide into various specialties and strive toward 'professional' status, the law requires an even higher standard of care in the performance of their duties."[21]

A difficult question is whether a producer has a duty to place insurance that is suitable for the needs of the client. In *Knox v. Anderson*[22] a life insurance agent was found liable because he induced the insured to rely upon his expertise. The insurance the producer placed was found to be unsuitable for the insured's purposes. The court found in *Knox* that the producer was not an agent of the insured and therefore was not a fiduciary with respect to the insured. Nevertheless, he was held liable because (1) his professed expertise had induced the client to rely upon his advice, and (2) the product the agent sold was unsuitable for the client's purposes.

Limitations on Agent's Authority

Limitations in the Policy

Insurers have the right to limit the powers of their agents. A typical policy limitation on an agent's authority is as follows:

This contract can be changed only by our President, Secretary, or one of our Vice Presidents, and then only in writing. We will make no change in this contract without your consent. No agent is authorized to change this contract.

Any limitations on an agent's powers contained only in the policy are ineffective notice for actions taken by the agent prior to the delivery of the policy. Limitations in the policy are effective after delivery, regardless of whether the insured has read the contract. (This is due to the general rule of law that a party to a written contract is presumed to know and to consent to all its terms.)

Nevertheless, if the insurer, by a course of conduct after delivery, effectively grants to the agent a power otherwise denied in the policy, then the contractual notice of limitation will be ineffective. In *Protective Life Ins. Co. v. Atkins*[23] the agent's misrepresentations of the policy terms contradicted the actual policy language. The policy also contained language that limited the agent's authority to make policy modifications. Because the contract was a mortgage insurance policy and the agent was also an officer of the bank making the mortgage loan, the court ruled that the policy limitation was insufficient to limit the agent's authority.

Limitations in the Application

It is common for insurance applications to have limitations on an agent's authority, as in this example:

> No insurance agent or medical examiner has the authority to make, alter, or discharge any contract, accept any risks, or waive any of our rights or requirements.

These limitations are seen (or deemed to have been seen) by the insured prior to the issuance of the policy and thus are early notice to the insured of the scope of the agent's authority. As with the policy, however, if the insured signs the application, he or she is deemed to have read and agreed to its terms. Also if the insurer permits the agent to take action inconsistent with the limitation, it will waive its rights to enforce the limitation.

Termination of Agency Authority

The method of terminating agency authority depends on the type of agency authority given to the agent. Actual agency authority (whether express or implied) may be terminated by complying with the relevant provisions of the agreement that created the agency between the parties. It may be terminated by the action of the principal (by dismissal of the agent) or by the action of the agent (by giving notice of resignation). Actual agency authority may also be terminated by operation of law, as when an insurance agent's license to sell insurance is revoked. Note that the termination of actual agency authority is between the agent and the principal; notice to third parties is not required. However, apparent agency authority may exist after actual authority has been terminated.

Independent of a grant of actual agency authority, the principal may permit a person to appear to have agency authority. This is known as apparent authority (discussed earlier in this chapter), and it lasts until the principal gives direct notice to third parties that the agency has been terminated or until the principal no longer permits the agent to appear to have agency authority. Apparent authority may also exist after an agent's actual agency authority has been terminated. In some cases the principal may fail to remove all of the indicia of agency authority from the agent's control. If so, any third party who reasonably relies upon that apparent authority will be protected in his or her dealings with the agent, and the principal will be bound even if actual agency authority has been terminated.

CHAPTER REVIEW

Answers to the review questions and the self-test questions can be found in the Supplement.

Key Terms

principal
fiduciary
capacity
broker
financial planner
holding-out provisions
actual authority

actual express authority
actual implied (incidental)
   authority
ratification
generalist level
dual-agency level
expert level

Review Questions

1. What are some of the different kinds of agency relationships?

2. What persons and entities have the capacity to be
    a.   a principal? Explain.
    b.   an agent? Explain.

3. Why do many state insurance codes differentiate between the terms *agent* and *broker*, and how do producers' licenses affect the distinction?

4. What difficulties are encountered in the regulation of financial planners?

5. Explain the different types of authority that are found in agency relationships.

6. Jim had been Dave's business agent for several years. Unfortunately, Dave and Jim recently had a falling out, and Dave terminated the agency relationship he had with Jim. A third party with whom Jim had previously conducted business on behalf of Dave had not opened his mail for a while and was unaware that Dave had mailed him a notice stating that Jim was no longer his agent. While talking with this third party, Jim realized he was unaware that the agency relationship had been terminated. Jim also saw the opportunity to make a profitable business deal for Dave with the third party. Hoping to get back into Dave's good graces, Jim, acting as Dave's agent but without authority, concluded the deal between the third party and Dave. Dave wants to accept the benefit of Jim's unauthorized acts. What should Dave do?

7. What basic duties does an agent owe to his or her principal, and what may result from a breach of these duties?

8. What duties are imposed on a principal by the agency relationship, and what may result from a breach of these duties?

9. Ben and Gerry have been best friends for many years. Ben is a life insurance agent for Insureco. Gerry wants to take out a large insurance policy on his life but knows that for various reasons his application will be denied. Gerry decides to apply for the insurance anyway and to falsify some of the information he provides in the application. Gerry is fairly certain Ben will cover for him. Ben is aware that Gerry has lied but does not inform Insureco. Is Ben's knowledge about the false information imputed to Insureco? Explain.

10. Insurance producers owe duties to others in what three specific categories?

11. Explain the duties a producer owes to the insured at each of the following levels:
    a. generalist level
    b. dual-agency level
    c. expert level

12. When might the limitations on an agent's powers by an insurer be ineffective?

13. What methods are used to terminate agency authority?

Self-Test Questions

T   F   1. Insurance companies conduct their business through three types of agents: salespeople, employees, and policyowners.

T   F   2. A relationship between an employer and an independent contractor is a contractual relationship rather than an agency relationship.

T   F   3. Any person and any entity may be a principal.

T   F   4. Sometimes the partners of a partnership are deemed to be the principal instead of the partnership as an entity itself being the principal.

T   F   5. There are fewer limitations on who can serve as an agent than there are on who can serve as a principal.

T   F   6. Only persons who are licensed by the state are permitted to act as insurance agents.

T   F   7. The insurance codes of some states do not have a provision that specifically defines the term *broker*.

T   F   8. The advantage of producers' licenses is that once a producer has obtained a producer's license, he or she is permitted to be the agent of numerous insurers based solely on the one license.

T   F   19. After many years of struggling to define the term *financial planner*, lawmakers and regulators have recently been able to effectively define the term and enact laws and regulations that apply separately to this profession.

T   F   10. One of the primary differences between the terms *authority* and *power* involves consent.

T   F   11. Actual express authority means that the principal's authority to the agent is in writing.

T   F   12. When there is a dispute concerning the extent of the authority an agent has been granted, the determination is based on what the agent, not the principal, reasonably thought the scope of the authority was.

T   F   13. The main distinction between apparent and actual authority rests with the reasonable perceptions of the third party with whom the agent has been dealing.

T   F   14. For a principal to ratify an agent's unauthorized act, the consent of the third party is required.

T   F   15. A principal's ratification of an agent's act becomes effective on the date of the act rather than on the date of the ratification.

T   F   16. If an agent decides to breach the agency agreement he or she has with the principal and not act on the principal's behalf, the principal has the right to sue the agent for specific performance of his or her duties under the agency contract.

T   F   17. Under the law a principal is deemed to have important knowledge about a transaction that an agent acquires within the scope of the agency whether or not the principal has been informed of the knowledge by the agent.

T   F   18. An agent is not a party to the agreement he negotiates between a third party and the principal.

T   F   19. It is possible for an insurance producer to be an agent of the insurer for certain purposes and an agent of the insured for other purposes.

T   F   20. It is common for an insurance application to contain some limitations on an agent's authority.

NOTES

1. This material is based on research by the author that has previously been published in the *Journal of the American Society of CLU & ChFC* and the *Journal of Insurance Regulation*.
2. Agents and Brokers Licensing Model Act, Sec. 2.a.
3. *Ibid.* Sec. 2.b.
4. *Ibid.* Sec. 3.
5. The formulation in table 16-1 is not the only way to characterize the various forms of agency authority. In Buist M. Anderson, *Anderson on Life Insurance* (Boston: Little, Brown & Company, 1991), p. 385, the author states that agency authority "includes (a) Actual powers,

which are (1) those expressly given, (2) those incidental to the express powers, and (3) those conferred by custom and usage; and (b) Apparent powers."

6. Restatement (2d) of Agency Sec. 7 (1958).

7. *Ibid.* Sec. 8.

8. The term *insured* is sometimes used collectively to refer to the policyowner, the insured, and the beneficiary unless the context indicates otherwise.

9. Bartram Harnett, *Responsibilities of Insurance Agents and Brokers,* Sec. 4.01 (1974).

10. *Ryder v. Lynch,* 42 N.J. 465, 201 A2d 561, 567 (1964). This case involved a property/casualty broker who is presumed to be acting for the insured rather than a life/health agent who is presumed to represent the insurer. Such distinctions between agents and brokers are not usually controlling in the disposition of agent liability cases.

11. *Quinn v. Samples*, 156 Ga. App. 168, 274 SE 2d 141 (1980).

12. *American Motorists Ins. Co. v. Salvatore,* 102 App. Div. 2d 342, 476 NYS 2d 897 (1984).

13. Levit, "The Liability of an Insurance Broker or Agent–Updated," *Ins. Counsel J.,* 207 (April 1974).

14. See Rokes, "Dual Agency of Insurance Agents and Brokers," 44 *Ins. Counsel J.,* 677 (1977) for a list of dual-agency cases.

15. *Blair v. Manhattan Life Ins. Co.,* 692 F.2d 296 (3rd Cir. 1982), applying Pennsylvania law.

16. See 3 Harnett and Lesnick, *The Law of Life and Health Insurance*, Sec. 11.04.

17. *Lazzarra v. Aetna Cas. & Sur. Co.*, 802 F.2d 260 (7th Cir. 1986).

18. *Lazovick v. Sun Life Ins. Co. of America*, 586 F.Supp. 918 (E.D. Pa. 1984).

19. Diane E. Burkley and Carol Ann Bischoff, *Liability of Agents, Broker and Intermediaries for Insurer Insolvency*, 343 (1989).

20. *Hardt v. Brink*, 192 F.Supp. 879 (W.D. Wash. 1961). See also *Moseley v. Coastal Plains General Company, Inc.*, 404 S.E.2d 123 (Ga. App. 1991).

21. *Ibid.* at 881.

22. *Knox v. Anderson*, 159 F.Supp. 795 (D. Hawaii 1958).

23. *Protective Life Ins. Co. v. Atkins,* 86 Ill. App. 3d 542, 42 Ill. Dec. 85, 408 N.E. 2d 462 (1980).

17

Advertising and Privacy

Burke A. Christensen

Learning Objectives

An understanding of the material in this chapter should enable the student to

17-1. Explain the impact of the Securities Act of 1933 on the advertising of certain insurance products.

17-2. Discuss the effect of the Uniform Securities Act on state laws and regulations involving the sale of certain insurance products.

17-3. Discuss how state and federal insurance laws restrict insurance advertising.

17-4. Describe the disclosure requirements imposed by the model rules on insurance companies and producers.

17-5. Identify the U.S. Constitution's limited recognition of a right to privacy.

17-6. Distinguish the different invasion-of-privacy torts and defenses to invasion-of-privacy complaints.

17-7. Discuss the implications of the Fair Credit Reporting Act on consumer reporting agencies and state privacy legislation.

17-8. To understand and explain the phone call restrictions and allowances set forth by the Federal Regulatory bodies that enforce the national do-not-call registry.

Chapter Outline

In recent years, allegations of misleading life insurance advertising practices by a few insurance agents have been reported widely in the news media. This is a serious concern to the ethical and professional life underwriter because such actions affect the public's willingness to listen to *any* insurance producer. This defensive reaction may enable people to protect themselves from bad advice, but it also prevents them from hearing good advice.

Many people feel that they need life insurance, but few people clearly understand life insurance. This combination of need and ignorance creates an opportunity for the unethical to take advantage of the public. As a result, the advertising and marketing practices of the insurance industry are subject to a high and increasingly higher level of regulatory scrutiny.

Protecting policyowners' privacy is also an important obligation of the insurance industry. As an example, the recent problem concerning public knowledge about whether a person has or has not tested positive for HIV infection has made the question of privacy a major issue. Life insurance underwriting practices require prospective insureds to reveal significant amounts of personal medical and financial information about themselves. The proper treatment of this kind of information, and other sensitive personal information, is a legitimate regulatory concern.

ADVERTISING

The great importance of life insurance protection to millions of consumers is widely recognized by the general public. This value has long been recognized by the Congress of the United States. As a result, the ownership of life insurance is encouraged by the U.S. federal tax system, which grants certain tax advantages to life insurance products. The two most important advantages are that the death proceeds of a life insurance policy are usually free from income tax, and the growth of the cash value inside an insurance policy is not normally subject to income taxation. In addition, most states grant special protection for life insurance cash values and proceeds from the claims of creditors. Many states also provide special statutory protection for life insurance in the event of a policyowner's bankruptcy.

Despite this encouragement and the general recognition of the importance of life insurance, many people do not clearly understand how life insurance works. A 1975 report issued by the Life Insurance Marketing and Research Association (LIMRA) noted that 73 percent of the respondents claimed that they had trouble understanding their life insurance policies. For example, 54 percent did not know the difference between the cost of the policy and the premium they paid for it. Since the life insurance product line has gotten far more complicated in the years since that survey was conducted, it is not likely that the public would do any better today than in 1975.

The basic concept of life insurance as a method to spread the risk and cost of premature death is fairly easy to explain and understand. After this point, all simplicity is lost, and the more one learns about life insurance contracts, the more complicated the subject becomes.

Giving advice about life insurance products is a particularly dangerous area for advisers (such as lawyers and accountants) who have not acquired specific expertise or education about insurance. While these advisers may be able to read and interpret the life insurance contract or analyze the numbers on an insurance illustration, these activities will not reveal the peculiarities of life insurance law or the nonguaranteed assumptions that created the illustration. The contract and illustration do not reveal the extent of the discretion the insurer retains to raise or lower the policyowner's costs with respect to the policy's nonguaranteed elements (mortality costs, interest crediting or dividend rates, expenses, and so forth). Consequently any advice given without access to and an understanding of these elements is inadequate.

Many Policy Illustrations Include These Nonguaranteed Elements

- mortality costs
- interest crediting
- dividend rates
- expenses
- miscellaneous features

For variable and variable universal contracts, which are subject to the disclosure rules relating to securities, this information can be discovered by a careful reading of the prospectus.

Since a life insurance policy is such a complex contract, accurate and fair communication of information about how particular types of life insurance work has long been a subject of regulatory concern. For this reason, the life underwriter must be familiar with a wide variety of state and federal laws that govern advertising life insurance products. These laws are applicable to life insurance marketing in general but, as we will see in the first part of this chapter, certain types of life insurance advertisements are subject to even more rigorous regulation.

FEDERAL AND STATE SECURITIES LAWS

Because of the growing popularity of variable annuities, variable life insurance, and variable universal life insurance products, insurance agents who sell these products now must be aware of the securities law requirements governing their sale. Since the account values in variable and variable universal products may be invested in securities, these variable products are themselves defined as securities. Under the Investment Company Act of 1940, the separate accounts through which a policyowner's money is invested in a variable policy meet the definition of an "investment company" and are subject to regulation in the same way a mutual fund is regulated. As a result, those who sell the life insurance policies with cash accumulation accounts that are invested in these "investment companies" are subject to the federal and state securities laws.

Life Insurance Policies Classified as Investments under the Investment Company Act of 1940

- variable life
- variable universal life

---

marketers

The *marketers* (the insurance producers) are regulated by the Financial Industry Regulatory Authority (FINRA) (formerly the National Association of Securities Dealers or NASD) as broker/dealers or as registered representatives of broker/dealers. The products and their issuers (the insurance companies) are regulated by the Securities and Exchange Commission (SEC). Both the producers and the companies must also comply with any applicable state securities laws.

Federal Legislation

The Securities Act of 1933 is the most important piece of federal legislation that has an impact on advertising insurance products classified as securities. This federal statute has a significant effect on advertising of variable products because it places requirements on the full and fair disclosure of relevant material information about newly issued securities. Civil and criminal penalties are imposed on agents and companies who violate the act.

The major impact of this law on insurance agents is the requirement that a prospectus be given to the applicant at or before the time the agent attempts to sell the contract. A prospectus is a summary of important information taken from the registration statement filed by the insurance company with the SEC when the policy was registered as a security. The prospectus contains information identifying the insurance company that issued the contract, the fees or expenses to be deducted, financial information about the insurer, and details about the policy. The act also requires that the prospectus for any security be updated and a new prospectus issued every 13 months. This means that agents selling products for which a prospectus is required must be sure that they are always delivering the most recent prospectus.

The act also prohibits any individual from using the U.S. mail or any other means of interstate commerce to sell a security that is not registered. It imposes civil and criminal penalties against any person who uses the mail or other means of interstate commerce to defraud any investor. Persons who omit material information or who make untrue statements designed to induce a sale of securities are also subject to sanctions of the act.

The SEC has enacted numerous rules that have an impact on advertisements of securities. These rules apply to variable insurance contracts. Under Rule 135A, generic advertisements that merely describe the insurance company and the value of its products are not considered to be equivalent to an offer to sell securities. However, under Rule 156, sales literature is strictly controlled. Sales literature is defined as any communication (written or oral) used by any person to effect the sale of a security. If a communication meets the definition of sales literature, it must be accompanied by a prospectus. Rule 156 prohibits the use of fraudulent or materially misleading statements in sales literature.

The increasing popularity of financial planning during the last 2 decades has broadened the scope of the insurance producer's market to include mutual funds, annuities, and other financial instruments. This has raised some as yet unanswered questions about the regulation of insurance producers by the state and federal securities administrators.

Prospectus

- It discloses detailed information about the investment.
- It must accompany sales literature.
- It must be delivered prior to or at time of the investment sale.
- Accompanying sales literature must be complete and must not be misleading.

The Investment Advisers Act of 1940 defines an investment adviser as any person who is engaged in the business of advising others for compensation about the advisability of investing in securities. The state blue-sky laws are patterned on the 1940 federal act and contain similar language. Those who hold themselves out to the public as providing those services are subject to additional regulation.

Some state and federal regulators have taken the position that holding oneself out as a financial planner is the same thing as being an investment adviser. Some have also taken the position that listing designations, such as the ChFC, on one's business cards or letterhead is also the equivalent of holding oneself out as an investment adviser and requires the person to comply with the registration, filing, and record-keeping requirements applicable to investment advisers. Underwriters with such designations, especially those who also sell variable products, need to stay abreast of the changing interpretations of the law. Those underwriters who are also in the business of giving advice about securities for compensation are clearly subject to the laws governing investment advisers.

The NASD (now FINRA) has enacted Rules of Fair Practice that apply to its members. Article III, Section 35(a) of those rules defines advertisement and sales literature as follows:

> ADVERTISEMENT—For the purposes of this section and any interpretation thereof, "advertisement" means material published, or designed for use in a newspaper, magazine or other periodical, radio, television or tape recording, videotape display, signs or billboards, motion pictures, telephone directories (other than routine listings), or other public media.

> SALES LITERATURE—For purposes of this section and any interpretation thereof, "sales literature" means any written communication distributed or made generally available to customers or the public, which communication does not meet the foregoing definition of "advertisement." Sales literature includes, but is not limited to, circulars, research papers, market letters, performance reports or summaries, form letters, seminar texts, and reprints of any other advertisement, sales literature or published article.

State Securities Laws

The states also have laws and regulations affecting the sale of securities. Kansas, in 1911, was the first to enact such a state law. Most of the other states soon followed with their own laws, but there were considerable differences among the laws. The obvious need for uniformity led to the design of a model state securities law to complement the federal laws. The

blue-sky laws

Uniform Securities Act, the model law upon which most state laws are now based, was developed in 1956. State laws based on this act are sometimes referred to as *blue-sky laws*. The laws of most of these states include variable insurance products within the definition of "securities." As a result, life underwriters who sell variable products need to be aware of relevant state securities laws.

The Uniform Securities Act permits the state securities administrator to require the filing of sales and advertising literature. As with the federal laws, this literature is defined as any communication distributed to clients or prospective clients with the intent to effect the sale of a security. Furthermore, the act prohibits the use of fraudulent or deceitful practices in the attempt to sell securities. The general rule of the act is that no person may make an untrue statement of a material fact or omit to state a material fact in the attempt to sell a security. Life underwriters must become familiar with the appropriate state version of the Uniform Securities Act to ensure that their advertising practices are consistent with the securities laws of the states in which they do business.

NONSECURITIES LAWS ON INSURANCE ADVERTISING

In addition to the state and federal securities laws, there are both state and federal insurance laws that restrict insurance advertising.

State Insurance Advertising Laws

The National Association of Insurance Commissioners (NAIC) has developed a set of model rules governing the advertising of life insurance. In fact, the NAIC has separate model rules that relate to advertising of particular types of insurance. There are model rules for advertising with respect to (1) accident and sickness insurance, and (2) Medicare supplement insurance. The NAIC has also prepared the Model Unfair Trade Practices Act.

These model rules are distributed to the state insurance commissioners as suggestions for consideration when the states adopt their own rules and regulations. All of the states have enacted laws governing the advertisement of insurance within their borders. A majority of the states have adopted legislation similar to or based on the NAIC model rules. Professional life underwriters should become familiar with the version of this law that is applicable to the states where they do business.

The purpose of the model rules is "to set forth minimum standards and guidelines to assure a full and truthful disclosure to the public of all material and relevant information in the advertising of life insurance policies and annuity contracts." Note that the law is intended to set forth only minimum standards of behavior. Life insurance professionals are encouraged to learn and follow the ethical standards of the several life insurance associations and organizations. The Professional Pledge of The American College, which provides as follows, is primary among these ethical standards:

> In all my professional relationships, I pledge myself to the following rule of ethical conduct: I shall, in the light of all conditions surrounding those I serve, which I shall make every effort to ascertain and understand, render that service which, in the same circumstances, I would apply to myself.

This high standard of ethical behavior is reinforced by the Society of Financial Service Professionals. The code's first imperative is that a member must competently advise and serve the client. This is interpreted to mean that a member must provide advice and service that are in the client's best interest. The practical effect of this imperative is that if there is a conflict of interest between the client and the member, the client's interests must take precedence. Misleading advertising or deceptive sales practices are clearly not acceptable behavior under the Pledge and the Code of Ethics.

Definition of Advertisement

advertisement

The definition of an advertisement for purposes of the state insurance laws is easily as broad as the definition used in the securities laws for the same term. An *advertisement* is any written or oral communication that is intended to create a favorable opinion about insurance or to induce the sale of insurance. The model rule defines advertisement as follows:

> For the purposes of these rules:
> 1. "Advertisement" shall be material designed to create public interest in life insurance or annuities or in an insurer, or in an insurance producer; or to induce the public to purchase, increase, modify, reinstate, borrow on, surrender, replace, or retain a policy including:
>   (a) printed and published material, audiovisual material, and descriptive literature of an insurer or insurance producer used in direct mail, newspapers, magazines, radio and television scripts, billboards and similar displays;
>   (b) descriptive literature and sales aids of all kinds, authored by the insurer, its insurance producers, or third parties, issued, distributed or used by such insurer or insurance producer; including but not limited to circulars, leaflets, booklets, depictions, illustrations and form letters;

      (c)   material used for the recruitment, training, and education of an insurer's insurance producers which is designed to be used or is used to induce the public to purchase, increase, modify, reinstate, borrow on, surrender, replace or retain a policy;

      (d)   prepared sales talks, presentations and material for use by insurance producers;

2.   "Advertisement" for the purposes of these rules shall not include:

      (a)   communications or materials used within an insurer's own organization and not intended for dissemination to the public;

      (b)   communications with policyholders other than material urging policyholders to purchase, increase, modify, reinstate or retain a policy;

      (c)   a general announcement from a group or blanket policyholder to eligible individuals on an employment or membership list that a policy or program has been written or arranged; provided the announcement clearly indicates that it is preliminary to the issuance of a booklet explaining the proposed coverage.

It is the nature of life insurance marketing that the great bulk of all communications between the insurance company and the public is created by the insurance producers. Frequently, the insurance company never sees this material. Nevertheless, the model rules place the responsibility for the accuracy and truthfulness of those communications directly on the insurers, stating, "Every insurer shall establish and at all times maintain a system of control over the content, form and method of dissemination of all advertisements of its policies. All such advertisements, regardless by whom written, created, designed or presented shall be the responsibility of the insurer." This assignment of liability for advertising to the insurer should explain to producers why companies are becoming increasingly restrictive about communications between producers and their clients.

Example: ***Responsibility for Advertisements***

Stewart, an agent for Colossal Life Insurance Company, created and placed an advertisement in the phone book's yellow pages stating the following: "Ask about our term life policies. The rate is guaranteed never to increase." In fact, the rates do increase at each renewal date; only the *schedule* of those rates is guaranteed never to increase. This is deceptive advertising for which Colossal Life can be held legally liable, even though it had no knowledge of Stewart's advertisement.

The form and content of advertisements is also regulated by the model rules as follows:

> Advertisements shall be truthful and not misleading in fact or by implication. The form and content shall be sufficiently complete and clear so as to avoid deception. It shall not have the capacity or tendency to mislead or deceive. Whether an advertisement has the capacity or tendency to mislead or deceive shall be determined by the Commissioner of Insurance from the overall impression that the advertisement may be reasonably expected to create upon a person of average education or intelligence within the segment of the public to which it is directed.

This section of the model rules goes on to prohibit the misleading use of certain terms such as investment, investment plan, deposit, profit sharing, savings, savings plan, and charter plan. Usage is misleading if it will lead a person to believe that he or she will receive (1) something other than an insurance policy or (2) a benefit not available to other similar persons.

Disclosure Requirements

The model rules also impose a lengthy list of disclosure requirements on insurance companies and their producers to ensure that advertisements will not be deceptive or misleading. A few of the 25 requirements are as follows:

- Any information required to be disclosed by the rules shall not be minimized or hidden within the text so as to make the advertisement confusing or misleading.
- No advertisement may omit material information or use any word if that omission or use has the capacity, tendency, or effect of misleading or deceiving purchasers. The fact that the policy is made available for inspection prior to the sale, or that an offer is made to refund premiums if the purchaser is unsatisfied, does not remedy misleading statements.
- An advertisement must clearly identify the product as a life insurance policy.
- If the insurer retains the right to change the premium during the policy term, the advertisement will be deemed inherently deceptive if it does not prominently describe this feature.
- An advertisement may not state or imply in any way that interest charged on a policy loan or the reduction of death benefits by the amount of outstanding policy loans is unfair, inequitable, or in any manner an incorrect or improper practice.

- No insurance producer may use terms such as financial planner, investment adviser, financial consultant, or financial counseling in a way that implies that he or she is generally engaged in an advisory business in which compensation is unrelated to sales unless that is actually the case.
- An advertisement cannot make unfair or incomplete comparisons of policies, benefits, dividends, or rates of other insurers. Nor can it disparage other insurers, insurance producers, policies, services, or methods of marketing.

Although it is not a part of the NAIC's model, at least one state (Alabama) has a law stipulating that an advertisement cannot imply that the beneficiary will receive the face amount of the policy and the cash value. While this provision makes some sense with respect to traditional whole life insurance, its applicability to universal and variable universal life policies, where the policyowner has selected death benefit option "B," is unclear. If the policyowner elects that option, the insurance company must keep the amount at risk at a constant level, and at the insured's death add the cash accumulation account to the at-risk portion so that the beneficiary will receive the face amount of the policy and the cash value. (This is just an example of how the rapidly changing industry has outpaced the regulations that govern it.)

Model Unfair Trade Practices Act

Model Unfair Trade Practices Act

The *Model Unfair Trade Practices Act* exists "to regulate trade practices in the business of insurance." In part, the model act prohibits any form of insurance advertising that is "untrue, deceptive or misleading." This model has been the basis for laws enacted in almost all of the states. In a way similar to that of the model act that governs insurance advertising, the Unfair Trade Practices Model Act includes false advertising on a list of specific actions—which also includes unfair claims settlement practices, defamation, unfair discrimination, and rebating—deemed to be unfair trade practices. False advertising is defined as any material that is "untrue, deceptive, or misleading."

The model act further defines false advertising to include these five specific types of misrepresentation:

- misrepresenting the benefits, advantages, conditions, or terms of any insurance policy
- misrepresenting the amount of future dividends or the share of the insurer's surplus that will be received by the owner of any insurance

policy. This extends to misrepresenting the amount of dividends previously paid by the insurer to the policyowner.

- misrepresenting the financial condition of any insurer. This prohibition also makes misrepresenting the nature of the legal reserve system (which is one of the fundamental principles of the insurance industry) a form of false advertising and an unfair trade practice.
- misrepresenting an insurance policy by the use of a deceptive or misleading name or title that obscures the fact that the product is an insurance policy
- misrepresenting the insurance policy so that the policyowner or applicant is led to believe that the policy is a share (or shares) of stock representing ownership in a corporation

Under the model act the insurance commissioner has broad powers to investigate allegations of unfair trade practices. The commissioner also has subpoena powers to compel insurers to appear and defend against such allegations. If an unfair trade practice has been committed with respect to the advertising prohibitions or any other prohibited practice, the commissioner can impose fines up to $250,000. If he or she finds that the violation was a willful act, the commissioner can suspend or revoke the insurer's license to do business in that jurisdiction.

Federal Insurance Advertising Laws

McCarran-Ferguson Act

Outside of the securities context, federal regulation of life insurance advertising is not a major issue. According to the *McCarran-Ferguson Act*, the federal government may regulate insurance practices only "to the extent that such business is not regulated by State Law." As the preceding discussion shows, state law is fairly comprehensive. As a result, there is little applicable federal regulation. The Federal Trade Commission (FTC) has the power to regulate commerce between the states, and it has attempted to exert regulatory authority over interstate direct response insurance advertising. Nevertheless, any FTC regulation is superseded in any state that has enacted its own insurance advertising rules and regulations.

In addition, both the United States Postal Service and the Federal Communications Commission (FCC) can exert some control over insurance advertising. The Postal Service can take action when the mail is used to transmit fraudulent advertisements or to defraud people. The FCC can exert an indirect influence on radio and television advertising. It is the FCC's responsibility to assure that the owners of broadcast licenses use the public airways in the public interest. Because the FCC has power to revoke a broadcasting license for a failure to operate in the public's interest, the owners of those licenses should carefully scrutinize proposed advertisements before they are transmitted. If the broadcaster believes that the FCC might determine that the proposed advertisement is not in the public interest, it should refuse to transmit the ad.

PRIVACY

Privacy can be broadly described as the right to be left alone. Contrary to many people's belief, the right to privacy is not a fundamental right guaranteed by the language of the United States Constitution. There is no reference whatsoever to anything like a right to privacy in the seven articles that make up the text of the Constitution. Indirect references to privacy can be found only in the amendments to the Constitution.

The first amendment forbids Congress from prohibiting the free exercise of religion. Although this provision has been interpreted to permit some restrictions on a person's religious freedom, there is an element of the right to be let alone inherent in it. The third amendment prohibition against quartering soldiers in private homes grants homeowners a limited right to be left alone. However, this prohibition can be overcome simply by passing a law permitting such forced hospitality.

The fourth amendment gives the broadest indication of a right to privacy. Even so, it is not described as a right to privacy, and the protection it grants against unreasonable searches and seizures can be overcome fairly easily. The amendment states, "The right of the people to be secure in their persons, houses, papers, and effects, against unreasonable searches and seizures, shall not be violated, and no warrants shall issue, but upon probable cause, supported by oath or affirmation, and particularly describing the place to be searched, and the persons or things to be seized."

Although the fourth amendment contains a specific reference to private property, that reference is only in the context of describing the process the federal government must follow to take it away: No one may "be deprived of life, liberty, or property, without due process of law; nor shall private property be taken for public use, without just compensation." The 14th amendment contains similar language and restricts (but does not eliminate) a state's power to deprive people of their life, liberty, or property.

It is important to note that the Constitution's limited recognition of a privacy right creates protections against invasions of one's privacy only against the federal and state governments. The Constitution says nothing at all about a right to privacy against invasions by one's neighbors, other private individuals, businesses, or the news media.

Thus the fact that the Constitution created some limited rights of privacy is clear evidence that a right to privacy did not exist in the common law when the Constitution was drafted. The right to privacy, as we understand it today, is a created right that began to evolve only during the 20th century, following the 1890 publication of an article in the *Harvard Law Review* titled "The Right to Privacy." Under the still-developing modern view, the right to be left alone also includes the right to have one's private affairs kept private. In her book, *Law and the Life Insurance Contract*, Muriel L. Crawford describes this right in the context of life insurance transactions as "the right to fair personal information practices."

Invasion of Privacy Torts

invasion of privacy

As a right to privacy developed in American law throughout the 20th century, courts recognized different ways in which that right might be violated. *Invasion of privacy* is the term used in the law to describe a violation of one's right to be left alone. Violation of a person's rights by another person is known as a personal injury, or a tort. Our legal system currently recognizes four different torts under the heading, "invasion of privacy."

The first tort is misappropriation of another person's name or likeness for one's own commercial or other benefit without that person's consent. Using someone's photograph or name in an advertisement is the usual example of this violation. It is possible that an insurance producer may commit this tort if he or she uses a prominent client's name as an endorsement of the agent's products or services without that client's permission.

The second invasion of privacy tort is an unreasonable intrusion into one's private space—one's home or apartment, work (in some cases), or wherever one has created an expectation of privacy. This tort also applies to invasions of one's temporary private use of otherwise public space—for example, a wiretap on someone's telephone conversations. However, if a person has no expectation of privacy, there can be no invasion. For example, a participant in the New York Marathon has no cause of action if a photographer takes a group picture of participants and spectators at the starting line and sells it to a magazine for publication. Another defense to this tort, and to invasion of privacy torts in general, is available to the mass media if the person is a newsworthy public figure. The media have a right to publish photographs and stories about permanently or temporarily newsworthy people.

The third version of the invasion of privacy tort is public disclosure of private facts. Insurance companies and producers have considerable amounts of personal, private information about their clients. Some of this information—especially about clients whose applications for insurance have been declined or who have been issued rated policies—may be embarrassing if it becomes public knowledge. Insurers should rigorously guard this information against unauthorized disclosure.

Note that this third version of the tort involves publication of facts, not opinions. Publication of one's opinion, whether good or bad, about another person is not an invasion of his or her privacy unless it is accompanied by the publication of private facts. Similarly, publication of inaccurate statements (not facts) about someone does not meet the elements of this tort even if the statements are slanderous. In that event, the appropriate tort is defamation, not invasion of privacy. Note that while truth is an absolute defense in a defamation lawsuit, it does not relieve the defendant of liability in a lawsuit based on invasion of privacy.

The final version of this tort occurs when a person by word or action places another person in a false light in the public eye. In 1949 it was held that Hearst Magazines had committed this tort when it published the picture of an honest waiter to illustrate a story about dishonest waiters.

Theoretically, the information revealed does not have to be unfavorable in order to meet the definition of a tort. Suppose, for example, that Sue is a wealthy, reclusive author with no charitable interests whatever. Sue requires anonymity in order to do research for her books. Suppose further that John publicizes Sue's photo and address widely, telling the public that Sue is a wonderful, charitable human being who is intent upon distributing $1 million in cash to homeless people. The information John publishes may well improve Sue's public image, but it is certainly a false light, and the result may well be an unreasonable invasion of her privacy.

Defenses to Invasion of Privacy

For purposes of the life insurance industry, two defenses to invasion of privacy torts are extremely important. The first defense is consent. If the insurer or producer can establish that the complaining party consented to the release of the private information, there should be no recovery. The second

privilege

defense is the assertion of a *privilege* to seek out and use otherwise private information. The law permits certain persons a limited right to investigate the lives of others to further those persons' legitimate interests. For example, prospective employers have a limited privilege to investigate potential employees' claimed experience and education.

Insurance companies use both defenses to avoid invasion of privacy lawsuits and to defend against those they cannot avoid. To avail themselves of these defenses, insurers include notices in their applications for life insurance policies specifying that they may investigate an applicant's background. Insurance companies ask the applicant to consent to the investigation, to the use of information gained thereby, and to the release of

Medical Information Bureau (MIB)

medical information from the *Medical Information Bureau (MIB)*. Sample language is as follows:

I/We authorize any physician, hospital or other medically related facility, insurance company, the Medical Information Bureau, Inc. (MIB) or other organization or person that has any records or knowledge of me/us or my/our health to give such information to the Company or its reinsurers. I/We acknowledge receipt of copies of the prenotifications relating to investigative consumer reports and the MIB. This authorization is valid for thirty (30) months from its date.

The applicant or initial owner is asked to sign this statement. If the insured is someone other than the applicant, then the insured is also asked to sign the statement.

In addition to the above statement, applications contain notices such as the following, which are given to the insured or applicant at the time the application is completed:

Information Exchange Notice

Information that you provide in your application will be treated as confidential. The Company may, however, make a brief report of the information received in some applications, including yours, to the Medical Information Bureau, Inc. (MIB), a nonprofit membership organization of life insurance companies that operates an information exchange on behalf of its members. Upon request by another member insurance company to which you have applied for life or health insurance coverage, or to which a claim is submitted, MIB will supply such company with whatever information it may have in its files, which may include information provided by the Company.

Upon receipt of a request from you, MIB will arrange disclosure of any information it may have in your file. However, medical information will be disclosed only to your attending physician. If you question the accuracy of any information in your file, you may contact MIB and seek a correction in accordance with procedures set forth in the Federal Fair Credit Reporting Act.

The Company may also release information in its file to other life insurance companies to whom you apply for life or health insurance or to whom a claim for benefits may be submitted if you have given written authorization to release this information to the particular company.

•   •   •

Notice of Investigative Consumer Report

As part of our normal procedure, an investigative consumer report may be prepared concerning your character, general reputation, personal characteristics and mode of living. This information will be obtained through personal interviews with your friends, neighbors, and associates. A complete and accurate disclosure of the nature and scope of the investigative consumer report, if one is prepared, will be provided to you upon written request to the Company.

Some companies provide the following additional notice for applicants in selected states:

Notice of Insurance Information Practices

Instructions to the Agent: Give this notice to the proposed insured/owner/applicant in the states of Arizona, California, Connecticut, Georgia, Illinois, Montana, New Jersey, North Carolina, Oregon, and Virginia.

1. Personal information may be collected from persons other than the individual or individuals proposed for coverage.
2. Such information, as well as other personal or privileged information subsequently collected, may be disclosed to third parties in certain circumstances, without authorization.
3. A right of access and correction exists with respect to all personal information collected.
4. A more complete notice describing our information practices in detail will be furnished to you upon request.

The above disclosure notices are merely samples; the actual language companies use varies considerably from contract to contract. The language of the notices also varies, in some cases, depending on the state in which the applicant resides. Once this information has been communicated to the applicant and insured, the insurance company may begin to investigate the proposed insured's background to determine whether it wants to accept his or her application for insurance.

Insurers' investigative practices are controlled primarily by a federal law known as the Fair Credit Reporting Act and at the state level by the several states that have enacted local laws based on that act. When the state and federal laws differ, the state version usually extends additional rights to the general public or further limits the powers of credit-reporting agencies. A minority of the states have also adopted local versions of the NAIC's model privacy act, which is formally known as the Insurance Information and Privacy Protection Model Act.

Fair Credit Reporting Act

During the 1960s, the United States Supreme Court announced several decisions that began to formalize a right to privacy against encroachment by state and federal authorities in certain limited circumstances. In response to public concern about the growing ability of private companies (primarily credit-reporting agencies) to use computers to collect and retain information about people, Congress created statutory protection of the public's right to privacy from these companies by enacting the 1970 *Fair Credit Reporting Act.*

The act enforces the privacy rights it creates by controlling the activities of consumer reporting agencies, which are defined as any entity that is in the business of preparing consumer reports or investigative consumer reports. The law applies to commercial agencies, which compile such reports and sell them to others for profit, as well as to cooperative nonprofit agencies such as the insurance industry's Medical Information Bureau. Interestingly, the Fair Credit Reporting Act protects only those consumers who are "natural persons" (people). It does not extend any privacy rights to businesses.

The purpose of the act is to require consumer reporting agencies and those who employ them to acquire, maintain, and report the collected information in a fair and impartial manner. The act specifies two kinds of reports that are subject to regulation: consumer reports and investigative consumer reports.

Section 603(b) of the act defines a consumer report as "any written, oral or other communication of any information by a consumer reporting agency bearing on a consumer's credit worthiness, credit standing, credit capacity, character, general reputation, personal characteristics or mode of living," when collected for the purpose of evaluating the consumer for the extension of credit, for prospective employment, or to determine the person's insurability.

Section 603(e) of the act defines an investigative consumer report as a report "obtained through personal interviews with neighbors, friends or associates of the consumer reported on, or with others with whom he is acquainted ...." The definition also includes interviews with any person who may have knowledge about the consumer being investigated.

The following are some of the numerous limitations and obligations the Fair Credit Reporting Act imposes on consumer reporting agencies and the persons who use them:

- Unless the agency is responding to a court order, it may release the information it has collected on a person only in response to that person's request or to an entity or person that can establish a legitimate business need for the information.
- If the consumer requests, the agency must disclose the nature and substance of the information it has collected. It must also reveal its sources of information and the persons to whom it has released the

information. There is an exception for medical information that the consumer requests. The agency is permitted to restrict its release of medical information in response to a consumer request only to the attending physician of the consumer making the request.

- The agency must establish procedures to safeguard the information it collects so that it will not be released to unauthorized persons.
- The act also prohibits the agency from releasing certain kinds of information if it is no longer up-to-date.
- Before any investigative consumer report may be obtained, the consumer must be advised that it might be sought and the extent of the investigation that may be conducted.
- The consumer must also be told how to access the information collected. If the consumer asserts that any portion of the collected information is in error, the agency must either confirm the accuracy of its information or delete the information from its files.
- If an insurer declines or rates an applicant based on a consumer report, the insurer must tell the prospective insured that a consumer report was the basis for the adverse decision. It must also tell the applicant the name and address of the consumer reporting agency that provided the report on which the adverse decision was based.
- If a person obtains a consumer report to which he or she is not entitled, the penalty is up to $5,000 in fines, one year of imprisonment, or both.

State Privacy Legislation

Some states have protected privacy rights through a collection of unrelated state laws. These laws focus on protecting personal privacy in areas such as state tax returns, adoption records, business and state employment personnel records, juvenile court files, and medical records, among others. Recently, some states have enacted special legislation designed to reinforce the confidentiality of medical records with respect to certain diseases, notably HIV and AIDS. With the exception of laws governing the confidentiality of medical records, these laws do not generally have a particular application to the insurance business. Nevertheless, insurers need to be aware of the variety of state laws that protect the privacy of applicants and insureds.

NAIC Model Privacy Act

Insurance Information and Privacy Protection Model Act

In 1979 the NAIC adopted a model privacy act—the *Insurance Information and Privacy Protection Model Act*. The model act is similar in purpose, and in many of its requirements, to the federal Fair Credit Reporting Act except that the NAIC Model Privacy Act is a state law and focuses solely on information gathered for the insurance industry, whereas the Fair Credit Reporting Act is applicable to many types of consumer reporting.

Like the Fair Credit Reporting Act, the model privacy act tries to minimize the intrusiveness of personal investigations and balances the insurer's need for personal information with the applicant's desire for confidentiality. The model act also gives people the right to discover and have access to the information that has been collected about them. It grants people the right to dispute the accuracy of collected information and requires information-collecting agencies to verify their information when the person being investigated disputes it. It also severely limits how the collected information can be disclosed. Finally, if an adverse underwriting decision is made based on information collected in the report, the model act permits the applicant or insured to learn the reason for the decision and the source of that information.

The NAIC has updated and revised the act several times, but only a small minority of states have adopted it. A larger number—but still only a minority of state jurisdictions—have privacy acts of any kind. Nevertheless, understanding the model act is important because most insurers comply with its requirements regardless of where an insurance policy may have been sold.

A summary of the model act's more important provisions is as follows:

- The act protects the privacy of natural persons, not businesses, and it is not applicable to persons who are acquiring insurance for business purposes. To obtain protection from the act, the person must be a resident of the state that enacted it.
- The model act prohibits *pretext interviews*—that is, investigations in which the interviewer misrepresents his or her identity in order to obtain information about someone. There is one exception to this rule: Pretext interviews are permitted in limited circumstances when an insurer is investigating a claim. To justify a pretext interview, the insurer must have some reasonable basis to believe that the claimant is engaging in a material misrepresentation with respect to the claim. Regardless of the insurer's suspicions, a pretext interview may not be conducted with someone who has a privileged relationship (for example, a lawyer, doctor, or spouse) with the person who is being investigated.
- Notification that an investigation may be conducted, the purpose of the investigation, and the potential extent of the investigation must be given prior to beginning the investigation. The insurer must obtain the consent of the person to be investigated, and the consent notice must expire within a specified time period (normally 30 months).
- If the state insurance commissioner determines at a hearing that the act has been violated, he or she may impose a cease-and-desist order

against the producer, the insurer, or other entity found to be in violation. If the party against whom the order is placed violates the order, he or she may be fined up to $10,000 for each violation. If the commissioner finds that the violation was part of a general business practice, the fine can reach $50,000. Under the act, the public is entitled to the assistance of injunctions or other court orders necessary to compel a party to comply with the act. Finally, as with the Fair Credit Reporting Act, a penalty of up to $10,000 in fines, one year in prison, or both may be imposed on anyone who obtains information about a consumer in violation of the act.

Example:	***Pretext Interview***
	A home office life insurance underwriter suspects that information about a recent hospitalization has been omitted from a life insurance application by the proposed insured. The underwriter calls the proposed insured's wife and poses as an employee of a survey research firm gathering people's opinions about the quality of care that they receive at the local hospital. One of the questions asked in the survey is how frequently the interviewee or members of her family have been treated at the local hospital in the past year. This conduct by the underwriter would be strictly prohibited under the NAIC's Model Privacy Act.

National Do-Not-Call Registry

national do-not-call registry

Congress enacted the Telephone Consumers Protection Act in 1991, which gave the Federal Trade Commission (FTC) and the Federal Communications Commission (FCC) authority to establish a national do-not-call registry.

Initially only the FTC was engaged in the creation of the registry at the national level (many states have also enacted do-not-call statutes). Lobbying efforts on behalf of the financial services industries gained exemption from the FTC rules. This relief was negated shortly thereafter when the FCC stepped in to apply essentially identical rules to the insurance industry, banks, and common carriers. Consequently, both the FTC and the FCC are involved in enforcing the FTC-maintained national do-not-call registry.

The registry is a list of residential and wireless phone numbers that people have requested not be called by telemarketers. That list exceeded 50 million phone numbers in October of 2003 when national do-not-call protection was initiated.

The applicable rules prohibit telemarketers from calling persons on the national do-not-call registry unless they have a business relationship with the party or have written permission to call. The rules prohibit calls before 8 a.m. or after 9 p.m. Callers are not permitted to block caller ID. All businesses, regardless of size, are required to maintain a company-specific do-not-call list of phone numbers they have been requested not to call again. Phone numbers on this company-specific list are not to be called, even if the party has established a business relationship with the company.

In addition to the national registry and company-specific do-not-call lists, there are at least 32 states that have do-not-call lists. The federal statute permits the states to impose more restrictive do-not-call standards but does not permit the states to weaken the federal standard with more lenient provisions. In other words, the FTC standard sets the minimal requirements that the states cannot undermine.

In many states, the do-not-call list is shared with the FTC to be included on the national registry. However, at least 10 states have refused to share their lists with the FTC and so businesses must check both the state list and the national registry to comply with both requirements in those states.

There are some exceptions to the national do-not-call registry. Political organizations and charities are permitted to call numbers on the do-not-call lists. Telephone surveys can also target numbers on the do-not-call lists. Calls that are not commercial or do not include unsolicited advertisements can be added to the protected group. A party on the do-not-call lists can give written permission to a business to call that number.

The establishment of a business relationship sets up a limited time exemption to the do-not-call restrictions. The business with a relationship can make calls for up to 18 months after a sale or transaction with a party associated with the protected phone number. Inquiries to the business open a window of 3 months for permitted calls to the associated protected phone number.

There are some strict rules that apply to telephone solicitations, even if they are directed at numbers not on the do-not-call lists. The caller must provide his or her name and the name of the company on whose behalf the call is being made. In addition, the caller must provide a phone number for contacting that company. If the caller leaves a prerecorded message, it must also include a number to contact to request inclusion on that company's own do-not-call list.

Violations of the FTC rules can be very costly. The law permits fines up to $11,000 per incident for infractions. There were more than 30,000 complaints filed with the FTC during the first 6 months of the national registry's operation. Complaints can be made to either the FTC or the FCC.

In addition to regulatory enforcement and fines, there is the possibility of civil litigation in the courts.

Upon request, consumers' phone numbers will be included on the national do-not-call registry. The initial request extends protection automatically for 5 years, and that protection is then dropped unless there is a separate request to extend the protection for another 5 years. Consumers can request that their phone number be deleted from the registry at anytime. Phone numbers will automatically be dropped from the registry if the phone number is disconnected (even temporarily, such as for a vacation). Upon reconnection, the consumer will have to initiate a new request for inclusion on the registry to restart the do-not-call protection. It takes 3 months to re-establish this protection.

Consumers can give written permission to a company to call a number that is otherwise protected by the registry.

Consumers can request not to be called by a company, which should result in the phone number being put on the company's own do-not-call list within 30 days of the request. This request is to be honored, even if the requesting party has an established business relationship with the company. Therefore, a company-specific do-not-call list may include phone numbers that are not on the national registry or a state do-not-call list. The company-specific do-not-call list may even include the phone numbers of some of its own customers.

Additional information is available from the FTC about the national do not call registry at the website http://telemarketing.dontcall.gov.

CHAPTER REVIEW

Answers to the review questions and the self-test questions can be found in the Supplement.

Key Terms

marketers	Medical Information Bureau
blue-sky laws	(MIB)
advertisement	Fair Credit Reporting Act
Model Unfair Trade Practices Act	Insurance Information and Privacy
McCarran-Ferguson Act	Protection Model Act
invasion of privacy	national do-not-call registry
privilege	

Review Questions

1. What types of products have to meet securities law requirements, and what groups are responsible for regulation?

2. The Securities Act of 1933 and the Securities and Exchange Commission have had a great effect on advertising insurance products classified as securities.
   a. Specifically, what is the major requirement this law imposed on insurance agents?
   b. What are some of the prohibitions imposed on insurance agents by this law?
   c. What specific effects have some of the rules enacted by the SEC had on advertising insurance products classified as securities?

3. How does the Uniform Securities Act affect life underwriters who sell variable products?

4. What is the purpose of the model rules developed by the NAIC?

5. What specific types of misrepresentation constitute false advertising under the Model Fair Trade Practices Act?

6. A right to privacy is indirectly referred to in amendments to the U.S. Constitution. Describe the amendment references to privacy.

7. What are the four invasion-of-privacy torts recognized in our legal system?

8. Betty and Sue are neighbors who have not been friendly to one another ever since Sue got a dog that barks incessantly. Betty is the only neighbor in the rural area who lives close enough for the barking to be annoying. One day when Betty was outside picking some flowers from her garden, Sue hollered over the fence, "You're not a nice person, and I am going to tell everyone at church." Can Betty file a lawsuit against Sue for invasion of privacy? Explain.

9. In the context of life insurance, what defenses to a claim of invasion of privacy are recognized in our legal system?

10. What is the purpose of the Fair Credit Reporting Act of 1970, and to whom or what does it apply?

11. What is the purpose of the NAIC Model Privacy Act, and how does it differ from the Fair Credit Reporting Act?

12. Indicate what calls are permitted to phone numbers on the national do-not-call registry.

13. Indicate the do-not-call lists with which a company is required to comply.

Self-Test Questions

T   F   1. Since so many people today own life insurance to protect their families and businesses financially, the majority of the adult population has a good understanding of how life insurance works.

T   F   2.   Variable life insurance and variable universal life insurance products and the issuers of these products are regulated by the Securities and Exchange Commission.

T   F   3.   Agents and companies who violate the requirements of the Securities Act of 1933 may be subject to civil and criminal penalties.

T   F   4.   Some federal and state regulators claim that if you hold yourself out to the public at large as being a financial planner, it is the same as being an investment adviser.

T   F   5.   Most states' blue-sky laws are based on a model law called the Uniform Securities Act.

T   F   6.   The model rules developed by the National Association of Insurance Commissioners (NAIC) governing the advertising of life insurance are intended to force state insurance commissioners to adhere to the format contained in the rules.

T   F   7.   The NAIC model rules purposefully exclude advertising disclosure requirements because it is recognized by insurance companies and producers that false advertising would harm their reputations.

T   F   8.   Under the Model Unfair Trade Practices Act, state insurance commissioners can impose fines up to $250,000 on insurers who violate the act's advertising prohibitions.

T   F   9.   There is little regulation at the federal level concerning life insurance advertising that does not involve products with a securities component.

T   F   10.   A clear right to privacy did not exist in the common law at the time the U.S. Constitution was written.

T   F   11.   When an insurance company declines a person's application for life insurance, the information contained in the application must be filed with the nearest municipal government office and become a matter of public record so that the company's refusal to insure can be reviewed.

T   F   12.   The Fair Credit Reporting Act was enacted in part to control the degree to which consumer reporting agencies can gain access to and report private information about people.

T   F   13.   Both the FTC and the FCC are involved in the national do-not-call registry complaint enforcement.

T   F   14.   Telemarketing calls are not permitted between 8 p.m. and 9 a.m.

18

Death and Dying

Edward E. Graves

<table>
<tr><td colspan="2">

Learning Objectives

An understanding of the material in this chapter should enable the student to
</td></tr>
<tr><td>18-1.</td><td>Become familiar with the issues that must be taken care of on behalf of a deceased person.</td></tr>
<tr><td>18-2.</td><td>Understand the issues of legal competency and delegation of health care and property management.</td></tr>
<tr><td>18-3.</td><td>Know the various types of power of attorney available for delegation of authority.</td></tr>
<tr><td>18-4.</td><td>Know the issues involved with the creation and implementation of living wills.</td></tr>
<tr><td>18-5.</td><td>Understand the importance of a donor card in making anatomical gifts.</td></tr>
<tr><td>18-6.</td><td>Know the relationship between wills and the laws of intestacy.</td></tr>
<tr><td>18-7.</td><td>Understand the matters that should be resolved by a will and the potential pitfalls of their resolution or lack of resolution.</td></tr>
<tr><td>18-8.</td><td>Understand the importance of regularly updating a will.</td></tr>
<tr><td>18-9.</td><td>Be aware of the responsibilities of a personal representative in handling the estate.</td></tr>
<tr><td>18-10.</td><td>Be cognizant of the emotional issues faced by the terminally ill and his or her survivors.</td></tr>
<tr><td>18-11.</td><td>Understand how an inventory of important information is a valuable aid to survivors and personal representatives who must settle the estate.</td></tr>
</table>

Chapter Outline

Everyone eventually faces death. Yet, surprisingly, few people know how to prepare for death or realize what must be done on their behalf after death. This is true of personal and business matters as well as interpersonal relationships involved.

When a person dies, a series of activities devoted to handling the final disposition of the body and settlement of the estate is initiated. This process is similar for all individuals. These matters are often handled by the surviving family members or friends, but since many have not gone through the process before, it is often perceived as difficult, complex, and confusing. They would like to carry out the deceased's wishes, but often these wishes were not discussed or otherwise made known, so they must guess at what the decedent wanted. There are many things that people can do while they are living to assist their survivors in making these important decisions.

Family discussions of what would happen if either or both parents were to die can be helpful. This raises the issues of funeral arrangements, estate distribution, future family income, educational desires for children, remarriage of the surviving spouse, donation of the deceased's body, custody and guardianship of any minor children, and so forth. These discussions should communicate each person's desires to the other family members. It is advisable to create written documents that will also communicate these final wishes and will be available after death. These documents should be distributed to all interested parties and potential care givers shortly after the documents are created so that decision makers will be aware of their existence.

PROCEDURAL ASPECTS OF DEATH AND DYING

Legal Capacity

Babies and children do not have legal capacity. Legal capacity is gained by reaching the age of legal majority (commonly age 18, depending on state statutes). *Black's Law Dictionary* defines *capacity* as "legal qualification (i.e. legal age), competency, power or fitness. Mental ability to understand the nature and effects of one's acts."

Various state statutes may grant specific capacities at different ages, such as the capacity to consent to marriage or the capacity to contract for life insurance (commonly age 15). Persons beyond the age of legal majority are assumed to be competent to contract on their own behalf, grant deeds, and create valid wills.

competent
Competent is defined by *Black's Law Dictionary* as follows:

> Duly qualified; answering all requirements; having sufficient capacity, ability or authority; possessing the requisite physical, mental, natural or legal qualifications; able; adequate; suitable; sufficient; capable; legally fit. A testator may be said to be competent if he or she understands (1) the general nature and extent of his property; (2) his relationship to the people named in the will and to any people he disinherits; (3) what a will is; and (4) the transaction of simple business affairs.

However, people can lose their competency for various reasons. A comatose person lacks both the physical and mental ability to make decisions or discharge duties. Insanity impairs one's mental ability and renders him or her incompetent.

Conditions leading to incompetency may be either permanent or temporary. Duress and intoxication are possible sources of temporary incompetency. Alzheimer's disease is usually a cause of permanent incompetency.

The most important aspect of competency for our purposes is the ability to make decisions about one's own medical care, property management, and creation or alteration of a will. A competent person can delegate medical care

attorney-in-fact
power of attorney

decisions and property management decisions to another party by appointing that party to be his or her agent (known as an *attorney-in-fact*).

The written document making such an appointment is called a *power of attorney* even if the person appointed as agent is not a lawyer. The person creating the power of attorney (the principal) can specify very explicit and limited powers to be conferred, such as the power to pay bills and to make bank deposits, or the powers may be general (full conference) powers. A general power of attorney cannot delegate the power to create or alter a will on behalf of the principal.

durable power
of attorney

One potential problem of a simple power of attorney is that it may terminate if the principal becomes disabled or incompetent (all powers of attorney terminate upon the death of the principal). A *durable power of attorney* can be established that will preserve the agent's power after the principal's disability or incompetency and thus extend the delegation up to the principal's death. Many people are reluctant to create a full and immediate durable power of attorney before they become disabled or otherwise experience diminished capacity. Consequently it has become an established practice to create a *springing durable power of attorney* that becomes effective only after the occurrence of specified events, such as disappearance or loss of physical or mental competency. This approach establishes the desired representation should it ever be necessary without delegating powers before they are needed or desired. A competent principal can terminate existing or springing powers of attorney at any time.

springing durable
power of attorney

Termination of Power of Attorney

- by action of competent principal to revoke the power of attorney
- by expiration terms set forth in the power of attorney itself (if any)
- at death of principal for a durable power of attorney
- at loss of competency for a simple power of attorney

Because a durable power of attorney can survive the principal's incompetency, the agent can carry on necessary transactions regarding property management and health care decisions without waiting for competency hearings and court appointment of a guardian. Further, the actions of the agent under a durable power of attorney need not become part of the public records (open to public scrutiny) as is the requirement for all actions of court-appointed guardians or conservators. The principal determines who can act on his or her behalf under a power of attorney, whereas a court-appointed guardian may be someone the principal would find less desirable than an agent he or she chose.

For estate planning purposes, it is desirable for the durable power of attorney to specify that it delegates the power to make gifts, implement any and all retirement plan transactions, and execute any property transactions consistent with the plans and desires of the principal. Failure to explicitly stipulate an intended power could result in subsequent litigation over whether the attorney-in-fact possessed that power. The IRS regularly challenges the power to make gifts unless it is specified in writing.

Sometimes the principal creates separate durable power-of-attorney documents for property management and for health care. Quite often, different people are chosen to represent the principal for these distinctly separate functions.

Powers That Can Be Included in a Power of Attorney

- make decisions about medical care and treatment
- manage finances
- manage property
- sell property
- make gifts of property
- acquire property
- manage trusts
- make retirement plan decisions and execute transactions

Note: No person can grant the power to create his or her own will.

Legislative interest in the health care durable power of attorney and the living will (discussed below) has prompted the states to adopt statutes acknowledging these advance medical directives. Some of these statutes refer to a durable power of attorney for health care as a medical power of attorney. The primary focus of these statutes is to allow the appropriate decision maker to reject long-term artificial life support when there is little or no hope for recovery, when death is imminent, and when the principal has written his or her desire to avoid prolonged artificial life support.

Living Will

living will

The written intent to avoid prolonged artificial life support is usually set forth in a document known as a *living will*. It addresses the principal's desires regarding use of artificial life-support systems when he or she is terminally incapacitated or permanently unconscious. Most states have statutes acknowledging living wills, but the statutes differ in how they define a terminal condition.

Because of these differences, it is advisable to draft a living will that conforms to the applicable law in the person's state of domicile. Persons who reside in more than one state need a living will that conforms to all of the applicable statutes in each state of residence.

Many physicians consider the living will to be an inherent conflict with their duty to prolong life. They may be unwilling to abide by a living will unless they are convinced that the combination of the specific document and the pertinent statute relieves the doctor of any civil or criminal liability for the death of the patient as a result of not initiating artificial life-support systems. Most of the statutes grant some immunity to health care providers acting in accordance with the patient's living will.

A strong case has been made for supplementing the living will with a durable power of attorney for health care. The attorney-in-fact (agent) for health care can make sure the physicians are aware of the living will. In order to get the health care providers to comply with the living will, the attorney-in-fact may have to take a strong stance as the patient's advocate. In some cases there may even be a conflict with a provider's religious philosophy. There is almost always a moral conflict because so many providers view a patient's death as a failure rather than a natural termination of the life cycle.

Example:

Excerpts from One Person's Living Will

I, _____ SSN: _____, do hereby appoint _____ as my attorney-in-fact to make health care decisions for me, if and only if I am incapacitated or otherwise unable to make decisions for myself. For purposes of this document, "health care decisions" means consent, refusal of consent, or withdrawal of consent to health care. Subject to any limitations in this document, I hereby grant to my attorney-in-fact full power and authority to make health care decisions for me and on my behalf in the event I should lose the capacity to make such decisions for myself. The term "health care" means any care, treatment, service, or procedure to maintain, diagnose, or treat an individual's physical or mental condition. In exercising this authority, my attorney-in-fact shall make health care decisions that are consistent with my desires as stated in this document or otherwise made known to my attorney-in-fact. My attorney-in-fact shall have the right to examine my medical records and consent to their disclosure.

If, at any time, I should have a terminal condition, or be in an irreversible coma or persistent vegetative state, and my attending physician or other health care provider has determined that there can be no reasonable medical expectation of recovery from such condition or state, where the application of medical treatment implemented for the purpose of sustaining life or the life process would serve only artificially to prolong the dying process, my attorney-in-fact is specifically instructed to direct that such medical treatment be withheld or withdrawn, and that I be permitted to die naturally with only the administration of medication or the performance of any medical procedure deemed necessary to provide me with comfortable care, or to alleviate pain. I specifically authorize the withholding or withdrawal of artificially provided food, water, or other nourishment or fluids.

Anatomical Gifts

uniform donor card

Some people decide to donate their body or parts of it to living persons or to medical research. Execution of a *uniform donor card* records such a wish and communicates it to those present at the time of death. A completed donor card eliminates the need for survivors to decide whether or not to donate the decedent's body, because it stipulates which parts of the body the donor intends to give. The card must be properly witnessed by two persons and carried by the donor so that it will be with the body at the time of death.[1] Doctors, relatives, friends, attorneys, or anyone else likely to participate in care decisions should be informed of the donor card. (A representative sample of the uniform donor card appears at the end of this chapter.)

anatomical gifts

Anatomical gifts enable living persons with impaired health to improve their health through transplants of healthy organs and/or tissue. Medical technology currently permits transplanting such organs as kidneys, livers, lungs, and hearts. This type of donation must be carried out within a few hours of death and can be accomplished only if the death occurs in a hospital. Thus intended donors who die outside of hospitals cannot donate their organs for transplants.

Other parts of the body that do not require that death occur in a hospital may also be donated. These include the cornea for the eye, bones for the inner ear, and skin tissue for healing severe burns. These gifts may restore sight or hearing to living people and enable burn victims to survive.[2]

Medical schools often take whole bodies for purposes of medical research and teaching, and those that accept full-body gifts also dispose of the body. When parts of the body have been donated, the family disposes of the rest of the body.

Body Parts That Can Be Donated to Living People

- heart
- lung
- liver
- kidney
- cornea

- inner ear bones
- skin
- hand
- bones

Making anatomical gifts does not preclude a funeral. Donated parts can be removed before the funeral, or the funeral can be held before the body is delivered for research. There are statutes in some areas that prohibit anyone from paying for dead bodies; however, the donee is allowed to pay transportation costs for cadavers.

It is important to realize that not all intended donations are accepted. The gift cannot be used if the tissue is either diseased or mutilated. Organs cannot be successfully transplanted unless there is a recipient with blood and tissue types similar to those of the donor. Sometimes medical schools even have more donations than they can handle and must reject some. For these reasons, anatomical gifts may or may not affect funeral plans.

Funerals

Just as it is important to know whether the deceased wished to donate his or her body or its parts, it is important to know what kind of funeral the deceased desired. There are many alternatives, and someone must make the arrangements. It is possible to bury or cremate the body without having a funeral or wake. Bodies from which organs have been donated are available for funeral preparation shortly after surgery has been completed; when the entire body has been donated, funerals can be held before the body is delivered to the donee. With the help of a funeral director, it is possible to make arrangements for funerals and burial or cremation before death when it is much easier to be objective.

The wide range of funeral services and caskets leads to wide variations in funeral costs. One recent survey disclosed that the lowest-cost service, including a casket, can vary by 300 percent from one provider to another. These costs do not include burial or cremation expenses. At the other end of the spectrum are full-service funerals with the most expensive caskets. These can cost over $20,000 exclusive of burial or cremation expenses. In some areas, memorial societies aid families in obtaining low-cost funerals and cremation or burial.

Burial

If the body is to be buried, a plot must be purchased and a separate fee paid for opening and closing the grave. Some cemeteries add a fee for perpetual care of the cemetery grounds, and some require that the casket be placed in a vault to prevent caving in if the casket deteriorates and collapses in later years. This adds additional expense to the burial.

Cremation

Cremation of the body is another method of handling the remains. This service will usually cost less if it is provided in conjunction with a funeral.

The actual prices for any funeral, burial, or cremation services depend on geographic location as well as on the kind and amount of services performed. Prices tend to be higher in large cities and in the eastern United States.

Custody of Children

One very important issue seldom considered prior to death concerns the care of children if both parents die. This involves a search to find a person or family whose lifestyle is conducive to raising the deceased's children in the way he or she would like. Even if such an environment is found, the person or family may not be willing to accept that responsibility if the need should arise. It is best to obtain agreement from potential guardians before naming them in a will or other written documents. Intended guardians for children must meet the approval of the court before they can be officially appointed. (A person nominates guardians in his or her will; usually the courts will honor these wishes.)

Will

will

The laws of each state give individuals the privilege of indicating how their property is to be distributed after death. This privilege is exercised by creating a *will* before death. If death occurs without a will, state laws of intestacy determine how the property is to be distributed. Even if all survivors know what distribution the deceased intended, they must distribute the property according to the state statute if no will is found or if the will is for any reason declared invalid.

Example: **Dying Intestate**

In someone dies without a valid will, the way his or her property will be distributed is dictated inflexibly by state law. The typical law provides a priority list starting with the surviving spouse, then the children of the decedent, the parents of the decedent, and the decedent's brothers and sisters. Note that there is no provision for a special friend or nephew of the decedent, for a favorite charity, or for other recipients the decedent might have preferred.

It is best to have a lawyer draw up a will so that it will be concise and unambiguous. The existence of the will and its location should be communicated to family members and friends to ensure that the will can be located and put into effect after death. If the will cannot be located, the estate will be settled as if there had never been a will.

The will should indicate who is to be executor of the estate, the trustee of any testamentary trusts, and who should be guardian of minor children in case neither parent survives. It should provide for the disposition of all assets the testator owned. The will should be redrawn or amended whenever it is appropriate, because assets not included in the will may be distributed according to the laws of intestacy.

The will should also be reassessed regularly. Whenever the family moves from one state to another or the family configuration changes due to births, deaths, marriages, incompetencies, or divorces, the will may need to be changed. Particular attention is necessary if a move involves both a common law state and a community-property state.

Important Papers

After a death, it is often a monumental task to locate all of the important papers necessary to settle the estate and secure death benefits for the dependents and spouse. The documents should be inventoried on a list that indicates both their existence and their location. One copy of the inventory should be kept in the home and a duplicate in a safe-deposit box or other safe location separate from the home. The location of all safe-deposit boxes should be known by both advisers and proposed executors. Spouses generally should either have access to the safe-deposit box or know where the key is located.

The inventory (a sample inventory is at the end of this chapter) should contain personal information for each family member, such as name, current address, date of birth, place of birth, Social Security number, and family relationship. There should also be a section of the inventory devoted to advisers. This section should give the type of services provided by each named individual, along with the provider's address and phone number. Accountants, insurance agents, investment brokers, clergy, funeral directors, executors, lawyers, and trust officers should be included in the adviser inventory.

A number of standard documents should be included in the inventory, which should also give the location of those documents in existence. (Originals should be kept in a safe-deposit box.) Such documents include birth certificates for all family members, marriage certificate(s), divorce papers, military discharge papers, passports, citizenship papers, death certificates of deceased family members, and adoption or guardianship papers. The inventory should indicate who drafted the latest will and where it is located. It should also reflect any trust agreements and their locations, as well as the name, address, and phone number of all trustees. This type of inventory is also an excellent place to record any prepaid funeral and/or burial arrangements, the location of any plots purchased, and the funeral home that is to handle the funeral.

There should be an exhaustive inventory of all insurance policies, giving the name of each company, the policy number, and the agent's name, address, and phone number. This portion of the inventory should include life insurance, health insurance, disability insurance, automobile insurance, home insurance, liability insurance, and any other policies in force.

Bank accounts and any other deposit account must be listed individually by account number. The name, address, and phone number of the institution is also necessary. Such accounts include certificates of deposit, as well as credit union accounts.

Holdings of stocks and bonds should be listed individually and should state the location of certificates. This is a good place to include purchase date and price or an indication of where that information can be found.

Any accounts or notes receivable should also be recorded on the inventory. The location of both the agreement and the payment record should be indicated, along with the debtor's name, address, and phone number. This is a good place to note the existence of any business agreements, the subject of each agreement, and its location.

Credit cards, too, should all be recorded on this inventory. The necessary information includes the name of the issuing company, the account number and number of cards, as well as the address and phone number of the issuing office. There are services that provide protection against lost or stolen credit cards. If such a service is being utilized, it should be identified in the inventory. After this service has been informed of a subscriber's death, the service should notify all credit card issuers.

Inventory of Important Papers

- Surviving personal representative(s) will have to locate all documents.
- An inventory list giving locations of documents will help those handling the estate settle it more rapidly.
- Intended personal representatives need to know of any inventory list and its location. (There should be multiple copies in separate locations for safekeeping.)
- The inventory should
  - give the location of safe deposit boxes and keys to those boxes
  - list real and personal property
  - include birth, marriage, divorce, annulment, death, military discharge, and passport documents
  - identify all trust documents and their locations
  - include all insurance policies and their locations
  - list all liabilities
  - list all pension or retirement accounts

In addition to credit cards, it is important to indicate all other unpaid debt accounts. This portion of the inventory should give the name, address, and phone number of the creditor, the purpose for the debt, and the location of both the agreement and the payment record.

No inventory would be complete without an exhaustive listing of personal property and approximate values. This portion of the inventory is essential for insurance claims after a fire or theft, as well as for settling the estate. Major items of personal property include household furnishings, paintings, books, cameras, tools, jewelry, furs, autos, trailers, boats, and planes.

All real property or real estate should be accounted for in this inventory. The necessary information includes a listing of the location of each parcel of property, a description of each, the names of all owners and their type of ownership, the identity of any mortgagee and the mortgage number, as well as the location of the deed, mortgage, and mortgage note for each property.

Finally, but not least important, comes a listing of all possible sources of nongovernmental retirement and death benefits. Employee or union pension plans, annuity contracts, individual retirement accounts, 401(k) plans, Keogh plans, and plans with fraternal organizations or professional associations should be detailed if any are applicable.

Once an inventory such as the one above has been compiled it should be updated annually. This information will be invaluable to the executor or administrator. Many life insurance companies have developed a checklist or inventory form similar to the one discussed here, but unfortunately, most of them only make such material available after death. Insurance companies that sell homeowners insurance usually have very good inventory forms for personal property and will share them with their policyowners.

Business Agreements

Individuals who have an ownership interest in either a partnership or a closely held corporation should create a business agreement. Such an agreement would determine how to settle the business ownership interests after the death or permanent disability of one or more of the part owners. These agreements should be very carefully drawn with the aid of competent legal counsel and must realistically ensure that there will be adequate funds available to carry out the specified terms. Insurance policies are usually used to provide the funds for these arrangements. (Business agreements are covered in CLU course HS 331.)

When death occurs without any established guidelines for settlement, the surviving owners are not likely to make a settlement that is as favorable to the deceased party's estate or beneficiaries. The absence of funding arrangements often forces liquidation of ownership interests at less than their market value. This occurs because most of the business assets are in capital goods instead of cash or working capital, and the capital assets usually cannot be quickly sold at a price that is equal to their value to the firm. Predeath planning and funding can avoid these problems, and it can ensure business continuation for the surviving owners.

Sharing Knowledge of Financial Planning

There have been cases where there has been sufficient predeath planning and funding, but the plans have not been shared with the family members. This may lead to survivors' improper utilization of assets and negate a well-planned program. It is just as important to share plans with intended beneficiaries as it is to make plans. This is because deviations from the plan may unnecessarily increase the tax burden and/or result in a loss from liquidating assets that should have been retained. These dangers are most prevalent when the deceased's family members or other of his or her beneficiaries have little knowledge of financial or business matters.

Funeral Arrangements

All lives terminate in death. At that time, responsibility for finally settling our affairs is generally passed to the one or more persons who survive us. Many of these responsibilities require prompt action, especially the arrangements for the deceased's body.

In the absence of prior arrangements, the decision to make anatomical gifts may rest solely with the survivors(s), and funeral arrangements must be made if a funeral is desired. Burial or cremation must be arranged as well unless the entire body has been accepted as an anatomical gift.

Even if the deceased has communicated his or her desires or has actually prearranged the funeral and final disposition of the body, a survivor will have the responsibility of notifying the funeral director or other appropriate representatives. The survivor may contact the wrong organization if he or she is not aware of prior arrangements and does not have access to an inventory or other notice of the deceased's plans.

Personal Representative

Survivors should obtain the original copy of the decedent's last will if a will exists. The will and any other papers should be reviewed to determine whether the deceased indicated who should be executor of the estate. Even if the will indicates an executor, it must be presented to the court for probate. (*Probate* means to prove that the will is in fact that of the decedent and that it was in fact his or her last will.) The court must officially appoint the *executor*. (A personal representative appointed in the will is called an executor.) If the person indicated in the will is deceased or refuses to accept the appointment, the court must appoint someone else to be the *administrator*. (When the court has to select the personal representative, that person is called the administrator.) The court must be petitioned to appoint an administrator to handle the estate if the deceased left no will or if no valid will could be located.

probate

executor

administrator

The personal representative is responsible for the collection of all monies owed to the deceased, payment of all debts owed by the deceased, payment of taxes, and the distribution of any remaining property. If there is no will, the property must be distributed according to the state intestacy statutes.

Death Certificates

There are many matters that must be settled after death, and most of them require that a death certificate be submitted. Copies of the death certificate can be obtained from the funeral director or from the local registrar of vital statistics. Settlement of even the simplest estate will often require a dozen copies of the death certificate, and complex estates may need three or four dozen copies of the death certificate.

Life Insurance

All of the deceased's life insurance policies should be located, and the agent or company home office should be notified. The information to be forwarded includes the name of the insured, the time and manner of death, and the policy numbers of all life insurance policies issued by that company covering the deceased.

Preferably the life insurance agent, who can assist by supplying the necessary forms and helping the beneficiary to understand the questions, should be contacted. The agent may advise the beneficiary about the different modes of settlement available if the insured did not select one. The beneficiary of the policy will have to complete a proof-of-death statement and return it, along with a copy of the death certificate, to the insurance company.

If the beneficiary is a minor or otherwise incapable of providing the proof-of-death-statement information, a duly appointed guardian or legal representative must complete the form. In these cases a copy of the court order appointing such guardian or representative must accompany the proof-of-death statement and death certificate.

In cases where the primary beneficiary predeceased the insured, a copy of the primary beneficiary's death certificate must accompany the customary papers. This will enable the insurance company to make the proceeds available to the contingent beneficiary or to the insured's estate if there is no contingent beneficiary.

Whenever the insured and the beneficiary die from the same cause, it is important to establish which person died first. If the beneficiary died first, the proceeds are payable to the contingent beneficiary. However, the proceeds will be payable to the beneficiary's estate if the beneficiary died after the insured. This result may be modified if a delay clause has been included in the beneficiary designation.

Insurance companies usually investigate more closely death claims that occur during the contestable period or claims in which death was not from natural causes and accidental death coverage was in force. In both of these cases the insurer will usually require a proof-of-death (physician's) statement to be filled out by the attending physician. This will be in addition to, rather than in lieu of, the beneficiary's statement and death certificate.

The agent should inform the beneficiary if there will be any delay in processing the claim and the reasons for that delay. The prompt payment of claims can be a great source of goodwill for insurance companies and agents, and it generates peace of mind for the survivors. Such an important task should not be jeopardized by unexplained delays. Professional servicing of death claims reaffirms the trust created when the policy was purchased. Prompt and courteous service of the death claim also gives the agent an opportunity to meet the surviving family members and impress them with his or her competency and trustworthiness. This is especially true when the choice of settlement option has been left open to the beneficiary. There is a strong tendency for beneficiaries to take a lump-sum settlement before they even realize that other options are available. It is often better for them to take a partial cash settlement that is sufficient to cover their immediate needs and leave the balance on deposit until they know more about their current and later needs. This protects their right to receive a life income or other form of settlement if that is desirable. Settlement options that are available from life insurance policies are usually more advantageous to the beneficiary than what would be available if an annuity were purchased separately.

All credit contracts should be checked for credit life insurance coverage that will pay off the outstanding debt. Notification of the death and a copy of the death certificate should be sent to the creditor.

Health Insurance

If the deceased was in poor health prior to death, there may be benefits payable in connection with health insurance or disability insurance contracts. The agent should be notified of the potential claim, the policy number involved, and the name of the insured. If any benefits are payable, the appropriate claim forms will have to be completed.

It is often necessary for the surviving spouse to assess the ongoing needs for health insurance coverage and adjust the coverage to meet these needs. If all health insurance was previously provided by group coverage through the deceased's employer, there may not be any current coverage for surviving family members.

There may be a conversion privilege in the group coverage that allows the dependent spouse to continue the coverage on an individual basis. The conversion request and premium payment must be made within one month of the death to continue coverage without a medical examination.

Medical expenses just before death are often very high, sometimes reaching many thousands of dollars. One study found that about one-half of deceased persons required treatment for at least a month before death, and one-fourth of them required treatment for more than a year before death. At current prices, hospitalization can cost more than $1,500 per day.

Other Insurance

After his or her spouse's death, the surviving spouse should check all policies covering the home, automobiles, and other property. The deceased person's name should be deleted from the policies and the survivor's name should be retained or added, if necessary. Necessary coverage should be continued and not allowed to lapse during the turmoil following a death. In some cases, the death will create the need for the surviving spouse to have new or different coverages than those already in force.

Social Security

Most working people are eligible for a $255 lump-sum death benefit from Social Security after death. This benefit can be obtained by filing the appropriate Social Security form and a certified copy of the death certificate with the local Social Security office. The benefit is payable to the funeral home or to a person who has paid for the funeral services. Funeral directors often file this form.

Quite often the deceased's spouse and any dependent children under 18 are eligible for survivorship benefits from Social Security. Widows or widowers of deceased workers may receive survivorship benefits if they have any single children under age 16 or if the widow(er) is over 60 years of age. The local Social Security office can provide the appropriate forms. A certified copy of the death certificate and the completed form should be submitted to the local Social Security office for processing. Certified birth certificates must also be furnished.

The level of benefits provided depends on the deceased's previous earnings. Benefits are also affected by the age and relationship of the beneficiary. Dependent children's benefits terminate when they either marry or reach age 18 (the age for full-time students).

Veterans' Administration

If the deceased has served on active duty in the United States armed forces and did not receive a dishonorable discharge, the Veterans' Administration (VA) will provide some form of burial benefits. This can be either burial in a national cemetery or a cash burial expense allowance of up to $400. The expense benefit may be applied for at any VA office and is payable to either the funeral director or to the person who paid the funeral expenses. If burial in a national cemetery is desired, application must be made to the superintendent of the national cemetery. Any local VA office can advise an applicant on how to apply.

Deceased veterans are also eligible for a headstone from the VA. This benefit can also be obtained through the local VA office.

Widows or widowers and dependent children under age 18 of deceased veterans who died as a result of service-connected disabilities are eligible for medical care from the VA.

There is a pension benefit available to widows or widowers of nearly all deceased veterans. The amount of the benefit depends on the beneficiary's income. The maximum monthly benefit is available if the recipient has an annual income lower than a specified threshold amount. As the income level increases, the monthly VA benefit available is reduced. No monthly benefit is available to a widow(er) with an annual income over an upper threshold unless the veteran's death was in some way related to military service. The local VA office can provide details and help an applicant file for any available benefits.

There are benefits provided for widow(er)s and children of veterans who died while serving in the armed forces. These benefits include a death gratuity equal to 6 months of the deceased's pay. In addition to the gratuity, the widow(er) and children are eligible for monthly pension benefits. The level of these payments depends on the deceased veteran's military rank. This benefit is called Dependency and Indemnity Compensation (DIC), and the payments will cease if the widow(er) remarries.

It is necessary to obtain the proper forms from a local VA office to apply for any VA benefits. The completed forms should be accompanied by copies of the death certificate, marriage certificate, and birth certificate for each dependent child and should be forwarded to the appropriate office. If the VA claim number for benefits is not known, it will be necessary to provide the following information about the deceased: military serial number, branch of service, inclusive dates of active duty, a copy of the discharge paper (form DD214), and the deceased's date of birth.

Many veterans have life insurance policies that were offered through the armed forces prior to 1966. After 1965, active members of the armed forces have been eligible for coverage that can be continued for up to 5 years after separation.

If the veteran had life insurance coverage under either Servicemen's Group Life Insurance (SGLI) or Veteran's Group Life Insurance (VGLI), the claims forms for this coverage can be obtained either from the Internet or by requesting them by phone. The Internet site is www.va.gov. The toll-free phone number is 800-419-1473. Completed claims forms should be mailed to Office of Serviceman's Group Life Insurance, 290 W. Mt. Pleasant Ave., Livingston, NJ 07039.

Civil Service

Deceased persons who worked under the Federal Civil Service for more than 18 months may have earned survivorship benefits for family members. For potential benefits, check with the Civil Service Bureau of Retirement Insurance and Occupational Health at 1900 E. Street, N.W., Washington, DC 20415, (202) 606-3500.

Private Business

It is possible that some of the pension plans covering the deceased provide death benefits and/or survivorship benefits to the spouse. Each potential source should be contacted individually. Former employers should be contacted and asked about the availability of benefits from group life insurance, pension plans, and employer-sponsored tax-deferred annuities. If the deceased was a union member, there may be benefits available from union plans. Professional and fraternal organizations to which the deceased belonged should also be contacted. If the deceased had established any separate retirement plans, there may be an unpaid balance payable to the surviving spouse. These separate plans are especially likely if the deceased was self-employed.

A registered letter (with a mandatory return receipt) similar to the following should be sent to each organization that could possibly be a source of benefits:

Dear_____,

This correspondence is to inform you that my spouse (full name) died on (day, month, year). I understand that he (or she) may have been eligible for death benefits or survivorship pension benefits through your organization. Please inform me of whatever information and documents you may require from me as beneficiary.

Sincerely,

Signature
TYPED ADDRESS FOR BENEFICIARY
(complete and accurate)

Estate Settlement

The person appointed by the court to be executor or administrator will have the responsibility of collecting monies owed to the estate, paying the deceased's outstanding debts, and distributing any property left in the estate. If there is no inventory like the one suggested earlier in this chapter (a sample inventory is included at the end of the chapter), the personal representative will have to create one. He or she will also have to update any existing inventory. Without such a guide it is possible that the representative will not be able to identify and collect all money owed to the estate. The representative should pay special attention to debts where credit life insurance may have been purchased. A claim for benefits must be made to the creditor or insurer by sending a copy of the death certificate.

Payment of debts owed will include federal and state income taxes up to the date of death as well as federal estate taxes—if the estate is large enough to owe any—and in most cases, state death taxes. A survey of some estates previously settled shows that expenses average between 4 percent and 6 percent of the estate assets; this percentage varies widely. As might be expected, the expenses are a large portion of the estate value for smaller estates and also for persons who die at younger ages. (CLU course HS 321 covers federal income taxes, and HS 330 covers federal estate taxes.)

The personal representative is eligible for compensation out of the estate and usually collects such compensation. When a family member or close friend is the representative, he or she sometimes serves without compensation.

Some pre-death planning can save the representative considerable work and, in some cases, emotional stress. In sizable estates with federal estate tax obligations, the taxes are due within 9 months after death and must be paid in cash. Very often there is not enough money available to pay the taxes unless the deceased's property or business or part of its assets is sold for cash. Adequate amounts of life insurance in force at the time of death may enable the property or business to be retained and distributed to survivors.

Customers and Clients

If clients and/or customers were dependent upon the services of the deceased, there may be a need to refer them to someone else for service. Case histories may have to be located and released to the client's new adviser. A doctor's patients may be advised to contact a new doctor immediately and obtain a new prescription for necessary medicine. Legal clients of deceased lawyers will need all of the information gathered by the deceased in order for their new counsel to proceed with impending litigation. Accountants who die may possess the business records that their clients must have in order to file their taxes on time. These records should be released to clients as soon as possible.

Office help and other employees will have to be terminated if the business is not to be continued. Some employees may be retained during the time the business is being closed out. These people will probably need references when they seek new employment. If no one is able to give these recommendations, the prospective employer should be informed by the executor that the death of the former employer makes it impossible to respond.

EMOTIONAL ASPECTS OF DEATH AND DYING

Death is a part of every life cycle, but the details of death vary immensely. In some cases, death is almost instantaneous as in some accidents, drowning, severe heart attacks, and so forth. In other cases dying may take awhile or even be very prolonged (for example, Alzheimer's cases).

In our society we do a poor job of preparing for and anticipating death, regardless of how rapidly it occurs. People who die instantaneously have rarely communicated their thoughts and desires about relevant issues to their closest family and friends who will have to handle the finances, property distribution, and ongoing support of dependents.

Ours is basically a death-denying society where the topic of death is avoided. We speak in euphemisms about a person's "having expired," "met his maker," or "passed away," rather than address death directly. The discomfort associated with the topic of death prevents many people from ever discussing their own inevitable death or taking positive steps in its anticipation, like making a will. This tendency to avoid preparing for death is so strong in the United States that even persons who are terminally ill continue to procrastinate and suppress their thoughts and feelings about death. Quite often the dying individual will withdraw from relationships and minimize contact with other people in an attempt to avoid dealing with the impending death.

Very often the people closest to a dying person have even stronger tendencies to avoid the topic than the dying person. They may retreat from contact and communication altogether or insist on changing the subject to something more positive if the subject of death emerges in conversation. Death is generally considered negatively and hence is not a welcome topic in our hedonistic society. For these reasons, many friends and close family members cease contact with the dying person even before the dying process restricts his or her mobility or other functions.

In one case with which I am familiar, even the grade-school-age children of a dying father withdrew from close contact and curtailed normal household conversation after becoming aware of their father's terminal cancerous condition. The father felt isolated and became severely depressed in that atmosphere of minimal emotional support. His only supporter was his dear and devoted wife.

In many cases of terminal illness, the spouse who is well is not able to sustain his or her strong emotional support all the way to the end of a trying and prolonged dying process. Sometimes the emotional strain of a prolonged decline even results in divorce prior to death.

There are many forces at work in our dynamic society that increase emotional stress on persons facing imminent death. Medical providers are very uncomfortable with death. They devote their careers to preserving and prolonging life. Many of them see death as an enemy and insist on bringing to bear every possible medical procedure in order to defeat or at least postpone death. What's more, they also have a well-founded fear of liability for negligence if they do not take heroic steps to extend life.

Consequently, medical providers generally will pressure the dying person and his or her family to pursue all avenues of intervention embraced by Western medicine. They are apt to show their distaste for living wills. Some physicians go so far as to cease pain relief medication once a living will is involved and a do-not-resuscitate directive has been issued.

Other societal sources of stress come from our extreme specialization that has resulted in many services being performed impersonally by strangers. Funeral directors, adult day care centers, transport services, nursing homes, hospitals, and emergency medical transport teams now perform functions that were previously furnished by the family, if at all. The services' businesslike manners often leave the customers feeling more like commodities than people. Lynn Caine gives a good example of this in her book *Widow,* where she describes the rules that prevented her young children from visiting their hospitalized father during the last 6 months of his life. Furthermore, we have also heard many accounts of inadequate care and hygiene in some nursing homes. Sometimes the deficiencies are so severe that health officials close the institution.

Moreover, the affluence of our economy and the wide geographic dispersal of family members have contributed to the breakdown of multigenerational families. Parents and grandparents almost always live apart, often in different states. This has lessened the frequency and duration of personal contact. Long-distance communication tends to discourage sharing details about day-to-day living and other experiences that strengthen emotional bonds in close-knit families.

Another indication of weaker emotional bonds in our society is the high incidence of divorce among healthy persons. This is concurrent with a weakening of spiritual commitment evidenced by declining support of many religious institutions. Many members of our society, submerged in their materialistic surroundings, are isolating themselves from direct human contact. They travel in a sealed air-conditioned car, and they work at home on their computer, connected to the outside only by a phone line; their entertainment is also computer generated. Will these shifts in society increase or decrease emotional stress? Will they alter the ways in which we react to death?

Grieving

There is an established body of literature dealing with the human emotions surrounding death. There are some universal reactions that survivors have after the death of a close friend, family member, or loved one. In fact, dying persons who are aware of their impending death experience essentially the same emotions (with slight variations) as survivors. These emotions were first identified in the literature by Dr. Elisabeth Kübler-Ross[3] as anger, denial, bargaining, depression, and acceptance. People coping with death often experience periods or stages when one of the five emotions dominates the others. Each of these emotions will be dominant in one or more phases, and there is no established order or duration.

Denial or anger surfaces as the first or an early phase of coping with death. Acceptance is often (but not always) the last phase. Most of these emotions can be experienced simultaneously, and people's conscious thoughts cycle frequently from one emotion to another.

Denial is often the first reaction to death (especially among the young who so often think of themselves as immortal). It is a temporary defense, often linked with magical thinking that, "if I ignore it, maybe it will go away." People often use denial to cope with painful and uncomfortable things in life. Both the physician and the dying patient may be covertly engaging in denial. Among survivors, denial often makes it easier to continue contact and communication during the terminal illness. After death, the survivors usually get over their denial and other grieving emotions within a year. However, in some extreme cases parents may extend the denial phase for years.

Anger is one way of expressing strong emotional trauma. It can be directed (usually without reason) at doctors, advisers, employers, relatives, or friends. Survivors often direct their anger at the deceased for leaving them.

Bargaining is an attempt to postpone the impending death. It is a plea to extend the duration of life another month, season, year, and so forth; in return the bargaining person intends to cease current vices, strengthen his or her commitment to family and loved ones, or increase support to religious or charitable organizations. Bargaining can prompt vigorous bursts of energy and enthusiasm.

Emotions Associated with Grieving

- anger
- denial
- bargaining
- depression
- acceptance

Depression may initially be triggered by the limitations of deteriorating physical health. It is also a manifestation of the loss of hope (the death of dreams). It saps the person's energy and often stops him or her from attempting things that he or she is still capable of doing. During times when depression is the predominant emotion of grieving, it is very hard to communicate with the person. Depression prompts individuals to withdraw from other people and focus on their inner thoughts and fears.

Acceptance of death may be short and recurrent. It may or may not be a prevalent emotion at the actual time of death. Acceptance of death is often accompanied by a cessation or reduced intensity of the emotional fight for survival. It is frequently marked by an increased desire and need or sleep. When acceptance is the final stage, death can be somewhat serene and tranquil.

When the dying process is long enough for the person to be cognizant of physical and/or mental deterioration, the dying person is aware of the loss of control of his or her own life and the loss of independence. Even in these impaired conditions there is a strong human need for dignity and self-respect. The dying person deserves humane treatment from those around him or her. Family members are often better at maintaining a warm nurturing environment if they have not already been stretched to their limits and experienced burnout.

Some religious and ethnic groups have developed ceremonies and procedures to accompany death. They are often devoted to extending dignity and humane treatment to those nearing death. They further promote respect for the deceased and support for survivors and their grieving. Survivors often require up to one year to adjust to the death and work through the grief. During that year their emotions are usually a roller coaster of extreme highs and lows. Survivors also need nurturing.

Surviving spouses are often so distraught that they make major lifestyle changes in hopes of easing their pain. Frequently these decisions are not good ones for the survivor's long-term best interests. Family and friends of survivors can provide some protection from making foolish decisions by playing the role of devil's advocate with the survivor and those who strongly influence him or her. All of us have the capability of making irrational choices. The likelihood of doing so seems to increase while we are grieving over the death of a loved one.

The grieving process is just as important to children as it is to adults. All survivors need to release their ties to the deceased. The stronger those ties were, the more painful the grieving process. Survivors who try to avoid the pain of grieving by not reacting to the death often display one or more of the following reactions: overactivity without a sense of loss, symptoms similar to those of the deceased prior to death, intense hostility toward specific persons, agitated depression, trouble sleeping and nightmares when sleeping, preoccupation with the deceased's image, and a long-term decrease in their level of social interaction.[4]

Communication with Survivors

Financial services professionals must themselves grieve for their deceased clients. At the same time, they must actively listen to the verbal and nonverbal messages from survivors and maintain a professional demeanor. They may be the only ones capable of playing devil's advocate on financial decisions facing survivors. Financial services professionals must suggest the correct moves financially even if doing so provokes angry confrontation now or in the future. Survivors generally will be able to make better rational evaluations and decisions 6 to 9 months after the death.

Aiding survivors is every bit as demanding as initial sales work. It requires empathy, diplomacy, patience, warmth, genuineness, and persistence. The communication can be and often is highly emotional. Strong negative emotions may be directed at professional advisers.

Consequently, financial services professionals must keep cool and maintain their composure. This may require some advance strategies for disengaging or otherwise calming the emotional fervor of conversations with survivors. This phase of service is the final stage for previously sold products and services, but it may be the initial stage for future product and service sales. Establishing credibility and reliability with survivors can expand potential referrals and thereby be a positive influence on future business. Each death creates the need to terminate an estate, but at the same time it reminds surviving family and friends that they have unfinished business to attend to before their own death. The financial services professional who performs extraordinary service for widows and widowers is enhancing his or her credibility. This may provide a handsome long-term dividend.

CHAPTER REVIEW

Answers to the review questions and the self-test questions can be found in the Supplement.

Key Terms

competent	uniform donor card
attorney-in-fact	anatomical gifts
power of attorney	will
durable power of attorney	probate
springing durable power of attorney	executor
	administrator
living will	

Review Questions

1. Indicate the two major activities survivors need to take care of on behalf of a deceased person.

2. Indicate which categories of persons lack the legal capacity to create valid wills and contract on their own behalf.

3. Indicate the kinds of powers that can be delegated by means of a power of attorney.

4. Distinguish between a power of attorney and a durable power of attorney.

5. Explain why some people prefer a springing durable power of attorney over the immediate creation of a durable power of attorney.

6. Why do some people create a separate durable power of attorney for
   a. property management
   b. health care

7. Explain how use of a durable power of attorney can preserve more privacy for an incompetent principal.

8. How can a principal minimize the likelihood of an IRS challenge of the attorney-in-fact's power to make gifts?

9. What is the primary focus of a living will?

10. Indicate why some physicians oppose the use of a living will.

11. Indicate the kinds of body organs and tissue that can be donated via a uniform donor card under the right conditions.

12. Explain why organs and tissue authorized for donation sometimes may not be transplanted when the potential donor dies.

13. What are the potential benefits of arranging before death for funerals and burial or cremation?

14. Indicate why it is strongly urged that the will nominate guardians for minor children.

15. Explain why it is important that surviving family members know about the existence and location of a will.

16. Explain why it is important to reassess a will regularly and amend it after new assets have been acquired.

17. Identify typical events that often justify changing a will.

18. Explain what steps can be taken before death to ease the burden on survivors who settle the estate.

19. Explain why survivors may not receive a fair settlement for the deceased person's business interest if there is no existing agreement specifying the terms of settlement.

20. Indicate why it is important for survivors and executors to know of and understand any existing financial plans.

21. Describe the responsibilities of the deceased's personal representative.

22. Indicate the information that should be supplied to life insurance companies when filing death-benefit claims.

23. Identify other potential sources of funds available to the estate and/or survivors.

24. Explain why it may be imperative to contact customers and clients of the deceased professional shortly after death.

25. Identify sources of increased emotional stress on persons facing imminent death.

26. Identify the five emotions people coping with death usually experience as part of the grieving process.

Self-Test Questions

T   F   1. Estate settlement is not necessary for deceased persons unless they owned real estate at the time of death.

T   F   2. Some states grant the capacity to contract for life insurance at age 15.

T   F   3. The test for competency of a testator is based on age, understanding some aspects of property transactions, and the potential recipient's relationship.

T   F   4. Intoxication can be a source of temporary incompetency.

T   F   5. It is not possible to lose competency permanently.

T   F   6. A durable power of attorney remains in effect after the principal's death.

T   F   7. A simple power of attorney terminates with the incompetency of the principal.

T   F   8. The actions of agents operating under a power of attorney must be recorded in the public record.

T   F   9. A person appointed in a durable power of attorney as an attorney-in-fact does not have to be approved by the courts.

T   F   10. An attorney-in-fact under a durable power of attorney generally has fewer restrictions than a guardian.

T   F   11. The IRS regularly challenges the power of an agent to make gifts unless it is specified in writing.

T   F   12. Some advisers suggest that a living will should be supplemented with a durable power of attorney for health care.

T   F   13. Intended donors of anatomical gifts who die outside of hospitals are usually not able to donate their organs (except corneas) for transplant.

T   F   14. Making anatomical gifts precludes the survivors from having a funeral for the deceased.

T   F   15. The courts must accept the nominated guardian named in the deceased's will.

T   F   16. Assets not included in the will may be distributed according to the laws of intestacy.

T   F   17. It is inappropriate to nominate the intended executor in the will itself.

T   F   18. Survivors who settle the estate will be helped by having an inventory of all assets and liabilities of the deceased.

T   F   19. The court must be petitioned to appoint an administrator for the estate if the deceased left no will.

T F 20. The surviving spouse may have to arrange for conversion of the deceased's group health coverage to individual coverage within one month of death.

T F 21. The United States is basically a death-denying society.

T F 22. The grieving process does not apply to children.

NOTES

1. A sample uniform donor card appears at the end of this chapter. Cards may be obtained from the National Kidney Foundation at 30 East 33rd Street, 11th Floor, New York, NY 10016, (212) 889-2210, www.kidney.org, or any other organization working with donor programs.

2. For more information about donor programs contact local funeral directors or those organizations directly involved with the programs. The National Kidney Foundation at 30 East 33rd Street, 11th Floor, New York, NY 10016, (212) 889-2210, www.kidney.org, is involved with organ donations and transplants. The foundation also has local chapters in many major cities. Lions Clubs are active in supporting the many eye banks in the nation. For information about skin tissue, contact the American Association of Tissue Banks, 1350 Beverly Road, McLean, Virginia 22101, (703) 827-9582. In many areas local representatives can provide information and uniform donor cards.

3. Elisabeth Kübler-Ross is the author of *On Death and Dying* (New York: Macmillan), 1968.

4. E. Lindeman, "Symptomatology and Management of Acute Grief," *American Journal of Psychiatry,* vol. 2 (1944).

INVENTORY OF IMPORTANT INFORMATION
NEEDED BY EXECUTORS OR ADMINISTRATORS

PERSONAL INFORMATION

Name_____

Address_____

Date of birth_____

Date of death_____Location of birth_____

Death certificate #_____Social Security #_____

Military service #_____Veterans' Administration claim #_____

DEPENDENTS
(Name, address, date of birth, Social Security #, relationship)

_____

_____

_____

_____

Employer _____Phone_____

Address _____

ADVISERS
(Name, address, phone)
Accountant_____

_____

Investment broker_____

_____

Insurance agent_____

_____

Trust officer_____

_____

Clergy_____

_____

Funeral director_____

_____

Executor or administrator_____

_____

CERTIFICATES

Where Located

o   Birth certificate(s) (every
    family member)

_____   _____

_____   _____

_____   _____

o   Marriage certificate   _____

o   Divorce papers   _____

o   Military records (especially
    discharge papers certificate)   _____

o   Passport(s) (every family
    member)   _____

o   Citizenship papers   _____

o   Death certificate (any deceased
    family member)   _____

o   Adoption papers   _____

WILL

I have made a will   (yes) _____ (no) _____

The original copy is located at _____ dated _____

    Name of attorney who drafted the will _____

    Address _____

    Phone _____

TRUST AGREEMENT

Location of trust agreement _____

    Name of trustee _____

    Address _____

    Phone _____

FINAL ARRANGEMENTS

- Burial   Location of cemetery plot _____

                           Location of deed _____

- Cremation

- Funeral

- Donation of organs and/or body to medical science

- Prepaid arrangements   Location of agreement _____

                           Name of organization _____

                           Address _____

                           Phone _____

INSURANCE

Life:

Policy # _____ Company _____

Agent address _____

Phone_____ Policy location _____

Policy # _____ Company _____

Agent address _____

Phone_____ Policy location _____

Policy # _____ Company _____

Agent address _____

Phone_____ Policy location _____

Policy # _____ Company _____

Agent address _____

Phone_____ Policy location _____

Policy # _____ Company _____

Agent address _____

Phone_____ Policy location _____

Policy # _____ Company _____

Agent address _____

Phone_____ Policy location _____

INSURANCE (cont.)

Health:

Policy # _____ Company _____

Agent address _____

Phone_____ Policy location _____

Policy # _____ Company _____

Agent address _____

Phone_____ Policy location _____

Disability:

Policy # _____ Company _____

Agent address _____

Phone_____ Policy location _____

Policy # _____ Company _____

Agent address _____

Phone_____Policy location _____

INSURANCE (cont.)

Auto:

Policy # _____ Company _____

Agent address _____

Phone_____ Policy location _____

Home:

Policy # _____ Company _____

Agent address _____

Phone_____ Policy location _____

Boat policy #_____ Company _____

Address _____ Phone _____

Plane policy #_____ Company _____

Address _____ Phone _____

Trailer policy #_____ Company _____

Address _____ Phone _____

Other policy #_____ Company _____

Address _____ Phone _____

Location of policy(ies)_____

BANK ACCOUNTS

Checking account # _____ Bank _____

Location _____ Phone _____

Checking account # _____ Bank _____

Location _____ Phone _____

Savings account # _____ Bank _____

Location _____ Phone _____

Savings account # _____ Bank _____

Location _____ Phone _____

Certificate of Deposit

Certificate # _____ Bank _____

Location _____ Phone _____

Credit union account # _____

Address _____ Phone _____

Records located _____

Income tax

    Location of tax returns _____

    Location of receipts _____

SECURITIES

Stock Company	# of Shares	Location of Shares	Location of Purchase Records

Note any stocks that are held in street name by the broker.

Bonds

Issuer	Serial #	Maturity Date	Location

Broker_____Phone _____

Address_____

Broker_____Phone _____

Address_____

SECURITIES (cont.)

Loans to Others (Notes Receivable)

Debtor's Name	Address	Phone

Location of record payment_____

Location of loan agreement_____

Business Agreements	Subject	Location

UNPAID DEBTS*

	Owed To	Address	Phone
1.			
2.			
3.			
4.			

	Purpose of Debt	Agreement Location	Payment Record Location
1.			
2.			
3.			
4.			

*Check for existence of credit life insurance that will pay the debt upon proof of death.

CREDIT CARDS*

Company_____ Account #_____ # of Cards_____

Address_____ Phone_____

Company_____ Account #_____ # of Cards_____

Address_____ Phone_____

Company_____ Account #_____ # of Cards_____

Address_____ Phone_____

Company_____ Account #_____ # of Cards_____

Address_____ Phone_____

Company_____ Account #_____ # of Cards_____

Address_____ Phone_____

Company_____ Account #_____ # of Cards_____

Address_____ Phone_____

Company_____ Account #_____ # of Cards_____

Address_____ Phone_____

Company_____ Account #_____ # of Cards_____

Address_____ Phone_____

*Check for existence of credit life insurance that will pay the debt upon proof of death.

PERSONAL PROPERTY

○   Safe-deposit box   Location _____

○   Household furniture
    (list most valuable items)   Location

_____   _____

_____   _____

_____   _____

_____   _____

_____   _____

_____   _____

_____   _____

_____   _____

○   Jewelry
    Description   Location

_____   _____

_____   _____

_____   _____

○   Furs
    Description   Location

_____   _____

_____   _____

PERSONAL PROPERTY (cont.)

o   Cameras

Make   Serial #   Location

_____

_____

o   Collection
   Stamps/Coins/Books/Paintings

Item   Value   Location

_____

_____

_____

_____

o   Tools and Shop Equipment
   Item   Serial #   Location

_____

_____

_____

_____

o   Automobile(s)
                    (1)   (2)   (3)

Make _____

Year _____

Model _____

Serial # _____

Location of title _____

Location of registration _____

PERSONAL PROPERTY (cont.)

o   Trailer(s)

(1)   (2)

Type _____

Manufacturer _____

Serial # _____

Location _____

o   Boat(s)

(1)   (2)

Type _____

Manufacturer _____

Serial # _____

Location _____

o   Plane(s)

Manufacturer _____ Model_____

Serial # _____ Location_____

REAL ESTATE

Property(ies)   Location

1._____   _____
2._____   _____
3._____   _____
4._____   _____

Type of Ownership of Properties Above

      Sole Owner   Held Jointly With

1.   ○   _____
2.   ○   _____
3.   ○   _____
4.   ○   _____

Mortgages on Properties Above

1. Mortgage held by_____ Mortgage #_____
     Address_____ Phone_____

2. Mortgage held by_____ Mortgage #_____
     Address_____ Phone_____

3. Mortgage held by_____ Mortgage #_____
     Address_____ Phone_____

4. Mortgage held by_____ Mortgage #_____
     Address_____ Phone_____

Deed Location for Above Properties

1. _____
2. _____
3. _____
4. _____

RETIREMENT PLANS

Identify each plan administrator and indicate how to contact.
(Give telephone number and address.)

○Pension

○Annuity Contracts

○Associations or Fraternal Organizations

○Union

○Keogh Plan (HR 10)

○Individual Retirement Accounts

○401(k) Plan

○SEP Plan

○403(b)

SAMPLE UNIFORM DONOR CARD

UNIFORM DONOR CARD

OF_____

       Print or type name of donor

In the hope that I may help others, I hereby make this anatomical gift, if medically acceptable, to take effect upon my death. The words and marks below indicate my desires.

I give: (a) _____ any needed organs or parts

         (b) _____ only the following organs or parts

_____

               Specify the organ(s) or part(s)

for the purposes of transplantation, therapy, medical research or education,

       (c) _____ my body for anatomical study if needed.

Limitations or
special wishes, if any: _____

Signed by the donor and the following two witnesses in the presence of each other:

_____

Signature of donor   Date of birth of donor

_____

Date signed   City and state

_____

Witness   Witness

This is a legal document under the Uniform Anatomical Gift Act or similar laws.

19

Readings from The Best of 'Strictly Speaking'

Ethics Readings from the Journal of the American Society of CLU & ChFC
(now called the Journal of Financial Service Professionals)

Learning Objectives

An understanding of the material in this chapter should enable the student to

19-1.   Understand the influence of Dr. Solomon Huebner in establishing a program to recognize professionalism among insurance producers.

19-2.   Know the institutions that have participated in the creation of professional designations, guidelines, codes of ethics, ethics awareness week, and other programs to enhance the reputation and image of professional insurance producers.

19-3.   Indicate the factors and guiding principles that are helpful in prompting ethical behavior within the insurance industry.

19-4.   Understand the complexity and challenges presented by illustrations, company ratings, rebating, and so forth.

19-5.   Be aware of common behavior in the insurance industry that is not conducive to a positive public image of the insurance industry.

19-6.   Explain the distinction between law and ethics.

19-7.   Understand common obstacles to ethical behavior.

19-8.   Be aware of common rationalizations people use to explain unethical behavior.

Chapter Outline

According to Burke Christensen and Ken Cooper, the editors of *The Best of "Strictly Speaking,"* "Today ethics is a major concern. The media regularly communicate ethical and legal transgressions that result in major embarrassments, convictions, fines, and a decline in public confidence. Industry leaders have stepped forward to assert new emphases of legal compliance and higher ethical standards. We believe the road to higher ethical standards starts with an understanding of the industry's heritage followed by an appreciation of how truly important ethics is. Leadership and education are the keys. Here the emphasis is on education. *The Best of 'Strictly Speaking'* drawing from the best of one of the industry's leading proponents of ethics, offers a beginning step."

From the 19 columns in *The Best of "Strictly Speaking"* we have selected 10 for inclusion in this book. We have also included "Why Do Good People Make Bad Choices?"—a "Strictly Speaking" column that was published after *The Best of "Strictly Speaking"* had been printed.

Ethics—the Pillar of Professionalism

John R. Driskill, CLU, ChFC

The year was 1904, our nation was much embroiled in the Industrial Revolution, the automobile was in its earliest stages of evolution, and the Wright brothers had just made their first machine-powered flight at Kitty Hawk, when a young professor of economics joined the faculty of the University of Pennsylvania's famed Wharton School of Business. His name was Dr. Solomon S. Huebner. This young academician was hired by the university to teach his students about the security and commodity exchange markets.

Mildred F. Stone, CLU, wrote of this remarkable man and educator in her book entitled *A Teacher Who Changed An Industry*.

Early in his career, Dr. Huebner developed a genuine fascination for the subject of insurance, property and liability as well as life and health. As a professor of economics, his early interest soon developed into a deep admiration for the economic value of this remarkable product and the important role it played in the financial and moral fiber of our nation's economy. His growing interest in our industry soon inspired him to write one of our nation's first recognized texts on life insurance, which subsequently led him to teach the first college level course on the subject.

Throughout his career, Dr. Huebner looked upon those persons who sold insurance as performing a socially redeeming service for all of society. It was this deep conviction, coupled with his research, writing, and teaching on the subject, that soon led him to the belief that the work of the life underwriter was so socially important to society that it should be recognized as a profession.

In the immediate years following the Armstrong Investigation of 1905, Dr. Huebner's thinking further crystallized. He became convinced that the life insurance industry must set about the task of professionalizing its unique calling by building upon those two basic pillars of professionalism, namely education coupled with professional ethics.

The rest of this story has become history. In 1914, Dr. Huebner made his first public speech regarding his idea of creating a professional designation program for the life underwriter before the Baltimore Association of Life

Underwriters. His idea was not one which caught the immediate fancy of the industry. But through deep personal *commitment* (a word we shall discuss later on in more depth) and perseverance he, in time, gained the moral and financial support of the industry. And in 1927, the American College of Life Underwriters was incorporated in the District of Columbia with the enabling assistance and enthusiastic support of the National Association of Life Underwriters.

The CLU movement was finally underway, with the first class of graduates receiving the designation in 1928 at NALU's annual meeting held in Detroit, Michigan. This first class was composed of 21 graduates including one woman and a trust officer of a New England bank—a mix of students which prophesied several industry trends which would develop in the decades to come.

By now you're probably wondering why we are discussing such historical events in a column dedicated to dissertations on ethics. The answer lies in the very early principles upon which Dr. Huebner dedicated his work. As a scholar he knew that no profession could ever be successfully formed without the presence of two important underlying principles: that of a unique body of knowledge which could be taught to aspiring students and the development of a code of professional ethics. These he knew were the twin pillars of professionalism.

As members of the Society we have already demonstrated our belief in and commitment to a lifelong process of education by acquiring our designation(s). Many of us have taken the second step by *committing* ourselves to keeping this knowledge viable and updated throughout our professional careers by participating in the Professional Achievement in Continuing Education program—PACE.

What is not always so clear, or as frequently discussed, is the absolute need for us to likewise *commit* ourselves to the highest standards of professional conduct as embodied in The American College's Professional Pledge. There's that idea of *commitment* again.

commitment
PACE

As has been so well stated by the Society's president, Donald H. Mehlig, CLU, ChFC, "Professionalism is built on *commitment;* a long-term commitment to education through programs such as *PACE*, and a lifetime of commitment to dealing with your clients with the highest degree of personal integrity and professional ethics." Don goes on to say, "This kind of professional commitment is not unlike the commitment which is required of one through marriage. We all know that you can live together, buy homes, raise families, without being married, but with marriage there is a very real difference. It's called *commitment.*"

This is the kind of ethical commitment our acceptance of the CLU designation demands of each and every one of us. It's embodied in our Judeo

Christian beliefs and expressed in the Golden Rule whose principles have been incorporated in our Professional Pledge.

Ethics is the cornerstone of our business because ethical conduct must be the anchor to which all social and business change must be tied. As our industry and practice evolve, they must move forward rooted on the very foundation of ethical behavior. Ethical behavior must be practiced not only by the life underwriter, but by our companies as well. If we were to lose this anchor, we would surely lose the ship of professionalism upon which we sail.

Our business is one of unique, long-term promises and long-term commitments made by the life underwriter on behalf of the insurance company; promises that are often not required to be fulfilled for 40 to 50 years. As a result, the industry's one and only real product is a promise to pay.

Is it any wonder then that ours is a calling rooted in trust? We ask our clients to place their faith in us and in our companies for the delivery on the carrier's promise—a promise that must be honored even when those clients are no longer alive to witness its fulfillment. It is clear that faith is the real commodity with which we deal. Without our commitment to ethical integrity to foster such trust, our industry would not survive long.

Our industry is moving into an era when this faith and trust will be severely tested by the marketplace and our clients. The past decade of policy replacements and illustration abuses has not strengthened our long-held position of trust. Therefore, it is even more important that you, the individual CLU, and your Society, take a leadership role in our industry to rebuild our position of trust with the public. If not us, who? If not now, when?

It is for the precise reasons that the Society has fostered the Professional Practice Guidelines to help curb policy illustration abuses by both agents and companies. It is why The American College has created a full-time professorship in Business Ethics and why the College, the Society, and our CPCU friends worked last year to create, for the first time ever, an insurance industry Ethics Awareness Week.

Our industry is coming under the magnifying glass of public scrutiny as our companies deal with the problems of financial security and profitability. Let us not expose ourselves to increased scrutiny through unscrupulous business practices. Because ours is an industry built on trust, it is imperative that we weed out unethical individuals whose conduct robs us all of public trust. We cannot be tolerant of the unethical practitioner.

In the process of rededicating yourself to ethical practice, set your personal standards high, base them on trust and the Golden Rule and, in so doing, develop a personal touchstone by which you may judge your own behavior.

John R. Coleman, PhD, former president of Haverford College and the author of "Blue Collar Journal," suggests that in your business and personal dealings with others, you check your ethical behavior by asking yourself the following question: "How would my children feel if they knew of my recent activities? Would they be embarrassed if they learned of my conduct or actions?"

Dr. Huebner did, indeed, have a dream. He did, in fact, change an industry by helping us to professionalize the noble calling of life underwriting. We have been endowed by a rich legacy left to us by the leaders of the past. But how will we treat this legacy? How will we leave this great business for the generation which is to follow? The poet, R.L. Sharpe, captured our opportunity best in these few simple lines:

> Isn't it strange
> That princes and kings
> And clowns that caper
> In sawdust rings
> And common people
> Like you and me
> Are builders for eternity?
>
> Each is given a bag of tools
> A shapeless mass
> A book of rules
> And each must make
> Ere life has flown
> A stumbling block
> Or a stepping stone.

What we have inherited in the form of public trust has come from the builders of the past!

What we do in the future with what we have inherited will be the legacy we leave to our successors.

As a CLU or ChFC, as a professional life underwriter, the choice to be better than the minimum requirements of the law is yours!

Life Insurance Issues: Yesterday and Today

Frederick H. Stitt, CLU*

Today I will share what I have begun to learn from our past, some trends I now see maturing, and my formula for a bright future for our industry.

I will discuss two chapters of history: the credibility of illustrations and the public trust, and how both affect current business.

Then I will speculate on three current issues: banks in the life insurance business, rebating, and commission design.

CREDIBILITY OF ILLUSTRATIONS

The credibility of illustrations is of greater concern today than it was in 1951, my first full year in our business. As background, you may recall that non-par, guaranteed-cost life insurance was then a strong part of the market. It performed steadily as advertised and projected well when compared to most of our fine mutual companies, which had been generally decreasing their dividends and projections since the 1930s.

An example comparing historical and projected performance in 1952 may surprise you. Suppose you and I went on a joint call that year to a 45-year-old male who was interested in $100,000 of whole life. We might offer two policies for consideration, both including disability waiver of premium:

- Mass Mutual at $4,089 per year with a 20-year average net payment projected at $3,195
- Travelers with a guaranteed 20-year average payment of $3,100

Note that the Travelers guaranteed payments were $95 less than Mass Mutual's projected net payments (without any adjustment for interest on the higher Mass Mutual premiums in the earlier years). Checking history, the 20-

---

* Mr. Stitt's remarks were presented on June 6, 1990, at the Annual Meeting of the Chicago Chapter of the American Society of CLU & ChFC after he received the Huebner Scholar of Chicago Award for 1990.

year average net payments of a Mass Mutual policy issued to a 45-year-old in 1932 had been $3,153, still $53 more than the premium guaranteed by the Travelers in 1952.

Based on both projections and history, the Traveler's policy was the clear winner.

Today, hindsight tells us that our client would have been far better off with Mass Mutual than Travelers. We know that the average 20-year net payment on a Mass Mutual policy bought in 1952 was not the $3,153 of history, nor the projected $3,195. It was, in fact, $2,526—$574 less than the non-par, guaranteed-cost life policy of Travelers, which, of course, did no more or less than promised. Further, these results predated the update programs that have resulted in almost unbelievable dividend increases in the 1980s, increases that have further reduced premium costs for participating policies from mutual companies. We all know that non-par, guaranteed-cost life insurance is no longer a factor in our market. And I know I am happy to represent Mass Mutual today along with other fine companies.

Many of us worship at the twin altars of histories and projections. We need to be more critical of our own dogmas.

While I believe that illustrations today are important tools, we must be more careful presenting them, and we need to know more about them. The assumptions behind illustrations in 1952 were far simpler than now. Most companies then used similar mortality, interest, and expense assumptions; and yet, as demonstrated by our example, we were still led astray by the steadily rising interest rates that, with improved mortality, caused dividends to soar. Today, every company has its own secret formula of yield, mortality, expense, and lapse assumptions that it uses for cooking illustrations; and I believe we need to get our hands on the recipe book.

hidden assumptions

We need to understand what we sell, and certainly our clients have a right to much of the now *hidden assumptions*. It is simply incredible that a client considering depositing $50,000 or more with a life insurance company cannot find out what is behind the figures projected on the illustrations that attract him. For example, the mortality assumptions alone can be based on

(1) an industry table
(2) the company's own experience over the past 5 years
(3) projected improvements well into the future
(4) unrealistic lapse assumptions
(5) any number of permutations on these methods

Also, we all quote current yield rates, but are they gross or net? If net, net of what? Investment expenses? Taxes? Are they based on a portfolio, separate account, index or new money rate? Do companies increase expense and/or mortality assumptions in order to advertise high-yield assumptions? Much of this data is under tight security as privileged information to be guarded by companies from the competition. I believe much of the company rhetoric justifying secrecy is nonsense, and I suspect that its origin was in the days, like 1952, when the industry wanted to obscure how inefficient it was.

I believe we all need to get involved in the effort to get more illustration disclosure. It seems to be a clear-cut professional issue that should be pursued by the Society and other agent and broker organizations.

PUBLIC TRUST

Now I come to the second chapter of history—public trust—and how it has been dangerously eroded.

When I started in our business in 1951, people believed all large life insurance companies were safe, sound, and secure. In the 20 previous years, the stock market had crashed and stayed wrecked for a long time. Most banks had gone broke, leaving their depositors high and dry (there being no FDIC). The savings and loans had followed the banks. Only the life insurance industry had weathered the economic strain of the 1930s without loss to our fellow citizens.

I remember stories of companies sending in additional personnel from home office to local office to help process policy loans promptly when banks were either closed, in default, or delaying payments on withdrawal requests. No one lost money in their life insurance. Our public was grateful. Life insurance was held in high esteem as a bastion of security, safety, and prudence.

Today we are in grave danger of losing that trust. If we do, we will be grouped in the public's eye with all financial institutions and will lose the unique position of trust we have enjoyed.

While our industry by 1951 had earned a reputation for being sound, there is little doubt that most, if not all, life insurance companies were overly cautious, inefficient investors. More recently, and greatly encouraged by those of us who insisted on more competitive products, some companies began to invest more aggressively. Other companies that up to then had been comfortable with the results of their captive agents soon found their distribution systems upset by companies with higher investment yields projecting better results. Business was lost, along with loyalty, and the pressure for better performance intensified throughout the industry.

I believe that investment strategy should not be as overly cautious as it once was, but, nevertheless, it must be tightly related to a company's preeminent responsibility for protecting policyholders. Policyholders do not want to worry about their death benefits or their cash values, and they would gladly trade some basis points and cost for greater security and peace of mind.

The strategy of seeking higher yields makes sense only if the client has absolute confidence not only in his company but also in the industry as a whole. Recently, we have seen the ratings of one large company plunge because of the questionable future of investments acquired aggressively. If one company can find itself in this situation today, so can other companies tomorrow. In the short term, of course, nonperforming junk is not unique to bonds. There are a lot of nonperforming mortgages and foreclosed real estate held by other companies. In the long term, if we see that one company's problems are a result of shortsighted management, how do we guarantee that other companies' managements will not become shortsighted in the 50 years or so our policies will be in force?

We need to regain the strong public trust we enjoyed in 1951. I believe we can all contribute to that worthy goal by changing our demands on our companies. While I will not back off in wanting companies to perform efficiently, I also want them to perform wisely. I will continue to insist that companies earn and sustain A+ Best ratings; but I now also want to see high ratings from Standard & Poor's, Moody's and Duff & Phelps—with AA being a current minimum and AAA being a realistic goal. When illustrating products, I disclose company ratings, and I find most of my clients like the security of high ratings and see no reason not to demand them. I also recommend studying copies of the rating services' analyses and sharing them with clients.

We should encourage our companies to seek and publish ratings from all the top four rating services, not just Best's or even Best's and Standard & Poor's. An unrated company, I believe, will become a suspect company.

While I admit I do not understand all of the problems that companies have, I do know that millions of dollars have been wasted in fruitless reorganizations, ill-conceived attempts to diversify into ancillary and other businesses, inefficient management, and foolish investment strategies. We have a professional responsibility to insist that our companies' management perform well, that they more ably fulfill their roles as our policyholders' fiduciaries.

To sum up my discussion of the two chapters of history and their effect on us today, I invite you to join me in letting home offices know how important we feel high ratings are. Tell them that you do not want them to pursue a more aggressive investment strategy that might increase dividends or yields but also might place the company's ratings at risk. Also tell them that you and your policyholders would like to know what the assumptions are behind your illustrations. You and I have a professional responsibility to find out, and our clients have a right to know.

BANKS

First, I believe that banks and other financial institutions will be in our business, and soon. You will recall that I said earlier that in 1952 we were clearly differentiated from banks and other financial institutions based on our unprecedented record of safety and performance. As we lose that differentiation in the public's eye, all of the reasons to keep the banks out of our business disappear. However, I believe that banks will not overwhelm us, that we will be able to compete very well against them. Do you remember when banks started marketing the concept of "Your Own Personal Banker?" Was that 15 or 20 years ago? I have many hundreds of clients I have kept for the past 15 or 20 years, and so do many of you. I wonder how many personal bankers they have had during that time. Banks will probably market our product the way they do personal banking. services, with young personnel. The greater insight and creativity they exhibit, the faster they will move on to other duties. They will tend to be short term, transaction oriented, and will treat insurance like a commodity.

REBATING

A second change which I believe to be more serious will be the elimination of barriers to rebating. California and Florida have struck down their rebating laws, and they seem to be leading indicators for the rest of the country. Extensive rebating will hurt all of us some, but it will most hurt those who will tend to sell life insurance as though it was a commodity, like it was a CD.

When clients view insurance as a simple commodity, they wonder at the reason for a commission; but if one must be paid they view it as a favor to be bestowed. Today, this favor is bestowed on a broker with power or one who is a friend. The banks will surely become a broker with power; and with rebating, the buyer's favor may be bestowed on his or her best friend, himself.

Therefore, we must market two fundamental concepts that confirm that life insurance should not be seen as a simple commodity:

(1) Insurance contracts, insurance planning, and insurance service are enormously complex and detailed and require not only routine administration but constant attention to changing circumstances, markets and laws.
(2) We are uniquely qualified to manage this complexity, and we are committed to providing these necessary present and future services. We will stay on the cutting edge of circumstances, markets, and laws.

COMMISSION DESIGN

I believe our companies will respond to rebating and expense problems by creating commission scales that are less heaped (i.e., more level). To those of us who have established practices, this will be a short-term inconvenience but should produce a better-performing product and therefore a product easier to sell. We may earn less on each sale, but we should sell more.

In coping with these and other changes to come, I try to keep in mind two rules of life that are true and dependable, however uncomfortable: (1) life is not fair; and (2) change is inevitable.

Adjusting to the jarring changes that have occurred in my 39 years in the life insurance business has been challenging and exciting.

How well we adjust to the coming changes not only predicts our happiness, but is also a strong indication of how successful we will be in the future.

Company Bashing

Frederick H. Stitt, CLU

Selling insurance is hard.
Even if there is no competition, it is hard.
It is harder if there is competition.
The agent/broker needs to make the sale to

- support himself or herself and his or her family
- meet whatever quotas or goals are imposed by his or her company or GA/manager
- perhaps satisfy his or her ego

In short, there is a lot of pressure to make the sale, and there may be a sense of panic if the sale seems to be slipping away, especially to another agent/broker.

So it is no wonder that we are tempted to use any tools at hand to make the sale, including pointing out our company's advantages and the competitor company's limitations. This activity can range from simply comparing ratings published by Best, Standard & Poor's, Moody's, and Duff & Phelps to slanderous remarks about the competing company.

company bashing   Slanderous remarks surely qualify as *company bashing* and should be avoided by all practitioners. In fact, evidence of such activity should be reported to the local Society chapter for possible disciplinary action (if the alleged wrongdoer is a CLU) and to the aggrieved company for possible legal action.

But disclosure and comparison of ratings seem to me to be not only acceptable behavior, but also possibly a professionally required step.

The client is certainly entitled to have all relevant information about the purchase he or she is contemplating, and this includes information about the company. I believe this relevant information includes (but is not limited to)

- ratings by Best, Standard & Poor's, Moody's, and Duff & Phelps or, perhaps as significant, lack of ratings (Ratings are an indication of current financial strength. Lack of ratings may mean the company is reluctant to expose financial weakness.)

- current surplus and recent earnings (leading indicators of future financial strength and/or product performance)
- extent of junk bonds and real estate investments (indicators of how "hard" or "soft" the company's surplus really is)
- percentage of troubled assets (Have they already been written down, or will this be a prominent *Wall Street Journal* story soon?)
- and, certainly, information on historical performance and current illustration integrity (History teaches us about the company's devotion to its policyholders. Is the current illustration based on credible assumptions?)

Our first obligation is to protect our client and not our company. The Society's Code of Ethics provides that in a conflict of interest situation, the interest of the client shall be paramount. To protect our clients' legitimate interests, all this relevant information should be freely available, and we should feel comfortable and, under many circumstances, compelled to present it along with the usual illustrations. Companies who wish to hide from the light of truth should suffer the discipline of our free market. Companies who are injured by falsehood should aggressively seek to overturn the falsehood and replace it with truth.

Perhaps this open market of information will help to encourage executives to manage companies more responsibly and producers to become more concerned about their companies' financial strength and ratings. This result would benefit both policyholders, agents/brokers, and the companies themselves.

I believe we cross the line into company bashing when we leave the objective presentation of information and, to use a word popular in politics, put an unduly negative "spin" on information. For example, what is the real difference between AAA and AA ratings?

Obviously, disseminating information that is false, or editorializing in a negative manner without using data at all, is even worse. Company bashing, so defined, is unprofessional and gives the whole industry a black eye. Further, it could easily result in litigation by the agent/broker who has lost a sale because of twisted information, by the client who has perhaps purchased a policy that was second best, or by the company who was slandered.

While I encourage agents/brokers to tell the truth about companies and interpret the truth fairly, I also encourage all of us, companies included, to take ethical and legal action against the type of company bashing just described. It has no legitimate place in our industry and it smears us all.

Can a Producer Effectively Evaluate Carriers?

John S. Moyse, CLU, ChFC

What is the responsibility of the producer to give advice to clients concerning the financial strength of insurance companies? This was one of the topics at the Society's Agent and Broker Liability Conference held in June 1990.

The question is very timely. Conference luncheon speaker Thomas B. Wheeler, CLU, president and CEO of Massachusetts Mutual Life, observed that the rate of insurance company insolvencies is increasing. In the event of policyowner loss arising from company insolvency, the producer is a natural litigation target. Material prepared for the conference by Thomas J. Ziomek, a partner in the Philadelphia law firm of White and Williams, noted that in the past 10 years the frequency of errors and omissions claims against insurance producers has increased, and the severity of those claims has become greater.

Conference speakers noted that, to lessen the danger of being sued, a producer should exercise care in selecting insurance companies to represent and in providing advice to clients insured by companies whose financial condition has deteriorated.

To emphasize the significance of insurance company insolvency to the producer, Dr. Joseph Belth pointed out that many producers carry errors and omissions coverage which does not protect the producer against claims based upon losses incurred due to an insurer insolvency.

It is the writer's opinion that, in communications to clients concerning the financial fitness of an insurer, a producer should follow the general principle of remaining within one's area of expertise and not pose as an expert in the financial analysis of insurance companies. In giving advice to clients concerning the financial strength of insurance companies, the producer should rely solely on published sources which have been prepared by industry specialists.

The initial step in any communication of this nature should be to inform the client of the insurance company's rating by A. M. Best Company and also, if available, of the ratings of other rating services—Duff & Phelps, Inc., Moody's Investors Service, and Standard & Poor's Corporation. The producer can help the client understand the ratings by providing each rating service's explanation of the applicable rating category. These rating categories assess the company's ability to meet its policy obligations.

Another published source is the National Association of Insurance Commissioners (NAIC), which calculates the Insurance Regulatory Information Systems (IRIS) ratios. Ratios applicable to 1989 results were published by NAIC in May 1990, and can be obtained for $50.00 by writing to the NAIC. Dr. Belth explained if a company has several ratios outside the usual ranges, that's a warning signal that should prompt the producer to obtain further information about the company.

A good source of additional information is the report provided by the rating services in connection with the issuance of (or change in) a company's rating. Should a cloudy picture of the company emerge, the producer may be wise to recommend another carrier. If the client is presently a policyowner of the company in question, the producer should review the facts with the client and consider recommending replacement of the product to protect the client's investment and/or insurability. At the same time, the producer is lessening the likelihood of being the target of a successful lawsuit.

If the producer is recommending the sale of a participating life insurance policy, Best's 10- and 20-year dividend comparisons indicate how the company performed in the past and how close it came to its illustrations.

The writer believes that a producer should limit communications to clients regarding the fiscal soundness of insurance companies to published facts which have been compiled by experts. This will minimize the risk of being accused of posing as an expert in areas where the producer lacks specific expertise. If the client desires some evaluation of these facts, the producer should respond by seeking additional published data. If appropriate data is not available, the producer should refrain from being tempted to "guess." For the client who persists in posing technical questions which are beyond the producer's expertise, the producer should attempt to locate an expert in insurance accounting.

The producer who provides clients with conclusions based on personal analyses of the annual statements of insurance companies is treading on dangerous ground. Even a professional in this field cannot perform a competent analysis of an insurance company's statement without a substantial amount of supplementary information.

An annual statement does not disclose a number of items which are important in assessing the financial strength of an insurer. For example, it does not reveal the extent to which the surplus position and earnings of the company are distorted by reinsurance arrangements. Many of these arrangements are very complex. A professional analysis requires not only a copy of the reinsurance agreement but also a numerical illustration showing its financial effect on the insurance company.

Should a producer rate companies on the basis of their ratio of surplus funds to liabilities? No. One company may have a higher surplus ratio than another but be in poorer financial condition for a number of reasons—it may have received surplus relief from reinsurance arrangements or from transactions involving premium loadings or first-year commissions. In addition, surplus needs differ between lines of business. The producer who wishes to review adequacy of surplus should consider using Moody's Risk Adjusted Capital Ratio. This is a more sophisticated measure than the pure ratio of surplus funds to liabilities and has the advantage of having been compiled by an expert. Company ratios along with Moody's company ratings for 1989 appear in *Moody's Industry Outlook—Life Insurance,* which was published in July 1990. Copies can be obtained by writing to Moody's Investors Service.

Should a producer rate companies on the basis of the quality of their investment portfolio? Not unless some reliable published material is available. More refined studies are becoming available on junk bonds. But how can the producer assess the quality of the mortgage portfolio or of the real estate portfolio? And what about investments in the company's affiliates?

Company insolvency can result in the policyowner's recouping nothing unless the policy is taken over by another insurer or is covered by a state guaranty association. Evaluation of financial strength is also important because a company in poor financial condition is more likely to fail to perform as illustrated even though it may remain solvent. A producer who acted as an expert in analyzing the financial statements of such a company runs a greater risk of being held liable for the failure in performance.

Failure to perform as illustrated can also arise from overly optimistic illustrations in instances where the insurance company is of unquestioned financial strength. Here again, the producer who assumes the role of an expert adviser and creates a reasonable expectation by the insured that the illustration is a guarantee could be held liable. The risk to the producer could be lessened through use of the information contained in a company's reply to the Society's Professional Practice Guideline.[1] This information can assist the producer in obtaining a better understanding of the underlying assumptions and in communicating these to the client.

NOTE

1. The Professional Practice Guideline was the forerunner of the Society's Illustration Questionnaire (IQ).

What Are Ethics?

Bobette G. Scribner, CLU, ChFC

Who determines what is ethical and what isn't? Why has it become a very important buzzword in our business lives? If we were to ask these questions of thousands of people, we would get many different answers, all of which could be correct. Therein lies the dilemma: Our ethics are determined by our individual set of moral standards. There is no fixed standard to cover each situation.

Americans are blessed (not everyone would use this word) with an extensive legal system which is challenged to keep us within the letter of the law. If we steal and we are caught, we can expect to be punished. If we injure someone and the damaged person decides to sue, we know the consequences. This is because law is precise: Specific acts lead to specific consequences.

Ethical principles, however, aren't specific and in most cases there isn't anyone enforcing our moral codes. So ethical behavior is the result of individual choice. Let's take a look at some ethical issues in the insurance industry and see how many choices there are.

Assume that we have a young couple with two small children. One of the adults works and provides for the family while the other adult manages the home. This couple has $400 to spend on life insurance. One life insurance agent will show this couple a $25,000 whole life policy which will give them some monies towards future needs. Another agent will show this same couple $200,000 of term insurance to protect the stay-at-home adult and the two young children. Which agent's advice is correct?

I offer to you that they may both be correct. Depending on our own personal biases, each of us will choose one of the two options above. However, regardless of our own opinions, only the client can determine which need and solution is most important to him or her.

The whole life product will allow the young couple to stop paying premiums at some point in the future and still retain the coverage. It will allow them to begin a savings program for their children's education or their own retirement. It will provide immediate cash for the family should something happen to the income provider.

What will term insurance do for this couple? It will provide a much larger death benefit for the couple should the income partner die too soon. This might permit the nonworking spouse to stay home until the young children are in school full-time. It will also allow the family to convert to a permanent plan sometime in the future, even if the insured becomes uninsurable.

What is more important to this young family? Which agent is the more right? If the salesperson is more concerned with the protection of this young family, he or she will suggest the term insurance. If the salesperson is more concerned with long-term planning, he or she will recommend the permanent policy.

Let's complicate the issue even more. What if the adults in the above case went to a seminar and first heard about the term insurance option only after having already purchased the whole life policy? They then spoke with the agent who was giving the seminar and told her that an immediate death benefit was much more important to them than the savings feature. They want to make sure that their current lifestyle can continue even if something should happen to the working adult. If this agent replaces the permanent policy with term, will the replacement be wrong? If the clients are committed to the need for the high death benefit, then how can anyone say the agent was wrong in replacing the whole life policy with term insurance?

In 40 years, if this young family happens to be one of the lucky ones, then in hindsight the term insurance probably wasn't the best choice. But some agents aren't willing to gamble on that many years of someone's life and so choose a different way. Who can say one is more right or wrong than the other? Isn't the right or wrong determined when we discover that the clients were only told of one plan and not the other? The first agent's error was made when the clients weren't given the opportunity to select among alternative solutions and decide what helps them the most.

Let's look at a different kind of ethical question. What should we do when a prospect asks for a proposal from a company that we know little or nothing about? The assumptions here are that the agent is selling for a number of companies and thus doesn't find it unusual to show two or more proposals to a prospect. A prospect has read advertisements about the great results a particular company is achieving and wants to buy the product from it. The agent does research and decides that he or she would not purchase a product from this company.

What are the choices the agent has to make? (1) Simply state: "I don't sell that company. You will have to buy from someone else." (2) Explain why the agent believes this is an inferior company and attempt to sell another carrier. (3) Sell the product and hope for the best.

In my opinion, it is imperative that we commit ourselves to never selling anything that we would not purchase for our own financial needs. I believe that the Professional Pledge of The American College leads us to this conclusion. The Pledge states: In all my professional relationships, I pledge myself to the following rule of ethical conduct—I shall, in the light of conditions surrounding those I serve, which I shall make every conscientious effort to ascertain and understand, render that service which, in the same circumstances, I would apply to myself.

If I'm selling to a young couple, I know that if I were in their place I would want to have a lot of death benefit so I would recommend the term insurance. If they want to buy a small permanent policy, I have to deal with the fact that, if I sell it and if there is a death claim, I will have to deliver the smaller amount to the survivors. Can I live with myself if I sell the smaller death benefit? If I were asked to sell or at least quote a company that I wouldn't buy myself, I could not do it. I can't justify in any way selling such a product to someone who understands less than I do about how insurance companies and their products work.

The tough, but ethically irrelevant, issue here is the need for regular commission income. In my first example, we are dealing with small commission differences, but in the second we may be dealing with many thousands of dollars. Can any of us honestly say we have never been lulled into rationalization by a big commission? Can any of us say that we are so pure we can stand in judgment of someone else's human frailty?

Our need to be compensated is a legitimate right. But if we claim to be professionals and advisers to our clients, our needs must be subservient to the needs of our clients. Our Society's Code of Ethics provides, "In a conflict of interest situation, the interest of the client must be paramount."

Your Society is taking action to help all of us address issues such as those listed above. These two were chosen to give very different examples, but there are many other ethical issues that we all must wrestle with daily. I believe ethics is treating others as we wish to be treated. The Society exists to build our business into a respected profession that the general public trusts.

Let's join together in helping all of our associates arrive at conclusions that are good for the industry and for the public. If we don't, I suggest that there are governmental units that will be helping us in the not too distant future. Now is the time to set policies which make sense to the people we are serving—the buying public.

Ethics Requires Practice

Burke A. Christensen, JD, CLU

On a recent business trip, I read an article on business ethics in an airline magazine. The article, entitled "Ethically Speaking," was written by Patricia Haddock and Marilyn Manning, PhD. It appeared in the March 1990 issue of *Sky* magazine.

The article began with a quotation from Mark Twain: "Always do right. This will surprise some people and astonish the rest."

For those who aspire to be professionals, this quotation cannot be applicable. We must live our business and personal lives in such a manner that people expect us to do the right thing and would be astonished if we did not.

The acquisition of such a reputation is absolutely vital if we are to conduct our business based upon our clients' trust rather than *caveat emptor.*

In their article, Haddock and Manning relate the following story about the effect upon a business of an ethical code.

"In 1932, a Chicago Rotarian was asked to save a business from bankruptcy by strengthening its moral character in order for it to stand out from its competition. The Rotarian came up with four key questions to establish a code of ethics for the company. This code has become known as The Four-Way Test. It requires that four simple questions be asked:

- Is it the truth?
- Is it fair to all concerned?
- Will it build goodwill and better friendships?
- Will it be beneficial to all concerned?"

Repeated use of The Four-Way Test caused the company to change its policies toward competitors. Employees stopped making adverse comments about the competitors' products, and when they found opportunities to speak well of the competition, they did so. They also applied The Four-Way Test to relationships with employees, suppliers, and customers.

The company went from near bankruptcy to becoming a multimillion-dollar business. It enjoys the increasing goodwill and confidence of its customers, competitors, and the public. The company believes that the application of The Four-Way Test is the reason for its success.

By applying The Four-Way Test, it is easier to make decisions that fall into gray areas. For example, when we talk about the features of our products, are we obliged to admit negative features if we are aware of them? Remember, The Four-Way Test would require us to ask such questions as "Is failure to disclose fair to all concerned?" and "Will not disclosing build goodwill?"[1]

While this story has a happy ending, Robbin Derry, chairholder and associate professor—management at The American College, has stated that one should not adopt ethics because it leads to financial success. There are many examples in history where adherence to a high moral standard has wrought terrible consequences. Instead, we should do the right thing because it is the right thing to do.

As a moral imperative, the last sentence of the previous paragraph will do nicely. However, a professional society and the members who support its Code of Ethics must struggle to answer a most difficult question: How do you get people to do the right thing always? Stated more simply: Can ethics be taught? The answer is that ethical behavior, like skilled piano playing, is acquired only by teaching and by practice.

Any parent can attest to the fact that we are not born with an innate sense of ethical behavior. Somewhere near the age of 2, we begin to learn that everything within reach is not "mine." According to Professor Michael Levin at City College of New York, "Moral behavior is the product of training, not reflection. As Aristotle stressed thousands of years ago, you get a good adult by habituating a good child to doing the right thing. Praise for truth-telling and sanctions for fibbing will, in time, make him 'naturally' honest."

I must stress that mere knowledge of what is right and what is wrong does not make a person ethical, any more than living in a garage will make a person a car. Great skill at the piano is acquired only when knowledge and technique become automatic. The same is true of ethics. In Levin's words: "Honest people don't have to think how to answer under oath."

It is clear that insurance producers are striving toward acceptance as professionals. It is an expensive road. Replacing customers and *caveat emptor* with clients and trust permits clients to sue when the advice is bad. Becoming an adviser to clients requires giving advice that is in the clients' best interest.

I once heard a prominent figure in the life insurance business say, "What obligation does a life insurance agent have to point out the deficiencies in his own product? Damn little I say!" That kind of thinking is not an example of professionalism. It is a roadblock in the path to professional status.

The Four-Way Test is a simple system, and a good one. But I submit that it is lacking one element to make it satisfactory for a profession. That element is altruism. For members of the Society, it is not enough that an act be merely fair and beneficial to all concerned. We have the ethical obligation to put our clients' interests before our own. That is a far higher standard because it requires us to act on our principles—sometimes to our own detriment.

As you conduct your practice, consider this idea from Professor Levin: "Telling right from wrong in everyday life is not that hard; the hard part is overcoming laziness and cowardice to do what one perfectly well knows one should. As every parent learns, only good examples and apt incentives can induce that strength."[2]

NOTES

1. "Ethically Speaking," by Patricia Haddock and Marilyn Manning, PhD, March 1990 issue of Sky magazine, pages 128-130.
2. "Can Ethics Be Taught?" by Michael Levin, *The New York Times,* November 25, 1989.

Ethical Behavior as a Core Value

Denis F. Mullane, CLU

Ethical behavior has been a core value of the Society from its inception. The Society's impressive programs and initiatives over the last few years are further evidence that this core value is alive and well today.

Clearly—by virtue of your professional designations and active membership in the Society—you exemplify the highest standards of professionalism. With all these wonderful initiatives—and with such a large and distinguished group of professionals committed to doing the right thing—why, then, does a crisis of confidence persist among consumers about the life insurance industry?

We know that consumers find insurance products to be very complex and technical. They have to trust the judgment of an "expert" to advise them, and people are frightened by that.

Then, of course, there's competition from elsewhere in the financial services industry. Consumers have more choices that appear less complex and more attractive than life insurance. To fight back, some in our industry have positioned life insurance products as tax-advantaged investments, rather than the major source of income protection. And that's led to some of the negative perception we face today.

Finally, all you have to do is read the papers, where the news is often too true to be good. As we all know, there has been tremendous fallout from media coverage about the illegal sales practices of a handful of agents from an even smaller handful of companies.

On the other hand, the news isn't all bad. One ACLI study shows that most policyholders are pleased with the performance of *their* agents and *their* companies. Sixty-eight percent of policyholders with recent agent contact consider that contact "very helpful." Seventy-five percent rate the service provided by their agent as "very good" or "excellent." Eighty-five percent agree that their own company provides good service. Sounds encouraging, doesn't it?

Despite all the positive things we "good guys" have been doing in the industry, why does the negative image persist? Some of it is due to circumstances beyond our control.

So let's look at what we can do to change the situation, because a lot of it is well within our control. Our problems are not solely because of a few "bad apples." Sure, they've gotten the headlines. But if the rest of us performed perfectly, then we could easily dismiss those bad apples as renegades and outlaws, and the public would agree with us.

Unfortunately, however, the public has a negative image of our industry because that image has a basis in fact. And we can't change the image until we change the basis in fact.

Now, we're all professionals. We're good guys, right? Yet, we routinely do things that leave consumers with a negative impression. I'm not talking about blatant abuses. Quite the opposite. I'm talking about activities and practices that are socially acceptable at NALU and CLU meetings and among elite example-setting agents everywhere.

Let me give you a list of things that many good agents do which are considered "socially acceptable" in our profession. Then I'd like you to ask yourself if you engage in any of these practices. If you answer "yes," then—despite your best intentions—you are contributing to the basis in fact for our negative image.

(1) Not telling the prospect "the whole truth"

I don't mean lying to prospects. But how often do we emphasize only the positive aspects of the product we're selling? How often do we stop short of telling them what the risks and downsides are? It's understandable. Pointing out a potential negative could scare off a prospect.

On the other hand, what clients don't know *can* hurt them—and hurt your business. If they are unpleasantly surprised somewhere down the road by the performance of the product, they will be upset with you, your company and the industry.

(2) Selling, instead of problem-solving

In an effort to gain or keep a client, have any of us sold either the cheapest policy, or simply what he or she asked for, instead of what the policyholder really needed? Maybe you were afraid the client wouldn't buy, or that a competitor would undercut you. Again, it's understandable. But if the client has a problem somewhere down the road, and the product can't solve the problem, we have an unhappy customer.

(3) Not talking to your customers as often as you should

I believe you can't talk to a customer too much—at the very minimum, once a year—face-to-face. Here's an example of what happened when my company's agents did not do that.

At one point in my career, I decided to do a computer search of our policyholder database, and found that many Fortune 500 CEOs had Connecticut Mutual Life policies. Unfortunately, the majority of them were orphans. Our agents sold them policies way back when those CEOs-to-be were just starting out, and never stayed in touch.

(4) Using illustrations rather than focusing on past performance

It's been said that the best predictor of future behavior is past behavior. But as we've all learned in recent years, predicting anything is risky business.

It used to be that our industry could routinely expect to meet or exceed dividend projections. As a result, our assumptions were as good as promises. But those days are long gone. So projecting "current assumptions" is flirting with disaster. Even if you carefully explain to the customer that "this is only an illustration," the customer takes that piece of paper and thinks "this is what's *going* to happen." Then, when it doesn't, the customer becomes disenchanted, if not downright angry.

When I talk about "focusing on past performance," I mean this: Look at the company behind the product. A company with a long, proven history of financial strength and sound business practice is likely to be there to write the check 20, 30, or 40 years down the road, when the client really needs it.

That is the essential promise that underlies any life insurance contract, and that's what the customer really needs and wants.

(5) Looking for "something for nothing" from insurance companies

This means saying to yourself, "This company will pay me a couple more points in commission," or "That company will tell me its policy performs better than my company's policy, so I'll sell that policy."

After all, it wasn't customers who said, "I need the kind of projections that Executive Life, Integrated Resources, and Baldwin United provided." Agents said it. They believed that those companies could do something that the rest of the industry couldn't do. And they paid the price, as did their clients.

If you want something for nothing from a company, and you promise customers something that the company really can't deliver, customers will eventually be unpleasantly surprised. Then they'll blame you, and they'll blame the insurance business.

(6) Misrepresenting who you are

Most agents, even the good ones, who tell clients they are "independent," are really career agents of some company. But not every consumer is savvy enough to ask an agent if he or she pays self-employed Social Security tax, which is the litmus test for independence.

I can understand the reluctance to admit to a company affiliation. A prospect may think you're not as objective as a so-called independent agent. But this is a classic case where honesty is, indeed, the best policy.

I was always candid with my clients on this point. I'd say, "I'm an agent of the Connecticut Mutual Life Insurance Company. I've chosen to be with that company because it's a wonderful company. It has good products that can, for the most part, meet your needs. But let me tell you something strange about our industry. If I bring an application for insurance on your life to any company in the business, it will happily pay me a commission. So if some other product will serve your needs better, or if you have a strong reason for wanting your policy to come from another company, I can do that for you, too."

I've had clients who told me, "Denis, I respect what you're saying, but you're tied to Connecticut Mutual. We've got a proposal from an independent agent, and we think he'd be more objective."

To which I'd say, "His company affiliation is a matter of public record. If I can prove to you he is a career agent with another company and has not been forthright about who he is, would that affect your decision?" Usually, it would.

You can be objective without being "independent," and if you're frank about it—up front—your client will believe it. The point is, you not only need to have the right behavior, you also have to tell the truth and have the guts to live that truth. In other words, you have to "walk the talk."

I have always believed that it will enhance your sales if you play it straight. And, frankly, given the erosion of consumer confidence in what we do, there's never been a more important time to "play it straight."

(7) Failing to pursue continuing education

Think of it this way. How would you like to be operated on by a surgeon who had not improved his technique or read a medical book since he graduated from medical school? I don't know how we can best serve our customers without being up to date. So, among other things, I would strongly urge you to participate in PACE, the Society's continuing education program for accreditation.

(8) Not delivering the policies

Let's face it. Most life insurance customers don't really know what they've bought. When the product fails to perform according to unrealistic expectations, the customer is dissatisfied.

I personally delivered every policy I ever sold. I sat down with the customer and reviewed it, paragraph by paragraph. I did not leave until I was sure the customer understood what he or she had just purchased. If you don't do this, you leave yourself—and the industry—open to negative fallout when the client's *misconception* about what he or she bought collides with the *reality* of what was bought.

TOTAL QUALITY SERVICE

The eight items I've listed are all things that *good* agents do. They aren't dishonest or unethical, but they contribute to the possibility that customers will be disappointed and upset. We can't change our negative image among consumers unless we change the behavior which contributes to the basis in fact for that image. So what can you do about it? How can you help improve customer confidence in our industry?

Let me suggest a plan of action to accomplish just that. It's what I call "Total Quality Service." It stems from four operating principles that I used as an agent. As a general agent, I encouraged all my agency associates to accept and follow them as well.

(1) Have a complete confidential information questionnaire in your file for every customer.

This is like an estate planning questionnaire, but it's not for the purpose of selling estate planning. It is a means of getting to know your customer thoroughly. After all, you can't properly serve a customer's needs unless you really *know* who the customer is.

(2) Hold all of your customer's financial products in your hand.

You should physically examine each existing insurance policy, mutual fund prospectus, or any other documentation the customer has. Remember, when it comes to insurance and investment, customers often don't know what they really bought. They may give you inaccurate information, not because they're trying to mislead you, but because they simply don't know what they have. If someone tells you he or she already has a million-dollar policy with another company, he or she may not realize that what was bought is a travel-accident policy. By pointing this out, you'll be doing your customer a service. And you'll probably make a sale.

(3) Actually deliver and explain the policy.

This is the only way to make sure the customer understands what he or she has purchased. If you explain things thoroughly and accurately, you reduce the possibility that the customer will be disappointed later by unrealistic or false expectations. You may wish to keep your client's policies in your safe, but you can still deliver the policy first.

(4) See the customer no less often than once a year.

This is the best way I know to keep your customers happy. And you'll be doing them a valuable service by keeping their insurance programs updated. What's more, regular client contact is perhaps the most effective public relations you could ever create—for yourself and for our industry.

My friend, Bob Tedoldi, CLU, ChFC, the current president of NALU, suggested a fifth idea which I liked so much, I plan to adopt it. After each interview, Bob sends a summary letter to the prospect or client. This is, in effect, "the minutes of the meeting." And he keeps these letters on file. He reports that many misunderstandings have been prevented by this file.

If people have confidence in someone they believe is really working in their best interest and making good recommendations, then they will be much more likely to implement appropriate financial programs.

We can be those trusted advisers, provided we get back to basics. That means understanding the clients' needs and showing how we can help them meet those needs, rather than focusing on why our product is better than someone else's.

This is a great time to be great in the life insurance business, because there's a market out there of people who are more affluent than they've ever been and who have a greater need for what we do than ever before.

I can't think of a better job today, or in the future, than being a life insurance agent. As soon as I retire, I'm looking forward to becoming an agent again. If we all go forward with that attitude and convey that kind of joy and enthusiasm to our clients, we can go a long way toward restoring consumer confidence in our industry. I hope you'll join me in that effort.

Facing Decisions and Making Choices

Burke A. Christensen, JD, CLU

The American College's Professional Pledge, which is applicable to all those who have earned the CLU and ChFC designations, is at the very core of your Society's Code of Ethics. It provides: "In all my professional relationships, I pledge myself to the following rule of ethical conduct: I shall, in the light of all conditions surrounding those I serve, which I shall make every conscientious effort to ascertain and understand, render that service which, in the same circumstances, I would apply to myself."

Some have maintained that the pledge sets a standard identical to that which our culture refers to as the golden rule: "Do unto others as you would have them do unto you." I suggest that it sets a slightly different standard which can be succinctly summarized: "Serve your client's interests as well as you serve your own." The distinction is significant, I think, because the latter version leads us to the next level of ethical behavior where we put the interests of others *ahead* of our own.

The Code of Ethics of your Society exhorts the member "to competently advise and serve the client." The Professional Pledge's focus on service to the client is also echoed in the Code of Ethics: "A member shall provide advice and service which are in the client's best interest."

These statements, like all ethical standards, share two consistent factors: They are strong on moral absolutes but weak on specific guidance for everyday situations. Our Code of Ethics only begins to approach a practical level of specificity when it provides, "In a conflict of interest situation the interest of the client must be paramount."

In order to make these moral imperatives work, the student must make numerous subjective value judgments. Sometimes, what seems right or wrong can change with each case. To complicate matters, it often happens that two ethical and reasonable people can honestly disagree on what is right. This is frustrating perhaps, but it is to be expected because all moral questions involve a subjective balancing of competing interests.

This dearth of specificity may be frustrating to the student or practitioner who is seeking to know the right thing to do in every circumstance, but the ethicist cannot provide such a detailed ethical road map.

The country through which we must walk has many inviting detours and hidden swamps; we cannot expect someone else to be there with a road sign to warn of every danger. The path is too often obscured by sudden fogs and storms for us to look for external signs to mark the way. While some might wish it to be so, there is no universally accepted iron rod of ethically correct behavior along the path to which we can hold when the way becomes slippery. Instead, each of us must acquire and maintain an internal *moral compass* which will point the proper way when we are tempted to put our own interests ahead of the interests of our clients.

moral compass

How do we acquire such a moral compass? It is important to understand that one does not learn ethics in the same manner that Advanced Underwriting or Estate Planning is learned. The student becomes expert in the latter topics by learning facts, such as the transfer-for-value rules or the mechanics of split-dollar agreements.

This is not applicable to ethics because the "facts" are often not facts at all. Instead, they are our differing interpretations of the constantly changing relationships and relative interests between the parties involved. Consequently, our subjective assessments of what is right or wrong may change as the relationships change. What is ethical in one situation is unethical in another.

As a result, the student must discover ethical behavior by comprehending a few grand absolutes: Lying is bad; honesty is good; giving informed, objective advice is good; taking advantage of a client's lack of knowledge is bad, etc. These broad guidelines must then be applied by the student to the shifting facts of everyday life.

In my ethics files I have a sheet of instructions entitled "Guidelines for Ethical Decision Making." Its source is unknown to me, but its message is useful to my point in this column. The guidelines are:

It would be impossible to formulate a list of morally right answers for every ethical dilemma since each situation has many unique aspects and considerations which must be weighed. But there are ways of reasoning and thinking about ethical conflicts which lead to reliable solutions. We encourage you to approach moral reasoning by asking yourself several important questions about the situation. As with any difficult decision, these questions demand serious reflection and require you to think broadly about the implications of your actions.

(1) Obligations: To whom do I have obligations and what are these obligations?

(2) Rights: Who has rights which must be protected?

(3) Moral Rules: What moral rules apply to this situation and should be upheld?

Take some time to answer these questions specifically and in depth. Then decide which of these obligations, rights, and moral rules are most important. The demands of some may conflict with others. You will need to prioritize them. Ethical decisions are inherently balancing decisions.

(4) Publicity: Would I publicly advocate this action? If my decision were publicized in the headlines of the *New York Times*, would I be able to defend my reasoning and choice?

This final question recognizes the importance of social values and standards in our individual ethical decisions. We don't make ethical decisions in a vacuum. We make them in the context of our communities and our world. Therefore each such decision has an impact on the shaping of our work and social environments. We must take this context into account as we practice better ethical decision making.

The way to becoming a good person and an ethical professional is a process, not an event. It involves facing decisions and making choices. It is inevitable that we will make some mistakes. We must learn from the bad choices as well as the good ones, so that there will be fewer wrong choices and more right ones. It's not a bad idea to adopt the view of Calvin Coolidge, who said, "I'd rather be right than president."

•   •   •

Example: ***Evaluating the Ethics of One's Behavior***

The financial rating assigned by A.M. Best to Building Blocks Life Insurance Company was recently downgraded from A to A–. Jason, an agent for another company, contacted several Building Blocks policyowners by phone informing them of this change, which he termed "extremely serious." Jason urged them to replace their policies immediately with policies in his company. He stressed to them that the added safety of being insured by his A-rated company could be gained "with the only cost being a slight increase in the premium." Some questions to consider:

- What obligations, if any, are owed to Building Blocks Life, its agents, and its policyowners?
- Do Building Blocks Life, its agents, and its policyowners have rights that must be protected?

- What moral rules (for example, honesty and fairness) apply to this situation?
- Would the agent, Jason, be willing to place an advertisement in the paper advocating that because of the "extremely serious" rating downgrade, Building Blocks policyowners should replace their policies with policies in Jason's company, "with the only cost being a slight increase in the premium?

Ethics and the Law

Burke A. Christensen, JD, CLU

The members of the Society are bound by a formal Code of Ethics which is based upon the pledge taken by all holders of the CLU and ChFC designations. The pledge states: "In all my professional relationships, I pledge myself to the following rule of ethical conduct: I shall, in the light of all conditions surrounding those I serve, which I shall make every conscientious effort to ascertain and understand, render that service which, in the same circumstances, I would apply to myself."

The purpose of the Code of Ethics is to provide a series of standards against which Society members may measure their business and professional activities. The Code contains two ethical imperatives which mandate that a member provide competent advice which is in the client's best interest and that a member shall act in a manner that will enhance the public regard for the professional designations held by members.

Laws exist to set a minimum level of behavior. Actions which do not conform to that level will result in the imposition of fines and penalties. Our legal systems set a line which separates acceptable from unacceptable behavior. That behavior which crosses the line is unacceptable outlaw behavior. Laws are not concerned, for the most part, with one's distance from the line. A shoplifter and a murderer are both outlaws. The magnitude of their crimes is relevant to the victim and the punishment, but not to the fact that both shoplifting and murder are illegal activities. Each has equally crossed the line into outlaw behavior when the theft or murder occurs. Further, insofar as the law is concerned, there is no distinction between a saint and a sinner, if neither has violated any temporal laws. A person cannot be acting more legally than another person who is also acting legally. There are no gradations of legal behavior. An act is legally acceptable or it is not.

ethical codes
Ethical codes, however, begin with the assumption that all of one's actions are acceptable; that is to say, all illegal activity is by definition unethical. If one accepts the principle that all ethical behavior is contained within legal behavior, then there must be some legal behavior which is unethical. If not, there is no distinction between law and ethics and we have no need for one term or the other.

But there is a distinction between the two. Ethical codes exist to elevate the behavior of men and women above the level of those who merely obey the law. The law may merely require that a person not tell a lie. This legal standard may permit one to give less than a complete answer.

For example, suppose I am trying to sell you an insurance policy and you ask me if it's a good idea. My answer may be, "I have a policy just like it on my own life." If that statement is true, it is a legal response. If the statement is true but I intend to replace the policy, then the legal response is unethical.

If ethics requires one to affirmatively disclose the truth, it may thereby require the disclosure of unsought information which, if revealed, may be adverse to the interest of the seller. Such a result should not be unexpected. The Code of Ethics provides that a member shall provide advice and service which are in the client's best interest. This means that a member has an obligation to use his or her professional expertise for the client's benefits and shall avoid taking advantage of that knowledge to the detriment of the client. It unavoidably follows that whenever a conflict arises between the interests of the client and the member, the interests of the client shall be paramount.

A violation of the Code of Ethics would expose a member to sanctions which range from a reprimand to revocation of membership in the Society. A member is in violation of the Code when a final judgment has been made that the member has failed to adhere to one or more of the specific guides listed in the Code. In most cases, a legal violation would automatically include our ethical breach. However, in the narrower field of business and professional ethics some infractions of the law—such as a parking ticket—would not be thought generally relevant to one's ethical business behavior. This does not mean that a member must have violated a civil law in order to be charged with a violation of the Code. It is entirely possible for a member to be acting legally and still be in violation of the Ethical Code. To make the pledge and the Code of Ethics meaningful, we must be willing to apply the Code so that the gap between acceptable behavior in the eyes of the law and ethical behavior according to the professional pledge is maintained and enforced.

•   •   •

Example: ***Legal vs. Ethical***

Barney, an insurance agent, has only a few days left to complete 3 hours of continuing education to meet his state's CE requirement for license renewal. The law will give Barney one hour of CE credit for each hour of attendance at a 3-hour seminar being conducted by the local NAIFA chapter next week. Barney signs up, attends the seminar, sits at the back of the dimly lit hotel ballroom for 3 hours doing crossword puzzles, and collects his certificate of attendance. Legal? Probably yes. Ethical? Probably not.

Happy Anniversary, "Strictly Speaking"

Ken Cooper, PhD

[. . . There will always be] a need to persistently keep ethics before us. It is a major issue in life insurance today. Two factors—the recent legal actions concerning ethical issues and the media's high-profile treatment of them—have focused attention on ethics. The result has been an even further decline in the public's respect for the life insurance industry. Today ethical transgressions are discussed using such euphemisms as "market conduct" and "business practices." The choice of words doesn't change a thing. Market conduct problems are ethics problems! While we might hope for the day when "Strictly Speaking" no longer needs to discuss ethics, it is not likely to happen in the foreseeable future.

The preface to the pamphlet containing The American College Code of Ethics emphasizes a rich heritage. It states that "Dr. Solomon S. Huebner, the pioneering educator who founded the College, seldom spoke of education without also speaking of ethics. To him a professional relationship between agent and client had to be based on sound ethical principles."

Both The American College and the Society have built their programs on the Huebner legacy. With this heritage, why is life insurance beset by ethics problems? Isn't earned trust an essential part of the agent-client relationship? Don't most—actually, nearly all—agents want to do what is morally right? My guess is that nearly everyone answered these questions in the affirmative.

For starters, today's ethical crisis wasn't invented by the life insurance profession. It is important to realize that others with noble callings and the desire to do what is morally correct have gone or are going through similar difficulties. Knowing *why* such problems develop can be the beginning of the solution.

Human beings have the ability to rationalize away and accept actions that once would have been viewed as clearly unethical. Those of you who have seen the Robert Redford film *Quiz Show* will recall the small, gradual steps by which a scholar from an intellectually disciplined family went from rejecting even the *thought* of receiving the answers before the quiz show to being able to justify why he should have them. On a larger and more shocking scale, who among us hasn't wondered how a typical German citizen—who probably acted ethically in other situations—got caught up in and supported Nazi atrocities during World War II?

The ability to rationalize and to blind ourselves to truths we have earlier understood and lived by exists for families, educators, government officials, professionals, and everyone else! No one is excluded, including those in the financial services fields. There is no need to look further. Examples abound, from assumptions made in preparing illustrations, comments offered or omitted in replacement policy sales, to "looking the other way" when applications are filled out less than truthfully. Our ability to rationalize is competitive with anyone else's.

Professor Saul Gellerman describes four commonly held rationalizations:

- The activity is within reasonable ethical and legal limits. It isn't "really" illegal or immoral.
- The activity is in the individual's or the corporation's best interests. It is "obvious" that it should be undertaken.
- The activity is safe because no one will ever find out what happened.
- The activity will benefit the firm, so it will be accepted and the employee will be protected.[1]

Perhaps you can add to the list. In little steps we learn how to justify that which we would have rejected months or even days earlier.

Gellerman further states, "The idea that an action is not really wrong is an old issue. How far is too far? Exactly where is the line between smart and too smart? Between sharp and shady? Between profit maximization and illegal conduct?"[2]

The boundaries between right and wrong or between ethical and unethical actions are clearer to us when we are emotionally unattached. Objectivity is more difficult when we have something at stake. We are then more likely to rationalize in the ways Gellerman describes.

Professor Stephen Robbins suggests factors that influence the how's and why's of moral behavior. First, he states, "People who lack a strong moral sense are much less likely to do the wrong things if they are constrained by rules, policies, job descriptions, or strong cultural norms that form such behavior."[3]

Codes can be inferred from Robbins's list. He goes on to suggest, as Gellerman does, that even those who are strong morally can be corrupted under certain circumstances. He proceeds to examine four factors:

- the degree that a person's moral decision is independent or dependent on others
- the degree of guidance that is provided by the employing organizations

- the impact of an organization's culture on employees. This is influenced by both the content and strength of the culture.
- the importance of the particular issue to the decision. How important is it to have the desired course of action undertaken?[4]

What influences whether we will act ethically? One factor is how independently we can act. A basically independent person can better withstand pressures from others to do something that would be clearly understood as wrong if there were no personal involvement. This perception of independence varies from person to person and situation to situation. For example, we feel less independent when we might have to act counter to the wishes of the boss.

If a clear code of ethical conduct is frequently communicated and methodically enforced, the odds are better that we will avoid unrealistic rationalization.

Some organizations have a long history of sound ethical practices. Many founders and other leaders of past generations have become heroes for the standards of conduct they established. Persons like Disney, Watson (IBM), Dayton (Dayton-Hudson), Penney, and—yes—Huebner (insurance education) remain legends for setting high moral standards and acting on them. Their impact on their organizations lasts long after their individual careers have ended.

The importance of a particular issue can also have a bearing. The extent of one's personal involvement with individuals who might be helped or hurt by the action plays a part. What is the likelihood that harm to someone will result from the act? How severe or harsh might that harm be? What is the nature of the impact? Emotional? Material wealth? Relationships? Career? How strong (or weak) is public opinion on this issue? How long will it be between the time of action and when others will find out (if ever)?

Two questions emerge from this discussion. The first—What can be done to ensure the ethical environment that financial services needs and deserves? Robbins's list of the *reasons* we rationalize unethical behavior into "acceptable" actions is a place to start. Be aware of these factors and seek to take the necessary steps to neutralize the negative impact each could have.

The second question—Who should be responsible for making sure that a profession-wide resurgence of high ethical conduct takes place? The "Strictly Speaking" answer to this remains unchanged. Eleven years ago and eleven years into the future the answer was and will be the same. The client-centered insurance agent should affirm the highest ethical standards in acting in the client's best interests. Happy Anniversary, "Strictly Speaking."

NOTES

1. Saul Gellerman, "Why 'Good' Managers Make Bad Ethical Choices," *Harvard Business Review* (July–August 1986): 88.
2. *Ibid.,* 88.
3. Stephen Robbins, *Management,* 4th ed. (Englewood Cliffs, N.J.: Prentice Hall, 1994), 130.
4. *Ibid.,* 130–134.

Why Do Good People Make Bad Choices?*

Burke E. Christensen, JD, CLU

Over the last several years, I have become familiar with the details of some civil lawsuits involving insurance producers. In a few of these cases, it was clear that the producer had made some bad decisions that resulted in harm to the insurance company or to the policyowner. I have frequently wondered how these producers—some of them with many years of otherwise unblemished histories—came to take the actions that brought them so much grief. In depositions, their attempts to justify those actions after the fact seem much like a little boy trying to blame the baseball for the broken window.[1]

It is my experience that most insurance producers (like most lawyers) are good people who seek to do the right thing. So, why do good people sometimes make bad choices?

An article in the *Harvard Business Review* asked the same question more specifically: "How could top-level executives at the Manville Corporation have suppressed evidence for decades that proved that asbestos inhalation was killing their own employees? What could have driven the managers of Continental Illinois Bank to pursue a course of action that threatened to bankrupt the institution, ruined its reputation, and cost thousands of innocent employees and investors their jobs and savings? Why did managers at E. F. Hutton find themselves pleading guilty to 2,000 counts of mail and wire fraud, accepting a fine of $2 million, and putting up an $8 million fund for restitution to the 400 banks that the company had systematically bilked? How can we explain the misbehavior that took place in these organizations—or in any of the others, public and private, that litter our newspapers' front pages . . ."[2]

I believe the answer is fairly simple. These people probably did not start out intending to do wrong, but, in the words of Warren Buffet, they let their moral compasses deviate from North. This premise requires us to begin with the assumption that most people take actions designed to achieve what they believe will be in their best interests. When problems arise as a result of

---

*This column did not appear in *The Best of "Strictly Speaking"* because it was published subsequent to the printing of that book.

actions a person takes, it is not because the problem was desired but because (a) the action was a mistaken attempt to achieve a correct goal, or (b) the person had an incorrect picture of what was best—he or she allowed his or her compass to shift away from North.

A mistake made while trying to do the right thing is only a mistake. At worst it might be an act of negligence, but it is not an ethical problem because an unethical act requires some intent to do wrong. However, an incorrect picture of what is best will usually tempt you to make bad choices and take bad actions. Perhaps an example will be useful.

Sue and Bob are preparing for an extremely comprehensive exam given by their employer. If they pass, they will be given more responsible positions and higher pay. Sue's goal is to master the material so that she will be completely prepared for any question that might be asked about that topic on the exam. Bob's goal is to be promoted and earn more money. Alan has a copy of the exam. He offers to sell the exam to Bob and Sue for $500 each. He explains that by studying the exam, they will know "all the important stuff" that they will need to pass the exam and to do the job. Bob buys the exam; Sue does not. Both pass and are promoted.

If the job for which they are now both "qualified" is making the telephone recordings about which movies are playing at the local theater, then you probably don't care very much about Bob's ethics. But what if the job is air traffic controller, commercial airline pilot, or elevator mechanic? What if passing the test allowed Bob to become your tax return preparer or heart surgeon?

With these latter jobs, it is clear that passing the test without gaining the knowledge was not in Bob's best interest (or ours). Clearly, Bob has made a bad decision based upon an incorrect picture of what was in his best interest. He thought it was in his best interest to simply pass the test; but if the job has any meaning at all, knowing how to perform all of the tasks required—not merely passing the test—is the minimum qualification. Readers of this column should see an obvious comparison in the life insurance business. Is there a difference between the producer who has merely passed the tests and the producer who knows the science and art of life insurance?

Consequently, the first principle we must follow in order to consistently make right choices is to examine our picture of what is best. For insurance producers who are members of the Society, I believe that this means putting the interest of the client ahead of our own. Our Code of Ethics is quite clear: "In a conflict of interest situation, the interest of the client shall be paramount."

There are two other principles:

(1) Have a greater regard for the truth than for the advantage you might gain by telling a lie. Honesty is not one of the better policies, it is the best policy. Aristotle taught that: "Contemplation is the best activity.

It is also the most continuous since we can contemplate truth more continuously than we can perform an action." Times have changed in 2,000 years, but Aristotle was right—it is easier to contemplate being truthful than it is to always tell the truth. Nevertheless, one who has always told the truth will sleep better than one who has not.

(2) Conquer ignorance. Not knowing the answer when you should, or when the client thinks you should, creates an almost overwhelming temptation to pretend that you do. There are only two resolutions to this problem: (a) Learn your business well and keep learning it. (b) When you don't know, admit it.

One day a Goat came to a Rabbit's peanut stand and purchased five cents worth of peanuts. She gave the Rabbit a dime and received a punched nickel in change. The next day she plugged the hole in the nickel and went back for another bag of peanuts. The Rabbit refused to take the plugged nickel. "But it's the same nickel you gave me yesterday!" said the Goat. "Not quite," said the Rabbit. "Yesterday the hole was open for all to see. I am not responsible if you were dumb enough to take it. Today, you offer me a plugged nickel and try to pass it off as the real thing. You are obviously an unethical goat and should be arrested for fraud." The Goat was not arrested, but she never bought any more peanuts from the Rabbit and neither did any of her friends. Moral: When dishonesty meets ignorance, everyone loses.

NOTES

1. For purposes of this article, let's exclude those producers who have broken the law and are the subject of criminal convictions and regulatory sanctions. Our focus here is upon why apparently ethical people violate their civil duties or moral obligations. Those who wish to learn why people commit crimes are advised to start with *Crime and Punishment* by Feodor Dostoyefsky.
2. Saul W. Gellerman, "Why 'Good' Managers Make Bad Ethical Choices," *Harvard Business Review*, July/August 1986, page 85.

CHAPTER REVIEW

Answers to the review questions and the self-test questions can be found in the Supplement.

Key Terms

commitment	company bashing
PACE	moral compass
hidden assumptions	ethical codes

Review Questions

1. Who wrote the first college-level text on life insurance?

2. When and where did Dr. Huebner first publicly announce his idea of creating a professional designation program for life underwriters?

3. What professional organization was instrumental in assisting Dr. Huebner's launching of the CLU program and the founding of The American College of Life Underwriters?

4. What did Dr. Huebner consider to be the twin pillars of professionalism?

5. Why did the American Society of CLU & ChFC (now the Society of Financial Service Professionals) foster the Professional Practice guidelines?

6. Who were the creators and supporters of the insurance industry Ethics Awareness Week?

7. What test does John R. Coleman, PhD, suggest for checking your own ethical behavior?

8. Indicate five different factors on which mortality assumptions for policy illustrations can be based.

9. Describe Frederick H. Stitt's view about the responsibility of professional life underwriters with respect to policy illustrations.

10. Cite two concepts that indicate life insurance should not be seen as a simple commodity.

11. How does Frederick H. Stitt believe life insurers will respond to rebating and expense problems?

12. Indicate the relevant information to which prospective life insurance purchasers are entitled, according to Frederick H. Stitt.

13. Indicate which parties are likely to initiate litigation in response to life insurance sales that were accomplished by company bashing.

14. What companies provide insurance company ratings?

15. Why does John S. Moyse discourage insurance producers from presenting information about insurer financial strength from anything other than reliable published materials?

16. Describe the four-way test developed by a Chicago Rotarian.

17. Identify eight things considered "socially acceptable" within the insurance industry that contribute to its negative image.

18. Identify the four principles of total quality service suggested by Denis F. Mullane.

19. Identify what Burke A. Christensen calls a "few grand absolutes" applicable to ethical behavior.

20. Explain what Burke A. Christensen considers to be guidelines for ethical decision making.

21. Explain the distinction between law and ethics.

22. What are four common rationalizations cited by Professor Saul Gellerman?

23. What are the four factors examined by Professor Stephen Robbins that can tempt morally strong persons?

Self-Test Questions

T F 1. Dr. Davis Gregg founded the CLU program in Bryn Mawr, Pennsylvania.

T F 2. Dr. Dan McGill wrote the first college-level text on life insurance in the U.S.

T F 3. Female students were not permitted into the original CLU class.

T F 4. PACE stands for Professional Achievement in Continuing Education, which requires participants to update their knowledge.

T F 5. The life insurance industry's real product is a promise to pay.

T F 6. John R. Driskill wrote, "Because ours is an industry built on trust, it is imperative that we weed out unethical individuals whose conduct robs us all of public trust."

T F 7. Rebating will most hurt those who tend to sell life insurance as if it were a commodity.

T F 8. Leveling commission scales will produce a less efficient (more costly to purchasers) life insurance product.

T F 9. Slanderous remarks about other insurers are a form of company bashing and should be avoided by all life insurance underwriters.

T   F   10.   The code of ethics of the American Society of CLU & ChFC (now called the Society of Financial Service Professionals) provides that in a conflict of interest situation, the interest of the insurance company shall be paramount.

T   F   11.   Putting an unduly negative spin on information can be considered company bashing.

T   F   12.   In the past decade, the frequency of errors and omissions claims against insurance producers has remained about the same, but the amounts of those claims have declined.

T   F   13.   Insurance producers who carry errors and omissions coverage are protected automatically from claims based on losses incurred due to an insurer insolvency.

T   F   14.   The producer who assumes the role of an expert adviser and creates a reasonable expectation by the insured that the illustration is a guarantee could be held liable for future failure in performance (if any occurs).

T   F   15.   In most cases there is no one other than ourselves enforcing our moral codes.

T   F   16.   Possessing the knowledge of what is right and what is wrong does not necessarily make a person ethical.

T   F   17.   The negative image of the insurance industry is solely due to a few "bad apples."

T   F   18.   Ethical behavior is merely a matter of following detailed guidelines and checklists developed by ethicists.

T   F   19.   A person cannot be acting more legally than another person who is also acting legally.

T   F   20.   Ethical codes begin with the assumption that all illegal activity is by definition unethical.

T   F   21.   It is entirely possible for a person to be acting legally and still be in violation of an ethical code.

T   F   22.   Market conduct problems are not ethical problems.

T   F   23.   Ethical and unethical actions are clearer to us when we have an interest in the outcome.

Glossary

absolute assignment • transfer of all of the ownership rights in property, such as a life insurance policy, by the owner to another party

absolute payment by check • payment in such a way that failure by a bank to honor the check will not affect the validity of the transaction for which payment by check was made

accelerated benefits • life insurance death proceeds that may be withdrawn prior to the insured's death under specified circumstances, such as if he or she incurs a medical problem that limits his or her life expectancy to 2 years or less

acceptance • manifestation of assent by one party to an offer made to him or her by another party

accidental means • in a life insurance policy, death directly, and apart from any other cause, by unintentional and unexpected means. Both the cause and the result must be accidental.

accidental result • in a life insurance policy, death directly by accidental bodily injury and no other cause. The result, but not necessarily the cause, must be accidental.

accord and satisfaction • see *compromise settlement*

accumulation period • the period in an annuity prior to the starting date of the annuity benefit payments

action at law • a lawsuit for money damages on the claim that one party to a contract had not performed according to the contract

action in equity • a lawsuit in which the plaintiff sues not for money damages but for other remedies that will put the parties to a contract in the position they were in before the contract was made

actual authority • authority, whether express or implied, that is intended to be given to an agent by a principal

actual express authority • the power of an agent for a principal as based on the oral or written grant from the principal

actual implied (incidental) authority • the power of an agent derived from an oral or written grant from the principal and reasonably believed by the agent to do those acts that are necessary to carry out the grant of express authority

administrative case law • case law that is developed by an administrative agency

477

administrator • the personal representative of a deceased person selected by a court because no executor was nominated or because the nominated executor is unable or unwilling to serve as such

advancement • money or other property transferred to someone prior to the anticipated time of payment or delivery

advertisement • as defined in the NASD's (now FINRA's) Rules of Fair Practice, "material published, or designed for use in a newspaper, magazine, or other periodical, radio, television or tape recording, video display, signs or billboards, motion pictures, telephone directories (other than routine listings), or other public media"

agency • the fiduciary relationship that exists when one party, the principal, manifests consent that another party, the agent, will act on behalf of the principal and the agent manifests the same type of consent

agent • one who acts for another, called the principal

aleatory contract • a contract in which performance by one party is conditioned on the occurrence of an uncertain event, so that the tangible values actually received by each party may be substantially different

alienate • voluntarily and absolutely transfer title to property from one party to another

alien enemy • a resident of a foreign country where a state of war with the U.S. exists

alien friend • a resident of a foreign country where no state of war with the U.S. exists

alien insurer • an insurer formed under the laws of a jurisdiction outside the U.S.

American Bankers Association (ABA) assignment form • a standard form developed by the ABA with collaboration by the Association of Life Insurance Counsel for use in effecting a collateral assignment of a life insurance policy, spelling out in detail which rights are and are not transferred by the assignor

American rule • a rule adopted in a majority of U.S. jurisdictions holding that, if there are multiple valid assignments of a life insurance policy, the first assignee in point of time will have a prior claim to the proceeds, unless he or she fails to require delivery of the policy at the time of the assignment; see also *English rule*

anatomical gift • a gift by a living or newly deceased person of a healthy part of his or her body to another by means of transplantation

annual statement blank • a detailed form developed by the NAIC that insurers must use in preparing and filing their annual financial statements with state regulatory bodies

antedating • see *backdating*

antirebate laws • state statutes in virtually all states that prohibit the practice of rebating

apparent authority • authority that people reasonably believe an agent has based on action or inaction on the part of the principal

appellate jurisdiction • jurisdiction to review the decision in a case heard by a lower court

applicant • the person who applies for life insurance on the life of the proposed insured (usually is the policyowner, but not necessarily)

approval type of conditional receipt • a conditional receipt for a premium that makes the life insurance coverage effective as of the date the insurance company approves the application

Armstrong Investigation • an investigation into the life insurance business conducted in the early 1900s by a committee of the New York state legislature that uncovered numerous abuses by insurance companies resulting in substantial policyowner losses

artificial person • legal entity that exists only because the law creates it (trusts, corporations, and partnerships, for example)

asset valuation reserve (AVR) • a balance sheet reserve that is similar to the mandatory securities valuation reserve (MSVR) but encompassing all invested assets, not just stocks and bonds

assignee • the entity to which some or all ownership rights in a life insurance policy are transferred

assignment • the transfer of some or all of the ownership rights in property, such as a life insurance policy, from one party to another

assignor • the entity that transfers some or all ownership rights in property, such as a life insurance policy, to another

assumption of the risk • principle that a person is presumed to expect and intend the probable or foreseeable consequences of his or her actions

attorney-in-fact • a party who is the agent or representative of another and who is given authority to act in place of and in the name of that other party

authority • the power to act that is given by one party to another party

automatic premium loan • a method of paying renewal life insurance premiums in which the policyowner authorizes the insurer, at the end of the grace period when any premium has not been paid, to create a policy loan in favor of the insurer (if there is sufficient unencumbered cash value) in the amount of the overdue premium

availability of coverage • a goal of insurance regulation that coverage should be obtainable on an affordable basis by all who wish to purchase it to cover their basic economic security needs

backdating • the practice of using any date prior to the effective date of a life insurance policy in order to, for example, establish the date on which premiums are payable or the amount of the premium to be paid

balancing test • a test as to whether state laws or regulations erect barriers against or unduly burden interstate commerce because legitimate state interests are too small relative to the degree of burden on interstate commerce

Bankruptcy Reform Act of 1978 • a federal statute that, among other things, exempts certain categories of property owned by a defaulting debtor from the claims of his or her creditors

bargaining contract • a contract whose terms are negotiated by the parties to it prior to its formation

basis (in a life insurance policy) • the taxpayer's total premiums paid, minus all dividends paid by the insurer, and minus any previous nontaxable withdrawals from the policy

beneficiary • the party designated to receive some or all of the proceeds of a life insurance policy at its maturity

beyond a reasonable doubt standard of proof • the highest level of proof required by the U.S. courts; used for proving guilt in criminal trials

bilateral contract • a contract in which each party makes one or more legally enforceable promises

bill of interpleader • an equitable device for settling conflicting claims for insurance proceeds or other benefits, whereby the insurance company pays the proceeds into court, admitting its obligation to pay and petitioning the court to adjudicate the conflicting claims and determine who is entitled to receive the money

blue sky laws • state laws that, among other things, define and regulate the conduct of investment advisers and the sale of securities

boycott • a group or concerted refusal to deal

broker • a party who acts primarily as the agent of the applicant in negotiating for and obtaining insurance

broker/dealer • a securities brokerage firm engaged in the business of buying and selling securities to or for customers

business of insurance • a test as to whether a particular activity carried on by an insurance company or agent is protected from federal regulation under the McCarran-Ferguson Act. It is so protected only if the activity is held to be part of the business of insurance.

capacity • the legal qualifications, competency, power, or fitness to accept authority or responsibility

case law • law that is developed by courts and administrative agencies in deciding on particular legal disputes

cash value accumulation test • a test to determine whether a life insurance policy qualifies as life insurance for federal income tax purposes. The test is met if the cash value is no more than the net single premium that would be needed to fund the policy's death benefit.

caveat emptor • literally, let the buyer beware; a harsh legal principle that a purchaser buys at his or her own risk

center of gravity (grouping of contracts) theory • a doctrine often used by courts to resolve a conflict-of-laws problem whereby the law applicable to a contract will be that of the state that maintains the most significant relationship or contacts with the subject matter of the controversy

chose in action • a right to bring action with respect to personal property, usually evidenced by a legal document and enforceable under the law

chose in possession • any type of property that a person possesses or may physically possess

civil law • most commonly, that part of the law that is concerned with noncriminal matters

class beneficiary • a member of a group that is designated as the beneficiary

Clayton Act • a federal statute that prohibits certain types of anticompetitive behavior, such as tying contracts, interlocking directorates, and mergers that may substantially lessen competition or tend to create a monopoly

clean hands • one of the three requirements of a plaintiff for entering a plea of equity; honest, fair behavior toward the other party and complete lack of fraud and deceit in the matter at hand

clear and convincing standard of proof • a standard of proof that, if met, will produce a firm belief as to the facts sought to be established; a standard of proof that is beyond the preponderance of the evidence standard but less than the reasonable doubt standard

collateral assignment • a transfer of some but not all of the ownership rights in property, such as a life insurance policy, by the owner to someone else, so that the property may serve as collateral for a loan

commerce clause • a clause in the U.S. Constitution providing federal jurisdiction over interstate commerce and limiting the power of states to erect barriers against or unduly burden interstate commerce

commitment • the state of being emotionally impelled to a future course of action

common disaster clause • a life insurance policy provision specifying that if the insured and beneficiary die in a common accident and there is no sufficient evidence that they died other than simultaneously, the insured will be assumed to have survived the beneficiary; accomplishes the same result as the Uniform Simultaneous Death Act

common law • as contrasted with statutory and case law, the law arising from the collection of court decisions, customs, and concepts of justice that define what is held by a society to be right and wrong

common-law system • as contrasted with the community-property system, the type of property law applicable in most states in the U.S., derived from English law and developed from judicial precedent in individual cases, rather than from statutes

community-property-law system • as contrasted with the common-law system, the type of property law applicable in a few states in the U.S., derived from French and Spanish law and developed from statutes, rather than from individual cases

commutative contract • a contract in which the tangible values each party expects to receive are approximately equal

commute • substitute one form of payment for another, such as to replace a stream of payments with a lump-sum payment

company bashing • making slanderous remarks about a competing company; disseminating false or misleading negative information about a competing company

competent • duly qualified or possessing the required physical, mental, material, or legal qualifications to engage in some activity

comprehensive-type statute • a type of state law that protects all kinds of life insurance benefits from the claims of all creditors

compromise settlement • a payment by an insurer to a beneficiary of an amount that is mutually acceptable although it is less than the full amount that is normally payable, usually because there is a dispute as to whether or not the beneficiary has the right to the full amount

concealment • in the context of insurance, a failure of the applicant to communicate to the insurer the applicant's knowledge of a material fact that the insurer does not know

conclusive presumption • a presumption that is so strong that no evidence, argument, or consideration will be permitted to overcome it

condition • a provision in a legal agreement that makes one event contingent on the occurrence of another

conditional contract • a contract in which one party's obligation to perform is conditioned upon fulfillment of certain obligations by the other party

conditional payment by check • payment in such a way that failure by a bank to honor the check will cause failure of the transaction for which payment by check was made

conditional receipt • a receipt for the first premium for a life insurance policy that binds the coverage, subject to one or more conditions, without reference to delivery of the policy; see also *approval type of conditional receipt* and *insurability type of conditional receipt*

conditional refusal to deal • as contrasted with an absolute refusal to deal on any terms, a refusal to deal except on certain terms

condition precedent • a condition that must be fulfilled by one party to a contract before any obligation is imposed on the other party to it

condition subsequent • a condition that must be fulfilled by one party to a contract in order to avoid releasing the other party to it from an obligation that has been created under the contract

conflict of laws • the body of law by which a court decides which law is to be applied in a case where the laws of two or more jurisdictions seem to be applicable to the case but where the individual laws conflict with each other

Connecticut rule • a minority legal view of the status of a member of a class beneficiary designation who predeceases the insured if the policy is silent on the question. Under this rule, the interest of the deceased class member belongs to his or her heirs; see also *New York rule* and *per stirpes distribution.*

consideration • something of value, such as property or a promise to do or refrain from doing something, given to someone in return for that person's also giving something of value, for the purpose of creating a contract

constitution • the fundamental law of a nation or state that sets forth the character of its government and the basic principles under which it is to operate

constructive delivery • an alternative to actual or physical delivery of a life insurance contract such that the policy is deemed to have been legally delivered when, properly stamped and addressed, it is deposited in the mail

contest • defined by most courts as a court action that challenges the validity of a life insurance contract

contestable period • a specified period at the beginning of certain insurance contracts during which the insurer retains the right to dispute the validity of the contract

contingent beneficiary • a beneficiary who takes the place of the primary beneficiary if the primary beneficiary predeceases the insured or otherwise loses entitlement to the proceeds before receiving them; may also be a beneficiary of unpaid proceeds that become payable following the death of the primary beneficiary

continuing representation, rule of • a view once held by the courts that a representation has to be true at the time the contract becomes effective, not just at the time the statement is made; if not, a misstatement provides a basis for rescission of the contract

contract • an agreement that is enforceable at law because it entails an offer and acceptance, consideration, competent parties, and a legal purpose

contract of adhesion • a contract that is not negotiated but rather drafted entirely by one party, with the other party to the contract not permitted to alter the contract terms but only to accept or reject the contract. Any ambiguities are to be interpreted in favor of the party that has not drafted the contract.

contract of indemnity • an insurance contract that reimburses the insured only for actual losses incurred

contract to pay a stated sum • a contract that is not one of indemnity but, rather, entails a promise to pay a specified amount of money in the event of a covered loss

convergence of financial services • the trend of various financial institutions to move across traditional boundaries limiting their scope of activities, of new financial products being developed to compete across traditional boundaries, and for nonfinancial companies to enter the financial services business

Conway decision • a decision of the New York Court of Appeals holding that an insurer is allowed to exclude certain causes of death, such as by aviation activities or war, from the operation of the policy's incontestable clause

courts of equity • as contrasted with courts of law, courts that apply rules of equity and good conscience

courts of law • as contrasted with courts of equity, courts that apply the rules of common law

death benefit requirement • one of the two prongs of a test to determine whether a life insurance policy qualifies as life insurance for federal income tax purposes. The test is met if the death benefit exceeds a specified multiple of its cash value at all times; see also *guideline premium requirement*

declaratory judgment • a court judgment designed to establish the rights of the parties to a dispute without imposing an obligation on either of them to do anything

defeasible vested interest • according to a minority view, the degree of interest held by a revocable beneficiary in an insurance policy—that is, that such beneficiary has a vested interest in the policy but the interest may be extinguished or terminated by the policyowner. Under this view, the policyowner may not give an assignee an interest in policy proceeds without the beneficiary's consent or without revoking the beneficiary designation.

defeasible vested interest concept • the view that because a beneficiary to an insurance policy has a vested interest in the policy, the beneficiary's consent is necessary to the exercise of any policy rights by the insured other than the right to change the beneficiary

delayed payment clause • a clause used by a few insurers specifying that policy proceeds will be payable to the beneficiary only if he or she is alive at the time of payment or, in some companies, only if he or she survives the insured by at least a specified number of days

delivery-in-good-health clause • a clause specifying that a life insurance policy that has been applied for will not take effect unless, at the time of delivery, the proposed insured is alive and in good health

discrimination against interstate commerce test • a test as to whether state laws or regulations erect barriers against or unduly burden interstate commerce because they treat domestic companies more favorably than out-of-state companies

distraint • the act of seizing

distributive-type statute • a type of state law providing that proceeds from life insurance policies payable to the insured's estate will pass to the spouse and children free of claims of creditors against the estate

diversity of citizenship • a situation in which the party on one side of a lawsuit is a citizen of one state and the party on the other side is a citizen of a different state or is an alien

dividend options • alternative ways in which a life insurance policyowner may choose to use policy dividends, usually to take them in cash, to reduce the renewal premium due, to buy paid-up additions, or to accumulate at interest, as well as, in some policies, to buy term insurance additions to the policy

divisible surplus • an insurance company's proceeds beyond expenses that may be apportioned among participating policies at frequent intervals and paid as dividends

domestic insurer • an insurer formed under the laws of the state in question

donee beneficiary • a beneficiary who has furnished no consideration in return for being designated as such

double-indemnity provision • an insurance policy statement that doubles the standard death benefit if the insured dies accidentally

dual-agency level • the level of duties an insurance producer owes to a client when the producer's actions create an agent-principal relationship between the producer and the client

durable power of attorney • a power of attorney that continues the agent's power even during the principal's disability or incompetency

effective date (of a policy) • the date on which coverage under the policy takes effect; see also *operative date (of a policy)*

effective regulation test • a test advocated by some that the McCarran-Ferguson Act's protection of insurance from federal regulation should apply not merely because insurance is regulated by state law but also that it must be effectively regulated by state law

election • a voluntary choice of one course of action over another with the intent to be bound by that choice

electronic funds transfer • a method of paying renewal premiums in which the policyowner, by phone or computer modem, authorizes his or her bank to electronically transfer funds from his or her account to that of the insurer

English rule • a rule adopted in a minority of U.S. jurisdictions holding that, if there are multiple valid assignments of a life insurance policy, the assignee who first notifies the insurer has primary claim to the proceeds, provided that, at the time of the assignment, he or she had no notice of a prior assignment

entire-contract statute • a state law specifying that the written life insurance policy and the attached application constitute the entire agreement between the insurer and the policyowner

equitable estoppel • an estoppel that arises when one party relies on a past action of a second party to his or her own substantial detriment, so that it would be inequitable to allow the second party to now reverse his or her earlier action

equitable remedy • the redress of an injury through means other than the award of money damages, such as enforcement of the terms of a contract that is in dispute

equity • the body of law that has been developed to provide a remedy or relief where legal remedies (that is, money damages) would provide no or inadequate relief; also, a goal of insurance regulation that insurers treat their separate policyowners fairly

estoppel • a legal principle that a party loses—that is, is precluded from using—a defense because of actions that are inconsistent with that defense

ethical code • a systematic, usually written compilation of the ethical principles and rules applicable to a particular group of people or organizations

ethics • a set of general moral principles or values; the discipline dealing with what is good or bad, what is morally acceptable or unacceptable, and what is a moral duty or obligation

exclusion ratio • the ratio of the amount invested in an annuity to the total amount expected to be received under the annuity; the proportion of each annuity benefit payment that is excluded from taxation for federal income tax purposes

executive power • an order or regulation issued by the President of the U.S. that, if published in the Federal Register, has the effect of law

executor • the personal representative nominated in a deceased person's will and approved by the court

exoneration statutes • laws in community-property states specifying that if an insurer pays benefits according to the terms of the policy and application, it will not be responsible if another party unknown to the insurer asserts a community-property interest in the policy

expert level • the level of duties an insurance producer owes to a client when the producer's representations of expertise induce the client to rely on that expertise

express authority • authority specifically given to an agent by a principal, either orally or in writing

expressio unius est exclusio alterius • a legal doctrine applied by a minority of courts that the expression of certain events as being excluded from a provision in a contract, such as the incontestable clause, implicitly means that all other events are not excluded

factual expectation • one person's expectation of financial advantage from the continued life of another person, which expectation is not based on a legal obligation

Fair Credit Reporting Act • a federal law designed to protect the privacy rights of individuals by controlling the activities of consumer reporting agencies

fairness • a goal of insurance regulation that insurers should treat individual policyowners equitably in such areas as claims practices, agent representations, and service provided

federalism • the goal of dispersing decision-making power away from the federal government and toward the states when possible

Federal Tax Lien Act of 1966 • a statute that overrides state exemptions for property of an individual in bankruptcy by allowing the federal government to require an insurer to withdraw life insurance policy loan values to satisfy a federal tax lien

Federal Trade Commission (FTC) Act • a federal statute that prohibits unfair business methods of competition and unfair and deceptive market practices

fiduciary • one who has a legal obligation, created by his or her undertaking to act primarily for the benefit of another in matters related to the undertaking. In agency law, an agent is a fiduciary with respect to the principal.

FIFO (first in, first out) method of taxation • a method of taxing a withdrawal from a life insurance policy whereby the amount withdrawn is treated first as a nontaxable return of basis and thereafter as income

fifth dividend option • a way in which life insurance policy dividends may be used by the policyowner to buy one-year term insurance in specified amounts to supplement the basic death benefit provided by the policy

Financial Industry Regulatory Authority (FINRA) • a self-regulatory organization created in 2007 to succeed the NASD in regulating securities marketing

financial planner • one who advises individuals on estate, tax, investment, and other such matters; usually regulated under laws pertaining to investment advisers

first-taker beneficiary • a beneficiary, whether primary or contingent, who is entitled to policy proceeds at the insured's death and who, unless the policyowner has already done so, is entitled to elect a settlement option and/or designate who is to receive any unpaid proceeds at his or her own death

foreign insurer • an insurer that is formed under the laws of a state other than the state in question

free-look period • a specified number of days following delivery of certain insurance policies during which the contract is in full force but the policyowner has the right to cancel and receive a full refund of the premium paid

free-look provision • a statement that gives a policyowner a certain number of days (usually 10, but sometimes 20) to examine a life insurance contract during which the policy may be returned and all premiums paid refunded

FTC • the Federal Trade Commission

garnishment • a legal proceeding whereby a person's property is involuntarily applied to the payment of a debt owed to another person

generalist level • the level of duties an insurance producer owes to a client to exercise reasonable skill, care, and diligence

geographical jurisdiction • jurisdiction that is limited to a particular geographic area, such as a state

gift • a transfer made without any reciprocal consideration

good health • for purposes of the delivery-in-good-health clause, usually defined by the courts to mean not absolute freedom from all physical infirmity but only such a mental and physical condition that one may discharge the ordinary duties of life without serious strain on one's vital powers

grace period • a period of time, usually 31 days, following the due date of a renewal premium, during which a life insurance policy remains in force

gratuitous beneficiary • see *donee beneficiary*

grouping of contracts theory • see *center of gravity theory*

guaranteed purchase (guaranteed insurability) option • an insurance policy provision allowing an insured to purchase the right to acquire additional insurance in specified amounts at specified ages without having to provide evidence of insurability

guaranty fund • a fund established by each state with money received from all solvent insurers licensed to operate there, the purpose of which is to protect state residents, at least partially, against losses due to insolvency of an insurer operating there

guideline premium requirement • one of the two prongs of a test to determine whether a life insurance policy qualifies as life insurance for federal income tax purposes. The test is met if the total premium that can be paid into the policy at any given time is less than an amount derived by a formula in the Code; see also *death benefit requirement*

health care power of attorney • a power of attorney that may be exercised only with respect to decisions regarding the extent of health care to be provided to a principal who is close to death

hidden assumptions • assumptions as to future results, such as in mortality, expense, interest, or lapse rates, that are not spelled out clearly in life insurance policy illustrations

holding-out provisions • provisions in the securities laws of some states specifying that individuals who hold themselves out as financial planners or financial consultants are subject to regulation as investment advisers

impermissible risk of inconsistent regulation test • a test as to whether state laws or regulations erect barriers against or unduly burden interstate commerce because the subject of regulation is national in nature or admits only one uniform system or plan of regulation

implied authority • authority that is not expressly given to an agent by a principal but is necessary so that the agent can exercise the power specifically given to him or her

imputed • attributed or assigned vicariously

incidental authority • see *implied authority*

incidents of ownership • elements of ownership or control over property, such as the right to name the beneficiary of a life insurance policy

incontestable clause • a provision in a life insurance contract that waives most of the insurer's rights to dispute the validity of the contract after it has been in force for a specified period of time, such as 2 years during the lifetime of the insured

incorporation by reference • inclusion in a contract of terms of another document without actually including the second document in the contract

index policy • an annuity contract whose accumulation rates are tied to external indexes

individual-insurer standard • a test of the materiality of a misrepresentation by referring to the normal underwriting standards of the individual insurer to decide whether, had it known the truth, it would have acted differently than it did

inside buildup • the cash value or investment fund in a life insurance policy

inspection receipt • a receipt for a policy, given by the applicant and specifying that the policy has been delivered to him or her only for purposes of inspection and approval and that the first premium for it has not been paid

insurability type of conditional receipt • a conditional receipt for a premium that makes the life insurance coverage effective as of the date of the application (or perhaps the date of the medical examination, if later) if the applicant is subsequently found to be insurable according to the general underwriting rules of the insurance company

insurable interest • an interest in the subject matter of an insurance contract such that the holder of the interest can reasonably expect to lose, usually financially, from the occurrence of the insured event, such as the death of the insured, or to gain, usually financially, if the insured event does not occur

insurance broker • see *broker*

Insurance Information and Privacy Protection Model Act • a model state law developed by the NAIC designed to protect the privacy rights of individuals by controlling the information-gathering and information-disclosure activities of the insurance industry

Insurance Regulatory Information System (IRIS) • an early warning system developed by the NAIC for monitoring the financial solidity of insurers; includes the calculation of several financial ratios for each insurer and a comparison of those ratios with what are deemed by the NAIC to be acceptable ranges for each one

insured • in life insurance, the person on whose life the policy is issued

interest-adjusted cost indexes • methods for expressing or comparing the cost of life insurance taking into account the time-value of money

interest maintenance reserve (IMR) • a required reserve on the balance sheet of an insurance company that is used to amortize over a period of time realized gains and losses in insurer investments resulting from falling or rising interest rate levels

interpleader • an equitable proceeding in which a party holds but does not claim to own property that is claimed by two or more other parties and asks the court to require that those other parties litigate their claims between or among themselves

interstate compacts • a proposed system of agreements entered into by the states with one another that would, subject to approval by Congress, help bring about uniform standards, rules, and enforcement mechanisms needed to regulate certain aspects of the insurance business more effectively

intestacy • the state of dying without leaving a valid will

invasion of privacy • the wrongful intrusion into someone's private activities by another party or by the government; includes misappropriation of one's name or likeness, unreasonable intrusion into one's private space, public disclosure of private facts, and placing one in a false light in the public eye

Investment Advisers Act of 1940 • a federal statute that, among other things, defines and regulates the conduct of money managers and investment advisers, the latter meaning those who are in the business of giving advice about securities for compensation

Investment Company Act of 1940 • a federal law that governs investment companies, including mutual funds, by requiring their registration, honest and unbiased management, security owner participation and control, adequate capital structure, proper financial statements and accounting, and acceptable selling activities

IRIS • see *Insurance Regulatory Information System*

irrevocable beneficiary • one who is named in an insurance policy as the person who is to receive the benefits after the death of the insured and whose designation may not be changed unilaterally by the insured or the policyowner

irrevocable beneficiary designation • a beneficiary designation that cannot be changed by the policyowner without the beneficiary's consent

issue date • the date on which the policy is prepared by the insurer and sent to the agent for delivery

jurisdiction • the authority or power to interpret and apply a law

jurisdiction over the person • jurisdiction that applies to the party involved in an action or proceeding

jurisdiction over the subject matter • jurisdiction that applies to a case of a particular type, such as a divorce case or an income tax case

laches • an undue delay in enforcing a right of action or negligent failure to act promptly

late remittance offer • an offer by an insurer, usually subject to conditions, to grant an additional period of time after expiration of the grace period for payment of a renewal premium

law • the set of rules of conduct established by the members of a society as binding on them and for which violators are penalized in some manner

legal estoppel • an estoppel that arises when one party relies upon a promised future action of a second party to his or her own substantial detriment, so that it would be inequitable to allow the second party to conduct himself or herself differently from the promised future action

legal remedy • see *remedy at law*

legislative law • law that is enacted by parliamentary bodies and promulgated through regulations of administrative bodies

LIFO (last in, first out) method of taxation • a method of taxing a withdrawal from a life insurance policy whereby the amount withdrawn is treated first as income to the extent of income earned in the contract and thereafter as a nontaxable return of basis

liquidation period • the period in an annuity after the starting date of the annuity benefit payments

living will • not really a will, but a document setting forth the wishes of a person concerning the use of extraordinary medical measures, such as artificial life support systems, if the person should become terminally incapacitated or permanently unconscious

mailbox rule • a legal principle that, even if a renewal premium does not arrive at the insurance company on time, it will be deemed to have been paid on time if the policyowner mailed it, properly addressed, in sufficient time that he or she could reasonably expect that it would be delivered on time

mandatory securities valuation reserve (MSVR) • a contingency fund formerly required to be established on the balance sheets of insurance companies to serve as a cushion or buffer against a decline in their surplus positions in the event of downward fluctuations in the market values of securities in their investment portfolios; now replaced by the asset valuation reserve (AVR) and the interest maintenance reserve (IMR)

market conduct • fair or unfair practices carried on by insurers and their representatives in the marketing of insurance—for example, truthful and complete advertising, discrimination against certain classes of consumers, rebating, and full disclosure of policy conditions

marketers • with regard to life insurance, the insurance producers; regulated by the National Association of Securities Dealers as broker/dealers or as registered representatives of broker/dealers

market value adjustment contract • an annuity whose proceeds payable in case of withdrawal are adjusted upward or downward to reflect changes in the market value of the securities underlying the contract

married women's statute • a type of state law that protects proceeds from life insurance policies taken out by or for the benefit of a married woman on the life of her husband from the claims of creditors of the husband

material • in the life insurance context, a test of the importance of a deliberate misrepresentation or concealment by an applicant. If the insurer was induced to take an action other than the one it would have taken if the truth had been known, the misrepresentation or concealment is deemed material.

maturity rights • rights in a life insurance policy that arise at the time it matures, such as the right to receive the death proceeds

McCarran Act • see *McCarran-Ferguson Act*

McCarran-Ferguson Act • a federal law enacted in 1945, shortly after the *South-Eastern Underwriters Association* decision, specifying that most regulation of insurance will be the responsibility of the states, not the federal government, except to the extent that the insurance business is not regulated by state law

MEC • see *modified endowment contract*

Medical Information Bureau (MIB) • a nonprofit membership organization of life insurance companies that operates an exchange of underwriting information for its members

medical power of attorney • see *health care power of attorney*

mere expectancy theory • the now prevailing legal theory that the interest of a revocable beneficiary in a life insurance policy represents only a contingent benefit that may be defeated by the policyowner by the exercise of various policy rights without the revocable beneficiary's consent, or perhaps even knowledge

misstatement of age or sex provision • a clause in a life insurance policy allowing the insurer, even after the contestable period, to adjust the death benefit payable in case the insured's age or sex was misstated. The usual adjustment is to the benefit amount that would have been purchased with the premium actually paid if the age or sex of the insured had not been misstated.

Model Unfair Trade Practices Act • a model law developed by the NAIC and adopted by almost every state to help assure appropriate market conduct by insurers and agents; includes provisions relating, among other things, to false advertising, misrepresentation, defamation, boycott, false financial statements, unfair discrimination, rebates, and failure to maintain complaint-handling procedures

modified endowment contract (MEC) • a life insurance policy that is subject to LIFO tax treatment of loans and most distributions from the policy, as well as a 10 percent penalty tax if taken prior to age 59½, because the policy fails the so-called seven-pay test in the Internal Revenue Code

Monahan decision • a decision by the Illinois Supreme Court holding that a life insurance policy is incontestable after the expiration of the period specified in the policy, even if the insured died during that period, unless the incontestable clause specifies otherwise

monopoly power • the power to control market prices or to exclude competition with respect to a particular product and geographic area

moral compass • an internalized system of principles and values that helps one determine what is or is not ethical behavior in a given situation

mutual assent • a manifestation of the intent of two or more parties to accept the terms of a contract; a "meeting of the minds"

mutual mistake • an error on the part of both parties to a transaction on the same matter

mysterious disappearance • the disappearance of a person, such as an insured, with no explanation, so that it is unclear as to how or even whether he or she has died

NAIC • see *National Association of Insurance Commissioners*

National Association of Insurance Commissioners • an unincorporated voluntary association whose members are the principal insurance regulatory authorities of the various states

natural person • a human being

Net Payment Cost Comparison Index • an interest-adjusted method for expressing or comparing the cost of life insurance using the assumption that cash values are left with the insurer and are part of the proceeds payable at the insured's death at an assumed future time, such as the end of the 20th policy year

New York rule • the predominant legal view of the status of a member of a class beneficiary designation who predeceases the insured if the policy is silent on the question. Under this rule, the interest of the deceased class member belongs to the surviving class members; see also *Connecticut rule.*

New York-type statute • a type of state law that protects life insurance cash values and death proceeds payable to a beneficiary other than the insured or applicant against creditors of the insured and of the applicant

nonforfeiture laws • legislation that requires provisions to be included in life insurance policies that accumulate a savings element to specify the method that must be used to compute the minimum size of the savings element and the minimum options under which it must be made available to policyowners

nonforfeiture options • the alternative ways in which a policyowner can choose to receive a life insurance policy's nonforfeiture values, at a minimum being in cash, as extended term insurance, or as a reduced amount of paid-up insurance

nonforfeiture values • the savings element in a life insurance policy that has to be returned or available to the policyowner

nontaxable policy exchange • an exchange of a life insurance policy for an annuity or for another life insurance policy, or an exchange of an annuity for another annuity, that is protected from taxation under the nonrecognition provision of IRC Sec. 1035

nonwaiver clause • a clause in a life insurance application and/or policy specifying that the soliciting agent does not have authority to modify any of the terms contained therein

offer • the manifestation of a willingness to enter into a contract, made in such a way as to indicate to another party that if the offer is accepted, a contract will be created

operative date (of a policy) • the date on the policy governing the status of various policy provisions after the policy has gone into effect; may or may not be the same as the effective date of the policy

opt-out statute • a state statute that eliminates the choice given by federal bankruptcy law to an individual filing bankruptcy to have the benefit of either the federal or state property exemptions, thus allowing the individual only the exemptions provided by the state's law

ordinance • a rule enacted by the legislative body of a municipal corporation or agency, such as a zoning board or city council

original jurisdiction • jurisdiction that applies to a case when it is first heard by a judge or jury

owner • the person, often the applicant, who owns the policy on the life of the insured (may also be the insured, but not necessarily)

owner-applicant • the party that applies for and owns a policy on the life of another person

ownership endorsement • a written endorsement to a life insurance policy, developed by or acceptable to the insurer, whereby all ownership rights in the policy are transferred from one party to another

PACE • see *Professional Achievement in Continuing Education program*

palpably material • of such extreme importance as to be obvious to any person of normal intelligence, so that failure to disclose may be evidence of fraudulent intent

parol evidence rule • a legal principle that oral evidence may not be used to modify the terms of a written insurance contract once it is issued except in case of fraud, accident, or mistake

partial assignment • the transfer of some but not all of the ownership rights in property from one party to another

Paul v. Virginia • a case in 1869 in which the U.S. Supreme Court decided that the insurance business is not commerce, so it cannot be interstate commerce, and therefore the states, not the federal government, have the authority to regulate it

per capita • the distribution of assets in a manner that gives equal shares to all individuals who are beneficiaries

person • any legal entity, including natural persons and artificial persons such as trusts, corporations, and partnerships

personal property • any property that is not land, a part of land, or attached to land

per stirpes • the distribution of assets in a manner that gives to a deceased person's issue or lineal descendants the share that the deceased would have taken had he or she survived

place-of-making rule • a rule specifying that, unless the two parties to a contract agree otherwise, the law of the state where the contract was made or brought into existence will be applied in the interpretation or enforcement of it

policy • a contract of insurance

policy date • see *operative date*

policy loan • an advance of money available to the policyowner from a policy's cash values, with no fixed time for repayment. Interest is accrued on the amount borrowed from the policy, and the amount of the loan plus any unpaid interest will be deducted from any policy values payable.

policy reserves • a liability on the balance sheet of a life insurance company to reflect the estimated amounts needed, together with estimated future premium and investment income, to provide the benefits promised under its life insurance and annuity contracts as those benefits become due

postclaim underwriting • reevaluating at the time of a claim information submitted by the applicant at the time the insurance was applied for, such as statements on the application about the proposed insured's age or health

power • the ability to say or do something

power of attorney • a written document appointing someone as an attorney-in-fact

preauthorized check plan • a method of paying renewal premiums in which the policyowner gives the insurer the right to order withdrawal of each premium directly from his or her checking account and authorizes his or her bank to honor such withdrawal orders

precedent • an earlier decision by a court that may provide an example or authority for a later court in deciding upon a similar case

preemption doctrine • a legal principle embodied in the supremacy clause of the U.S. Constitution whereby state laws and regulations must give way to—are preempted by— federal jurisdiction if such is the clear purpose of Congress or if federal and state laws are extremely inconsistent

prematurity rights • rights in a life insurance policy that may be exercised before it matures, such as the right to dividends or to change the beneficiary

premium adjustments • amounts that may be added to or subtracted from death benefits of a life insurance policy based on the contract or state law. For example, if a premium was paid for coverage after the month when the insured died or if premiums were paid in advance for periods after the insured's death, such amounts may be refundable. Furthermore, a reduction in the death benefit may occur if there are any premiums due but unpaid at the date of death or if there are unpaid premium loans or interest on those loans.

prepaid premiums • premiums paid to the insurer in advance of the date on which they are due

preponderance of the evidence standard of proof • a standard of proof in a civil case that, if met, means that the evidence presented is more convincing than the opposing evidence

prima facie evidence • evidence that, on its face or at first sight, seems adequate and free from palpable defects

primary beneficiary • a beneficiary who has first claim to the proceeds of a life insurance policy if the conditions on which they are payable, such as that he or she must outlive the insured, are fulfilled

principal • one for whom an agent acts

private laws • laws that, unlike public laws, are directed at one named individual or a specific group of individuals

privilege • an exceptional or extraordinary exemption employed by certain parties and not available to parties in general

probate • the act of proving that a deceased person's will is in fact his or her genuine and last will

procedural-type statute • a type of state law that protects a small amount of life insurance death proceeds from the claims of all types of creditors, including creditors of the beneficiary

proceeds and avails (of a life insurance policy) • the policy's death benefit, cash surrender and loan values, waived premiums, and dividends

Professional Achievement in Continuing Education (PACE) • a formal program jointly adopted by The American College and the Society of Financial Service Professionals for the continuing education of CLUs and ChFCs

promisee • one to whom a promise is made, as in a contract

promisor • one who makes a promise, as in a contract

promissory estoppel • see *legal estoppel*

promissory note • a written promise to pay a specified sum of money according to specific terms

proof of the insured's death • a death certificate or other official evidence, which must be provided by a beneficiary for a life insurance company to consider the claim

property • the exclusive right of ownership; the right to possess, enjoy, transfer, or dispose of a thing or interest, as well as the thing or interest that is the subject matter of that right

prospectus • a document given to prospective purchasers containing detailed information about the issuer and provisions of newly issued securities, including variable insurance and annuity products

prudent-insurer standard • a test of the materiality of a misrepresentation by referring to what insurers in general would do in their underwriting of the case if they had known the truth

public laws • laws that, unlike private laws, apply to the public as a whole

purposeful disappearance • the disappearance of a person, such as an insured, wherein a reasonable explanation for his or her absence can be established

ratification • the validation by a principal of an unauthorized act of an agent

readable contract laws • state statutes establishing minimum standards to make insurance contracts understandable to average consumers with only high school educations

real property • land and those things that are a part of or attached to land

reasonable doubt standard of proof • a standard of proof in a criminal case that, if met, means that the evidence presented is so conclusive and complete that all reasonable doubts would be removed from the mind of an ordinary person

reasonable expectations doctrine • a legal principle occasionally applied by a court in the interpretation of a contract of adhesion specifying that the reasonable expectations of the nondrafting party will control even if the language of the contract is contrary and unambiguous

reasonableness • a goal of insurance regulation that insurers in their market conduct should treat their policyowners as a group in a fair manner, particularly with respect to price and product quality

rebating • giving a prospective purchaser of life insurance any economic benefit not specified in the policy as an inducement to purchase it

rebuttable presumption • a presumption that can be overcome through the introduction of sufficient contrary evidence

reciprocal enforcement provision • a provision in the NAIC's Unauthorized Insurers Model Act giving a particular state enacting the provision the power to enforce judicial decisions of courts in other states having done the same as if they were judicial decisions of the particular state

reformation • an equitable remedy by which erroneous terms of a contract are revised to conform to the actual intention of the parties

regulations • rules of conduct issued by administrative agencies and having the force and effect of law

reinstatement • the process of restoring a life insurance contract that has lapsed to its former status

reinstatement provision • statement by an insurer allowing a policyowner's reacquisition of insurance coverage under a policy that has lapsed, providing certain conditions are met

release • the intentional relinquishment of a right to do or to have something, usually given in exchange for some consideration

remedy at law • the redress of an injury, most commonly by the award of money damages

renewal premium • a premium whose payment, while unrelated to the creation of an insurance contract, is essential to its continuation for another period of coverage

replacement • a transaction in which a new life insurance or annuity contract is sold and it is or should be known that because of the sale, the policyowner will terminate, convert, or otherwise reduce in value an existing life insurance or annuity contract

representation • a statement made during the creation of a contract, but not a part of the contract, that induces the other party to enter into the contract

rescission • the termination or cancellation of a contract

resulting trustee • a trustee status that is created by implication of law in cases where it seems from the nature of a transaction that the parties intended to create a trust

reverse common disaster clause • a life insurance policy provision specifying that if the insured and beneficiary die in a common accident and there is no sufficient evidence that they died other than simultaneously, the beneficiary will be presumed to have survived the insured

reversionary irrevocable designation • an irrevocable beneficiary designation in which, if the beneficiary predeceases the insured, all rights in the policy revert to the policyowner

revocable beneficiary • one who is named in an insurance policy as the one to whom the benefits are to be paid after the insured's death but the policy allows the policyowner unilaterally to change the designation to someone else

revocable beneficiary designation • a beneficiary designation that can be changed by the policyowner at any time without the beneficiary's consent

rider • an amendment to an insurance policy

right of subrogation • the right of an insurer to take the place of the injured insured and sue the party responsible for the damages incurred

right to assign • the right of a policyowner to transfer some or all of his or her rights to another person

Risk-Based Capital for Life and/or Health Insurance Model Act • a model law developed by the NAIC that describes several regulatory action levels to be implemented against an insurer whose actual capital falls short of its risk-based required capital

risk-based capital requirement • a system of enhancing the financial solidity of insurance companies by periodically establishing the minimum capital and surplus needed by each insurer in light of its particular exposure to various types of risks. The greater the riskiness, the greater the minimum capital and surplus required.

Robinson-Patman Act • a federal statute that amends the Clayton Act and prohibits unfair price discrimination

rule of continuing representation • a doctrine that a representation made in the policy application has to still be true at the moment a contract becomes effective

rules of statutory construction • rules to be applied to determine and give effect to the intent of the legislative body that created a statute

sales literature • as defined in the NASD's (now FINRA's) Rules of Fair Practice, "any written communication distributed or made generally available to customers or the public, which communication does not meet the . . . definition of 'advertisement'"

secondary beneficiary • see *contingent beneficiary*

second taker beneficiary • a contingent beneficiary who becomes entitled to life insurance policy proceeds at the death of a primary beneficiary who has been receiving them under an installment option. Payments to the second taker usually must continue under the same distribution pattern as applied to the primary beneficiary.

Securities Act of 1933 • a federal law requiring full and fair disclosure of relevant material information about newly issued securities, including variable insurance and annuity products, to potential purchasers

Securities Exchange Act of 1934 • a federal law governing the trading of already outstanding securities through disclosure requirements, prevention of fraud and manipulation, regulation of securities exchange markets and the over-the-counter market, and control of credit in securities markets

Securities Valuation Office • a unit within the NAIC to value, on a uniform basis, the stocks and bonds held in the investment portfolios of insurance companies in the U.S.

service of process • the communication of notice and court papers to a defendant, by physical delivery or otherwise, concerning upcoming legal proceedings against him or her, giving the defendant the opportunity to appear and be heard in connection with those proceedings

seven-pay test • a test to determine whether or not a life insurance policy falls under the definition of a modified endowment contract. It meets the definition if the policy takes in too much premium in its first 7 policy years or in the 7 years following a material change in the policy.

Sherman Act • a federal statute that specifies that every contract, combination, or conspiracy in restraint of trade is illegal

simple power of attorney • a power of attorney that may terminate if the principal becomes incompetent or disabled before death

socialization of risk • a goal of insurance regulation that economic security in certain areas, such as that threatened by on-the-job accidents and illnesses, should be extended broadly throughout the population

soliciting agent • a member of an insurer's field sales personnel

solidity • a goal of insurance regulation that insurers should remain not only technically solvent but also sufficiently strong financially so that they can be relied upon to properly perform their functions in society

South-Eastern Underwriters Association case • a case decided by the U.S. Supreme Court in 1944 reversing the *Paul v. Virginia* decision and holding that the insurance business can fall under the authority of the federal government to regulate it as interstate commerce

"specifically relates" requirement • a provision in the McCarran-Ferguson Act that no law of Congress impairs or supersedes state law unless the federal law "specifically relates" to the business of insurance, meaning that to preempt state law, the federal law must specifically express the intent to do so and to render the McCarran-Ferguson Act inapplicable

specific beneficiary • a beneficiary who is designated by name or in some other manner that clearly sets him or her apart from all other parties

spendthrift clause • a clause in a life insurance policy or settlement agreement that denies the beneficiary the right to commute, alienate, or assign his or her interest in the proceeds

spendthrift-type statute • a type of state law that protects life insurance proceeds payable under a settlement agreement from claims of creditors of the beneficiary as long as the proceeds are still in the hands of the insurer

split-dollar life insurance • a plan whereby a life insurance policy's premium-payment obligations and policy benefits are in some manner split between two individuals or entities, such as an employer and one of its key executives

springing durable power of attorney • a power of attorney that becomes effective only after the occurrence of certain events, such as loss of the principal's physical or mental competency

standard provisions • policy provisions that must be included in insurance contracts, either as set forth in a statute or in such a way as to accomplish the same effect as the statutory wording

Standard Valuation Law • a model law of the NAIC prescribing the method by which life insurers must calculate their minimum policy reserves

stare decisis • literally, let the decision stand, meaning that a legal decision in an earlier, similar case will also be applied in the present case

state action • an action of a private party that is exempt from the federal antitrust laws because, although it is a restraint on competition, it is clearly articulated and affirmatively expressed as state policy and actively supervised by the state

state action doctrine • a doctrine approved by the U.S. Supreme Court that "state action" is not subject to the Sherman Act

Statute of Frauds • a statute in nearly every state requiring that certain types of contracts, but not life insurance contracts, be in writing in order to be enforceable

statutes of limitation • laws that control how long a person may wait before bringing a lawsuit of any sort against another party

succession-in-interest clause • a life insurance policy provision that becomes operative in the absence of contrary instructions by the policyowner and that controls the disposition of the interest of any class beneficiary who dies before becoming entitled to payment of his or her share of the policy proceeds; typically specifies that the deceased's share goes to the surviving members of the class

suicide • the intentional taking of one's own life

suicide provision • a statement excluding insurance coverage for a death by suicide within a certain period (typically 2 years) after the issue date

suit for reformation of the contract • a legal action for an equitable remedy in cases where an error has been found in a life insurance policy to make the written instrument conform to the intention of the parties

supremacy clause • a clause in the U.S. Constitution declaring that all laws made in pursuance of the Constitution and all treaties of the U.S. are the supreme law of the land and have legal priority over any conflicting provisions in a state constitution or law

Surrender Cost Comparison Index • an interest-adjusted method for expressing or comparing the cost of life insurance using the assumption that cash values are withdrawn at an assumed future time, such as the end of the 20th policy year, at which time the policy is surrendered

termination dividend • a special policy dividend some insurers pay upon termination of a policy through death, maturity, or surrender if the policy has been in force for at least a specified period of time

third-party beneficiary • a beneficiary other than the insured or the insured's estate

time-value of money • the adjusted nominal value of money paid out early rather than late or received late rather than early after lost interest earnings in the interim are taken into account

tontine system • a system that is now illegal and that pays policy dividends under participating policies only to those policyowners whose coverage is still in force at the end of a lengthy specified period, with all other policyowners forfeiting the right to dividends

tort • a civil wrong other than breach of contract; breach of a legal duty other than contractual that exists by reason of society's expectations concerning interpersonal conduct

total disability • an insured's inability because of disease or bodily injury to perform any of the essential acts of his or her job or of any other job for which he or she is suited based on schooling, training, or experience (each insurer creates its own definition of total disability)

transfer-for-value rule • a provision in the Internal Revenue Code specifying that, subject to certain exceptions, death proceeds payable under a policy that has been transferred from one policyowner to another for valuable consideration are taxable to the beneficiary, minus the total paid by the transferee for the policy

treaty • an agreement made between two or more independent nations, formally signed and ratified by each

treble damages • an award that may be recovered under the Sherman and Clayton Acts in an amount equal to three times the damages that a court or jury would normally find a party entitled to if he or she is injured in his business or property by reason of conduct forbidden in the antitrust laws

trustee • one who holds legal title to property for the benefit of another and who is charged with carrying out specified duties with regard to the management and/or disposition of the property

twisting • inducing a policyowner, through the agent's distortion or misrepresentation of the facts, to discontinue and replace a life insurance or annuity contract

unauthorized insurer • an insurer doing insurance business in a particular state but without a license to do so in that state

Unauthorized Insurers Model Act • a model law created by the NAIC that subjects unauthorized insurers to the jurisdiction of the insurance commissioner and courts of the enacting state

Unauthorized Insurers Service-of-Process Act • a law in every state designating the insurance commissioner or other state official as the agent of any unauthorized insurer operating there for purposes of accepting service of process

unearned premium • a premium in the possession of a life insurer that it is not yet allowed to keep, usually because it has not yet assumed the risk

unfair discrimination • inequality of treatment among policyowners that is not justified by underwriting considerations or sound business practices or that is deemed unacceptable because of external public policy objectives

uniform donor card • a standardized card that specifies a person's wishes concerning the donation of his or her body parts at the time of his or her death

Uniform Securities Act • a model securities law upon which most state blue sky laws are based

Uniform Simultaneous Death Act • a statute in almost every state specifying that, if two or more people die and there is no sufficient evidence that they died other than simultaneously, each will be presumed to be the survivor as regards his or her own property

unilateral contract • a contract in which only one party makes one or more legally enforceable promises

unilateral mistake • an error on the part of only one of the parties to a transaction

universal life insurance • a whole life policy with flexible premiums, an adjustable death benefit, a cash value credited with current interest rates, funding through the insurer's general account, and unbundling of the various elements of cost

valid • having legal force so that the matter is incapable of being rightfully overturned or set aside

valued policy • a policy that pays a stated sum of money if the insured event occurs, regardless of the amount of the financial loss at that time

viatical settlement company • a company that purchases life insurance policies from owners on living insureds, in return for which the company receives the death benefit when the insured dies

voidable contract • a contract in which one of the parties has the right to disaffirm it, thereby terminating the agreement

void contract • no contract at all because it is unenforceable by either of the parties

waiver • the voluntary, intentional relinquishment of a known right

waiver-of-premium provision • requirement that the insurer will waive payment of premiums during the term of the insured's disability

waiver situation • a situation that may lead to loss of an otherwise valid legal defense because that defense has been waived by the party formerly entitled to it

warranty • a statement that is made a part of a contract and guaranteed by the maker to be true in all respects

will • a document created during one's lifetime specifying how his or her property is to be distributed following his or her death

withdrawal • the taking of some of the money out of a life insurance contract's savings element in a nonloan format while the insured is still alive

Index

Name, misappropriation of, 374
National Association of Insurance Commissioners (NAIC)
  Accelerated Benefits Model Regulation, 181
  Agents and Brokers Licensing Model Act, 340
  Insurance Regulatory Information Systems ratio of, 446
  model acts and regulations, 6
  model advertising rules, 367
  Model Privacy Act, 379–81
  Model Unfair Trade Practices Act, 371–72
  Standard Policy Provisions Model Act, 172
  Unfair Claims Settlement Practices Model Act, 256
  Unfair Life, Accident and Health Claims Settlement Practices Model Regulation, 257
National Association of Securities Dealers (NASD, now FINRA), 364
  Rules of Fair Practice, 366
National do-not-call list, 381–82
New Jersey, interest of revocable beneficiary in, 303
New York
  applications at beneficiary's instigation in, 77
  courts of, 16
  exception to suicide exclusion in, 73
  exemption statute of, 323–26
  incontestable clause in, 145–46, 172
  Insurance Law, 80–81
    materiality tests of, 103
  succession in interest rule, 276–77
New York Life Insurance Company v. Statham, 202
Nonforfeiture provisions, 175–76
Nonpayment
  forfeiture and, 177
  renewal premiums and, 202–3
Nonwaiver clause, 127
  payment of first premium and, 131–33
North Carolina, applications at beneficiary's instigation in, 77–78

Occupation, misrepresentation of, 105
Offer, valid, 24
Oklahoma, exemption statutes of, 325
Operative date of policy, 57–59
Opinion
  versus fact, 105–6
  misrepresentation of, 99–100
Oral agreement, legality of, 85–86

Oral representation, 95–96
Original jurisdiction, 13
Owner-applicant, 265. *See also* Applicant
Ownership
  concept of, 303–5
  incidents of, 299
  interests
    of creditors, 234
    due to wrongful killing of insured, 234–35
    marriage and divorce effects on, 228–34
  provision, 179
  rights
    ABA assignment form and, 308–10
    absolute assignments and, 307–8
    of beneficiary, 279–80
    collateral assignments and, 305–7
    notice of assignment and, 310–12

Parol evidence rule, 44
  exception to, 163 n. 24
Parties, legal capacity of, 36–41
Partnerships
  insurable interest in, 83–84
  as principals, 339
Patterson, Edwin W., 121
Payment
  conditional, 68
  dates, 204–6
  extensions of time, 209–10
  of first premium, 47–48
  methods, 210–16
  of premium, 195–200
  presumption of, 198
  by someone other than policyowner, 195–98
Pension benefits, veterans, 403–4
Per capita clause, 279
Per stirpes, 278–79
Person
  jurisdiction over, 13
  legal definition, 38
Personal property, 225–28
  intangible, 225–28
  inventory of, 398
  tangible, 225
Personal representative, 400. *See also* Executor
Pierce v. Homesteaders Life Association, 182–83
Place-of-making rule, 17
Plan change provision, 179–80
Police Courts, 15
Policy

THE AMERICAN COLLEGE
ALUMNI
ASSOCIATION

Your Bridge to a Lifetime of Professional Achievement

We encourage you to take advantage of knowing more about The Alumni Association. Together we can create a stronger community and explore new opportunities for professional success.

Call us at (610) 526-1200

e-mail: russell.figueira@theamericancollege.edu

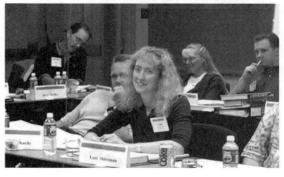